CHILDREN &
YOUNG PEOPLE'S
WORK

LEVEL **2**
CERTIFICATE

MIRANDA WALKER

 Nelson Thornes

Published in 2012 by:
Nelson Thornes Ltd
Delta Place
27 Bath Road
CHELTENHAM
GL53 7TH
United Kingdom

13 14 15 16 / 10 9 8 7 6 5 4 3 2

A catalogue record for this book is available from the British Library

ISBN 978 1 4085 1538 9

Cover photograph by Rob Hainer / Shutterstock

Page make-up by Pantek Media, Maidstone

Printed in China by 1010 Printing International Ltd

Contents

About the author   **viii**

Introduction   **ix**

How to use this book   **x**

SHC 21 Introduction to communication in children and young people's settings   **1**

    L01 Understand why communication is important in the work setting   **2**

    L02 Be able to meet the communication and language needs and wishes and preferences of individuals   **26**

    L03 Be able to overcome barriers to communication   **31**

    L04 Be able to respect equality and diversity when communicating   **38**

    L05 Be able to apply principles and practices relating to confidentiality at work   **44**

SHC 22 Introduction to personal development in children and young people's settings   **53**

    L01 Understand what is required for competence in own work role   **54**

    L02 Be able to reflect on own work activities   **61**

    L03 Be able to agree a personal development plan   **68**

    L04 Be able to develop knowledge, skills and understanding   **73**

SHC 23 Introduction to equality and inclusion in children and young people's settings   **80**

    L01 Understand the importance of diversity, equality and inclusion   **81**

    L02 Be able to work in an inclusive way   **91**

    L03 Be able to access information, advice and support about diversity, equality and inclusion   **100**

TDA 2.1 Child and young person development — **105**

LO1 Know the main stages of development of children and young people **106**

LO2 Understand the kinds of influences that affect the development of children and young people — **133**

LO3 Understand the potential effects of transitions on the development of children and young people — **142**

MU 2.2 Contribute to the support of child and young person development — **149**

LO1 Be able to contribute to assessments of the development needs of children and young people — **150**

LO2 Be able to support the development of children and young people — **165**

LO3 Know how to support children and young people experiencing transitions — **169**

LO4 Be able to support children and young people's positive behaviour — **175**

LO5 Be able to use reflective practice to improve own contribution to child and young person development — **187**

TDA 2.2 Safeguard the welfare of children and young people — **192**

LO1 Know about the legislation, guidelines, policies and procedures for safeguarding the welfare of children and young people, including e-safety — **193**

LO2 Know what to do when children and young people are ill or injured, including emergency procedures — **202**

LO3 Know how to respond to evidence or concerns that a child or young person has been abused, harmed or bullied — **208**

MU 2.4 Contribute to children and young people's health and safety — **225**

LO1 Know the health and safety policies and procedures of the work setting — **226**

LO2 Be able to recognise risks and hazards in the work setting and during off-site visits — **234**

LO3 Know what to do in the event of a non-medical incident or emergency — **241**

LO4 Know what to do in the event of a child or young person becoming ill or injured — **247**

LO5 Be able to follow the work setting's procedures for reporting and recording accidents, incidents, emergencies and illnesses — **250**

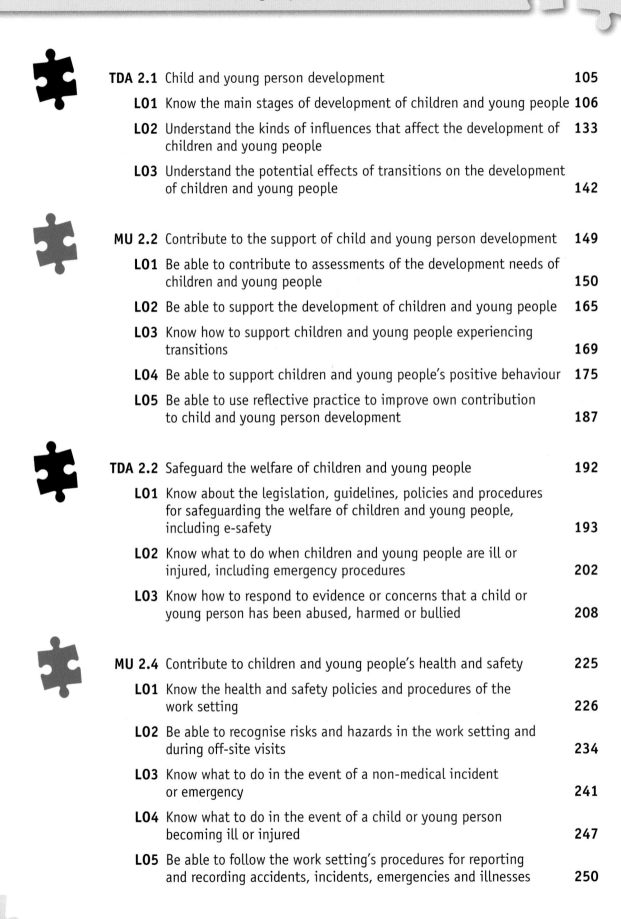

LO6 Be able to follow infection control procedures   **254**

LO7 Know the work setting's procedures for receiving, storing and administering medicines   **260**

TDA 2.9 Support children and young people's positive behaviour   **263**

LO1 Know the policies and procedures of the setting for promoting children and young people's positive behaviour   **264**

LO2 Be able to support positive behaviour   **271**

LO3 Be able to respond to inappropriate behaviour   **277**

MU 2.8 Contribute to the support of positive environments for children and young people   **289**

LO1 Know the regulatory requirements for a positive environment for children and young people   **290**

LO2 Be able to support a positive environment that meets the individual needs of children and young people   **299**

LO3 Be able to support the personal-care needs of children and young people within a positive environment   **305**

LO4 Understand how to support the nutritional and dietary needs of children and young people   **314**

MU 2.9 Understand partnership working in services for children and young people   **323**

LO1 Understand partnership working within the context of services for children and young people   **324**

LO2 Understand the importance of effective communication and information sharing in services for children and young people   **330**

LO3 Understand the importance of partnerships with carers   **341**

PEFAP 001 Paediatric emergency first aid   **353**

LO1 Understand the role of the paediatric first-aider   **354**

LO2 Be able to assess an emergency situation and act safely and effectively   **358**

LO3 Be able to provide first aid for an infant and a child who is unresponsive and breathing normally   **362**

LO4 Be able to provide first aid for an infant and a child who is unresponsive and not breathing normally   **366**

LO5 Be able to provide first aid for an infant and a child who has a foreign body airway obstruction — 368

LO6 Be able to provide first aid for an infant and a child who is wounded and bleeding — 371

LO7 Know how to provide first aid for an infant and a child who is suffering from shock — 374

MPII 002 Managing paediatric illness and injury — 378

LO1 Be able to provide first aid to an infant and a child with a suspected fracture and a dislocation — 379

LO2 Be able to provide first aid to an infant and a child with a head, neck and back injury — 382

LO3 Know how to provide first aid to an infant and a child with conditions affecting the eyes, ears and nose — 386

LO4 Know how to provide first aid to an infant and a child with a chronic medical condition or sudden illness — 390

LO5 Know how to provide first aid to an infant and a child who is experiencing the effects of extreme heat and cold — 397

LO6 Know how to provide first aid to an infant and a child who has sustained an electric shock — 401

LO7 Know how to provide first aid to an infant and a child with burns or scalds — 403

LO8 Know how to provide first aid to an infant and a child who has been poisoned — 405

LO9 Know how to provide first aid to an infant and a child who has been bitten or stung — 408

TDA 2.7 Maintain and support relationships with children and young people — 413

LO1 Be able to communicate with children and young people — 414

LO2 Be able to develop and maintain relationships with children and young people — 417

LO3 Be able to support relationships between children and young people and others in the setting — 429

TDA 2.14 Support children and young people at mealtimes and snack times — 435

LO1 Know the principles of healthy eating for children and young people — 436

LO2 Know the benefits of healthy eating for children and young people 442

LO3 Know how to encourage children and young people to make healthier food choices 445

LO4 Be able to support hygiene during mealtimes or snack times 450

LO5 Be able to support the code of conduct and policies for mealtimes or snack times 452

TDA 2.15 Support children and young people with disabilities and special educational needs 457

LO1 Know the rights of disabled children and young people and those with special educational needs 458

LO2 Understand the disabilities and/or special educational needs of children and young people in own care 469

LO3 Be able to contribute to the inclusion of children and young people with disabilities and special educational needs 473

LO4 Be able to support disabled children and young people and those with special educational needs to participate in the full range of activities and experiences 476

TDA 2.16 Support children and young people's play and leisure 483

LO1 Understand the nature and importance of play and leisure 484

LO2 Be able to support children and young people's play and leisure 498

LO3 Be able to support children and young people in balancing risk and challenge 505

LO4 Be able to reflect on and improve own practice 510

OP 2.15 Contribute to the support of children's communication, language and literacy 513

LO1 Understand the importance of communication, language and literacy 514

LO2 Be able to contribute to children's learning in communication, language and literacy 523

LO3 Be able to evaluate own contribution to children's learning in communication, language and literacy 532

OP 2.17 Contribute to the support of children's creative development   **535**

LO1 Understand the importance of creative development   **536**

LO2 Be able to contribute to children's creative development   **543**

LO3 Be able to evaluate own contribution to children's creative development   **554**

Reflective practice   **558**

Glossary   **563**

Index   **565**

ABOUT THE AUTHOR

Miranda Walker has worked with children from birth to 19 years in a range of settings, including her own day nursery and out-of-school clubs. She has inspected nursery provision for Ofsted, and worked at East Devon College as an Early Years and Playwork lecturer and NVQ assessor and internal verifier. She is a regular contributor to industry magazines and an established author.

INTRODUCTION

The Level 2 Certificate for the Children and Young People's Workforce is a brand new qualification. Before it was introduced, people wanting to work in various jobs within the workforce would undertake completely different qualifications. The government wanted to address this as part of its work to create a unified workforce which shares a common identity and values. The qualification will also help to ensure that a common professional language is shared by practitioners – this will overcome some difficulties which occurred in the past when words such as "observation" and "assessment" had different meanings to different practitioners.

Structure

The structure differs to that of previous qualifications, because there are three different pathways (study routes), which meet the needs of learners wishing to work in three different areas of specialism within the children and young people's workforce. The three pathways are:

- Early Learning and Childcare Pathway
  This is the pathway you have selected, suitable, for example, for those working in a day nursery

- Children and Young People's Social Care Pathway
  Suitable, for example, for those working in children's residential care

- Learning, Development and Support Services Pathway
  Suitable, for example, for Connexions advisers and learning mentors

The qualification has three "shared core units". These are mandatory units that will also be included in other Level 2 qualifications across the children and young people and adult social care workforce. There are ten mandatory core units for the children and young people workforce, which must be undertaken by everyone studying for this Certificate. (Some of these units are shared with other pathways.) These reflect the knowledge and skills of the common core. The common core describes the skills and knowledge that everyone who works with children and young people is expected to have. Learners will also select units from the optional unit bank. Each unit has a credit value. The options selected must total a minimum of 4 credits.

The shared units of this new qualification makes it much easier for practitioners to transfer into other areas of work within early learning and childcare during their careers, as it will be possible to undertake additional pathway and optional units rather than starting another different qualification from scratch.

Learning and assessment

How you will be taught and assessed will be explained to you fully by your college or training centre. There will be differences in the learning methods offered by colleges and centres. There are also differences in the way in which the three awarding bodies – CACHE, City & Guilds and Edexel – assess the qualification. Specific advice on preparing for assessment by each of the awarding bodies is given for each unit so you can be confident that you'll know what to do. All learners must be assessed in the workplace as they carry out practical work. Additional commonly used assessment methods include discussion with a tutor or assessor, answering oral or written questions, completing assignments and projects, completing tests and reflecting on your own practice.

Credits and level

Each unit has a credit value which reflects how long it is expected to take the average learner to achieve. This time includes private study and guided learning hours (time spent in lessons or tutorials) time spent undertaking practical work (at work or on placement) and time spent on assessment (including completing tasks and assignments, and being observed). As a rough guide, one credit is equivalent to approximately ten hours of learning. You must gain 35 credits across the qualification in order to gain the Certificate. Once you have completed all of the mandatory units required you will have accumulated 31 credits, so you must select optional units to study with a combined total of at least 4 credits. There are currently 15 to choose from in the "option bank." Your college or training centre will advise you on your selection of optional units – they may not offer them all.

The Certificate is ranked at Level 2 on the Qualification and Credit Framework. Some of these optional units are ranked as Level 3. These are ideal for learners who want to go on to gain the Level 3 Diploma in the future. Howerver, many learners will solely choose optonal units ranked at Level 2.

Structure of units

Each unit consists of a number of learning outcomes. These specify what you will know and understand in order to achieve the unit. Learning outcomes also tell you what you will be able to do competently in practice to achieve the unit - or in other words, what practical skills you will have.

All learning outcomes must be assessed. Assessment criteria is provided for each learning outcome. This specifies and breaks down the standard/level of knowledge and understanding and practical competence that must be demonstrated.

The content of this book covers all of the knowledge and understanding required for the units included.

HOW TO USE THIS BOOK

Welcome to the *Level 2 Certificate for the Children and Young People's Workforce* student book. This section explains the features of this book and how to use them as a tool for learning. It's important that you read this section.

Throughout certain units, there are references to the home countries, e.g. 'You should follow the curriculum framework that applies in your home country.' This is because there are some differences in laws, requirements, curriculums and procedures in England, Wales, Scotland and Northern Ireland.

Learning outcomes

All units are divided into learning outcomes. The first page of each unit lists the relevant learning outcomes.

LEARNING OUTCOMES

The learning outcomes you will meet in this Unit are:

Focus on...

This feature appears at the beginning of each learning outcome to explain the focus of the outcome. It also makes a link to the Assessment Criteria.

FOCUS ON ...health and safety

Link Up!

The Link Up! feature frequently appears in the text to direct you to other units that relate to the subject currently being covered.

Did you know?

This feature provides interesting and useful facts that will be valuable to your learning and will enhance your knowledge.

Key terms

During your course you'll come across new words and new terms that you may not have heard before. When these words and terms are first used in the book the key terms feature appears. This gives you a clear definition of the word or term.

Have a go!

The Have a go! feature asks you to do small tasks based on the text you have read. The tasks will help you to understand and remember the information. Some tasks are linked to your placement. These will help you to apply your learning to your practical work.

Good practice

It's important that you always work to high standards and do the best for the children in your care. This feature highlights good practice.

Practical example

Practical examples (case studies) are included to help you understand how theory links with practical work in real settings. After each Practical example a question or two is provided to help you think about how you can use your learning in real situations.

Practical example

Stars Out of School Club interprets legislation

Ask Miranda!

Your expert author, Miranda Walker, answers all the burning questions you may have as you work through the units and supports you on your way to success!

Ask Miranda!

Progress Check

At the end of each unit you will find a list of questions. Answering these will confirm that you have understood what you have read.

▶ Progress Check

Are you ready for assessment?

This feature offers advice on preparing for the different types of assessment you will be required to complete for each unit. The feature is divided into three sections: CACHE, City & Guilds and Edexcel, so you can be confident you will know exactly what you have to do. A tip on how to prepare for assessment is also given. If your awarding body does not have a set task or an assignment for you to do for a specific Unit, the tip will relate to gathering evidence or preparing to be observed.

Are you ready for assessment?

Reflective Practice

A key component of professional development is learning from past experience. This is known as 'reflective practice'. You need to demonstrate that you can think about your practice, notice areas for development and plan how to improve your knowledge, understanding and skills, as you work through your qualification. To help you achieve this, a Reflective Practice section is included at the end of the book. It provides suggestions to help you focus on relevant aspects of your professional development.

REFLECTIVE PRACTICE

UNIT 21

Introduction to communication in children and young people's settings

LEARNING OUTCOMES

The learning outcomes you will meet in this unit are:

1 Understand why communication is important in the work setting

2 Be able to meet the communication and language needs and wishes and preferences of individuals

3 Be able to overcome barriers to communication

4 Be able to respect equality and diversity when communicating

5 Be able to apply principles and practices relating to confidentiality at work

INTRODUCTION

It's very important for you to learn how to communicate effectively because communication is at the heart of our work as practitioners. We communicate constantly with the children and young people in our care, their families and our colleagues. We do this for a wide range of reasons and in many different ways. You'll learn about these during this unit.

... understanding why communication is important in the work setting

In this section you'll learn about the reasons why people communicate and how effective communication affects all aspects of the practitioner role. You'll also learn why it's important to observe an individual's reactions when communicating with them. This links with **Assessment Criteria 1.1, 1.2, 1.3.**

Communication

When communication is mentioned, talking is often the first thing that springs to mind. This is of course a very important verbal method of communication. But there are also several non-verbal (non-spoken) methods of communication that are just as important.

Key methods of communication are:

■ verbal conversation

■ written communication

■ body language and gesture

■ facial expression

Did you know?

It's important to remember that conversation involves listening as well as talking!

There are several methods of communication

eye contact

touch

sign language

visual communication (such as pictures that convey a meaning)

behaviour.

You'll learn more about communication methods on pages 10–20.

Reasons for communicating

People communicate for several reasons, as shown on the diagram below.

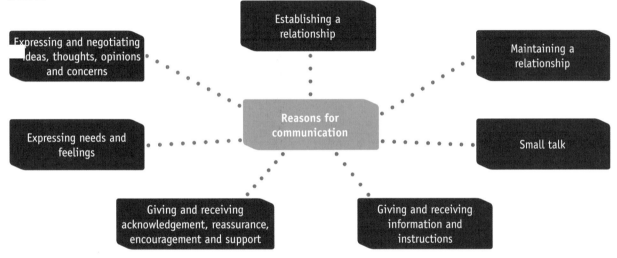

Establishing a relationship

Expressing and negotiating ideas, thoughts, opinions and concerns

Maintaining a relationship

Reasons for communication

Expressing needs and feelings

Small talk

Giving and receiving acknowledgement, reassurance, encouragement and support

Giving and receiving information and instructions

Reasons for communicating

We'll look at these reasons in turn. We'll also consider how communicating effectively for each reason affects your work.

Establishing a relationship

We use communication to establish (start) relationships with other people. For example, when we meet someone we:

make eye contact

smile

say hello

introduce ourselves.

We may also shake hands.

Already we're using body language, facial expression, the spoken word, gesture and touch, and we've only just met the person!

How this affects your work

Communicating in this way lets the person know that we're friendly and interested in them. We're also striking up a rapport (a connection).

Because there will always be new children, families and colleagues to meet, it's important that all practitioners learn to establish relationships well. A little bit of confidence and a smile go a long way, because they help people to feel at ease with us.

The more people you meet, the more natural and enjoyable this process becomes. This applies to learners on placement as well as employed staff.

Maintaining a relationship

All relationships need maintaining. On the most basic level, we do this each time we communicate with someone who we have already established a relationship with – each time we say hello or wave to someone we've already met for instance.

How this affects your work

If someone you know fails to acknowledge you, it can leave you feeling awkward and insecure. This can also happen within the setting, so it's important that you make an effort to communicate with people, as long as this is appropriate. For instance, if another member of staff is dealing with a parent, it isn't appropriate to interrupt, but you can smile as you pass by.

Small talk

'Small talk' is also known as 'casual conversation' or 'chit-chat'.

How this affects your work

Small talk also helps us to maintain relationships. For instance, if a parent tells you that they're looking forward to a visit from a family member this evening, you might ask them tomorrow if they had a good time.

Have a go!

Think about a time when someone you know failed to acknowledge you – when you passed them in the street perhaps, or saw them in a shop. How did you feel?

Small talk helps us to maintain relationships

Giving and receiving information and instructions

Lots of information is exchanged in settings every day and many instructions are given. These may be:

- verbal
- on paper
- in electronic files (such as emails and attachments).

Practitioners will exchange information and instructions with a number of people, including:

- children
- parents and carers
- colleagues
- supervisors and managers
- outside professionals, for example social workers, speech and language therapists, etc.

How this affects your work

Some of the information will be confidential, which means that not everyone will have access to it. You'll learn more about confidentiality and how this affects your work in Learning outcome 5.

Good practice

Keep small talk with parents and carers to a brief conversation only, or it will prevent you from getting on with other aspects of your work. Although small talk with colleagues is also important, this should be kept for break times. It is not good practice for staff to be discussing personal matters when they are with the children.

Information and instructions should always be shared appropriately and given clearly, so that they are properly understood. Many settings have procedures in place to ensure this. You must always work in line with these systems. For instance, there may be:

■ a system for passing on day-to-day information at the end of a practitioner's shift

■ whiteboards recording when sleeping babies were last checked

■ message forms to fill in when taking phone messages

■ a home/nursery daily contact sheet for recording when babies fed and how much feed they had

■ a chain of command so it's clear which members of staff are responsible for giving instructions to less senior colleagues.

If you are unsure about the meaning of any information or instructions given to you, always ask for clarification rather than making a mistake. If you do make a mistake, always inform the appropriate person straight away so that it can be sorted out.

It's also important for you to choose an appropriate method of communication when exchanging information or instructions. For example, should you tell someone something in person or write it down? You'll learn more about this as you work through the unit.

See Learning outcome 3 for information on ways to ensure that communications have been understood.

There may be message forms to fill in when taking phone messages

Practical example

Communicating with families

Venetta works in a children's centre. At the end of every day, she sits down with each of her key children and asks them what they enjoyed doing today. She then writes this down briefly in the child's home/setting diary.

Venetta also takes photos of the children's activities throughout the week. Then every Friday (with the permission of the parents and carers), she chooses one or two pictures of each child and emails them home to their family.

Giving and receiving acknowledgement, reassurance, encouragement and support

Giving and receiving acknowledgement, reassurance, encouragement and support are important for everybody's emotional well-being. To know just how crucial they are, you only have to imagine for a minute what it would be like to have no one to reassure you when you're worried, or no one to support you when you do something challenging, such as starting a new job or college course.

This is especially true for children and young people because their lives are full of new experiences and situations. They need to know that the adults in their life care for them and take an interest in them, and that they are there to support them.

Give practical help when it's needed

How this affects your work

Practitioners meet children's needs for acknowledgement, reassurance, encouragement and support constantly through their communicative interactions. This occurs in many different ways, including:

- gentle touch when attending to physical care (such as changing nappies)
- verbal praise
- encouraging nods and smiles
- eye contact
- giving practical help when it's needed
- comforting a child who is upset
- behaving appropriately around children and young people
- giving a child who is apprehensive about going down the slide time and space to watch others.

Expressing needs and feelings

Both adults and children need to express what they need and how they feel. This is crucial to emotional well-being because people cannot respond to someone's needs and feelings unless they know what they are.

Did you know?

Being caring towards children at all times is at the heart of communicating acknowledgement, reassurance, encouragement and support.

Practitioners need to interpret the communications of babies and young children

Unit TDA 2.2 Safeguard the welfare of children and young people.

Unit MU 2.8 Contribute to the support of positive environments for children and young people.

Unit TDA 2.16 Support children and young people's play and leisure.

Unit OP 2.17 Contribute to the support of children's creative development.

How this affects your work

Babies and young children in particular have limited ways to express their needs and feelings. This means that practitioners need to interpret their communications. For instance, a cry from a baby could mean a number of things, including:

- I'm hungry
- I'm tired
- I'm uncomfortable
- I'm in pain
- I need company.

If the practitioner cannot interpret the communication effectively, the child's physical and emotional needs may not be met. This would have a negative impact on their well-being. You'll learn more about meeting the needs of babies and young children in Unit MU 2.8.

Children and young people need practitioners to give them opportunities to express their needs and feelings, otherwise they may become frustrated or overwhelmed. In time, they will learn to recognise and deal with their feelings in more sophisticated ways. Creative activities are a common way to encourage expression. You'll learn about these in Units MU 2.8, TDA 2.16 and OP 2.17.

Expressing and negotiating – ideas, thoughts, opinions and concerns

Settings function best when practitioners work effectively as a team. This requires each team member to share their ideas, thoughts, opinions and concerns. Most settings will make time for this in general team meetings. There will also be time for everyone to 'put their heads together' when planning activities or reviewing policies and procedures. In Unit TDA 2.2 you'll learn how to raise serious concerns about the quality of the setting (whistle-blowing) and what to do if you are concerned that a child is being harmed. There's also some relevant information in Learning outcome 5.

It's good for children and young people to express their own ideas, thoughts and opinions in their play and their conversations. Paying attention to ideas, thoughts and opinions helps us to:

- show children that we value what they think and say

- build children's confidence and self-esteem

- get to know children well as individuals

- learn about children's levels of understanding and development.

Practitioners share their ideas, thoughts, opinions and concerns in team meetings

How this affects your work

It takes a bit of confidence to share your ideas, thoughts and opinions at work, but it is an important part of your role. Settings know this, and usually make an effort to encourage newer staff to contribute, so it's important that you do respond. In time, it will be second nature to join in at staff meetings, etc.

In your practical work with children and young people, be sure to regularly ask them for their thoughts, opinions and ideas. This can be done in numerous ways, including:

- asking young people at a holiday club for their theme or activity ideas

- asking a child whether they'd like their snack indoors or outdoors today

- asking children what they think will happen next in a story

- asking young people which way of doing something they prefer, for example what method of painting they prefer and why.

Ask an experienced practitioner if you can pay attention to how they encourage children to express their thoughts, opinions or ideas over the course of a session. Make a brief note each time you notice a form of encouragement.

Later, you can reflect on this. You will probably find that the practitioner encouraged expression numerous times, as it's a very natural part of interacting well with children. What can you learn from the methods you observed? Can you weave them into your way of interacting with children?

Everyday communications

A huge number of individual communications take place within settings each day. For instance:

How many more daily communications can you think of to add to this list on the right? There are many more that occur between adults. Also, think about the numerous communications between children and between children and adults.

■ Parents tell practitioners how their child is in the morning and give any special information or instructions, for example they'll be collecting them a little early, or please remove the skin from their pear at lunchtime, etc.

■ At the end of the session practitioners tell parents how their child was, for example what they did, whether they were happy, if they slept, what they enjoyed, how much they ate. A written note may also be given, particularly for babies and younger children.

■ Supervisors allocate daily jobs and responsibilities to colleagues.

■ Colleagues discuss the best way of carrying out an activity.

■ Practitioners answer the phone and may write down messages for colleagues.

Communication methods

There are many different methods of communication.

■ Some methods are verbal.

■ Some methods are non-verbal.

Verbal and non-verbal methods are shown in Table SHC21.1.

Table SHC21.1: Verbal and non-verbal methods of communication

Verbal methods of communication	Non-verbal methods of communication
Face-to-face conversation	Sign language and Makaton (the simple form of sign language)
Telephone conversation	Facial expression
Video clips	Eye contact
Audio clips	Touch
Video/webcam link	Gesture and body language
	Behaviour
	Email
	Text
	Letter
	Pictures and symbols
	Reports and newsletters

Choosing an appropriate method

You should always aim to communicate clearly in a way that is appropriate for individuals and appropriate to the situation. To do this, you should start by thinking about the nature of what you need to say.

Urgent or non-urgent?

An important consideration is whether or not the communication is urgent, as this will dictate whether someone needs to be contacted straight away.

Examples of urgent communications include:

■ Informing a parent that their child has vomited and that they need to be collected and taken home. In this case, it would be appropriate for a practitioner to call the parent's workplace straight away.

■ A large piece of outside play equipment has broken during a session, and another group of children is due out to play shortly. It will be necessary to let the supervisor know promptly so that the item can be removed or placed safely out of bounds.

■ A child who was expected has not arrived at an after-school club based on school grounds. Practitioners must follow the setting's 'missing child' procedures immediately, beginning by speaking to the child's teacher to find out if they were in school today.

If a child is sick, their parent/ carer should be called straight away

Examples of non-urgent communications include:

■ A child has been coughing on and off throughout the afternoon. It's appropriate for a practitioner to wait and tell the parent in person when they collect their child.

■ One of the footballs has been punctured. A practitioner throws it away and remembers to tell the supervisor at the end of the day so that a replacement can be ordered.

■ There's going to be a Christmas party. Invitations can be popped in children's bags to take home.

Good practice

It's good practice to think about confidentiality too, for example who should know about the content of the message. For instance, it may be appropriate to put a general, round-robin note or newsletter in children's bags for them to take home. But a formal, confidential letter would need to be sealed in an envelope, addressed and marked 'confidential'. It should then be posted, or handed, to the appropriate adult. (You'll learn more about confidentiality in Learning outcome 5.)

Table SHC21.2 shows the range of communication methods you can choose from. Advantages and disadvantages are given for each, along with a tip for their use within the setting.

Styles of communication

You also need to think about whether your approach should be formal or informal. As a general rule, this depends on the tone and circumstances of:

■ what you have to say

■ who you are communicating with.

This will also impact on the tone, pitch of voice and the vocabulary (the actual words) that you use.

Table SHC21.2: Methods of communication: advantages and disadvantages

Method of communication	Key advantages	Key disadvantages	Tips for using the method
Face-to-face conversation	Often the quickest, easiest and most effective way to communicate on a day-to-day basis with children, young people, colleagues, parents and carers. Effective for social interaction, discussion, giving and receiving information and feedback, asking questions, and meetings of all sizes.	Can be difficult to arrange a) a time to talk and/or b) a place to talk in private when necessary. Detailed information may not be remembered. Barriers are common for people with communication difficulties and for people whose first language is not English.	Speak clearly and concisely, make eye contact and listen actively (see page 18). Take notes when appropriate to ensure that you remember details – it's easy to make mistakes with times, dates, etc. If you have specific information to give verbally, make notes and refer to them to ensure you cover everything. Check that you have understood correctly or, if appropriate, that others have understood you (see Learning outcome 3 on page 35).
Sign language/ Makaton	The primary and most effective way for many deaf people to communicate on a day-to-day basis as long as those they wish to communicate with also know sign language. Makaton may be used by children and/or those with learning difficulties.	The majority of people do not know sign language or Makaton. Different sign languages are used in different countries/ cultures. You need to be able to see one another.	If sign language/Makaton is used in your setting, learn some key signs. An introduction course to sign language or Makaton is recommended. Your setting's SENCO should know about local courses (see page 102).
Telephone call	Ideal for contacting people in an emergency, arranging/ confirming appointments and meetings, giving/receiving information from parents, outside professionals, etc. Messages can be left on voice mail when people are unavailable.	Not everyone has access to a landline and/or a mobile phone. People with communication difficulties may find that phones present a barrier to clear communication. People with English as an additional language may also experience difficulty.	Think about what you want to say before you call. Speak clearly, give your message concisely. Make sure you call from an appropriately quiet room and in private if your message is confidential.
Letter	An excellent way of communicating both formally and confidentially, and of putting important details in writing. For example, a letter may be sent to confirm that a place has been booked at the setting for a new child, or a supervisor may write a letter of reference for a student who has worked with them on placement and is now applying for jobs.	The written text may not be accessible to people who have difficulties with literacy, those with visual impairments and those with English as an additional language.	Write your message clearly and concisely, and check for spelling and grammatical errors. Always be sure to address people appropriately (for example 'Dear Mrs Foreman'). Mark envelopes 'private and confidential' if this applies. Use the setting's letterhead if appropriate.

Method of communication	Key advantages	Key disadvantages	Tips for using the method
Text message	A useful way to send round-robin reminders a) to colleagues (for example 'Reminder: staff meeting starts at 6pm this evening'), b) to young people to let them know what is happening at a setting (for example 'Youth club karaoke this Fri and disco on Sat!') and/or c) to parents/carers (for example 'Reminder: Pre-school fête, 3–5pm this Saturday!')	Not suitable for everything but very informal, short messages, and best used for reminders rather than messages that must be received by a certain time. Not everyone has a mobile phone, and those who do may not check messages regularly. The issues with written text as described in the section on letters (page 13) also apply.	Do not use text abbreviations (for example 'u' instead of 'you'). Be wary of how you address people – in many settings 'Hi Sarah' would not be considered appropriate for a parent. You must have permission from the setting and parents before texting children or young people. Only ever text from a work mobile phone, not your personal number.
Internet	A popular way to order supplies and resources. A website is a useful way for a setting to communicate about its services and provision, particularly to new families interested in using the setting. Blogs can be used to give information about the setting's events and activities.	Information on the internet is in the public domain and can be accessed by anyone, including those with negative intentions for its use. Not everyone has access to the internet, and not everyone is familiar with such technology. The issues with written text as described in the section on letters (page 13) also apply.	Be very careful about the information that is placed on the internet, including the use of photographs of children and young people. Most settings will have very strict guidelines about this, and these must be followed to the letter. If ordering online, ensure websites have secure payment systems.
Email	It is easy to create groups of people to whom you send the same message, for example a group of parents, a group of committee members, a group of colleagues, etc. This makes email a great way to distribute a range of information such as newsletters or minutes from the staff meeting. You can attach additional documents easily and provide weblinks. Messages are received in the recipient's inbox instantly. You have an electronic copy of all the messages you send and receive. It is simple to forward messages when appropriate. You can have one-to-one correspondence with someone at a time that suits you both, as people can read and respond to messages when convenient.	Not everyone can use the technology. Not everyone has internet access or email accounts. Those who do send emails may not check messages regularly. Emails are quick to write, and there is a danger of a) sending messages that have not been thought through (particularly if you are feeling annoyed), b) sending an email that has not been written to a professional standard and/or c) sending too many emails.	Avoid sending too many emails, and ensure the ones you do send are clear and concise. Be wary of how you address people (see the section on text messages above). You must have permission from the setting and parents before emailing children or young people. Only email from a work address, not your personal account. Think about confidentiality, especially when copying other people in. Check for spelling and grammatical mistakes. Avoid replying to emails when you are annoyed in case you send a message that you later regret.

For example, a formal approach is required:

- in written reports

- when approaching or liaising with a professional outside the setting

- when discussing something of a sensitive/serious nature with colleagues or families.

An informal approach is suitable for:

- typical everyday conversations with colleagues

- everyday conversations with parents who you already have a relationship with

- your day-to-day interactions with children and young people.

Tone

Tone of voice has a lot to do with the way we interpret the communications made to us. Some studies have indicated that people often take more notice of tone than they do of what someone actually says to them. The Have a go exercise and the Practical example below demonstrate this.

Have a go!

Think back to when you were at school. Imagine that your teacher says to you in a casual, warm tone, 'There's something I need to talk to you about. So stay behind after class please.' How would you feel? Curious, perhaps? Now imagine they say exactly the same words in a harsh and formal tone. How would you feel now? Worried? Maybe even a bit scared that you are in trouble?

Practical example

Arguments

Arlo is a three-month-old baby. His parents are having an argument. Although they don't shout at each other, they do use some harsh, angry tones. Arlo hears this. He cannot understand the words his parents are using or why they are having an argument, but Arlo starts to cry because he is distressed by the tone of the voices he is hearing. Arlo's parents realise what has happened. They give him a cuddle and use soothing tones to comfort him. It takes a little while, but this eventually settles him down.

Harsh tones are distressing for children, even if they do not understand what is being said

So, when communicating on a day-to-day basis with children, colleagues, parents and carers you should use tones that are:

- warm

- friendly

- respectful.

Pitch

'Pitch' refers to how high or how low your voice is. Children respond best to a variation in pitch, because a voice that rises and falls is interesting to listen to. This can be a really useful tool to engage children, particularly when you're reading a story or when you're carrying out a group activity that requires you to hook everyone's interest at once. Try it! Pay attention to other practitioners too, and you'll see how well this works. Practitioners who really engage children usually make very good use of their voice.

A low pitch can be effective when we want to adopt a serious tone, and it can be useful if we need to step in to stop inappropriate behaviour. A firm, low 'No' can be very effective.

Vocabulary

Language is closely linked with thinking and children's overall intellectual development. When working with children and young people, it's important to use language that is appropriate to their stage of development. If you use language that's too complex with a group of pre-school children during a planned play activity, many opportunities for them to learn and enjoy are likely to be lost. The same is true if you use overly simple language for a group of primary-school children.

With experience, pitching your vocabulary at the right level will become second nature to you, and you will find that you can adjust your level with ease when communicating with children of different ages and stages of development even within the same group setting. Many job roles require an ability to do this well – working at a holiday club that caters for children aged 4–12, for instance. Most new practitioners and students learn this skill by simply absorbing the vocabulary used by their colleagues in their workplace settings.

Did you know?

Babies in particular respond well to a high-pitched voice. Many people naturally adopt a higher pitch, and perhaps a sing-song tone, when they interact with a baby.

However, it's important to understand that new words can and should be introduced regularly as this is how children's own vocabularies grow. You'll learn more about how children's vocabularies develop in Unit TDA 2.1.

Unit TDA 2.1 Child and young person development.

Good practice

Some forms of communication, such as face-to-face conversation for example, can be either formal or informal. However, other methods, such as texting or messages left on post-it notes, are generally regarded as strictly informal and inappropriate in certain circumstances. Be sure to follow any rules your setting has about the methods of communication used to contact parents, carers and outside professionals.

Communicating with adults

It is essential to communicate clearly to ensure that your message is received. Once you have chosen the appropriate communication method for the situation and the individual, you are on the right track. But there is a key question to ask yourself prior to communication – what exactly are you trying to say? You need to be clear about the point of your message before you try to communicate it to someone else. At the start of their careers, it's not unusual for students and new practitioners to feel a bit nervous about communicating in certain circumstances. But the following strategies can help:

It's important to use language appropriate to a child's age and stage of development

- Thinking through/writing down key points in advance so that you don't forget anything and you feel focused.

- Practising or seeking advice. If you are unsure about how to phrase something, practise a few different ways aloud, or in writing, or seek advice from a colleague.

- Considering whether a certain response or answer is required. Do you need to wait for a reply or some information in response?

Unit TDA 2.7 Maintain and support relationships with children and young people.

Communicating with babies, children and young people

For specific guidance on communicating with babies, children and young people, see the information on forming relationships with them, in Unit TDA 2.7.

Active listening

Communication is a two-way street, so how well you listen is just as important as how well you express yourself. It certainly impacts on the quality of the communication between you and other adults, and between you and the children and young people in your care.

Listening well shows that you value what children say and feel

Active listening demonstrates to children that you value what they say and feel. This has a positive effect on their levels of confidence and self-esteem. Active listening strategies include the following:

■ Letting children and young people see you are interested in what they are saying. Establishing eye contact, getting down to the children's level whenever necessary. Smiling and nodding encouragingly if appropriate.

■ Giving children time. Children need time to formulate their ideas as they speak. Listen for long enough to let them finish what they have to say, even if they need to pause for thought.

Asking children and young people questions about their topic. This encourages them to talk further (and to think). They will know you are interested if you are asking for more information.

Clarifying and confirming. You can ask questions to check you are following what a younger child is telling you. Making sure you are interpreting correctly is part of listening well. You can repeat the essence of what a child says, asking afterwards, 'Is that right?' Or you can ask questions to clarify, for example, 'So you borrowed three books from the library on Saturday?'

Reacting to what children say. Showing empathy for children's feelings when they are expressed. Be aware of your facial expressions – look happy for children, or concerned, or whatever is appropriate.

Responding. Make sure that you answer children and young people when they talk to you. Even if they have not asked you a direct question, you should still respond appropriately, perhaps just to say, 'That's interesting' or, 'That sounds like fun'. These acknowledgements are important. They let children and young people know that you have received their communication, and that you appreciated their message.

You can use the same strategies to equally good effect when you are listening to adults.

Behaviour to avoid

The following types of behaviour could indicate to children and young people that you do not value their ideas and feelings:

- Not really listening.

- Not making eye contact.

- Looking bored.

- Not contributing to the conversation.

- Not responding.

- Not acknowledging or answering.

- Interrupting.

Some behaviour could indicate that you don't value the ideas and feelings of children or young people

■ Rushing them to get to the point.

■ Not acting upon their ideas.

■ Not thanking or praising them for their contributions.

Sometimes, particularly in group discussions, children and young people will be keen to share their thoughts and may interrupt one another. Allowing interruptions sends the message that one person's thoughts are more important than another's. The Practical example below demonstrates an effective way of dealing with this without putting children off contributing eagerly.

Practical example

Andreas controls a group discussion

Andreas works in a holiday club. Next week's theme is the rainforest, and he has been asking the children for some activity ideas. Eight-year-old Lennon is telling Andreas which animals he'd like to find out about, when seven-year-old Kerry interrupts, eager to share her own idea to make some parrots. Andreas acknowledges her, but encourages her to wait by saying, 'Hold on to that idea Kerry. Let's finish listening to Lennon, and then we'll hear from you.'

Good practice

Your general behaviour communicates just as much, if not more, than what you say. For instance, someone may say things that you'd expect to hear from a caring practitioner. But if they do not behave in a caring way towards others, this is meaningless to everyone. You may like to think for a moment about what uncaring behaviour communicates to everyone about the practitioner, and how the behaviour is likely to affect children.

Make sure your communications and your behaviour match up, so you both *communicate* and *behave* appropriately and consistently.

Observing reactions when communicating

When you're communicating with someone it's important to notice how the other person is reacting. This helps you to judge whether you should adjust what you're saying or the way in which you're saying it. For instance, if someone seems upset or worried, it may be necessary to adjust the tone or pitch of your voice. You might also ask if they want to discuss any concerns. Or, if someone seems confused, you may need to simplify the language that you're using to get your message across or to further explain what you mean.

There are five main indicators of reaction, as the diagram below shows.

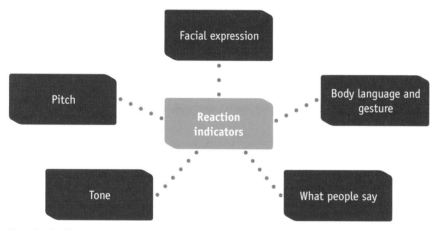

Reaction indicators

We will look at these in turn. However, it's important to recognise that facial expression, body language/gesture, tone and pitch can mean different things to people of different cultures and ethnicities. We'll explore this further in Learning outcomes 3 and 4.

Facial expression

As you've learnt, it's good practice to make eye contact when you communicate with someone face to face. This also helps you to notice and to read someone's facial expression, which is a good indicator of how your message is being received. For instance, you will be able to recognise if someone looks worried, confused, excited, bored, etc.

Have a go!

What facial expressions might you notice in the following situations?

- Someone agrees with something you've said.
- Someone disagrees with something you've said.

Body language may indicate when someone feels tense

Body language and gesture

Body language can also be very revealing. There are whole books dedicated to the subject, but you're probably already quite familiar with what basic body language postures indicate. For instance:

■ If someone is looking at something/someone other than you when you're talking, they may be distracted or uninterested.

■ If someone steps back from you, they may feel you're standing a little too close and encroaching on (or 'invading') their personal space.

■ If someone has a relaxed posture with shoulders back, they may be feeling confident.

■ If someone leans towards you with an open posture (no folded arms or legs), it can signal friendliness and being at ease with you.

■ If a child reaches out to you, they may want a cuddle.

■ If someone crosses their arms tightly, or has tight lips or clenched fists, they may be angry or tense.

■ If someone turns their body away from you, they may not be willing to listen to what you have to say.

■ If someone has raised shoulders, they may be feeling tense.

■ If someone has a slouched posture, they may be lacking confidence or enthusiasm/motivation.

Many of us 'talk with our hands' by gesturing when we're speaking, and we're not consciously aware that we're doing it! This is because it's such a natural, ingrained part of our behaviour. This occurs as a response to communication too, giving us further feedback. You may observe signals such as these:

■ Someone who is in agreement nodding along.

■ Someone who disagrees shaking their head.

■ Someone who wishes to interject (have their say) holding the palm of their hand towards you as if to stop you.

Have a go!

What body language reactions might you notice in the following situations?

■ Someone doesn't really have time to stop and talk to you.

■ Someone wants to politely end a conversation with you now.

Tone and pitch

What people say – the particular words they use – is of course very important, but the tone and pitch they use provides us with plenty of extra reaction feedback. See the Have a go section below for an example of this.

Imagine the following scenario:

You're explaining to a mum that her child, Joe, has deliberately pushed over another boy today, and it's not the first occasion. She responds by saying, 'I'll talk to him again at home. Come on, Joe.'

Now think about how her pitch and tone could indicate her reaction. For example, how might she be reacting emotionally to the event if she says this in a calm, even tone? What if she raises her voice and looks at Joe while she's speaking? Or if she looks down and says it very quietly?

Some assumptions are made about pitch and tone of voice – that a quiet voice indicates nervousness for instance, or that a high-pitch voice indicates excitement. In reality, though, it can be very difficult to read (or judge) these unless you are familiar with the way that an individual usually talks. But once you are 'tuned in' to this, it's possible to detect differences quite easily. For example, you can probably tell if a friend is feeling down just by their tone of voice on the phone.

Good practice

If you aren't communicating with someone face to face, you won't be able to observe facial expressions or body language, so you'll need to pay close attention to the other reaction indicators.

Your reaction to others when they are communicating

You should also respond with appropriate facial expressions, body language/gesture, touch and tone of voice when someone is communicating with you. These things are just as important as what you actually say when you reply.

It may be appropriate to show empathy or concern, or perhaps that you are pleased for someone. Luckily, we often do this naturally! If you are talking to someone who becomes upset, you will probably drop the tone of your voice and speak more softly and slowly. You may also find that you naturally mirror (copy) people when interacting. For instance, you might:

■ smile at someone who's happy to be telling you their good news

■ repeat the babblings of a baby back to them in their own tone

■ frown in concern when a worried child approaches you

■ nod when someone is talking to show that you agree, or to encourage them to continue

■ tilt your head to one side a little, showing you're interested

■ raise your eyebrows in response to a happy surprise

■ touch the arm of an adult who is upset

■ put your arm around an upset child, or give them a cuddle.

Did you know?

In some cultures, touch is unacceptable as a method of communication and should not be used.

It's important to show interest when you are communicating

The overall effect of communication on relationships in the setting

Communication is at the heart of making and maintaining relationships with children and adults within the setting. This includes parents and carers as well as colleagues and outside professionals. It's also central to your training and learning relationships – with tutors, assessors and mentors.

When positive relationships are formed it is easier for everyone to give and receive:

- trust
- information
- support
- help
- advice
- encouragement.

You'll learn more about this in Unit TDA 2.7.

It is also more likely that skills and knowledge will be shared, and that any problems arising between adults will be resolved positively. (You'll learn more about resolving conflict in Unit TDA 2.9).

In summary, good teamwork, effective learning and the effective shared care of children and young people depend on positive working relationships, which in turn depend on effective communication.

Did you know?

Positive working relationships between colleagues lead to a pleasant environment. This is good for the adults and the children or young people.

Link Up!

Unit TDA 2.7 Maintain and support relationships with children and young people.

Unit TDA 2.9 Support children and young people's positive behaviour.

Did you know?

The quality of the relationships you form and how well you work in practice depends on your communication skills. This means that effective communication is one of the most important skills for you to develop.

LEARNING OUTCOME 2

... being able to meet the communication and language needs and wishes and preferences of individuals

In this section you'll learn how to find out about an individual's communication and language needs and wishes and preferences. You'll also learn about using appropriate communication methods to meet them, and how and when to seek advice about communication. This links with **Assessment Criteria 2.1, 2.2, 2.3**.

Part of your role is to find out about the communication and language needs and wishes and preferences of the people you work with – colleagues, parents, children and young people. Once practitioners know about someone's needs, wishes and preferences, they plan how to meet them so that effective communication occurs and good relationships are built and maintained.

Often, the best way to find out about needs, wishes and preferences is to directly ask the people concerned, and this includes the children and young people. If this is inappropriate, remember that families will generally know their children better than anyone, and they are usually happy to help. Most settings will ask families about their communication and language needs and wishes and preferences when they first register with the setting. This means that effective communication measures can be taken from the start.

Wishes and preferences

While individual people's wishes do vary, an important general rule is to always be professional when interacting with others. This means communicating and behaving politely and courteously at all times.

Good manners show respect for other people. More importantly, a lack of manners is often interpreted as a lack of respect for other people. You can probably think of many times when you've been offended by someone who has spoken to you rudely, interrupted you or failed to say please and thank you.

Always remember that good manners are to be used when you are talking to children as well as adults. Manners are an important part of establishing and maintaining positive relationships with everyone, and they influence the behaviour of children too. You are a role model for children, so always talk to them as you would like them to talk to others.

You should also use people's names correctly. A name is part of someone's individual identity and you must respect this. Here are some helpful tips:

- Find out how people would like to be addressed.

- Don't assume that it's acceptable for you to use a parent's first name.

- Don't make assumptions about people's titles (for example, not all mothers go by the title 'Mrs').

- Not all parents share the same last name as their child.

- Never shorten the name of an adult or a child unless you are invited to.

- If someone asks to be called by a shortened version of their name, stick to using this.

Recall a time when someone has called you by the wrong name. Perhaps they shortened your name without asking, or called you the wrong name altogether. How did it feel?

When appropriate, also consider the communication methods preferred by other people. (You learnt about communication methods in Learning outcome 1.) For example, unless there's an urgent reason for contacting them, some people prefer email to phone messages. Families may also have preferences about the time at which you communicate with them. For instance, a working parent may prefer to discuss an issue at the end of day when they collect their child rather than at the beginning when they drop them off, because they need to rush off to work.

Communication and language needs

To understand communication and language needs, you must know the meaning of the key terms relating to speech, language and communication. These are explained in page 28. A good understanding of the patterns of children's speech and language development is also important. This is covered in Unit TDA 2.1. It's a good idea to read this information as part of your study of this unit.

Unit TDA 2.1 Child and young person development.

- Speech: this is the process of vocalising language. It is produced by muscle actions that occur in the head, neck, chest and abdomen. When learning to speak, children are discovering how to regulate and coordinate muscles to produce a number of sounds which, when combined, result in words that others can understand. There are more than 40 sounds to master in the English language.

- Language: this is a symbolic communication system. The symbols can be spoken aloud, written down or signed. There are conventions (rules) about the way these symbols are used, but once they are understood, the rules allow people to say anything they want within the limitations of their vocabulary. For example, we can say sentences that we have never heard said before. Each of the symbols in a language system have meaning, but these are often abstract, which makes them hard to learn.

For instance, the word for 'egg' in no way resembles an egg. The only way a child will learn the meaning of the word for egg is if they hear it used in context – when they are being offered a boiled egg, for instance. However, they will also need to learn that the term 'egg' applies to a raw egg, a scrambled egg, a fried egg, etc. Although lots of species of animals communicate, only humans use a learnt symbolic system. So it's often said that language is the 'essence of being human'.

Language may be spoken, written down or signed

- Communication: this is an umbrella term that refers to the way in which people send messages or signals to one another. Communication methods can be both verbal and non-verbal, as you learnt in Learning outcome 1. For communication to be effective, each person communicating needs to both:
  - understand what others are communicating to them
  - express themselves in a way others can understand.

What are language and communication needs?

Language and communication needs can arise from the following factors:

- An impairment/difficulty.

- Culture.

Ethnicity.

Speaking more than one language.

Lack of confidence.

You will learn about language and communication impairments below. In Learning outcomes 3 and 4, we'll look at the needs that arise due to culture, ethnicity, speaking more than one language and a lack of confidence.

Language and communication impairments (or difficulties)

People with language and communication impairments experience difficulty communicating with others across one or more of the elements of speech, language and communication, as described above. For instance, some may have difficulty vocalising language, for example a child with a cleft palate. Some may not be able to hear speech well, for example a child who is partially deaf. Others may have a learning difficulty, for example a child with autism.

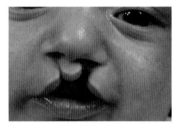

Some children may have difficulties vocalising language

A language and communication impairment usually means that someone:

cannot express themselves, or

experiences difficulty expressing themselves, or

has difficulty understanding what people say to them, or

finds that other people have difficulty understanding the ways in which they communicate.

It's not uncommon for more than one of these factors to apply.

Each setting will have appointed one of the practitioners to take on the role of Special Educational Needs Coordinator (**SENCO**). The SENCO takes responsibility for ensuring that the individual needs of children and young people are met within the setting. This includes children who have communication and language difficulties. The SENCO will work in partnership with the family and the child's key person, and will also have contact details for outside professionals and services that can be accessed for information and support. A plan

key terms

SENCO Special Educational Needs Coordinator. An appointed practitioner within a setting who is responsible for ensuring that the individual needs of children and young people are met.

will be drawn up to show how the child's needs will be met. This will be reviewed at regular intervals.

If you are not a child's key person (or if you are a student on placement), the SENCO is a good person to approach within the setting for advice on how to communicate effectively with those who have language and communication needs.

Also see the information on identifying and overcoming language and communication barriers in Learning outcome 3.

Did you know?

Children's language and communication difficulties may be minor or they may be complex. The difficulties may be experienced temporarily over a short period, temporarily over a long-term period, or they may last throughout their life.

Good practice

During your career you can expect to work with children and adults with a range of language and communication needs. You should be able to choose the communication methods best suited to the needs of each individual. You may like to refer back to the information on communication methods in Learning outcome 1.

Ask Miranda!

Q I've had some great feedback from my assessor on my communication skills and my relationships with young children. But I still find that I have problems getting children to express their feelings instead of getting frustrated and cross with each other. Sometimes they do things I've asked them not to do many times, like taking someone else's toy. Am I failing to communicate this to them clearly in a way they can understand?

A **Probably not. It sounds as though it's probably down to the fact that children are still learning about communication and how relationships work. It takes time and life experience to learn to deal with and communicate feelings and impulses appropriately. It's normal for children and young people to fall out with others many times as these lessons are learnt, just as we did at their age. But we do eventually learn to recognise and explain our feelings when we're upset, and to ask before we take something that belongs to someone else.**

LEARNING OUTCOME 3

FOCUS ON

... being able to overcome barriers to communication

In this section you'll learn how to identify **barriers to effective communication**, how to overcome them and how to ensure that your communications have been understood. You'll also learn how to identify services and sources of information and support that enable more effective communication. This links with **Assessment Criteria 3.1, 3.2, 3.3, 3.4.**

key terms

Barriers to effective communication factors that prevent effective communication.

Barriers to effective communication

We refer to factors that prevent effective communication as 'barriers'. You learnt how important effective communication is in Learning outcome 1, so you'll understand why it's part of a practitioner's role to:

■ identify barriers

■ find a way to overcome barriers.

Barriers that are experienced in settings generally fall into one of the following categories, and may apply to adults, children and young people. Suggestions of how each barrier may be overcome are given in the table on pages 33–4.

Language barriers

■ Someone only speaks a language other than English.

■ Someone is learning English as an additional language and there are gaps in this learning. Gaps are common for children who are being brought up to be **bilingual** (able to speak two languages) or **multilingual** (able to speak three or more languages).

■ Use of jargon or over-complicated language prevents communication from being clearly understood, or the message itself is unclear, misleading or confusing.

key terms

Bilingual able to speak two languages.

Multilingual able to speak three or more languages.

Cultural barriers

■ Aspects of communication have different meanings in different cultures, for example shaking the head may mean 'yes' rather than 'no'.

■ Certain aspects of communication may be inappropriate in some cultures, for example touch.

Physical barriers

Out-of-date technology may present a physical barrier to communication

■ Inefficient or out-of-date communication equipment or technology, including computers, phones and sound systems.

■ Noisy environment (usually background noise).

■ Environment is physically spread out, making communication from some locations difficult.

■ Settings operating from more than one site.

Personal barriers experienced by individuals

■ Language and communication needs (as described in Learning outcome 2).

■ Lack of confidence.

■ Lack of motivation (this could be due to emotional problems or concerns, or it could be related to health or psychological conditions, for example someone may be withdrawn or depressed).

Attitudinal barriers

■ Personal conflict between staff.

■ Professional conflict between staff (such as opposing views on how things should be done).

■ Practitioner's poor attitude to fulfilling their job role.

■ Lack of motivation (which may be due to poor leadership or a lack of consultation between management and staff).

Organisational barriers

■ Insufficient training in effective communication.

■ Lack of structure and guidance on lines of communication within the setting (who should communicate with whom, and how).

- Lack of effective systems for communication (such as the handling of post and email).
- Lack of access to sources of communication support (you'll learn more about this on page 36).
- Lack of non-contact time (time away from the children) in which practitioners can communicate.
- Incorrect information given.

Overcoming barriers to effective communication

Once practitioners have identified a barrier, they must think about how it can be overcome. Sometimes there is a fairly straightforward solution. For instance, if noise is preventing effective communication, it may be a case of simply turning off background music during free play time. In other situations, solutions may take longer to achieve. For instance, it may be necessary to access a translation service.

Table SHC21.3 gives examples of solutions to the barriers discussed above.

Table SHC21.3: Examples of measures to overcome barriers to effective communication

Barriers	Example measures to overcome the barriers
Language barriers: - Someone only speaks another language. - Someone is learning English as an additional language and there are gaps in this learning. - Use of jargon or over-complicated language prevents communication from being clearly understood, or the message itself is unclear, misleading or confusing.	- Access support from interpretation and translation services. - Access information online about agencies able to offer information, advice and support in relation to language barriers. This can be done via the Department of Education (www.education.gov.uk) and the setting's local authority. - Staff training on effective, straightforward and clear communication.
Cultural barriers: - Aspects of communication have different meanings in different cultures, for example shaking the head may mean 'yes' rather than 'no'. - Certain aspects of communication may be inappropriate in some cultures, for example touch.	- Research the meanings and appropriateness of communication methods (for example body language, gesture, touch, etc.) for the culture. Again, local agencies that can offer information, advice and support can be found via the local authority. - Staff training on the subject.

Barriers	Example measures to overcome the barriers
Physical barriers: ■ Inefficient or out-of-date communication equipment or technology, including computers, phones and sound systems. ■ Noisy environment. ■ Environment is physically spread out, making communication from some locations difficult. ■ Settings operating from more than one site.	■ Staff meeting to discuss and identify all problems experienced with equipment and technology. Plans made to update/ replace. ■ Turning off background music. ■ Tweaking the activity plans to ensure there's a balance of quieter and busier play activities available, which will reduce the overall noise level. ■ Systems to aid communication over a large area, for example walkie-talkies within a holiday club. ■ Systems to aid communication between two or more sites, for example mobile phones as well as land lines, manager to visit each site daily, regular joint staff meetings and events.
Personal barriers experienced by individuals: ■ Language and communication needs. ■ Lack of confidence. ■ Lack of motivation.	■ Consultation on how best to meet language and communication needs/lack of motivation between families, key person, the SENCO and outside professionals such as speech and language therapists. ■ Planned strategies to support confidence, such as one-to-one conversation opportunities with the key person, giving the child plenty of time to respond, avoiding putting the pressure on the child to communicate in group activities. ■ Play activities that promote communication, for example toy telephones, rhymes, etc.
Attitudinal barriers: ■ Personal conflict between staff. ■ Professional conflict between staff. ■ Practitioner's poor attitude to fulfilling their job role. ■ Lack of motivation.	■ Meetings between staff to discuss conflict and agree a resolution and way forward. A senior colleague mediates. ■ A discussion between the employer and employee about work performance and how this can be improved, for example communication training, appointing a mentor for the practitioner. ■ The arrangement of regular staff meetings to consult everyone about the policies, procedures and daily events at the setting.
Organisational barriers: ■ Insufficient training in effective communication. ■ Lack of structure and guidance on lines of communication within the setting. ■ Lack of effective systems for communication. ■ Lack of access to sources of communication support. ■ Lack of non-contact time in which practitioners can communicate. ■ Incorrect information given.	■ Staff training. ■ A period of staff consultation leading to the introduction of written communication policies and procedures. ■ Administrative systems introduced. ■ Reorganisation of work schedules to allow adequate non-contact time. ■ A part-time administration worker appointed. ■ SENCO asked to do some research and compile a file on sources of communication support. ■ System put in place to ensure information given in documents such as newsletters is proofread to ensure it is accurate.

Ensuring communication has been understood

As you've learnt, steps taken to overcome barriers should be regularly and formally reviewed. But it's also good practice to ensure that individual communications have been understood when barriers apply. This is a two-way street. You need to be sure of the following points:

■ That others have understood the communications you have made to them. You can check that the message or information you have given verbally has been understood by asking the other person if everything is clear, and inviting them to ask any questions. If you think they may have misunderstood but they are not aware of this, you can always ask them to summarise. So you may say to a young person, 'Just to make sure we're both clear, can you tell me what you'll need to bring on the trip out next week?' If you are communicating in writing or by email, you can ask for a reply.

Good practice

The likelihood of your message being understood is greatly increased if you have chosen a communication method that meets the person's communication and language needs, wishes and preferences (which you learnt about in Learning outcome 2).

■ That you have understood the communications made to you. The key technique here is active listening, which you learnt about in Learning outcome 1. This will help you to focus on understanding the message.

Good practice

You should also ask questions to clarify and confirm as part of your active listening. For example, you may say to a parent, 'So you want to cancel your nursery booking for Tuesday. Is that next Tuesday only? Or do you want to cancel every Tuesday?'

Services and sources of information and support

Sometimes settings need extra information and support to enable more effective communication. In these circumstances, the following services can be called on:

- Translation services.

- Interpretation services.

- Speech and language services.

- Advocacy services.

We'll look at each in turn below.

Translation services

Translators are bilingual or multilingual. They will translate writing/text into other languages for people who cannot understand them in English. They will also translate writing/text in other languages into English. For instance, a setting may arrange for their policies to be translated into Polish to meet the needs of a family new to the setting. Writing/text can also be translated to or from Braille.

Interpretation services

Interpreters are bilingual or multilingual. They will attend a setting to facilitate (or enable) a conversation between two people who do not speak the same language, by interpreting what each is saying. Even if a family has some understanding of English, many settings find it helpful to use the services of an interpreter when something important or formal is being discussed. This helps to ensure that everyone understands all of the details.

A sign-language interpreter at work

A 'signer' is another sort of interpreter. The signer will facilitate conversation between a deaf person who uses sign language and someone who does not, by interpreting what each is saying. If a deaf person is attending a meeting where there will be discussion amongst several people, two signers may be booked. In this case, one will sign what everyone else is saying so the deaf person can understand. Meanwhile, the other signer will translate the deaf person's sign language into the spoken word, so everyone else can understand.

Good practice

When a setting first begins working with someone for whom English is an additional language, or someone who uses sign language, it can be particularly helpful to discuss future communication needs via an interpreter or signer to avoid misunderstandings about this important topic. This smoothes the way for successful communications in the future.

Speech and language services

When a problem with speech or language has been identified, a speech and language therapist will meet with a child or young person to work on ways in which their speech and language can be developed and supported. An important part of this role is providing advice and guidance on how families and settings can effectively communicate with children and young people. Suggestions may include activities that encourage them to engage in communication, as well as advice in the use of specific methods of communication, such as using Makaton (the simple form of sign language) or a communication deck (children point to pictures printed on a deck of special cards).

Advocacy services

'Advocacy' means supporting or representing the interests of people who are likely to be disregarded or have difficulty in gaining attention.

Under legislation called the UN Convention on the Rights of the Child, children have a right to be consulted about matters that are important to them. The role of an advocate is to talk to children and young people who may not otherwise have their opinion listened to, about things that are important to them and their lives, and to represent their best interest. Through the advocate, a child or young person's opinions and feelings are passed on to the appropriate person or authority.

Advocates have an extremely important role to play in ensuring the voices of children are heard. They are likely to work with children and young people who are looked after by their local authority, as well as those with communication or learning difficulties.

Did you know?

Your setting's SENCO will generally have contact information for support services available in your local area.

LEARNING OUTCOME 4

FOCUS ON

... being able to respect equality and diversity when communicating

In this section you'll learn about how people from different backgrounds may use or interpret communication methods in different ways. You'll also learn about communication that respects equality and diversity. This links with **Assessment Criteria 4.1, 4.2.**

Interpretation and different backgrounds

We are all different, but people who have a shared experience of a particular background will often interpret communication methods in similar ways. This could be to do with a shared experience of:

■ culture

■ experience

■ knowledge

■ childhood

■ family background.

Shared experience gives us a kind of 'shorthand' when it comes to communicating with others who have a similar background to our own. We just seem to understand each other. This may lead you to assume that people in general will interpret your communications as you intend. However, you shouldn't necessarily expect this.

The reason for this is that people from different backgrounds may use and interpret communication in different ways, as the following section explains. The experience young children have of communication in the home will have a particularly strong impact on their own communication methods and style as their communications outside the home and family will be limited.

Have a go!

Think of a child you know who is of pre-school age. How many different adults do you think he or she regularly spends significant time communicating with? It's likely to be few.

Home language and culture

There may be a complete or partial language barrier. Different forms of the same language may be spoken in different regions of the same country, and accents and pronunciation may vary. Words that have more than one meaning in English can be particularly misleading.

People who do not have English as their first language may use and interpret tone and pitch in a different way. For example, they may not use rise and fall in their tone.

Gestures and body language may be interpreted differently. For instance, eye contact may rarely be used in some cultures. Touch may be unacceptable. Subjects considered sensitive or unsuitable for 'polite conversation' may differ greatly. There may be different sensibilities in terms of things that are considered rude or offensive.

Home and family background

Different families interact and communicate in very different ways. Some homes are busy and noisy and calling to one another from two rooms away is normal behaviour. Others are quieter and calmer, and voices are rarely raised.

Some children will hear and perhaps use more than one language at home. Swearing may be heard in the home or on TV, or it may not be tolerated at all. Adults may be highly communicative or relatively quiet – they may engage in banter with one another and with

Did you know?

In the Western world, it's often considered rude to point directly at someone, but it's fine to point out objects to other people. But in some Asian countries it's considered rude to point with the finger at anything. Instead, it's acceptable to gesture towards an object with an open palm that is facing upwards.

Some homes are busy and noisy

children, or it may be rarely heard. Individual children may be used to interacting with other children at home, or they may spend most of their time with adults.

Personality, confidence and self-esteem

These are closely linked. Some children are naturally more outgoing, while others are more reserved. Some children approach practitioners frequently with something to say, but it's important to also initiate communication with the children who are less likely to do so.

Avoid pressurising those who are reluctant to speak in group activities or when someone new is present, or there's a danger they may avoid certain situations and become isolated. Negative experiences can seriously impact on children's confidence and self-esteem. If a child is ridiculed for the way they communicate or for mistakes that they make (written or verbal), it can affect them for years to come. They may grow up believing they are no good at writing, for instance, and this could become a block to their learning.

Personality also influences the way in which children and young people respond. Some are an 'open book' – they may vocalise their excitement, enthusiasm, unhappiness or anger. While others communicate this more subtly, the intensity of their emotion may be the same.

Literacy and technological ability

As discussed in Learning outcome 2, literacy skills vary in adults as well as in children and young people. This could be due to a negative or unsuccessful learning experience, a lack of learning opportunity, a learning difficulty or learning English as an additional language. Confidence can also be an issue – some people do not feel confident expressing themselves in writing, or they fear making a mistake if reading aloud.

Practitioners should provide information verbally as well as in writing when necessary. When working with young children it is important to provide activities that promote literacy skills and confidence. People who do not have fluent literacy skills may also be at a disadvantage in terms of technological knowledge or ability, as sending emails and browsing websites relies on these skills.

Have a go!

Think back to when you were a child. How did you express your feelings? Were you an 'open book' as described opposite? Or did you communicate your feelings more subtly?

Written instructions for technology, such as the use of a digital camera or a smart phone, can use unfamiliar and complicated language. But people who are highly literate may also struggle here – they may not have learnt how to use modern technology (or they may not have access to it), so never assume everyone will sign up to the setting's blog or check the website for updates.

Learning two or more languages

We live in a culturally diverse society, so it is important for practitioners to recognise that many children will learn more than one language. You should understand the following:

■ Children who are learning two or more languages at the same time sometimes show a delay in their communication. This is generally put down to the fact that they are absorbing two languages – or twice as much. However, with support, children's overall communication development need not be affected.

■ Some experts believe that children pick up a second language more easily if it is introduced to them after they have mastered the basic use of one language.

■ Someone who speaks two languages is known as bilingual. Someone who can use three or more languages is multilingual.

■ Children tend to learn languages best by simply absorbing them naturally. This happens when people frequently interact and talk with children in a language.

■ Bilingual and multilingual children may confuse languages at times, mixing up simple words, sentences or phrases. This might be because they have not yet learnt the particular word they want in the language they are currently speaking. For instance, if a child usually eats their meals at home where they speak only Italian, they may not know mealtime words in English, even though they speak English at their pre-school every morning. So when they play with a tea set at pre-school, they may introduce some Italian words into their spoken English.

■ Word games and activities (such as picture lotto) can help to fill children's vocabulary gaps.

■ It's thought that children learn to separate different languages most easily when they clearly identify them with people and places. For instance, if grandparents only talk to their grandson in Chinese, he is likely to only communicate back in that language. If a child only speaks English at a setting, they are less likely to switch between English and their home language when they are there. Difficulties are more likely to occur when children hear adults switching in and out of languages frequently when they talk.

■ You may speak just one language with a bilingual or multilingual child, but it's important to recognise that they are developing their communication skills in other languages too. This achievement should be acknowledged.

■ Bilingual and multilingual settings should ensure that all languages spoken are recognised and valued as part of children's culture.

Respecting equality and diversity

In Learning outcome 3 you learnt how to identify and overcome barriers to communication. By following these procedures, practitioners can ensure that everyone is given equal opportunities in terms of communication. If a setting fails to identify and overcome communication barriers, the people who experience them are likely to

Link Up!

Unit SHC 23 Introduction to equality and inclusion in children and young people's settings.

Playing lotto can help to fill children's vocabulary gaps

become very isolated. Their ability to participate equally in all aspects of the provision would certainly be severely affected.

The languages we speak and the other ways in which we communicate are part of our own individual identity. If we do not value a child's language or communication methods, then we are not properly valuing that child. The same applies to the adults within our settings.

By broadly celebrating cultural and background diversity and meeting needs that arise from them, settings show that they value difference and respect equality and diversity.

Practical example

Karen prepares for a bilingual child

Karen works at a day nursery. A new child, three-year-old Amalie, will be starting soon, and Karen will be her key person. The manager tells Karen that he has arranged for Amalie's parents to visit the nursery, meet Karen and fill in the registration forms. The manager also tells Karen that Amalie's parents are French. They speak English fluently and they are bringing Amalie up to be bilingual.

Karen thinks about this, then makes a note of the language issues she should discuss with the family. Questions on her list include:

1. What is the family's approach to bringing Amalie up to be bilingual? (Is she currently learning both English and French?) What language does she use at home? (Who talks to her in French, and who talks to her in English?)
2. How fluently does Amalie speak each language? (Does she understand most of what is said to her? Does she confuse languages? Has there been an impact on her communication development?)
3. How would the family like practitioners to communicate with Amalie? (Totally in English? Some of the practitioners do know a little French, although no one is fluent.)
4. How can the setting and the family work together to support Amalie's bilingual communication development?

LEARNING OUTCOME 5

FOCUS ON

... being able to apply the principles and practices relating to confidentiality at work

In this section you'll learn what **confidentiality** is and how to demonstrate it in day-to-day communication. You'll also learn about situations when confidential information may need to be passed on and how and when to seek advice about confidentiality. This links with **Assessment Criteria 5.1, 5.2, 5.3, 5.4.**

key terms

Confidentiality this refers to the rights of people to have information that is held or known about them kept privately and safely.

What is confidentiality?

The word 'confidentiality' refers to the rights of people to have information that is held or known about them kept privately and safely. It's a key issue for practitioners because they know many personal details about the families that they work with. The Data Protection Act of 1984/1998 makes it a legal requirement for settings to handle appropriately the confidential information that they collect and hold about people.

When working in a setting, you may be given confidential information verbally, and depending on your position you may have access to confidential files and records. These may be paper based or electronic. Even as a student you will become aware of some information about children and families that must not be shared outside of the setting.

Have a go!

All settings have a confidentiality policy that explains the procedures they will follow in order to comply with the Data Protection Act. Make sure that you read and understand your setting's confidentiality policy. Speak to your supervisor if there's anything that you don't fully understand.

Good practice

Passing on information when you should not do so can have serious consequences for students and employees alike. As well as breaking the rules, trust may be lost, and this will damage working relationships and upset individuals. Your professional reputation can be affected, and disciplinary action may be taken by employers.

For instance, you may come to know about a child's disability.

Types of confidential information

You should treat any personal information about the people at your setting as confidential. That includes information relating to children, parents, carers, other family members and colleagues.

Types of confidential information include:

- Personal details such as those recorded on the registration form, including addresses, telephone numbers and medical information.

- Information about children's individual development and needs, including observations and the type of information held in development reports and on special educational needs registers.

- Letters, emails or reports from outside professionals working with children or families.

- Details about family or social relationships or circumstances, including things you may know about the current or past relationships within families or details about people's jobs or events in their lives.

- Financial information, including details about how children's places are funded and how any fees are paid.

- Information relating to past incidents or experiences of a sensitive nature. For instance, a family may have suffered a traumatic event. Or perhaps you know that social workers, therapists or other professionals are working within a family.

'Need-to-know' basis

Settings will only make sensitive information available to practitioners on a 'need-to-know basis'. In other words, the information will only be given to those practitioners who need to know it in order to carry out their work. The Practical example on page 46 demonstrates this.

Practical example

Sapphire deals with a sensitive issue

Sapphire works in a nursery where she's the team leader of the baby room. She notices that 12-month-old Marium's mum seems upset when dropping off her baby, so she asks if everything is all right. Marium's mum reluctantly says perhaps they should talk. Sapphire takes her to the office where they can talk in private.

Marium's mum explains that Marium's grandmother has been diagnosed with a terminal illness, and that the family is very upset. Marium's parents are also under practical strain, as between them they are spending a lot of time visiting the hospice.

Sapphire tells Marium's mum that she's keen to support her, and assures her there's no need for the information to go any further. She suggests that it might be a good idea just to let Marium's key person know, as she works so closely with the family and Marium. She will be able to assist by offering understanding and support, and will be ready should Marium react to the strains that are currently within the family. Marium's mum agrees this is a good idea, then leaves for work.

Sapphire calls Marium's key person into the office and shares the information with her. Sapphire explains that none of the key person's other colleagues need to know, so this must be kept confidential.

Good practice

It is never good practice to gossip in the workplace.

So, different practitioners in the same setting will not necessarily have access to the same information. This means that you should not discuss confidential matters with colleagues unless you are sure that it's appropriate to do so, and it can be done privately. If you find yourself wondering if it's all right to say something to someone, *don't say it*! If you are not sure about any issue of a confidential nature, always check with your supervisor before disclosing information to anyone else. You'll learn more about seeking advice on confidentiality on page 51.

Confidential records

A large amount of confidential information is contained within the records of a setting. These could be paper based or electronic (kept on computers, laptops, disks, memory sticks, etc.). All of this data must be handled with care and stored securely. You should never leave sensitive paperwork or electronic files where people who do not need to know will have access to them. Parents and carers should be aware of, and party to, information held about them and their children.

Never leave sensitive files where people who do not 'need to know' can access them

Data Protection Act of 1984/1998

As confidentiality is such an important issue, there is legislation in place to ensure that people's right to confidentiality is protected. In accordance with the Data Protection Act of 1984/1998, any organisation that collects and stores personal records must be registered on the Data Protection Register. To summarise, those registered must only collect information that is:

- accurate at the time it is collected

- obtained legally and without deceit

- relevant for its purpose and not excessive.

Collected information should:

- only be used for the purpose explained when it was collected

- be kept confidential from anyone who does not have the right to see it

- be kept up to date

- be made available to the person it is about, meaning that individuals are entitled to see information held about them or their children

- be kept securely – there must be security measures in place protecting against unauthorised access (for example locked filing cabinets, passwords on electronic files, etc.)

- only be kept as long as is necessary.

Have a go!

You can find out more about the Data Protection Act at www.ico.gov.uk.

Sharing confidential information

Discussing confidential matters

It's sometimes necessary to discuss a confidential matter with a colleague or outside professional either in person or on the phone. Always make sure that you can talk privately without being overheard. In a busy setting, this can be achieved by scheduling a conversation at a time when you are free to go to a private space, such as the office, where the door can be closed.

Sometimes a confidential matter needs to be discussed with a parent or carer. Again, it's up to the practitioner to arrange to talk privately, ideally in another room. Consideration should also be given to whether it's appropriate for the parent's child to hear the discussion, which may well be about them or about an issue that affects them.

Sharing confidential paper-based or electronic files

Settings routinely share some of the information they collect and hold, such as information about children's achievements as recorded in the Early Years Foundation Stage (EYFS) profile. Further statistical information (statistics or facts and figures), such as the ethnicity of families, may also be collected and passed on to local authorities. This must always be done in line with the setting's confidentiality policy. Families should be aware of the exchange of information and should give their consent. Further information about the EYFS profile can be found in Unit MU 2.2.

Link Up!

Unit MU 2.2 Contribute to the support of child and young person development.

Maintaining confidentiality in day-to-day communication

As you've learnt, understanding your setting's confidentiality policy and good everyday working practices will enable you to maintain confidentiality and treat confidential documents, files and conversations with respect. The diagrams that follow show ways in which you can maintain confidentiality in your day-to-day communications and handling of information in three key categories:

- Paper-based information and communication.

- Electronic-based information and communication.

- Verbally shared information and communication.

Paper-based information and communication

While settings increasingly keep confidential electronic files, some information such as observations and children's drawings or work generally remain paper based. As paper documents are easily moved and read, it's important to ensure they are looked after appropriately to prevent them from becoming lost, damaged, inappropriately accessed or photocopied. Settings generally keep confidential paper-based items in lockable filing cabinets or cupboards. It's important that relevant staff members have keys so they can access the information easily. These keys must be kept securely.

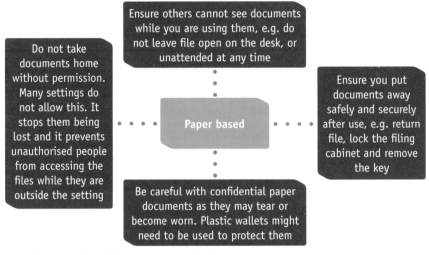

Ensure others cannot see documents while you are using them, e.g. do not leave file open on the desk, or unattended at any time

Do not take documents home without permission. Many settings do not allow this. It stops them being lost and it prevents unauthorised people from accessing the files while they are outside the setting

Paper based

Ensure you put documents away safely and securely after use, e.g. return file, lock the filing cabinet and remove the key

Be careful with confidential paper documents as they may tear or become worn. Plastic wallets might need to be used to protect them

Maintaining confidentiality: paper-based information

Electronic-based information and communication

Settings are increasingly keeping information on computers, laptops, discs, memory sticks and external hard drives. This may include emails, electronic documents, photos, video clips, audio clips, etc. Passwords can be used to protect access to computers and to particular files. This system can effectively allow practitioners who share a computer to access different files on a need-to-know basis.

Computers should have security in place to prevent them being accessed externally. They should be protected against viruses, and virus checks should be completed regularly. Back-up copies of electronic files should be made to prevent the loss of information.

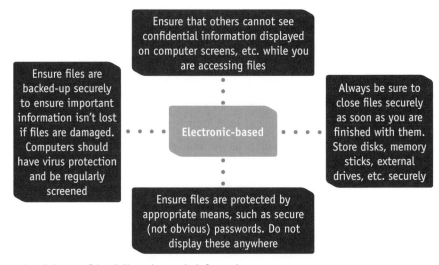

Maintaining confidentiality: electronic information

Verbal information and communication

Practitioners, parents and carers exchange confidential information verbally all the time, so it is important not to become complacent (or casual) about it. Stop and think about whether the things you are told should be kept to yourself. If it's appropriate and necessary to pass confidential information on to someone else, make sure you do so privately. Give some thought to whether you can be overheard – this also applies when you are on the phone. As already mentioned, it's never good practice to gossip. If you make it your rule not to gossip in the workplace, you will be less likely to accidentally reveal or hear confidential information inappropriately in your casual conversations.

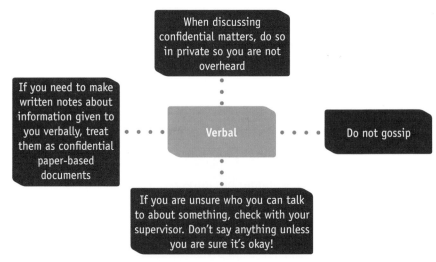

Maintaining confidentiality: verbal information

Situations where confidential information might need to be passed on

If confidential information about children or young people and their families needs to be passed on or discussed, parental permission must be sought in most cases. For instance, a practitioner may wish to contact an outside professional (such as a speech therapist) so they can work in partnership to support a child with communication difficulties. Or they may wish to make the child's records available to a body such as Ofsted during an inspection of the setting.

The exception to this is when not passing on information could affect a child or young person's welfare. For example, if you suspected that a child or young person was being abused or committing abuse, you would have a duty to **disclose** your concerns and the information they are based on, but only to the relevant person or authority. You would also need to report to the relevant person or authority any concerns that you had relating to the quality of care provided by the setting, including concerns about the practice of individual practitioners.

Practitioners may also be required to breach (or break) normal confidentiality if a crime has been committed, in which case it may be necessary to give information to the police.

For full details about how to disclose information relating to the concerns outlined above, see Unit TDA 2.2.

Seeking advice about confidentiality

As already mentioned, if you are ever in doubt about information that could be confidential, it's important that you seek advice from a senior colleague before sharing it with anyone else. You should also go to your line manager if:

- you have any questions about confidential matters

- you feel concerned or worried about information you have been asked to keep confidential within the setting.

key terms

Disclose pass on confidential information in certain circumstances, in line with confidentiality procedures.

Did you know?

Details of how to disclose information and raise concerns will be included in your setting's confidentiality policy and its child protection policy.

Link Up!

Unit TDA 2.2 Safeguard the welfare of children and young people.

How are things going?

▶ Progress Check

1. Explain five reasons why people communicate. (1.1)

2. Why should you observe someone's reactions when communicating with them? (1.3)

3. What do the following terms refer to:

   ■ communication and language wishes and preferences

   ■ communication and language needs? (2.2)

4. Give three examples of barriers to communication. (3.1)

5. What can a setting do to show that they respect equality and diversity in language and communication? (4.2)

6. What does the term 'confidentiality' mean? (5.1)

7. In what circumstances might confidential information need to be passed on? (5.4)

Are you ready for assessment?

Learning Outcomes 2, 3 and 4 must be assessed in real work environments.

CACHE

Set task:

■ In an induction scenario, you must provide information that shows you can identify the different reasons people communicate, explain how effective communication affects all aspects of your work, and explain why it is important to observe an individual's reactions when communicating with them.

You can prepare by rereading pages 2–25 and making relevant notes.

City & Guilds

In preparation for assessment of this Unit, it will be helpful to record in your reflective journal instances when you have identified and overcome barriers to communication.

Edexcel

In preparation for assessment of this Unit, it will be helpful to record in your reflective journal instances when you have identified and overcome barriers to communication.

Introduction to personal development in children and young people's settings

LEARNING OUTCOMES

The learning outcomes you will meet in this unit are:

1 Understand what is required for competence in own work role

2 Be able to reflect on own work activities

3 Be able to agree a personal development plan

4 Be able to develop knowledge, skills and understanding

INTRODUCTION

You must continue to develop your professional skills and knowledge throughout your career. This will help you to stay up to date with new developments in the industry, enabling you to meet regulations on an ongoing basis. It will also help you to improve your practice. This impacts on the quality of the care and learning that you provide.

In this unit you'll learn that a key part of professional development is learning from past experience. Practitioners think about their practice, notice areas for development and plan how to improve their knowledge, understanding and skills. This is known as 'reflective practice'.

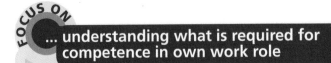

FOCUS ON

... understanding what is required for competence in own work role

In this section you'll learn about the duties and responsibilities of your work role, and the standards that influence the way the work is carried out. You'll also learn ways to ensure that personal attitudes or beliefs do not obstruct the quality of your work. This links with **Assessment Criteria 1.1, 1.2, 1.3.**

Duties and responsibilities of your work role

During this qualification you will learn and develop the basic knowledge and skills required of a level 2 assistant. But there is a huge range of jobs in the early years sector, within all kinds of settings. So you can expect the duties and responsibilities of different assistant roles to vary a great deal.

Throughout your career, it's important that you understand what is required of you in the specific job roles you take on. This applies whether you are:

■ a student on work placement

■ already employed

■ taking on a new role or responsibility at your current workplace

■ looking for a new job.

Did you know?

Everyone wants to do well at work. But you will only be able to do a good job if you understand what's expected of you. This will be influenced by what's expected from the setting by regulatory bodies such as Ofsted.

Job descriptions

Settings explain what they expect from employees by writing a job description for each role. This will be sent to job applicants who want to apply for any vacancies. It will also form part of the employment contract for the successful candidate.

The duties and responsibilities for a job role will often be expressed as tasks. For instance, if you are working as an assistant in the baby room of a nursery, tasks listed on your job description may include:

Assist in meeting the emotional and physical-care needs of babies with sensitivity.

Assist in making regular observations and assessment of the development of babies.

Most colleges and training centres will issue students with work placement guidelines. These are similar to a job description because they explain the duties and responsibilities of the student within the setting. Some settings also like to provide their own written guidance for the students who come to them on placement. Remember that nobody will mind if you need to ask a few questions about what is expected of you.

Person specification

Job descriptions often include a section called **person specification**. This lists the knowledge, experience and attributes that the practitioner will need in order to fulfil the duties and responsibilities. In our example, this may include:

Experience of meeting physical-care needs of babies, for example making up feeds, feeding and changing nappies.

Experience of meeting the emotional needs of babies, for example interacting with sensitivity and respect.

Ability to provide appropriate toys and play activities.

■ Good knowledge and understanding of baby and child development.

Good teamwork skills.

Ability to interact well with parents and carers.

A caring attitude.

Conscientious.

Basic food hygiene certificate.

Have a go!

If you're not yet employed, ask your placement supervisor if you could have a look at a job description for a level 2 post. It's a great way to see what is likely to be expected of you when you finish your course and apply for jobs.

key terms

Person specification part of a job description which lists the knowledge, experience and attributes a practitioner will need to fulfil a job role.

Read job descriptions carefully

Settings may identify some items on the job specification as 'desirable'. This means that, although they would ideally like a candidate to have a particular skill, knowledge or attribute, the setting will consider a promising candidate who does not have this. If offered the job, the candidate will be given the relevant training instead. It's worth keeping this in mind when you're applying for jobs. If you don't currently tick every box, let employers know that you're keen and willing to undertake further training, and you may still get the job.

Ask Miranda!

Q I want to work as an assistant in a school holiday club. Will all holiday clubs' job descriptions and person specifications be the same?

A No, they won't. Even the same kind of settings will develop their own and tailor them to suit their individual needs. You can expect similarities. For example, everyone will be looking for a caring person who relates well to children and young people, and someone who can contribute to establishing a fun, relaxed environment. Other points may be more unique. For example, a holiday club with regular access to the school swimming pool may list 'confident in the water' in their person specification.

Good practice

Once you have a job, always keep a copy of your job description. It's useful to refer back to when you're reflecting on your practice (you'll learn more about this in Learning outcome 2), and you may need it if your employer wants to make changes to your work role in the future. It will also come in handy if you want to apply for a new job. Job application forms will ask you to give details about your duties in your past positions, and your job descriptions will help you to give the correct information succinctly.

Your first placement or job

Everyone feels a little bit apprehensive during the first few days in any job or placement. There will certainly be a lot to learn. But all settings know this, and they will have developed an **induction programme** to help new workers settle in. Someone will be given the job of showing you around and introducing you to colleagues, children and parents. You'll also be told who to go to if you need any help or advice. Important information about the way the setting is run and how things are done will be explained, and you'll have plenty of opportunity to ask questions. There are two key pieces of advice to keep in mind:

- If you're unsure about anything, or if something hasn't been explained, always ask rather than guess. It avoids mistakes.

- Remember to smile!

key terms

Induction programme the system by which an employer or placement supervisor introduces a new staff member or student to the setting.

Standards that influence job roles

External standards

To ensure the safety and well-being of everyone who uses early years settings, groups can only operate if they meet certain external National Minimum Standards, which are set out in legal regulations and requirements of the setting's home country. For example, in England, early years settings must meet the Early Years Foundation Stage Safeguarding and Welfare Requirements. You'll learn more about this in Unit MU 2.4. You'll also learn about the curriculum frameworks that apply to settings or, in other words, the learning opportunities that children and young people must be given.

Settings must also meet the standards set out in additional laws and codes of practice. Some of these, such as the Children Act 2004 (see Unit SHC 23, page 94), apply specifically to children and young people's settings, while others are general. For example, the Health and Safety at Work Act (see Unit MU 2.4, page 226) applies to all employers in all industries – from playgroups to factories.

In addition, relevant National Occupational Standards (NOP) should also be met. Generally, these are sets of standards used by awarding bodies and others to develop qualifications and courses in our industry that provide appropriate learning at the right level.

Link Up!

Unit SHC 23 Introduction to equality and inclusion in children and young people's settings.

Unit MU 2.4 Contribute to children and young people's health and safety.

Settings have a number of policies and procedures

Unit OP 2.17 Contribute to the support of children's creative development.

Internal standards

Internal standards are the policies and procedures that individual settings develop. They will express how the setting will work to ensure that all required external standards are met or exceeded. For instance, the setting's health and safety policy and procedures will tell practitioners how things must be done within the setting, from who is responsible for ensuring the first-aid box is kept fully stocked to how frequently the toys in the baby room must be sterilised. By following all of the setting's internal policies and procedures, practitioners should be meeting the external standards.

Settings will often have additional standards that they have chosen to uphold. This might relate to the ethos or principles of the setting. This would apply to Montessori groups or Steiner schools for instance. Or a setting may place strong emphasis on a certain area, such as developing creativity (you'll learn more about this in Unit OP 2.17). Some groups choose to undertake a quality assurance scheme to prove that their work is of a high standard. This entails making a commitment to attain a set of published standards that exceed the minimum requirement. This will be assessed by an external body. For example, the National Day Nursery Association runs a quality assurance scheme for nurseries, and 4Children runs a scheme for out-of-school clubs.

The influence on job roles

When settings are devising their job descriptions and person specifications they will consider the relevant standards that they expect their new staff member to meet. Settings will not reach the external and internal standards required if the practitioners they employ are not up to scratch. The types of standards that will be considered are shown in the diagram on page 59.

Personal attitudes and beliefs

We all have our own personal attitudes, beliefs and values, and these shape our opinions and our behaviour. As part of personal development, all practitioners need to ensure that their attitudes and beliefs don't get in the way of the quality of their work. This is important because we are all influenced to some degree by the way we were brought up and educated, by what happens to us and by what we believe.

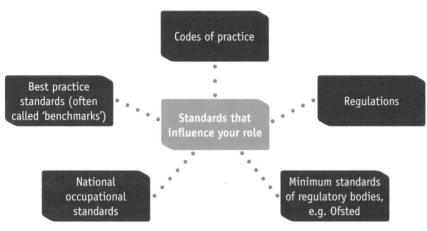

Standards that influence your role

This can show itself in many ways. For example, if you dreaded having to play team games in PE as a child, you may avoid including them in your activity programme for young people. A further Practical example is given below.

Practical example

Pia's attitude to mealtimes

Pia worked as a nanny for some time before deciding to try a new role. She has just started her first job in a nursery.

Pia notices that her colleagues at the nursery take a more relaxed approach to mealtimes. They don't insist that children eat all of their meal, and Pia normally would. She asks about this, and the team leader explains that they feel that mealtimes should never become a battleground, or young children may go on to experience unhealthy food issues in the long term.

Pia thinks about her own attitude. It occurs to her that she herself was brought up to finish everything on her plate as a sign of respect for the person who prepared her meal. She has been automatically expecting the children in her care to do the same. Pia realises that this could be affecting the quality of her work and that she needs to make a change.

Question:
What could Pia do to address the issue?

Our attitudes and beliefs change over time in response to our experiences and the things we come to learn and understand. To allow this to happen, it's important to keep an open mind and to consider and respect opinions and views that are different to your own. You must also respect the preferences and choices of families in terms of how their children's care needs are met. You'll learn more about this in Unit MU 2.8.

Strategies to avoid obstructing the quality of work

Becoming a reflective practitioner is one of the most effective ways to ensure that your own attitudes and beliefs don't obstruct the quality of your work. You'll learn about reflective practice strategies in Learning outcome 2. Also see:

- the information about reflecting on your own assumptions in the Good practice section on page 85 of Unit SHC 23

- the related Reflective practice section on page 558.

Good teamwork and communication skills will also help you to be open to other opinions and ways of working. (See Unit MU 2.9 for further information.) In addition to the everyday informal discussions that staff have as they go about their work, most settings will also devote time to air views and opinions on current issues in staff meetings. This encourages everyone to reflect and to see things from all sides. It also deepens understanding. Always remember that ways of working are not necessarily 'right' or 'wrong'. There are often several effective ways to do something.

Practitioners air views and opinions on current issues in staff meetings

▶▶▶Link Up!◀◀◀

Unit MU 2.8 Contribute to the support of positive enviornments for children and young people.

Unit SHC 23 Introduction to equality and inclusion in children and young people's settings.

Unit MU 2.9 Understand partnership working in services for children and young people.

Did you know?

To work well within a team it's important to learn two key things:
- That there could be several effective ways to do something.
- That we are not the only one who has good ideas!

... being able to reflect on own work activities

In this section you'll learn why **reflective practice** is an important way to develop knowledge, skills and practice. You'll also learn about assessing how well your knowledge, skills and practice meet standards, and how you can reflect on work activities. This links with **Assessment Criteria 2.1, 2.2, 2.3**.

key terms

Reflective practice the process of thinking about and analysing your work to improve your practice.

Personal development plan a plan that details how a practitioner will gain new knowledge and skills.

What is reflective practice?

Reflective practice is an important form of ongoing self-evaluation. It involves thinking carefully about your work in terms of what you do and what you achieve. It helps you to see what you are doing well and where development or changes may be necessary.

Sometimes reflective practice may lead you to try a new way of doing something – taking a music session outdoors instead of indoors for instance. This will be fairly easy to implement. At other times reflective practice may reveal a need to develop your knowledge and skills through further learning opportunities. This will involve making a **personal development plan** that sets out how you will gain the knowledge and skills – through a short course at the local college for example. You'll learn more about personal development plans in Learning outcome 3.

Even very experienced practitioners benefit from reflection because everyone has room for personal development and improvement. Also, there's always something new happening in early years that practitioners need to think or learn about.

What do reflective practitioners do?
Reflective practitioners regularly:

■ put time aside to think about their practice

■ analyse what they do well

key terms

Reflective practitioners
workers who use reflective
practice regularly.

- think about where they should make improvements

- identify work activities they could try doing differently

- record notes on their reflections, perhaps in a journal

- discuss their reflections with others

- use feedback from others to improve their own evaluations.

This helps them to:

- **identify their strengths:**
  - 'What do I do well or to a high standard?'

- **identify their weaknesses:**
  - 'What don't I do all that well? What don't I feel confident doing?'

- **notice their achievements:**
  - 'Where have I made progress? What targets or goals have I reached?'

- **identify their development needs:**
  - 'Which areas of my work or knowledge should be developed? What new information or skills should I learn?'

- **solve problems:**
  - 'What problems do I currently have and how can I tackle them?'

- **improve practice:**
  - 'What can I do to improve my practical work with the children, parents or my colleagues?'

Make notes in your reflective
journal

The ability to reflect on work activities

Practitioners aim to reflect on many different aspects of their work over time. But, initially, you might like to focus on some of the key areas suggested in the diagram on page 63.

Suggested areas for reflection

Reflection methods

Several methods can be used to reflect on your practice. Imagine a practitioner has experienced previous difficulty keeping children seated at story time. Today, one child got up and took another's cushion, causing them to cry. On reflection, the practitioner may:

- **question what, why and how:**
  'What actually happened and why did the event occur? How did I respond and why?'

- **seek alternative ways of doing something:**
  'How else could I have handled things?'

- **keep an open mind:**
  'There could be a better way to handle or prevent such situations.'

- **view from different perspectives:**
  'How might colleagues have responded? How were the children involved feeling at the time?'

- **ask 'what if?'**
  'What if I'd given the children more time to settle in their seats?'

- **think about consequences:**
  'A colleague came to deal with the situation while I tried to carry on with the story. But what would have happened if I'd stopped reading the story to the rest of the group until the situation was resolved?'

■ **learn from past experiences:**

'What similar events have I experienced, and were they handled effectively? Could techniques used then work in this situation? '

■ **talk it over with a colleague and combine ideas:**

'I've thought about the issue myself and discussed it with a colleague. She thinks that it's good to take time to settle children at story time. It can help them to concentrate and feel engaged during the session.'

■ **seek, identify and resolve problems:**

'On reflection, I think the problem was that the children had not settled before I started reading. Next time I will try giving them more time, and I will ask if they are comfortable and can see the book.'

Good practice

Good reflective practitioners learn to use all of these techniques, applying one or more of them to each situation or issue that they reflect on.

Reflection improves work practice

Have a go!

You may be able to see how changes have happened in your lifetime. Think back to how you learnt and played in various settings when you were a child, and compare this with how children are encouraged to learn and play now.

Assessing how well standards are met

As you have learnt, there's always room for personal development and improvement, and there's always something new happening in early years. Ideas about the best way to do things change over time, and new theories and changes to curriculums such as the Early Years Foundation Stage are common. (In fact, in England a revised Early Years Foundation Stage is currently being introduced, and will be followed in settings from September 2012.) Legislation, standards and other requirements also evolve as a result.

Without reflection and ongoing personal development, a practitioner's
knowledge, understanding and skills would soon be out of date. This
would affect their ability to keep meeting the required standards that
you learnt about in Learning outcome 2.

Feedback from others

A key way for you to assess how well your knowledge, skills and
understanding meet the required standard is to consider the feedback
you receive from others, including those shown in the diagram below.

Did you know?

Personal development
should be continuous,
so practitioners should
plan regular reflection
time. This ensures the
process is not forgotten
and that you have the
time to think.

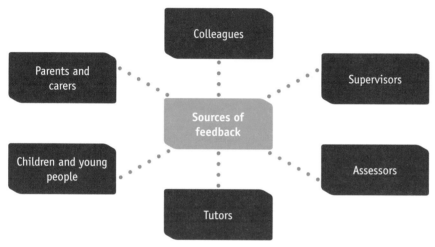

Sources of feedback

Informal feedback

Much of the feedback that we get from others is informal, and it's
available to us all of the time. It's just a matter of stopping to notice
and question what the responses we receive from others tell us. Some
of the responses will be verbal, but others will be more about how
people – including children – behave (or, in other words, how they
act). Consider these examples:

■ Imagine you have provided a play activity for a group of children.
How keen children are to participate and how engaged they are
gives feedback about how suitable the activity is. For instance,
if children needed lots of help, the activity may not have been
pitched at the right level – it may have been more suitable for
older children. If children tended to play only for a moment before
moving on, it may not have been challenging enough or presented
in an interesting way.

■ You tell the children a story that you know well without using a book. You notice how different it was to have continual eye contact with children at story time, and how well they listened (behavioural feedback). Your supervisor says, 'That was unexpected. Well done.' The next day a parent tells you their child couldn't wait to tell them all about the new story they had heard.

■ There's only one ride-on tractor in the nursery garden, so the children take turns to use it. This morning, the dad of four-year-old Luke tells you that Luke was upset when he got home yesterday because he didn't get to have a turn, even though you had told him he could have a go 'next'. You realise that you did make the promise, but forgot about it when the supervisor asked you to do a job for her indoors.

■ You've been learning about child development at college. During a classroom session, you answer several of the tutor's questions correctly.

■ Usually your colleague leads music and movement activities and you join in with the children. But today you swapped roles for the first time. When you're chatting later, you ask her if she's got any advice for you for next time.

Formal feedback
Appraisals

In most workplaces (not just children's settings), managers give employees an annual appraisal. Generally, senior staff will make an appointment to talk with each worker individually. The staff member's work performance will be discussed jointly. Strengths and weaknesses will be considered, and as a result a personal training/development plan will be agreed. Practitioners get the most out of an appraisal when they reflect on their own strengths, weaknesses and development needs before the meeting, and contribute their own thoughts during the meeting. It's common for settings to give practitioners a self-appraisal form to complete in advance, to help them to reflect. Once completed, this is handed in to an appraiser and it informs the appraisal discussion.

Feedback on work performance is given during an appraisal

Inspections

Also, the setting as a whole will receive formal feedback in the form of a report following inspections by their regulatory body. For example, in England this would be an Ofsted inspection.

Other formal feedback

You'll receive other forms of formal feedback at more regular intervals. This includes:

- Feedback following assessment in the workplace.

- Feedback given on learning work products such as assignments for college.

- College reports.

- Session/activity evaluations written by colleagues in the workplace, which will cover events and activities you have been involved in.

- Staff meeting and parent meeting discussions (formal because meeting notes known as 'minutes' will usually be kept).

When should you reflect?

As you've learnt, you should plan regular time to reflect. But in addition, you may decide to reflect in response to:

- a naturally occurring event, for example when you come across a new situation, or feel something has gone particularly well or badly

- informal feedback received

- formal feedback received

- new ideas about the best way to do something

- changes to legislation, regulations or standards

- policy/procedure reviews in the work setting, for example a review of the setting's health and safety policy or how well the setting works in partnership with parents. You can learn more about policies and reviews in Unit MU 2.4.

- taking part in quality assurance schemes.

Have a go!

Spend some time thinking about the formal feedback you're likely to receive in the near future (for example a workplace assessment, a marked assignment or an appraisal). How will you learn from reflecting on it?

Ask Miranda!

Q Won't focusing on what I do wrong knock my confidence?

A **Focusing on strengths and achievements can increase confidence and self-esteem, which is of course good. But identifying your weaknesses is also a very positive thing to do. Once you're aware of them, you can take steps to learn and to develop your practice. Then you can feel good about improving your overall work performance. Aim for a balance of reflection on things you do well and things you can improve.**

LEARNING OUTCOME 3

FOCUS ON

... being able to agree a personal development plan

In this section you'll learn about sources of support for your own learning and development. You'll also learn about the process for agreeing your personal development plan, and how to contribute to drawing it up. This links with **Assessment Criteria 3.1, 3.2, 3.3.**

Drawing up personal development plans

A personal development plan sets out how you will gain the knowledge, understanding and skills that you have discovered you need through reflection and feedback. Personal development plans will be an important tool in your learning throughout your career as a practitioner. If (or when) you are employed by a setting, the employer will take responsibility for overseeing your development planning. If you are currently a student, your tutor or assessor will take on the overseeing role.

A personal development plan should be a written plan of action against which progress made can be monitored. Plans can take many formats and can be given different names by different organisations. Your setting or training centre may call your development plan a 'personal profile' for instance, and they may or may not have a standard planning form for you to fill in.

But all plans should include clear objectives, which are often called 'SMART objectives.' 'SMART' stands for specific, measurable, achievable, realistic and time bound. This is explained in Table SHC22.1.

Table SHC22.1: SMART objectives

Specific	State exactly what you are planning to achieve and how you will achieve it so that you can focus clearly on your objective.
Measurable	Decide in advance how you will know when you are on the way to meeting your objective. How will you know when you have achieved it?
Achievable	Make sure your objective is achievable. Large goals are sometimes best broken down into several achievable objectives. The task then feels more manageable and you can see that you are making progress.
Realistic	Worthwhile objectives can be challenging, but be realistic about how and when you can achieve things or you may become disheartened and discouraged.
Time-bound	Timescales help you to get on with working towards your objectives, and can really motivate you. Set dates for when each objective should be met and monitor your progress.

Sources of support for learning and development

There are several sources of support (people who can support you)
with your learning and development. The support you receive can be
informal, such as the advice given by a colleague during a chat. Or
it may be formal, such as support given by assessors or appraisers.
The diagram below shows common sources of support. This includes
people working both within and beyond your own organisation.

In Learning outcome 2 you learnt about using feedback to evaluate
your own performance and to identify when personal development is
needed. You'll see from the diagram that the people who provide this
feedback are often also sources of support.

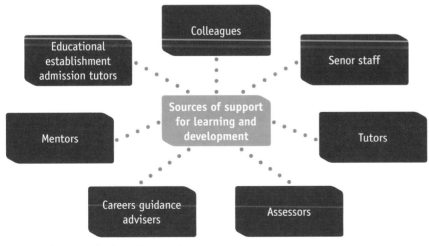

Sources of support for learning and development

Appraisals

You learnt about appraisals in Learning outcome 2. Your appraisers (senior staff members) are a particularly good source of formal support for your learning and development. As part of the appraisal process, you'll be helped to draw up a personal development plan that covers how you will gain any necessary knowledge, understanding and skills. But you can ask for additional support towards achieving your plan at any time – you don't have to wait for the next appraisal time to come around.

Senior colleagues will support your personal development planning

Colleagues

Colleagues are in a very good position to offer you informal, straightforward tips and advice to help you develop your practice. For instance, an experienced colleague may suggest a better way of handling a child's behaviour. They are also well placed to answer your questions, and generally on hand to talk to easily. They may also suggest learning activities that you might want to look into, such as a good course available online, or a book they have found helpful. They can also pass on information that they have picked up at training courses and seminars. Passing on this learning is known as '**cascading**'.

Tutors, assessors and mentors

If you are on a course, tutors, assessors and mentors are an excellent resource and will have good knowledge about your necessary learning and development. They will also understand any learning needs you may have.

Common methods of learning and development

Practitioners learn and develop in many ways. These can be:

- formal or informal
- full time or part time
- workplace based or outside the setting.

Methods include:

- Distance learning via mail or the internet.
- Workplace learning on assessment-based courses.
- Attending staff meetings (at which new information and new thinking in the industry is discussed). Staff will also talk about, review and make plans for all aspects of the provision, including the setting's policies and procedures. Staff may also cascade new information or learning to their colleagues.
- Attending in-house training (this means that a training session is delivered in the work setting, often by an outside trainer). These sessions may be run in the evening or at the weekend so that all staff can attend.
- Attending tutored courses.
- Attending training workshops.
- Attending seminars and conferences.
- Research via books, articles, the internet and training materials, including DVDs.
- Observing or shadowing other practitioners.
- Visiting other settings.

Did you know?

Over the course of their careers, practitioners can expect to use most of the different learning and development methods.

Ask Miranda!

Q How will I know what method of learning or development to choose?

A First of all, find out about the methods of learning available to you for the specific subject. For instance, to gain a first-aid certificate you must attend an accredited training course – that is the only option. Where there is a choice, think carefully about your learning needs. Which method best meets your learning objectives and the way you personally like to learn? Next, consider the access requirements of any methods that appeal to you – do you need qualifications or a certain amount of experience to get on to a course for example? Also make sure you understand the time and commitment necessary, from being available to attend learning sessions to being willing and able to spend time and effort on any homework or assignments. On a practical note, ensure the method is cost effective. Can you afford it, or is the setting prepared to pay for it? Also think about how you will get to and from any events or lessons that you need to attend, and any travel costs involved. If any fall in work time, will your workplace be happy for you to attend? And if you do, will you still get paid? If you're still undecided, talk the options over with your workplace manager, and remember to get your setting's agreement before signing up for anything.

Agreeing personal development plans

Once you have drafted a SMART personal development plan, it's good practice to agree it with the other people involved in your personal development. Within the setting this may include your supervisor, manager or employer. It may also be appropriate for outside professionals such as tutors, assessors and mentors to approve the plan. If you are under 18, a parent/carer or advocate may also be involved. (You learnt about advocates in Unit SHC 21, page 37.)

Make sure that you agree about the aspects of your personal development that you should focus on first. Prioritising what you should do is sometimes just a matter of timescales. For instance, if your first-aid certificate will be expiring shortly, it will be a priority to renew it. If a new piece of legislation is coming in, you may need to learn about it as soon as possible. Or you may want to take advantage of an opportunity coming up soon – a short course starting at the local college for example. If your workplace will be supporting your personal development by paying for training, they may well tell you how and when they'd like you to meet your personal development needs.

You should also agree how and when you will review your development and monitor your progress towards your plan. (See the SMART objectives on page 69.) This should not be left until the next appraisal – you must work towards your objectives and monitor your progress throughout the year.

Once your plan has been reviewed and prioritised, you can produce a final draft. Many settings will require staff to hand this in to their supervisor or manager who will keep a copy for the setting's records. If the setting will be supporting your development financially (by paying for training perhaps), it is usually at this stage that the money is officially allocated in the budget.

Good practice

Once a plan is agreed, make sure that you understand who is responsible for any organisational details. For instance, should you make a booking for yourself to attend a course, or will the supervisor do it and make payment at the same time?

LEARNING OUTCOME 4

FOCUS ON

... being able to develop knowledge, skills and understanding

In this section you'll find out how learning activities, reflection and feedback from others can improve your knowledge, skills and understanding. You'll also learn how to record progress in relation to personal development. This links with **Assessment Criteria 4.1, 4.2, 4.3, 4.4.**

Showing the impact of learning activities

So far in this unit, you've learnt:

- ■ what you must know and what you must be capable of doing to fulfil your job role

- ■ the value of reflecting on your current practice to identify your learning needs

- ■ how to develop a plan to meet your learning needs.

However, there's still one piece of the jigsaw left. You must now consider and show how any learning activities that you undertake improve your knowledge, skills and understanding.

Generally, the best way to do this is through further reflection, using the reflection techniques that you learnt about in Learning outcome 2. This process creates a cycle, as shown on the diagram below.

Show how learning activities improve your knowledge, skills and understanding

Understand your current duties and responsibilities (which will change over time)

Develop a plan to meet your learning needs

Reflect on current practice to identify learning needs

Personal development cycle

It's really important to reflect on what you've learnt and to think about how you'll put new learning into practice. Otherwise, your new knowledge and skills will be wasted, and you won't progress as planned in terms of personal development. To change your practice, you need to put in some thought and effort after the learning has taken place.

Once you have taken steps to put your new learning into practice, you'll need to use reflection to evaluate the effect that your learning activities have had on your practice. But be aware that it's normal to take a while to get used to new ways of working, and this may also apply to the children, young people and colleagues who you're working with.

If you embrace working as a reflective practitioner as described in Learning outcome 2, the notes that you make in your reflective journal will build into a record that documents how your reflection has led to improved ways of working.

Showing the impact of feedback from others

In Learning outcome 2 you learnt about using feedback to evaluate your own performance and to identify when personal development is needed. This can help us to overcome the difficulty of being objective about ourselves. We may sometimes be too close to see things clearly. For instance, we may worry that we're not doing something properly when in fact we're doing a great job, or we may not be aware that there is something we need to improve on or to learn.

Feedback on your performance may come from a number of sources, including colleagues, supervisors, assessors/tutors, parents, carers or children. It may be given formally or informally. For instance,

We may worry that we're not doing something properly

Good practice

When you have completed something on your personal development plan, get into the habit of using your reflective journal to reflect on what you've learnt, giving emphasis to how your learning will impact on your practice. For instance, if you'd been on a short course about promoting positive behaviour, you would reflect on the key learning points. Then you might think about how you'll introduce into your practice some of the new behaviour management strategies you've learnt, and plan accordingly. You might also consider how well you responded to the learning activity – was the level right for you? Did the type of learning (attending a course with others, distance learning at home, research, etc.) suit you? This information will help you to improve your learning activity choices in the future.

an assessor will give formal feedback during an assessment and an employer will give formal feedback during an appraisal, while a parent may make an informal passing comment about their child's care.

Good practice

It's good practice to reflect regularly on the feedback you receive. Your reflective journal will build into a record that shows how feedback from others has developed your knowledge, understanding and skills. You must also keep any documentation given to you as part of formal feedback, such as appraisal forms.

Recording progress in relation to personal development

It's very important to record your progress in relation to professional development. If you're currently studying for this qualification on a college course, your progress will be recorded on the Individual Learning Record (or an equivalent document). Some settings provide professional development files for practitioners, in which they keep all related information. The Practical example on page 77 shows an excerpt from such a file.

If you don't have access to these, start your own file – it will be with you throughout your career. Take good care of qualification certificates, and also file certificates of attendance (such as those issued on local authority training courses). These are your proof of learning and evidence of your professional development progress. If you want to change jobs or apply for training or study, potential employers and admissions tutors will want to see them. In the same file you can keep any written feedback that you receive about the progress you make.

Usman's self-evaluation

Usman is a trainee at a large children's centre. He attends college one day a week. When he joined the centre he was given a personal development file. It contains information about how the setting supports personal development, and includes a self-evaluation document for Usman to complete over time. Each section focuses on a different area of professional knowledge, understanding and practice. Usman is required to give himself a score and to record evidence to back it up. He can also make notes about any development needed. Today he's filling out the 'providing activities for children' section. Here is an extract.

Usman's professional development record

Knowledge, understanding and practice	Competency score 1–5 (score 0 if you have no knowledge, understanding or practical experience)	Evidence	Future development notes
Provide play activities for children aged 1–2 years.	0	I haven't worked with children aged 1–2 years yet.	*Ask the supervisor if I can spend a bit of time working in the Toddler Room in the near future. *Ask the Toddler Room team leader if I can pop in for a couple of minutes to look at their daily session plan each day (which is displayed on the Toddler Room notice board). It will help me to learn about the types of activities provided for this age group.
Provide play activities for children aged 2–3 years.	3	I've learnt about providing activities for this age at college. I've planned and carried out five play activities in the Nursery Room: a music session, finger painting, a feely bag activity, a lotto game (which I made) and circle games. The music was observed by my tutor and I got good feedback.	I still need to plan and carry out another activity for this age group for my college course. Now I have a bit of experience and feel more confident about providing activities, I'll try to contribute some activity ideas of my own at the next Nursery Room planning meeting.

Your setting

Your setting will want copies of your certificates for their own files too, as these can be used as evidence during inspections by regulatory bodies such as Ofsted and during quality assurance assessments. Your setting may manage information about staff training and qualifications by using an online database known as the Early Years Workforce Qualifications Audit Tool. A senior person in the setting will be nominated to upload the information for everyone working there. Your personal details will not be held on the database, and information about you and your colleagues' training and qualifications cannot be accessed by the public or other settings. However, the Children's Workforce Development Council and local authorities do have access. This helps them to identify the training and development needs of practitioners in the area, which informs their planning of training courses and other opportunities.

Your setting will also keep copies of any formal feedback that they give you. Appraisal documents are a good example of this.

Good practice

It's a good idea to keep another file containing the notes you make and any handouts you're given during learning activities, so that you can refer to them in the future.

How are things going?

▶ Progress Check

1. What standards influence the way your role is carried out? (1.2)

2. How can reflection help you to develop your knowledge, skills and practice? (2.1)

3. Describe three reflection techniques. (2.3)

4. Name three sources of support for your learning and development. (3.1)

5. Who should be involved in agreeing your personal development plan? (3.2)

6. What information should be included in a personal development plan? (3.3)

7. Explain how keeping a reflective journal can show how a learning activity has improved your knowledge, skills and understanding. (4.1, 4.4)

Are you ready for assessment?

Learning Outcomes 2, 3 and 4 must be assessed in a real work environment.

CACHE

Set task:

■ In an induction scenario, you are asked to show your line manager that you can describe the duties and responsibilities of your role, identify standards that influence the way your role is carried out and describe ways to ensure that your personal attitudes or beliefs do not obstruct the quality of your work.

City & Guilds

In preparation for assessment of this Unit, it will be helpful to reflect on your role and responsibilities, making notes in your reflective journal. You may like to review a job description for your role as part of the process.

Edexcel

In preparation for assessment of this Unit, it will be helpful to reflect on your role and responsibilities, making notes in your reflective journal. You may like to review a job description for your role as part of the process.

UNIT 23

Introduction to equality and inclusion in children and young people's settings

LEARNING OUTCOMES

The learning outcomes you will meet in this unit are:

1 Understand the importance of diversity, equality and inclusion

2 Be able to work in an inclusive way

3 Be able to access information, advice and support about diversity, equality and inclusion

INTRODUCTION

All children and young people and their families have the right to be treated fairly. This means they must have equal opportunities to learn, play and participate within the settings that they attend. Everyone who works with children and young people has a part to play in ensuring this, and there are laws and policies to guide us.

Equality has a positive impact on children's well-being. But when families experience discrimination, the negative effects can be serious and far-reaching. So it's important that you learn how to promote equality, and how to recognise ways in which discrimination can occur.

LEARNING OUTCOME 1

FOCUS ON

... understanding the importance of diversity, equality and inclusion

In this section you'll learn what is meant by diversity and discrimination. You'll also learn about ways in which discrimination may occur in the work setting, and how promoting equality and inclusion reduces the likelihood of discrimination. This links with **Assessment Criteria 1.1, 1.2, 1.3, 1.4.**

Terminology

There are several terms that you need to understand in relation to diversity, equality and inclusion. These are explained in the sections that follow. You can return to these pages if you need to check a definition as you work through this unit.

What is meant by prejudice?

The word prejudice means to pre-judge. People who are prejudiced make unfair, sweeping judgements about others based on a 'group' that they believe the person 'belongs to'. They already have a negative view before they even meet the person or find out anything about them. Commonly held prejudices about 'groups' of people are known as stereotypes. Here are some examples of stereotypes:

■ Wheelchair users are helpless and unable to contribute to society.

■ Travellers steal.

■ Black people are less intelligent than white people.

The assumptions of people who are prejudiced are often rooted in their country's historical belief that their own particular ethnicity or background is superior, or that *their* religion or way of living is the best one or right. These sorts of prejudice may still exist, but they are no longer considered acceptable in modern, multicultural Britain.

Sadly, you may have experienced prejudice yourself. You will certainly be aware of negative comments made about the way other people live their lives – perhaps about the way they dress or speak.

Not allowing boys to play with dolls within the setting would be discrimination

What is meant by discrimination?

Discrimination occurs when people act on prejudice. For example, a prejudiced person might believe that playing with dolls is only for girls. They will be discriminating if they don't allow boys to play with dolls in the setting. You'll learn much more about discrimination below.

What is meant by equality?

Equality is achieved when all children have equal opportunities to participate within a setting. Taking the same care to promote opportunities for every child is known as showing 'equal concern' for everyone.

Showing equal concern doesn't mean treating everyone the same. It means that we should meet the needs of all children and families. Their needs will be different, so we need to work in different ways with different children to give them equal opportunities. To achieve this, we need to get to know individual children well. This means that you must avoid making assumptions about a child's characteristics, needs and preferences based on the group they belong to or you perceive them to belong to. Instead you should take the time to know, understand and value them as individuals.

For example, you may know about a condition such as Down's syndrome, but you will not know how that condition impacts on an individual child you have just met. You won't know what adult support they may need. You certainly won't know about their personality or their likes and dislikes. If we make assumptions about what children need or want, how they will behave and what they will be able to achieve, we are in danger of having limited expectations for them. This means they may not be given all of the opportunities that should be available to them, which will affect their learning and development. As a result, they may have low expectations of their own abilities, and this can lead to low aims for their future lives.

Many other assumptions can also lead to inappropriate expectations. For example, expecting an Asian child to excel in certain subjects at school, or thinking that a young Polish person will probably go on to work as a manual labourer. You can probably think of many more. (Also see the section on discrimination on page 85.)

Did you know?

Getting into the habit of seeing all children as individuals is at the heart of equality, and it is the best way to avoid discrimination.

Practical example

Showing equal care

Ashray is an only child who has just turned three years old. At home, he enjoys playing on his own and with his parents. He recently started attending pre-school and he enjoys many of the activities. But when it comes to playing outside, Ashray appears overwhelmed by the hustle and bustle – the playground can get quite noisy when the children are busy running around, riding trikes, etc. Ashray frequently becomes upset and clings to a member of staff, which prevents them from giving attention to other children.

The staff discuss this. They agree that Ashray needs some one-to-one attention outside at the moment to reassure him and to give him confidence, and to slowly encourage him to join in. They make provision in their plans for an extra person to go outside and work solely with Ashray until he's feeling more secure in the playground. This will ensure that both his needs and the needs of the other children are fully met.

Question:
How are the staff showing equal care for the children?

See all children as individuals

Did you know?

Although some children may need to be given more time and attention than others, everyone should be equally valued and treated with the same concern.

What is meant by respecting diversity?

You have learnt that you need to understand and to value individual children's characteristics, needs and preferences. 'Respecting diversity' is the term given to the acknowledgement and respect of differences between individuals and within and between groups of people in society. Diversity may arise from a number of factors, as shown on the diagram below.

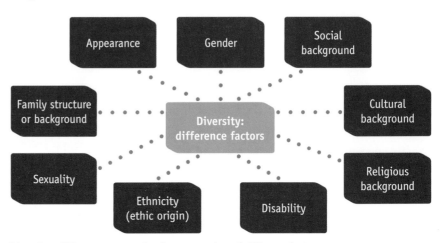

Appearance

Gender

Social background

Family structure or background

Diversity: difference factors

Cultural background

Sexuality

Religious background

Ethnicity (ethic origin)

Disability

Diversity: differences may arise from a number of different factors

What is meant by inclusion?

Inclusion occurs when a setting embraces diversity and makes sure that all children, young people and families are able to fully participate – or, in other words, they ensure that everyone is fully included. To work inclusively we need to find out about any barriers that may prevent a child or young person from being fully included, and take action to overcome them. For instance, a ramp may be put in place so that a child who is a wheelchair user has full access within the building. Or an activity may be adapted to enable them to participate – a sandpit may be placed on a stand or table instead of on the floor perhaps.

Think carefully about the assumptions you make about others

Good practice

Inclusive settings will also ensure that they welcome all families and make them feel wanted and valued. In this respect, inclusion is as much about your attitude as it is about your actions. You'll learn more about inclusive practice in Learning outcome 2.

Occurrences of discrimination

As you've learnt, discrimination occurs when people are treated unfairly because of prejudicial views that are held about them. There are all kinds of prejudices, and people treat others unfairly based on a broad range of them. But discrimination is commonly based on:

disability

ethnicity

culture

race

religion

gender

age

sexuality

low socio-economic group (financially poorer families).

Discrimination may occur either deliberately or inadvertently:

Deliberate discrimination:
Someone intentionally and knowingly sets out to do something discriminatory, for example a worker believes all disabled children should attend special settings rather than mixing with non-disabled children. So they tell the family of a disabled child that the setting is full when it isn't.

Inadvertent discrimination:
Someone discriminates without meaning to do so, for example when volunteers are needed to move chairs at the end of assembly, a teacher asks for some 'big strong boys' to help him. It doesn't occur to him that he's not giving girls the chance to volunteer. He may go on saying the same thing to different classes for years.

Good practice

Practitioners who work with children and young people are generally caring and keen to give them all the best experience possible, but they may sometimes still inadvertently discriminate. So everyone who works with children and young people must think carefully about the assumptions they make about others. This can be quite hard to do. But it's important, because once we are aware of our own assumptions, we can examine and challenge them, and make sure that we don't discriminate in any way. You will have the opportunity to do this in the Reflective practice section at the end of the book.

Types of discrimination

There are four types of discrimination as shown on the diagram below.

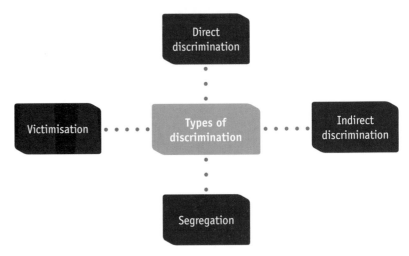

Types of discrimination

We'll look at these in turn.

- ### Direct discrimination:

   This occurs when obvious action is carried out to the detriment of a person because of their disability, ethnicity, culture, race, religion, gender, age, sexuality or socio-economic group. In the example on page 85, a member of staff lies to the family of a disabled child about the setting being full. This is direct discrimination.

- ### Indirect discrimination:

   This occurs when a condition is applied that will favour one group over another unfairly. For instance, in a setting where families speak languages other than English, a setting will be indirectly discriminating if they offer extra childcare places to parents on completion of forms, but only supply the forms in English.

- ### Segregation:

   This is when people are unfairly separated when there is no reason for this. For instance, a setting with a separate area set aside for disabled children to eat in.

- ### Victimisation:

   This occurs when people are intentionally treated unfairly after complaining about previous discrimination. For instance, a parent complains that they were not given a chance to book an extra

Did you know?

If discrimination occurs because an organisation will not meet the needs of someone, or because workers are jointly discriminating, the term 'institutionalised discrimination' may be used.

childcare place because they could not understand the form. As a result the supervisor says there has been a double booking, and their child will not be able to come at all.

Effects of discrimination

The emotional effects of discrimination are very serious. Once experienced, children can go on being affected by discrimination throughout their lives. Discrimination can lead to:

The emotional effects of discrimination are serious

- low self-esteem

- low confidence

- reduced sense of self-worth or self-value

- confused identity

- fear of rejection.

Discrimination can also result in missed opportunities that may affect a child or young person's learning and/or development.

The negative effects of discrimination will impact on the individual being discriminated against, but they can also be expected to affect the following:

- Families or friends of the individual. A child may be separated from their friend due to segregation for example.

- Those who inflict discrimination, because antisocial behaviour has negative consequences.

- Wider society. Discrimination and prejudice affects us all as we share the atmosphere of our environment.

Did you know?

If one child or family is stopped from participating within a group, then the rights of all the children and families to participate equally, alongside one another, are affected.

Good practice

Discrimination is criminal behaviour, and children and young people should not be exposed to it. But, sadly, some children and young people do pick up this behaviour and may go on to inflict discrimination. This is damaging not only to their victims but also to themselves and the wider society.

Promoting equality and inclusion

As you have learnt, everyone who works with children and young people has a duty to promote equality and inclusion. This is important because it reduces the likelihood of discrimination occurring within the setting. In particular, paying attention to equality and inclusion helps us to avoid inadvertently discriminating. As well as considering our own prejudices and assumptions, we can use the setting's environment to promote equality and inclusion by promoting positive images of people. Read on to learn more.

Promoting equality and inclusion through positive images of people

All settings should seek to show, through the way they portray people, that all different kinds of people are valued positively in the setting. This can be done by ensuring that the pictures that children and young people see in books, displays, on puzzles, etc., show males and females, people of all sizes, ethnicities and cultures, and people who have impairments. The aim is to reflect the wider society and modern, multicultural Britain. This is known as 'promoting positive images of people'.

Positive images should also be reflected in the toys that you choose whenever these represent people. For instance, within the setting's collection of baby dolls, practitioners may include dolls of different

Positive images should be reflected in the toys that you choose

ethnicities, and within the puppets they may have different ages represented. Your doll's house may feature a ramp and a doll with a wheelchair, or perhaps on crutches or with a hearing aid. The purpose is to represent society's diversity overall. It would be unrealistic to attempt to cover every eventuality in each collection of resources.

We must also ensure that people are shown in a positive light. Strong images of those people who may be discriminated against are particularly important. Some examples of resources that have strong images include:

- A set of jigsaw puzzles that each show a family of a different culture eating a meal together.

- A poster on the theme of celebrations, that shows six families of different religions celebrating.

- A set of picture postcards showing athletes competing in the Paralympics.

- A set of doll's-house dolls, featuring four elderly couples of different ethnicities.

- A set of puppets with the theme of 'People who help us' – including a female police officer and an Asian doctor.

- Stories that show men taking care of their children.

- A set of jigsaw puzzles showing children helping, which includes a child with special educational needs washing a car.

- Stories that are not about a child's disability, but the lead character just happens to be disabled.

Have a go!

Positive portrayals of people that avoid stereotypes can often help to shape children's aspirations for their own future. This is particularly true when a child can personally relate in some way to the people they see. For example, a disabled child may identify with the image of athletes competing in the Paralympics, and may aspire to participate in sport. Can you identify other examples from the bulleted list above?

Have a go!

Imagine what it might be like for a child to enter a new setting where there are no images or resources that they identify with. For instance, it could be that they are Asian and all the images portray white European people. There may be no clothes like the clothes their family wears, or little familiar food. How do you think they feel? How do you think their family may feel in terms of whether the setting values their culture?

Promoting equality and inclusion through other resources

Settings also promote equality and inclusion by reflecting our diverse culture through their use of other resources. Different styles of clothing can be represented in the dressing-up clothes for instance. A broad range of cooking utensils and foods can be included in the home corner. Crayons, paint and paper can be purchased in a range of flesh tones for art activities. Music from around the world can be played. There are many possibilities.

Practical example

Showing equal care

Ally is a new nursery assistant who has been asked to plan the music sessions that will take place at the setting over the next couple of weeks. She wants to include some recorded music for children to listen to and dance along with. She looks through the setting's CDs and notices that there is no music from other cultures. She talks about this with the supervisor. The supervisor tells Ally that they often borrow World Music CDs from the local library. Ally borrows the setting's library card and arranges to do this herself.

Question:
What else could Ally do to reflect diversity in her music sessions?

Ask Miranda!

Q Are any resources that show a range of people okay?

A No, you need to think carefully about the images you select. Not all images of people from groups who are likely to be discriminated against are positive. Some may even reinforce stereotypes. For instance, in a story or picture older people and disabled people are sometimes shown as being dependent or inactive, perhaps they are being cared for or pushed in a wheelchair. Or female characters may be portrayed as the underdog to male characters. Toy figures of wheelchair users are sometimes made from one moulded piece of plastic, so that the person will never come out of the chair. Even modern TV programmes, stories and comics frequently portray people with asthma as weak in body and character. Make sure you avoid these resources. If in doubt, always check with your team leader or supervisor.

LEARNING OUTCOME 2

FOCUS ON

... being able to work in an inclusive way

In this section you'll learn about legislation and policies relating to equality, diversity and discrimination, and what they mean to your role. You'll also learn about interacting with individuals in a respectful way, and how to challenge discrimination in a way that promotes change. This links with **Assessment Criteria 2.1, 2.2, 2.3.**

Working in an inclusive way

To work inclusively, you need to:

- be aware of equality legislation and codes of practice

- work in line with your setting's equal opportunities policy

- interact with others in a way that respects their beliefs, culture, values and preferences

- know how to challenge effectively any discrimination that you come across.

We'll explore each of these points in turn.

Legislation and policies

Over the years legislation has been put in place to protect children's rights, equality and inclusion. An outline of the key legislation follows on pages 92–5. You'll also be introduced to a new Act – the Equality Act 2010 – which is now bringing former pieces of legislation together. However, the legal implications for practitioners will stay essentially the same.

Your setting will also have its own equal opportunities policy in place, which must be in line with the relevant requirements of your home country. It's important that you read and understand your setting's policy and work in accordance with it at all times.

Good practice

If you haven't seen your setting's equal opportunities policy or if you don't fully understand it, ask your team leader or supervisor for assistance.

UN Convention on the Rights of the Child

The UK government made this convention law in 1991, giving children a number of rights.

- Children have the right to non-discrimination. Practitioners should aim to let children know (within the context of the setting) that they have equal rights, and will be accepted for who they are and respected when they are there. They also have the responsibility to respect other children and adults within the environment. This will be communicated by your actions and attitudes towards young children, but it is appropriate to be more direct as children grow up.

- Children have the right to rest, play and leisure, and opportunities to join in with activities including those that are cultural and artistic.

- Practitioners should ensure that disabled children have full opportunities to join in, since they may experience inequality in this area. A range of different cultural activities should be provided for all children, whatever their own culture.

- Children have the right to freedom from exploitation. For example, they should not be forced to work.

- Practitioners must ensure that children are not abused, bullied or used (see Unit TDA 2.2).

- Children have the right to a cultural identity. Settings should recognise, respect and value the cultural identity of individual families, and celebrate diversity throughout the group. Disabled children have the right to live as independently as possible, and to take a full and active part in everyday life. Practitioners must consult with families to support disabled children's independence in the most effective way.

- Parents and guardians have the right to support in carrying out their parental responsibilities.

- Practitioners must work in partnership with all families.

- Children have the right to have their views heard.

- Practitioners should consult with children, particularly about decisions affecting them, and take notice of what they say. They should seek out and respect the views and preferences of children.

Link Up!

Unit TDA 2.2 Safeguard the welfare of children and young people.

This may be achieved through discussion, 'All About Me' theme work, or even through artwork. Practice should be adapted to suit the child or young person's age, needs and abilities.

- Children need a strong self-image and self-esteem.

- Children should feel valued and accepted for who they are within the setting. This is achieved through showing children respect.

Every Child Matters: Change for Children

Full information is provided in Unit MU 2.8 but, in short, Every Child Matters was introduced to improve outcomes for all children and, in doing so, to ensure equality of opportunity for all.

The Disability Discrimination Act 1995 and 2005

The Disability Discrimination Act (DDA) was devised to support the rights of disabled people to take a full and active part in society. It gave them equality of access or, in other words, the same opportunities to participate in society as non-disabled people. It also gave disabled people (adults and children) rights regarding the way in which they receive services, facilities or goods. This included education, care and play services, and meant that practitioners became required by law to make reasonable adjustments for disabled people if necessary. This included providing extra assistance, and taking action if physical barriers such as doorways or steps caused access problems.

Link Up!

Unit MU 2.8 Contribute to the support of positive environments for children and young people.

Ask Miranda!

Q I'm not sure who 'qualifies' as being disabled.

A **A disabled person is defined as someone who has a physical or mental impairment that adversely affects their ability to carry out normal day-to-day activities. This will be long term – it will have lasted for 12 months or be likely to last for more than 12 months. This includes some chronic illnesses, such as ME, which affect some people's ability to carry out normal day-to-day activities.**

Children have the right to have their views heard

For information and further legislation relating to the Special Educational Needs Code of Practice, also see Unit TDA 2.15 Support children and young people with disabilities and special educational needs.

Settings must also meet the welfare requirements of their home country. You'll find details of this in Unit MU 2.4 Contribute to children and young people's health and safety, on pages 229–31.

key terms

Multidisciplinary working when professionals with different job roles work together, in this case for the benefit of children and young people.

Unit MU 2.9 Understand partnership working in services for children and young people.

Children Act 1989

This Act required all settings to have an equal opportunities policy that is regularly reviewed and that takes account of children's:

- religion

- racial origin

- cultural background

- linguistic background (language background).

Children Act 2004

The overall aim of this was to encourage integrated planning and delivery of services as well as improvement of **multidisciplinary working**. Multidisciplinary working is when professionals with different job roles work together for the benefit of children and young people. You'll learn more about this in Unit MU 2.9.

The Human Rights Act 1998

This Act allowed people in the UK to enforce within the British courts rights given to them under previous laws. Before the Act it was necessary to take cases relating to those laws to the European Court in Strasburg, which was time-consuming, expensive and inconvenient.

Race Relations Act 1976

This Act stated that racial discriminatory practice is unacceptable, and defines in law what that means. The Act was introduced to make discriminatory practice illegal in the UK.

Racial and Religious Hatred Act 2006

This Act created the new criminal offence of stirring up hatred against people on religious grounds.

The Equality Act 2006

This made it unlawful to discriminate on grounds of religion or belief in a number of circumstances. This is applicable in a variety of situations, such as education and the provision of services (for example a childcare service) or facilities (for example a playground).

The Equality Act 2010

At the time of writing, this new Act is bringing together and harmonising equality law with the aim of making it more consistent, clearer and easier to follow, in order to make society fairer. The new Act will replace previous equality legislation. However, the legal implications for practitioners will essentially stay the same. The government is looking at the best ways for the Act to be fully implemented, and announcements will be made in due course.

Interacting with respect

In Learning outcome 1 you learnt that it's important to get to know children, young people and their families as individuals because there will be a lot of variation in terms of the beliefs, culture, values and preferences of the families that you work with. It's also important that you interact with each individual in a way that shows you have respect for them and the way they live their lives – even if your own beliefs, culture, values or preferences are quite different. Your interactions with others are about what you say and what you do. Read on to find out more.

This also links with your learning in Unit SHC 21, about meeting the communication and language needs and preferences of others.

Link Up!

Unit SHC 21 Introduction to communication in children and young people's settings.

Interact with each individual in a way that shows respect

Listen closely to the terms used by tutors

Have a go!

You can read more up-to-date information about the Equality Act 2010 at http://homeoffice.gov.uk/equalities/equality-act, where you can also access a guide for service providers.

What you say
Use of language

The way in which we use language needs to be considered because the words and phrases we use can cause offence. The best way to pick up the appropriate terminology is to listen closely to the terms used by tutors during any classes or courses that you attend, and to take notice of how things are phrased in any modern textbooks or journals that you read, including this one. You can also learn by listening to staff within your setting and referring to the language used in your setting's policies and procedures.

Many terms that were once use widely are now considered inappropriate, particularly in relation to disability. For instance, we now use the term 'disabled' rather than the word 'handicapped' or 'crippled'. We also now use the term 'wheelchair user'. We don't say 'wheelchair bound' or 'confined to a wheelchair', as these terms suggest that the disabled person is inactive, dependent and perhaps even a victim. This doesn't portray in a positive way someone who uses a wheelchair.

We also take care not to label people by the terms we use. This respects the fact that impairments or health conditions do not define who someone is. For instance, rather than saying, 'Holly's an epileptic asthmatic', it's better to say, 'Holly has epilepsy and asthma'. Likewise, you will not work with a 'Down's syndrome child' but a 'child with Down's syndrome'.

It's also important to use appropriate terms that relate to people's ethnicity and culture. For instance, you would say 'black' not 'coloured', or 'Chinese,' 'Japanese' or 'Asian' rather than 'oriental'.

Discussing differences

Part of respecting diversity is valuing the differences between people. Children do notice differences quite early on, and may well ask questions or make observations about skin tone, gender, hair colour, clothing or an impairment for instance. There's no need to feel uncomfortable about this. In fact, it's a good opportunity to talk openly about differences, and to let the children see that diversity is a welcome part of everyday life. So always try to answer children's questions in an open, age-appropriate way.

Did you know?

The word 'handicapped' is thought to have come from the phrase 'cap in hand', which refers to having to beg.

Good practice

Always remember that you are a role model for children. They will learn to use the language they hear around them.

Ask Miranda!

Q I didn't think the term 'special needs child' was politically
correct anymore. But I've heard my setting's supervisor use it
when talking to the parents of a disabled child. Is she in the
wrong?

A **You're right, it's no longer politically correct to use that term. 'Special'
is just another word for 'different' after all. But it's something of
a grey area as some parents find the phrase 'special needs' more
acceptable than 'disabled', particularly in the early years when a
child is young and the family may be coming to terms with their
circumstances. In this case, staff may well use the term 'special needs'
in conversation with those particular parents only.**

**The term 'special educational needs' is still acceptable when used
to talk specifically about educational needs. It should not be used as
a general term to refer to impairments or conditions.**

What you do

Practitioners have many ways to show respect for individuals' beliefs,
culture, values and preferences through the actions that they take.
These include:

- Promoting equality and inclusion through positive images of
  people and through your choice of resources (see Learning
  outcome 1).

- Spending time talking to individual families to ensure proper
  understanding of individual beliefs, culture, values and
  preferences.

- Always taking care to meet needs arising from beliefs, culture,
  values and preferences, for example providing vegetarian or kosher
  meals (kosher food will have been prepared in a way that reflects
  Jewish law).

- Being aware of important events happening in a child or young
  person's cultural life and responding to them in an appropriate
  way, for example taking an interest in a religious or cultural
  festival and contributing to a celebration if appropriate, or sending
  an appropriate greetings card.

■ Incorporating multicultural foods on the setting's menu.

■ Translating signs, notices and newsletters into other languages as appropriate.

■ Exploring music and stories from around the world.

Good practice

Practitioners need to think carefully before planning the celebration of festivals outside of their own faith or culture, as there is likely to be a strong cultural or sacred significance that you cannot fully identify with. You may also cause offence if you 'role play' celebrating something that does not have any real significance for you and others within the group. This is particularly true if sacred aspects, such as lighting candles, are performed. This doesn't mean that festivals should not be celebrated, but it is advisable for settings to consult with families first, and to involve them as much as possible if a celebration goes ahead.

Challenging discrimination

As a practitioner, you should promote your setting's equal opportunities policy in your own work at all times. But you should also think of yourself as a guardian of the policy. This means that if you come across discrimination of any sort, you have a responsibility to challenge it in a professional way likely to promote change.

Children and young people

As you've learnt, it's a sad fact that some children and young people pick up negative attitudes towards diversity, and may say or do things that upset others in the setting. This is true even in the pre-school years.

It is important to comfort the person on the receiving end of this treatment. Reassure them that the behaviour is not acceptable in the setting and that you will deal with the issue. When you talk with the child or young person who has acted inappropriately, you have an opportunity to educate them about equality, in line with their level of maturity. Make it clear that such behaviour will not be tolerated.

It may be appropriate for a member of staff to speak to the parents/carers of the children involved when they are collected, and to make an entry in the incident book. You must follow your setting's procedures for this. Often, Level 2 assistants will be required to report the incident to their team leader, and they will take things from there.

You must always step in and put an immediate stop to verbal abuse of any sort

Parents and carers

Parents and carers sometimes hold views that do not respect diversity. If a parent or carer makes a comment or a request that does not promote equality, it may be necessary for staff to explain the policy of the setting and let them know where they stand. If a parent is unable to accept the setting's policy, they can of course leave the setting.

Colleagues

If you feel a colleague is discriminating or in any way showing prejudice through their behaviour or what they say, you must not ignore it. You have a duty to raise the issue, even if it's difficult to do. It's important to remain calm and professional, and to tackle the situation in a non-confrontational manner at an appropriate time and place. You'll learn more about this in Unit MU 2.9. Also see Learning outcome 3 for information on how to access advice and support if you need it.

> **Good practice**
>
> The old adage 'sticks and stones may break my bones but words will never hurt me' couldn't be more wrong. Words do hurt people, even though comments may be laughed off (particularly by older children and teenagers who are feeling humiliated). Never dismiss it as 'acceptable teasing'. A hurtful comment about someone's appearance, based on the fact that they wear a brace on their teeth for instance, can be just as upsetting as a racist comment. You must always step in and put an immediate stop to the situation.

Practical example

Showing equal care

A mum tells pre-school worker Aisha that she does not want her child playing with a boy in the group who has learning difficulties. Aisha explains that children are not segregated within the setting as this would be against their equal opportunities policy. Aisha asks the mum why she's made the request. The mum says that she has seen the child rocking back and forth, and is afraid that her child could pick up the same behaviour. Aisha arranges for the mum to have a word with the setting's SENCO, who talks through her underlying worries and concerns and attempts to put her mind at rest.

Question:
If the mum still refuses to allow her child to mix with the boy who has learning difficulties, what should the setting do?

Did you know?

It's easy to be angry when someone acts in a discriminatory way. But anger usually only results in the other person becoming defensive – it does not pave the way for an open professional discussion.

LEARNING OUTCOME **3**

FOCUS ON

... being able to access information, advice and support about diversity, equality and inclusion

In this section you'll learn about situations in which additional information, advice and support about diversity, equality and inclusion may be needed. You'll also learn how to access the support, etc. This links with **Assessment Criteria 3.1, 3.2.**

When you may need information, advice and support

All practitioners regularly need additional information, advice and support about diversity, equality and inclusion. One of the most common times is when a new child starts at the setting and practitioners need to get to know the family on an individual basis.

This may entail finding out more about a range of issues including culture and beliefs, or impairments or conditions, and how these impact on the child concerned.

As you've learnt, issues relating to diversity, equality and inclusion can be complex and very sensitive. You are not expected to know everything. So if you don't understand something or you're not feeling confident about what to do or say, it's important to always seek out the help or information that you need without delay. (See Learning outcome 2 for information about consulting with families on significant cultural and religious events.)

You will need additional information, advice and support when a new child starts

How to access information, advice and support

Practitioners can access information, advice and support about diversity, equality and inclusion from several sources. These include:

■ **The child or young person's family**:
  As you learnt in Learning outcome 1, practitioners must always find out about beliefs, culture, values, preferences and needs from families. Having some general knowledge about these things is useful, but it won't tell you about the implications for an individual family or child. For instance, a Jewish family may or may not require kosher food.

Unit SHC 22 Introduction to personal development in children and young people's settings.

Unit TDA 2.15 Support children and young people with disabilities and special educational needs.

Unit MU 2.9 Understand partnership working in services for children and young people.

Good practice

You must also make sure that the information you access is relevant to your home country. Check with your team leader or supervisor if you are unsure.

■ **The child or young person**:

As children mature they will increasingly be able to tell you about the way their family lives. Disabled children and young people are also best placed to tell you if their needs are being adequately met. For instance, they may say whether or not an adaptation needs to be made to a game to ensure they can participate. You'll learn more about this in Unit TDA 2.15.

■ **Colleagues**:

You will have some experienced colleagues at your setting who have a wide knowledge base between them, so don't be shy about asking them for information, support and advice. They are particularly well placed to help you deal with practical issues that you may come across, such as how to adapt an activity to meet a child's needs (see Unit TDA 2.15), or how to approach celebrating a festival without causing offence. In addition, the manager has a responsibility to see that you are well informed and well trained, so you should talk to them if you feel you would benefit from further learning in this area. You can also ask colleagues for feedback on your current performance.

■ **Special Educational Needs Coordinator (SENCO)**:

All early years settings have a SENCO. This is a nominated member of staff who has been trained to oversee how children with special educational needs (SEN) are supported. Part of the SENCO's role is to support staff working with children who have SEN, so they should be your first port of call for information, support and advice about this.

■ **Outside professionals**:

Your setting will sometimes work in partnership with outside professionals to meet a child or young person's needs, for example a speech therapist or a social worker. These professionals will have expert knowledge, and part of their remit is to support and advise those who care for the child. For further details about working in partnership with professionals, see Unit MU 2.9.

■ **Organisations**:

There are a number of reputable organisations that give information and advice to practitioners about diversity, equality and inclusion. Your manager will generally have a list of relevant organisations, which will include those within your local area. SENCOs will also have a list of organisations that specifically focus on disability, impairments or conditions, for example the Down's Syndrome Association and the National Deaf Children's Society. You can also use a search engine to find organisations on the internet.

Books are a good source of information

■ **Books**:

There are many books that focus solely on promoting diversity, equality or inclusion. This includes books that cover related subjects in detail – discrimination for instance, or meeting a disabled child's needs. Your setting may own some of these, and you can also access them via libraries and bookshops. A search of online bookshops will show you what is available. Simply type in 'discrimination' for example. It's important to make sure that you refer to books that are up to date.

■ **Magazines and journals**:

As you learnt in Unit SHC 22, it's part of your professional practice to keep yourself up to date with developments such as changes to legislation. You also need to know about the current opinions on best practice as these change over time. The best way you can do this is by reading industry magazines and journals such as *Nursery World* or *Child Care*.

■ **The internet**:

The internet gives you a wealth of information at your fingertips. All you need to do is conduct a search of your topic. However, not all information on the internet is correct or current, so make it an absolute rule to only use sites that you can be sure are reputable and professional. This will include sites such as the Department for Education, the NHS and BBC sites. National organisations (as mentioned above) will also have their own reputable sites.

■ **Television/radio**:

Some excellent documentaries are made about issues relating to diversity, equality and inclusion, and these are a great way to add depth to your knowledge and to stay up to date with current thinking and developments.

Did you know?

During your career, you'll find it beneficial to refer to these books:

Hyacinth Malik, *A Practical Guide to Equal Opportunities*, 2nd edn (Cheltenham, Nelson Thornes Ltd, 2009).

Angela Dare and Margaret O'Donovan, *Good Practice in Caring for Children with Special Needs*, 3rd edn (Cheltenham, Nelson Thornes Ltd, 2009).

How are things going?

▶ Progress Check

1. Explain what is meant by:
   a diversity
   b prejudice
   c equal opportunities and
   d inclusion. (1.1)

2. Explain what is meant by discrimination. (1.2)

3. Give an example of inadvertent discrimination within a setting. (1.3)

4. What is the name of the new Act that is bringing together previous equality legislation. (2.1)

5. If you heard a child make a racist comment, what would you do to challenge this in a way that promotes change? (2.3)

6. Suggest a situation in which you may need information, advice and support about diversity, equality or inclusion. (3.1)

7. Give three sources of information, advice and support about diversity, equality or inclusion. (3.2)

Are you ready for assessment?

Learning Outcome 2 must be assessed in a real work environment.

CACHE

Set task:

■ In an induction scenario you are asked to show that you can explain what is meant by diversity, equality, inclusion and discrimination, describe ways in which discrimination may occur in the work setting and explain how promoting equality and inclusion reduces the likelihood of discrimination. You are then asked to identify a range of sources of information, advice and support about diversity, equality and inclusion, and to describe how and when to access relevant information, advice and support.

You can prepare by asking your workplace SENCO about local sources of information, advice and support. You can also reread pages 81–90 and 100–103 and make relevant notes.

City & Guilds

In preparation for assessment of this Unit, it will be helpful to ask your workplace SENCO about local sources of information, advice and support about diversity, equality and inclusion.

Edexcel

In preparation for assessment of this Unit, it will be helpful to gather information and local sources of information, advice and support about diversity, equality and inclusion – it's a good idea to consult your workplace SENCO as part of the process.

UNIT 2.1

Child and young person development

LEARNING OUTCOMES

The learning outcomes you will meet in this unit are:

1. Know the main stages of development of children and young people

2. Understand the kinds of influences that affect the development of children and young people

3. Understand the potential effects of transitions on the development of children and young people

INTRODUCTION

It's absolutely essential for all practitioners to have a good understanding of children and young people's development. This underpins many aspects of our everyday work with children and young people. For instance, we draw on our development knowledge in order to pitch our interactions with children of different ages at the appropriate level, and to provide appropriate activities for them.

We also use our knowledge to monitor and assess the development of the individual children and young people who we work with. This enables us to support and promote their development effectively.

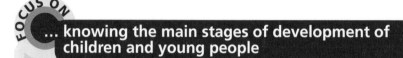

FOCUS ON

... knowing the main stages of development of children and young people

In this section you'll learn about the expected patterns of child and young person development from birth to 19 years. You'll also learn how different aspects of development can affect one another. This links with **Assessment Criteria 1.1, 1.2.**

Understanding child development

Expected development patterns

Tables within this unit give an approximate guide as to when babies, children and young people are likely to achieve certain milestones in their development, such as learning to walk.

These are the accepted expected development patterns. But it's important that you understand that children develop at *different* rates – this is entirely normal and should be anticipated. Always remember that the guides are only *approximate*.

Children of the same age will not reach all of the milestones at the same time. Some children will achieve milestones earlier than the **expected development rates** and some will achieve them later. The same child may well be ahead of expected rates in some areas and behind them in other areas. For example, a child may crawl and walk early but begin to talk a little late.

Sequence of development

Children generally develop in broadly the same sequence (or order). For example, babies will learn to roll over before they sit up, and children will say single words before they string two or three together in early sentences. However, there are exceptions to the **sequence of development**. For instance, disabled children and young people and those who have specific needs may develop differently. You'll learn about this is Learning outcome 2.

key terms

Expected development rates the approximate ages at which most children will achieve key developmental milestones.

Sequence of development the expected order in which most children will achieve key developmental milestones.

Babies will learn to roll over before they sit up

Using the expected patterns of development

Practitioners monitor and evaluate individual children and young people's development by making comparisons between a child's actual developmental stage and the expected development rates. This enables practitioners to:

■ understand the child's current stage of development

■ anticipate the next stage of a child's development.

This allows the practitioner to provide activities and experiences that will challenge and interest children, promoting their learning and development.

Monitoring and evaluating individual children and young people's development also helps practitioners to notice when children are not progressing as expected.

Although children develop at different rates, significant delays in one area of development or many delays in several areas can be an indication that children need intervention and extra support. You will learn more about the areas of development below. In Learning Outcome 3, you will learn about recognising and responding to concerns about the development of children and young people.

Practitioners monitor and evaluate development by carrying out observation and assessment of individual children. You'll learn about this in Unit MU 2.2.

Link Up!

Unit MU 2.2 Contribute to the support of child and young person development.

Aspects of development

For our convenience, we break child development down into different aspects (also called 'areas'). We do this because child development is complex, so we often need to focus on just one bit of it at a time. For instance, we talk about a child's physical development and their communication development.

But in practice, children's development is holistic. This means that children don't learn or develop in a compartmentalised way, but they learn and develop in many ways at the same time. For instance, a child will be learning to walk and talk at the same time. You'll learn more about this as you work through this unit.

Children can also use skills from across the aspects of development while doing one activity. You'll learn more about this on page 132.

But first, we'll break down child development into the aspects/areas shown on the following diagram.

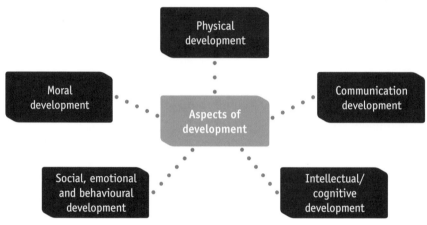

Aspects of development

Physical development

Physical development is about how children gain physical control of movements made with their bodies.

A newly born baby, known as the **neonate**, has **reflexes**. These are physical movements or reactions that they make without consciously intending to do so. For example, the neonate will move their head in search of the mother's nipple or the teat of a bottle when their lips or cheek are touched. This is known as the 'rooting reflex'. The baby will also suck and swallow milk. These reflexes help them to feed and therefore survive.

You may have experienced the grasp reflex – a baby will clasp their fingers around yours if you touch their palm. You will have probably seen the startle reflex too – a startled baby will make a fist and their arms will move away from their body. This can often be seen if there is a loud noise or if the baby wakes suddenly. The standing and walking reflex can be seen if a baby is held upright in the standing position with their feet resting on a firm surface, such as the floor. They will make stepping movements with their legs.

Gross motor skills

Gross motor skills are an aspect of physical development. The term 'gross motor skills' is used to refer to all whole-body movements such as:

- sitting up

- crawling

- walking

- kicking a ball.

These skills develop rapidly during a child's first five years. Some practitioners may use the term 'large motor skills', which has the same meaning.

Crawling   Sitting from lying down   Bear-walking

Walking with two hands held   Walking with one hand held   Walking alone

Gross motor skills involved in the development of walking

Fine motor skills

Fine motor skills are also an aspect of physical development. The term 'fine motor skills' is used to refer to the delicate, manipulative movements that are made with the fingers. (Some practitioners may use the term 'small motor skills', which has the same meaning.) Fine motor skills and the development of vision are linked. This is often referred to as 'hand–eye coordination'. Fine motor skills and hand–

eye coordination are used when a child is threading cotton reels for example – the child will look carefully at the position of the hole in the reel, and manipulate the string accordingly.

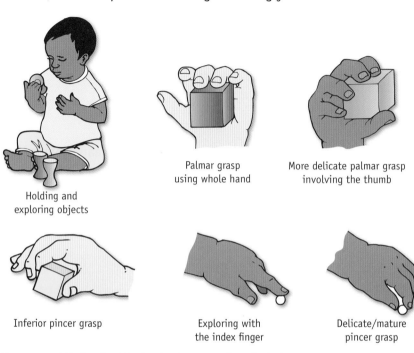

Holding and exploring objects

Palmar grasp using whole hand

More delicate palmar grasp involving the thumb

Inferior pincer grasp

Exploring with the index finger

Delicate/mature pincer grasp

Fine motor skills involved in the development of manipulation

Communication development

Communication development is the way in which children master speech, language and communication with others. There is a range of communication methods, including talking, body language, gesture, reading, writing and sign language. There are close links to intellectual/cognitive development because children need to think about and understand the communications that they receive from others as well as what they want to communicate themselves. Acquiring language also helps children's thinking processes. You'll learn more about language development in Unit TDA 2.7. Additional information is also provided in Unit OP 2.15. It's a good idea to read this as part of your study of this unit.

Intellectual/cognitive development

Intellectual/cognitive development is concerned with developments in the way the brain processes the information that children constantly receive from their surroundings and from people. It is a vast area of development, including:

Link Up!

Unit TDA 2.7 Maintain and support relationships with children and young people.

Unit OP 2.15 Contribute to the support of children's communication, language and literacy.

- memory

- concentration

- imagination

- creativity

- problem solving

- knowledge

- understanding.

There are close links between cognitive development and communication development, as explained on page 110.

Cognitive development and communication development are closely linked

Social, emotional and behavioural development

This is about the way in which children experience and handle their own emotions, which gives rise to behaviour. Frustration at not being able to do something is a good example of this. Children gain increasing control of their emotions as they develop. This area is also concerned with children's attachments to key people in their lives and their relationships with others, including how they relate to them.

Social, emotional and behavioural development has strong links to cognitive and communication development. Communication and understanding is at the heart of all relationships, and so is the act of expressing feelings and emotions.

Moral development

Morality describes the values and principles that we have. These inform our behaviour and decisions. This includes values and principles that are enforced by society (for example, that stealing is wrong), and those that are considered subjective (such as whether we have sex before marriage for example).

There are strong links to social, emotional and behavioural development because morality encompasses social acceptance, the control of feelings and the impact this has on behaviour. For instance, a child may know that it's wrong to hit someone, but controlling anger and behaviour so as not to hit someone is another matter.

There are also strong links to intellectual/cognitive development because developing values and principles requires the ability to think about issues and make decisions about them (whether or not to eat meat for example).

The development tables

On the following pages a concise overview of each stage of development is given in the rate and sequence of development tables. These are a snapshot in time, representing the big picture of a child's expected development at any given age. Within this, the expected development milestones for each of the areas of development appear in colour-coded segments. This enables you to track specific aspects of a child's development within the big picture, as you would do in reality. For example, if you want to track physical development from 0 to 19 years, follow just the blue segments on every page.

In the tables, you will come across the term 'neonate', which, as mentioned, refers to a newly born baby. You'll also see the term '**prone**' (which describes the position that a baby is in when lying on their front) and the term '**supine**' (which describes the position that a baby is in when lying on their back).

Table TDA2.1.1: Development tables

BIRTH–3 WEEKS

OVERVIEW

Full-term babies are born at around 40 weeks. If born more than three weeks before the due date, babies are premature. They will then be expected to take a little longer to meet the early development milestones. Newborn babies need to begin bonding with their primary carers from birth. Babies spend more time sleeping than they do awake.

PHYSICAL DEVELOPMENT

Reflexes as described on page 108

Usually holds hands tightly closed

In supine position, lies with head to one side

In prone position, lies with head to one side and tucks knees up under the abdomen

COMMUNICATION DEVELOPMENT

Cries to communicate hunger, tiredness and distress

INTELLECTUAL/COGNITIVE DEVELOPMENT

Recognises mother's voice

SOCIAL, EMOTIONAL AND BEHAVIOURAL DEVELOPMENT

Begins to bond with primary carers from birth. Needs close physical contact with them for security and when care needs are met

Totally dependent on others

OVERVIEW

Babies will have developed rapidly in the four weeks since birth. They will be sleeping a little less frequently and some may be settling into a sleeping and feeding routine. They begin to communicate through sounds as well as crying, and will begin to smile.

PHYSICAL DEVELOPMENT

When sitting: head falls forwards (known as head lag), and the back curves

Posture more 'unfurled'

Reflexes persist, startle reflex is seen less frequently

Gazes attentively at faces, particularly when fed and talked to

COMMUNICATION DEVELOPMENT

Communicates needs through sounds

Communicates needs through crying

Communication occurs through physical closeness

Begins to coo and gurgle in response to interaction from carers

INTELLECTUAL/COGNITIVE DEVELOPMENT

May be soothed when crying by a familiar voice or music

Senses are used for exploration

SOCIAL, EMOTIONAL AND BEHAVIOURAL DEVELOPMENT

Smiles from about 5 weeks

Begins to respond to sounds heard in the environment by making own sounds

Engaged by people's faces

3 MONTHS

OVERVIEW

Babies will now be far more alert, and some may have settled into a routine that includes sleeping through the night. Being more settled and engaging and interacting more with carers and the world, generally results in babies crying less often.

PHYSICAL DEVELOPMENT

Turns from side to back

In supine: head in central position

In prone: head and chest can be lifted from the floor, supported by the forearms

When sitting: little head lag remains, back is straighter

Arms can be waved and brought together

Legs can be kicked separately and together

Alert, the baby moves head to watch others

Engages in hand and finger play

Holds rattle briefly before dropping

COMMUNICATION DEVELOPMENT

Recognises and links familiar sounds such as the face and voice of a carer

Will hold 'conversations' with carer when talked to, making sounds and waiting for a response

Can imitate high and low sounds

Returns a smile when smiled at – may smile often

INTELLECTUAL/COGNITIVE DEVELOPMENT

Through use of senses, begins to understand he/she is a separate person

Begins to notice objects in immediate environment

SOCIAL, EMOTIONAL AND BEHAVIOURAL DEVELOPMENT

Begins to discover what he/she can do, and this creates a sense of self

May cry if a primary carer leaves the room, not yet understanding that person still exists and will return

Shows feelings such as excitement and fear

Reacts positively when a carer is caring, kind and soothing

If a carer does not respond to a baby, the baby may stop trying to interact

OVERVIEW

Rapid development will have continued. Babies are physically stronger and very alert. They can now clearly express enjoyment and excitement through smiling, laughing and squeals of delight, which encourages carers to interact with them playfully. They can also reach for objects they're interested in, allowing them a new degree of autonomy in exploration. (The items must be within their reach.)

PHYSICAL DEVELOPMENT

Turns from front to back, and may do the reverse

In supine: head can be lifted and controlled when pulled to sitting position

In prone: head and chest can be fully extended supported by arms, with the hands flat on the floor

Sits unsupported for some time, with back straight, and plays in this position

Uses hands to play with feet, and may take them to the mouth

Weight-bears when held in standing position

Uses palmar grasp to pick up objects

Takes objects to the mouth for exploration

Passes objects from hand to hand

COMMUNICATION DEVELOPMENT

Sounds are used intentionally to call for a carer's attention

Babbling is frequent. The baby plays tunefully with the sounds he/she can make

Rhythm and volume explored vocally

Enjoys rhymes and accompanying actions

INTELLECTUAL/COGNITIVE DEVELOPMENT

Interested in bright, shiny objects

Very alert

Watches events keenly

Takes objects to mouth for exploration

SOCIAL, EMOTIONAL AND BEHAVIOURAL DEVELOPMENT

Shows a wider range of feelings more clearly and vocally

May laugh and screech with delight, but cry with fear at the sight of a stranger

Clearly tells people apart, showing a preference for primary carers/siblings

Reaches out to be held, and may stop crying when talked to

Enjoys looking at self in the mirror

Enjoys attention and being with others

9 MONTHS

OVERVIEW

Mobility makes a huge difference at this stage. Babies can now explore the environment, and increased strength means that they will also sit up and play for extended periods of time. Cognitive development and communication development are coming on hand in hand, with babies understanding some familiar words. There's an important emotional milestone as babies begin to understand that carers who leave the room will return (object permanence).

PHYSICAL DEVELOPMENT

Sits unsupported on the floor

Will go on hands and knees, and may crawl or find an alternative way to move around

Pulls self to standing position using furniture for support

Cruises around the room (side-stepping, holding furniture for support)

Takes steps if both hands are held by carer

Uses an inferior pincer grasp to pick up objects

Explores objects with the eyes

Points to and pokes at objects of interest with index finger

COMMUNICATION DEVELOPMENT

Initiates a wider range of sounds, and recognises a few familiar words, including 'no'

Knows own name

Greatly enjoys playing with carers and holding conversations

Makes longer strings of babbling sounds

Intentionally uses volume vocally

INTELLECTUAL/COGNITIVE DEVELOPMENT

Likes to explore immediate environment (as long as a primary carer is within close proximity)

Begins to look for fallen objects (object permanence)

SOCIAL, EMOTIONAL AND BEHAVIOURAL DEVELOPMENT

Enjoys playing with carers, e.g. peek-a-boo games and pat-a-cake

Offers objects, but does not yet let go

Increasing mobility allows baby to approach people

Begins to feed self with support

Understands that carers who leave the room will return

12 MONTHS

OVERVIEW

Babies are becoming increasingly mobile and are beginning to walk. Fine motor skills are also developing with the emergence of a sophisticated pincer grasp and the ability to feed themselves with a spoon. Other key milestones include increased babbling leading to speaking the first words, and the development of memory, which opens up a whole new world of learning.

PHYSICAL DEVELOPMENT

Sits down from standing position

Stands alone briefly and may walk a few steps alone

Throws toys intentionally

Clasps hands together

Uses sophisticated pincer grasp, and releases hold intentionally

Feeds self with spoon and finger foods

COMMUNICATION DEVELOPMENT

Increasingly understands the basic messages communicated by carers and older siblings

Can respond to basic instructions

Babbling sounds increasingly like speech, and leads to the first single words being spoken

Shows understanding that particular words are associated with people and objects, by using a few single words in context

INTELLECTUAL/COGNITIVE DEVELOPMENT

Looks for objects that fall out of sight, understanding they still exist although they can't be seen
Memory develops

Remembering past events enables the anticipation of future familiar events (e.g. a baby may show excitement when placed in their high chair ready for lunch)

Begins to anticipate what comes next in the daily routine, e.g. a nappy change before nap time

SOCIAL, EMOTIONAL AND BEHAVIOURAL DEVELOPMENT

The sense of self identity increases, as self-esteem and self-confidence develop

Waves goodbye, when prompted at first, and then spontaneously

Content to play alone or alongside other children for increasing periods of time

OVERVIEW

At this stage, language is really developing, with children understanding more and using an increasing number of single words. Walking is steadier, and as independence develops, there will begin to be frustration when the child is prevented from doing certain things, or when they are unable to do something they want to do themselves. As they are 'into everything' and fully mobile, careful supervision is necessary.

PHYSICAL DEVELOPMENT

Walks independently

Crawls upstairs. Crawls downstairs feet first

Sits in a child-sized chair independently

Tries to turn the pages of a book

Makes a tower of two blocks

Makes marks on paper with crayons

Holds own cup when drinking

COMMUNICATION DEVELOPMENT

Understands the concepts of labels such as 'you', 'me', 'mine', 'yours'

Use of single words increases, and more words are learned

INTELLECTUAL/COGNITIVE DEVELOPMENT

Will put away/look for very familiar objects in the right place

Uses toys for their purpose, e.g. puts a doll in a pram

Shows a keener interest in the activities of peers

SOCIAL, EMOTIONAL AND BEHAVIOURAL DEVELOPMENT

Curious. Wants to explore the world more than ever, as long as carers are close by

May show signs of separation anxiety (e.g. upset when left at nursery)

May 'show off' to entertain carers

Can be jealous of attention/toys given to another child

Changeable emotionally. Quickly alternates between wanting to do things alone and being dependent on carers

May respond with anger when told off or thwarted. May throw toys or have a tantrum

Can be distracted from inappropriate behaviour

Possessive of toys and carers. Reluctant to share

Child 'is busy' or 'into everything'

OVERVIEW

Children are increasingly keen to have independence, and become frustrated easily if incapable of doing something. This may lead to asserting will strongly, showing angry defiance and resistance to adults. Children cannot yet control their emotional responses, and need sensitivity from their carers when they become overwhelmed by their feelings. They will understand a lot of what is said to them, so communicative stimulation is important. Children will begin to enjoy mark-making and use trial and error in exploration, for example, trying to post several shapes in the hole of a shape sorter.

PHYSICAL DEVELOPMENT

Walks confidently. Attempts to run

Walks up and down stairs if hand is held by carer

Bends from the waist without falling forwards

Balances in the squatting position

Pushes and pulls wheeled toys

Propels ride-on toys along with legs

Rolls and throws balls, attempts to kick them

Uses delicate pincer grasp to thread cotton reels

Makes a tower of three blocks

Makes large scribbles with crayons

Can use door handles

COMMUNICATION DEVELOPMENT

Understands a great deal of what carers say

More words spoken. Uses people's names

INTELLECTUAL/COGNITIVE DEVELOPMENT

Uses trial and error in exploration

SOCIAL, EMOTIONAL AND BEHAVIOURAL DEVELOPMENT

Has a better understanding of being an individual

Very curious, and more confident to explore

Becomes frustrated easily if incapable of doing something

Follows carers, keen to join in with their activities

Plays alongside peers more often (parallel play), and may imitate them

Still very changeable emotionally

May show sympathy for others (e.g. putting arm around a crying child)

Can be restless and very determined, quickly growing irritated or angry

May assert will strongly, showing angry defiance and resistance to adults

Can still be distracted from inappropriate behaviour

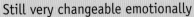

2 YEARS

OVERVIEW

By now, children's individuality and uniqueness is evident, and emerging more all the time. The long journey of learning to express this in words as well as behaviour will begin as short sentences are spoken. More confident physical movements lead to new experiences such as running, climbing and sliding, and appropriate outside apparatus will be enjoyed. Children still struggle with their overwhelming emotions, but are beginning to understand that actions have consequences. This is an important cognitive and behavioural development.

PHYSICAL DEVELOPMENT

Runs confidently

Climbs low apparatus

Walks up and down stairs alone holding hand rail

Rides large wheeled toys (without pedals)

Kicks stationary balls

Makes a tower of six blocks

Joins and separates interlocking toys

Draws circles, lines and dots with a pencil

Puts on shoes

COMMUNICATION DEVELOPMENT

Will often name objects on sight (e.g. may point and say 'chair' or 'dog')

Vocabulary increases. Joins two words together, e.g. 'shoes on'

Short sentences used by 30 months. Some words used incorrectly (e.g. 'I *goed* in')

INTELLECTUAL/COGNITIVE DEVELOPMENT

Completes simple jigsaw puzzles (or 'play-trays')

Understands that actions have consequences

Builds towers of bricks

SOCIAL, EMOTIONAL AND BEHAVIOURAL DEVELOPMENT

Beginning to understand own feelings. Identifies sad and happy faces

Experiences a range of changeable feelings, which are expressed in behaviour

More responsive to the feelings of others

Often responds to carers lovingly, and may initiate loving gestures (a cuddle)

Peals of laughter and sounds of excitement are common for some

May use growing language ability to protest verbally

May get angry with peers, and lash out on occasion (e.g. pushing or even biting them)

OVERVIEW

As children gain the ability to express themselves with language, behaviour related to frustration (e.g. tantrums) decreases. This facilitates moral development. Many children start pre-school. This is timely, as at this stage interest in being with peers increases, and most children will enjoy playing with others of a similar age. This is also easier, thanks to an increasing ability to share and take turns. Many children will experience planned learning activities for the first time.

PHYSICAL DEVELOPMENT

Walks and runs on tip-toes

Walks up and down stairs confidently

Rides large wheeled toys using pedals and steering

Kicks moving balls forwards

Enjoys climbing and sliding on small apparatus

Makes a tower of nine blocks

Turns the pages of a book reliably

Draws a face with a pencil, using the preferred hand

Attempts to write letters

Puts on and removes coat

Fastens large, easy zippers

COMMUNICATION DEVELOPMENT

Enjoys stories and rhymes

Vocabulary increases quickly

Use of plurals, pronouns, adjectives, possessives and tenses

Longer sentences used

By 42 months, most language used correctly

INTELLECTUAL/COGNITIVE DEVELOPMENT

Child is enquiring. Frequently asks 'what' and 'why' questions

Use of language for thinking and reporting

Can name colours. Can match and sort items into simple sets (e.g. colour sets)

Can count to 10 by rote. Can only count out three or four objects

Begins to recognise own written name

Creativity is used in imaginary and creative play

SOCIAL, EMOTIONAL AND BEHAVIOURAL DEVELOPMENT

Can tell carers how he/she is feeling

Empathises with the feelings of others

Uses the toilet and washes own hands

Can put on clothes

Imaginary and creative play is enjoyed

Enjoys company of peers and makes friends

Wants adult approval

Is affected by mood of carers/peers

Less rebellious. Less likely to physically express anger as words can be used

MORAL DEVELOPMENT

Increasingly able to understand consequence of behaviour and the concept of 'getting in trouble'

Understands the concept of saying sorry and 'making up'

4 YEARS

OVERVIEW

Many children will make the transition to school during this year, which marks a huge change in their lives. They will also be fluent talkers, confident movers and increasingly adept socially. Their play will contain definite ideas, which they can now verbalise. Their concentration span will be increasing all the time, and many children will now be experienced in taking part in planned learning activities.

PHYSICAL DEVELOPMENT

Changes direction while running

Walks in a straight line successfully

Confidently climbs and slides on apparatus

Hops safely

Can bounce and catch balls, and take aim

Makes a tower of 10 blocks

Learning to fasten most buttons and zips

Learning to use scissors. Cuts out basic shapes

Draws people with heads, bodies and limbs

Writes names and letters in play as awareness that print carries meaning develops

COMMUNICATION DEVELOPMENT

Uses language fluently

As an understanding of language increases so does enjoyment of rhymes, stories and nonsense

Speech is clear and understood by those who don't know the child

INTELLECTUAL/COGNITIVE DEVELOPMENT

Completes puzzles of 12 pieces

Memory develops. Child recalls many songs and stories

Attention/concentration span increases

Fantasy and reality may be confused

Imagination and creativity increases

Problem solves ('I wonder what will happen if...'), and makes hypothesis ('I think this will happen if...')

Sorts objects into more complex sets

Number correspondence improves

SOCIAL, EMOTIONAL AND BEHAVIOURAL DEVELOPMENT

May be confident socially

Self-esteem is apparent

Awareness of gender roles if exposed to them

Friendship with peers is increasingly valued

Enjoys playing with groups of children

Control over emotions increases

Can wait to have needs met by carers

As imagination increases child may become fearful (e.g. of the dark or monsters)

Learning to negotiate and get along with others through experimenting with behaviour

Experiences being in/out of control, feeling power, having quarrels with peers

Some considerate, caring behaviour is shown to others

Distraction works less often, but child increasingly understands reasoning

Co-operative behaviour shown

Responds well to praise for behaviour, encouragement and responsibility

MORAL DEVELOPMENT

Experiences being blamed, blaming

Has a good understanding of familiar, basic rules

If exposed to swearing, is likely to use these words in their own language

OVERVIEW

Children will now be in formal schooling. Many will enjoy the cognitive stimulation and challenge of the classroom and the independence they have at playtimes. But for some there may be a negative experience, particularly if reading and writing do not interest them, or they experience difficulties with these areas of learning. Friends are very important to children now. Physical development has now slowed, but coordination increases.

PHYSICAL DEVELOPMENT

Coordination increases

Controls ball well. Plays ball games with rules

Rides bike with stabilisers

Balance is good, uses low stilts confidently

Sense of rhythm has developed. Enjoys dance and movement activities

Controls mark-making materials well (e.g. pencils). Writing more legible

Writes letters and short, familiar words

Learns to sew

COMMUNICATION DEVELOPMENT

Learning to read. Recognises some words

Vocabulary grows

INTELLECTUAL/COGNITIVE DEVELOPMENT

Options/knowledge of subjects are shared using language for thinking

Enjoyment of books increases as child learns to read

Thinking skills and memory increase as vocabulary grows

Spends longer periods at activities when engaged

Shows persistence

Children learn from new experiences at school

Learning style preferences may become apparent

The school transition may be unsettling

Enjoys group play and co-operative activities

Increasingly understands rules of social conduct and rules of games, but may have difficulty accepting losing

Increasing sense of own personality and gender

Keen to 'fit in' with others. Approval from adults and peers desired

Friends are important. Many are made at school

Many children will have new experiences out of school (e.g. play clubs, friends coming for tea)

Increasingly independent, undertaking most physical care needs for themselves

May seek attention, 'showing off' in front of peers

Often responds to 'time out' method of managing behaviour

MORAL DEVELOPMENT

Feels shame/guilt when adults disapprove of behaviour

Keen to win and be 'right'

6–7 YEARS

OVERVIEW

Children are strongly influenced by what they learn at school, and can increasingly consider this alongside what they learn at home, and draw their own conclusions. This contributes to personality being established more firmly and attitudes developing. Development slows now (it is most rapid in the 0–5 years period), but confidence increases, and so does learning in terms of the school curriculum. Many children will be developing wider interests, and may attend club and classes outside of school hours (e.g. dance, music, drama).

PHYSICAL DEVELOPMENT

Can hop on either leg, skip and play hopscotch

Rides bicycle without stabilisers

Confidently climbs and slides on larger apparatus in school and in parks

Can catch a ball with one hand only

Sews confidently and may tie shoe laces

COMMUNICATION DEVELOPMENT

Language refined and more adult-like

Enjoys jokes and word play

INTELLECTUAL/COGNITIVE DEVELOPMENT

Imagination skills are developed

Fantasy games are complex and dramatic

Many children read and write basic text by age 7, but this varies widely

Ability to predict and to plan ahead has developed

Understands cause and effect well

Can conserve number

Does simple calculations

Understands measurement and weighing

SOCIAL, EMOTIONAL AND BEHAVIOURAL DEVELOPMENT

Enjoys team games and activities

Towards age 7, a child may doubt their learning ability ('I can't do it')

May be reluctant to try or persevere, becoming frustrated easily

Personality is established more firmly as attitudes to life are developed

Solid friendships are formed. The relationship with 'best friends' is important

More susceptible to peer pressure

Cultural identity also established

Has learned how to behave in various settings and social situations (e.g. at school, play club, a friend's house)

MORAL DEVELOPMENT

Attitudes to life beginning to be developed – these are the basis of future moral codes

Can understand increasingly complex rules, impacting on the sense of right and wrong

OVERVIEW

Children will now be reading and writing well. They will know what they like and don't like, and feel they know how and what they learn best. However, an emotionally rocky period can be expected with the transition to secondary and the onset of puberty (although the age at which this occurs varies widely). An interest in TV, computers, console games, DVDs may mean child is less active, so a balanced, active lifestyle should be encouraged.

PHYSICAL DEVELOPMENT

Physical growth slows at first, so fewer physical milestones reached

Puberty generally begins between 11–13 years (see 13–19 years table)

Coordination and speed of movement develops

Muscles and bones develop. Has more physical strength

Begins to run around less in play

Interest in TV, computers, console games, DVDs may mean less active

Does joined-up writing, which becomes increasingly adult-like

Has computer skills. May type well and control the mouse as an adult would

Can sew well, and may be adept at delicate craft activities such as braiding threads

COMMUNICATION DEVELOPMENT

May read for enjoyment in leisure time

Can make up and tell stories that have been plotted out

Verbal and written communication is fluent, often with correct grammar usage

Enjoys chatting to friends/adults

INTELLECTUAL/COGNITIVE DEVELOPMENT

Range of new subjects may be learned at secondary school

Child may follow their interests, learning outside of school

Sense of logic develops. Thinking in abstract by age 10 (can consider beliefs, morals and world events)

SOCIAL, EMOTIONAL AND BEHAVIOURAL DEVELOPMENT

May feel unsettled when making the transition from primary school to secondary school, and as puberty approaches

Stable friendships are relied upon. These are generally same-sex, although children play in mixed groups/teams

May be reluctant to go to a play club or event unless a friend will be there too

More independent

Makes more decisions

May play unsupervised at times

May travel to school alone by end of age band

Mood swings may be experienced during puberty (see 13–19 years table)

MORAL DEVELOPMENT

Conflict with parents due to desire for increasing independence ('Why can't I stay home alone?')

May feel rules are unfair ('But all my friends are allowed to do it!')

May refuse to go along with some decisions made by parents (e.g. refusing to wear certain clothes purchased for them as they feel they have the right to choose for themselves)

Thinking in abstract by age 10 (see intellectual/cognitive development)

There's a huge variation in terms of when young people mature in this age band. There's a lot happening too – puberty, relationships based on attraction, exams, leaving school, making career choices, establishing one's own ethics and morals – all of which happen in response to many new experiences. Practitioners need to be responsive to how young people respond to pressure at this age, while allowing increasing independence.

PHYSICAL DEVELOPMENT

The bodies of both boys and girls change throughout puberty. Variation in age at which this occurs

Girls generally enter puberty by 13 years, becoming women physically by 16 years

Boys generally enter puberty by 14 years, becoming men physically by 16 or 17 years

Sporting talents may become more apparent

May learn/refine new manipulative skills (e.g. drawing, stitching, carpentry, woodwork, playing an instrument)

Talent in the arts or crafts may become more apparent

COMMUNICATION DEVELOPMENT

May be reluctant to directly ask adults for the advice or information they need. May prefer to access it anonymously

INTELLECTUAL/COGNITIVE DEVELOPMENT

Academic knowledge increases as exam curriculum is followed

Towards age 16, decisions made about the future (college course/career)

SOCIAL, EMOTIONAL AND BEHAVIOURAL DEVELOPMENT

Desire to express individuality, but also a strong desire to fit in with peers

Becomes interested in own sexuality and feels attraction to others

Develops romantic relationships

Develops sexual relationships

May express self creatively through art/music/dance or creative writing

May worry about aspects of physical appearance

May express self/experiment with identity through appearance (e.g. dress, hairstyles, piercings, tattoos)

Pressure at school mounts as exam curriculum is followed

Young people may feel overwhelmed or anxious

A balance of school work/leisure time is important, especially if young people take on part-time jobs

Likely to communicate innermost thoughts and feelings more frequently to friends than to adults

May prefer to spend more time with friends than with family. May stay in bedroom more at home

May swing between acting maturely, and saying/doing 'childish' things (e.g. may watch a young children's TV programme, or sit on a swing in the park)

May experiment with smoking, alcohol, drugs or early promiscuity. This behaviour is linked with low-self esteem

May experience mood swings. Tense atmospheres are lightened when adults remain in good humour

MORAL DEVELOPMENT

Developing own morals, beliefs and values outside of parents' influence

May disregard the opinions/values of parents if they conflict with those of the peer group

Acting on own values may cause conflict at home (e.g. becoming a vegetarian)

Towards end of age band, may protest to make their feelings known and to act on a desire to change the world (e.g. online petitions, student protests)

How aspects of development can affect one another

At the beginning of this section you learnt that aspects of development are linked. This means that they affect one another. It's important for you to remember that children learn holistically, and to understand that the play and learning opportunities provided for them can promote several aspects of learning at once, as the following Practical example shows.

Practical example

Harrison's development task

Harrison is a student on placement in a pre-school. For his college course he has been asked to choose a common play activity provided by his setting. He must then identify which areas of children's development it promotes. He must record the information on a diagram.

Here is his work so far.

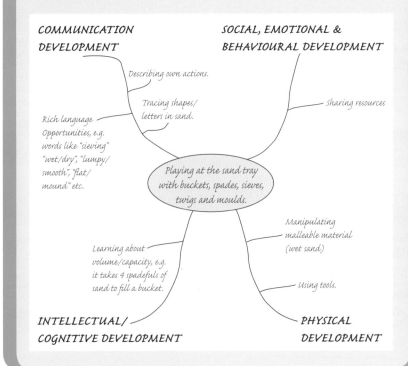

COMMUNICATION DEVELOPMENT

SOCIAL, EMOTIONAL & BEHAVIOURAL DEVELOPMENT

Describing own actions.

Sharing resources

Tracing shapes/ letters in sand.

Rich language Opportunities, e.g. words like "sieving" "wet/dry", "lumpy/ smooth", "flat/ mound" etc.

Playing at the sand tray with buckets, spades, sieves, twigs and moulds.

Manipulating malleable material (wet sand)

Learning about volume/capacity, e.g. it takes 4 spadefuls of sand to fill a bucket.

Using tools.

INTELLECTUAL/ COGNITIVE DEVELOPMENT

PHYSICAL DEVELOPMENT

Have a go!

In the practical example opposite, Harrison has yet to finish his diagram. Spend a few minutes thinking about his play activity. What information would you advise him to add?

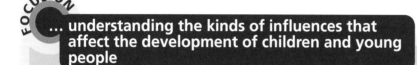
FOCUS ON

... understanding the kinds of influences that affect the development of children and young people

In this section you'll learn about the influences that affect the development of children and young people. You'll also learn about the importance of recognising and responding to concerns about children and young people's development. This links with **Assessment Criteria 2.1, 2.2**.

Nature and nurture

Below, you'll learn about the influences that affect the development of children and young people. These fall into two main categories:

- Nature: development occurs in response to the way children are genetically programmed from birth to be able to do certain things at certain times. This is referred to as 'nature'.

- Nurture: development occurs in response to the experiences that individual children have from the time they are born onwards. This is referred to as 'nurture'.

Why is nature and nurture relevant?

It is important for you to understand that the development of individual children and young people and their levels of maturity will depend partly on when they are genetically programmed to do something and partly on the experiences they have had. If you don't understand this, you will have unrealistic expectations of children's development.

Children have different experiences at different times, and so they develop at different rates. Children can't be expected to achieve aspects of development that are largely down to nurture if they haven't yet been exposed to experiences that encourage this development. This is shown in the Practical example on page 134.

Ask Miranda!

Q Can an aspect of child development be influenced by both nature and nurture at the same time?

A **Yes. Language is a good example of this. Studies have shown that babies all round the world make coos, gurgles and other sounds that are very similar. The potential to speak and a common ability to make similar pre-language sounds would seem to be down to nature. But children learn to speak the language they are exposed to. This is down to nurture.**

Marianna's physical play experience

Marianna is a refugee who has been in the UK for only a few weeks. She is three-and-a-half years old when she starts attending pre-school. When playing outside, her peers ride a tricycle confidently, pedalling and steering their way around the garden with ease. Marianna is keen to join in, but she struggles – her feet keep slipping off the peddles, she stops and starts continually and often bumps into things. Rather than steering, she stands and lifts the tricycle to change direction.

Pre-school trainee Melody notices this and mentions it to her team leader. The team leader explains that Marianna has come from a country where a war meant she had few opportunities to play safely outside. Marianna had not played with any sort of ride-on toy before joining the pre-school, while many of her peers played with ride-on toys from the age of around 18 months.

Influences that affect development

There are a number of influences that affect the development of children and young people. We'll break these down into the aspects shown on the following diagram and look at each in turn.

Children have different experiences at different times, and so they develop at different rates

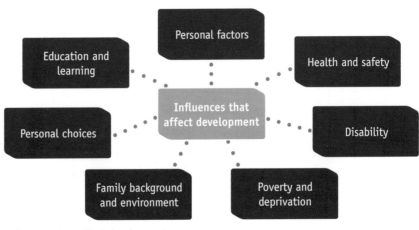

Influences that affect development

Personal factors

Personal factors are things that are an intrinsic (or built in) part of the child. They start to influence a child's development at the moment of conception.

All of the cells in our bodies contain 46 chromosomes, which are made up of 23 pairs. Each chromosome consists of long chemical threads, which we know as DNA. Each of the threads contain genes. The father's sperm and the mother's egg each carry their genetic information, and when the sperm and egg fuse, the chromosomes pair off, with the baby getting half of their chromosomes from the mother and half from the father. Experts now think we have in the region of 50,000 genes.

A number of factors are decided genetically, including aspects of health and appearance such as:

- hair colour

- eye colour

- face shape

- height (although external factors such as a poor diet can also affect growth).

The reason why children from the same parents aren't all the same, and the reason why we all have our own unique DNA, is that the selection of chromosomes in the sperm and the egg is completely random. Identical twins are the exception to the rule, because in their case one fertilised egg splits into two sections.

Further personal factors can arise during the pregnancy and birth. For instance:

- If the mother picks up certain infections, they can affect the baby's development.

- Harm can also be caused by drinking alcohol or taking drugs during pregnancy.

- If a baby is born prematurely, the usual full-term development will not be complete, and this can have long-term physical and/or cognitive effects.

Did you know?

Some people refer to DNA as our 'genetic fingerprint'.

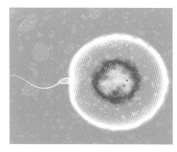

Personal factors influence a child's development from the moment of conception

135

Physical impairments or learning difficulties can be caused by all of the above. There can also be difficulties at birth that can impact on development, including a lack of oxygen, which can cause learning difficulties. You'll learn more about this below.

Health and safety

Ill health can have a big impact on a child's development for the following key reasons. It can cause children to:

- miss time or experiences at school or at a setting (due to being off sick or being physically unable to participate in all experiences)

- miss out on being with their family (most commonly due to stays in hospital)

- miss out on playing with friends and participating in other activities during their leisure time.

All of the above can result in a child missing out on experiences that contribute to development. When attending school or a setting, children may not have the energy or stamina to participate fully. In these cases, practitioners can devise strategies to support the child, as shown in the Practical example below.

To develop well, children also need to have opportunities to be physically active, to get enough sleep, to eat healthily and to be kept safe. You'll learn more about this in Unit MU 2.8.

▶▶Link Up!◀◀

Unit MU 2.8 Contribute to the support of positive environments for children and young people.

Practical example

Dervla's routine

Dervla is a childminder who cares for four children aged 5–8 during the school holidays. Eight-year-old Rosie has ME (myalgic encephalomyelitis), which causes debilitating tiredness. Although there isn't always a pattern to Rosie's fatigue, more often than not she is particularly tired after lunch. Dervla schedules quieter whole-group activities – such as sharing stories – to coincide with this time, so that Rosie needn't miss out while she has a rest on the sofa.

There are various causes of health problems. Some health conditions, such as certain heart problems, are present at birth, and the child will be affected by them to some extent from the start of their life.

There can be a disposition (or tendency) to develop other conditions, but a child will only develop them if they are triggered by external factors. Asthma can be triggered by living in a damp house for instance, or in an area with high levels of traffic pollution.

Disability

Disability can result from:

- genetic makeup

- pre-birth experiences (such as the mother taking drugs)

- birth experiences (such as a lack of oxygen at birth).

In addition, a non-disabled child or young person may become disabled during their life as the result of an accident, injury or illness. Any aspect of children's development can be affected by disability. An important part of a practitioner's role is to ensure that all children:

- can participate within the setting

- have the individual support they need.

This can limit the effect of impairments on future development. You'll learn more about this in Unit TDA 2.15.

Poverty and deprivation

Poverty shapes children's development. Living in poverty is extremely stressful for families. There may be constant worries about:

- having enough food to eat

- having appropriate clothes to wear (including school uniform)

- having heat in the winter

- affording to pay for everyday basic supplies of power (electric/gas) and water

- affording to pay for housing (for example making rent payments).

Did you know?

Health conditions for which there is no genetic disposition can also be caused by external factors, including a poor diet, poor health care and living in poor conditions. You'll learn more about the effects of poverty below.

Link Up!

Unit TDA 2.15 Support children and young people with disabilities and special educational needs.

Children living in poverty may worry about having appropriate clothes to wear

This can have an effect on everyone's mental health, as well as an impact on physical health. Poor-quality food and poor housing are particularly common problems. They can lead to a lack of opportunities to play safely, impacting on learning experiences.

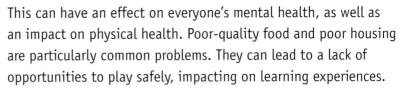

Did you know?

Children and young people may also experience the stigma of poverty, which affects their self-esteem and self-respect. This impacts on social and emotional development. It also lowers children's expectations for their own future.

Unit SHC 2.3 Introduction to equality and inclusion in children and young people's settings.

Family background and environment

How a child is brought up has a huge impact on their development. As you learnt in Unit SHC 23, children develop within unique families that exist within their own different social and cultural systems. This means that different families influence children in widely different ways and have different parenting styles. You may like to reread the information on culture and religion in Unit SHC 23 as part of your study of this unit.

However different children's homes may be, in most cases, children are well cared for by a parent/family who loves them. They do their best to feed them well, to keep them safe and to give them the emotional support and encouragement that they need. Many parents want their child to do well in life, so when they start at school they help with homework and take an interest in events. Children have things to do and places to play in their leisure time. This all has a positive effect on development and on the children's life outcomes.

Difficulties at home

However, parenting styles can sometimes cause difficulties despite the best intentions of families. For example, some parents find it difficult to provide their child with the emotional support they need. They may find it challenging to show affection physically (for example with a hug) or verbally (for example by telling a child that they love them). Some parents have difficulties with consistency, particularly in terms of responding to children's behaviour. They may alternate

Parents can impact on development by helping children to learn

between being overly strict and overly permissive, which is extremely confusing for children and can lead to insecurity as well as difficulties controlling their own behaviour.

While all families have periods of stress and strain, in some families arguments at home may be commonplace. These can be extremely upsetting, whether they are between adults or siblings, particularly if accusations are made. Children may feel under fire, uncared for or unloved. Some parents, carers or other family members may have issues in their life that affect their parenting and therefore the child's development. This could include drug or alcohol abuse, domestic violence, depression or other mental health issues. It's also a sad fact that some people deliberately harm their own children. (You'll learn more about this in Unit TDA 2.2.)

All of these factors may lead to children and young people spending less time at home, and they may become overly independent at a young age. This can make them vulnerable in terms of personal safety, particularly if they are hanging about on the street or staying out late. In this case, there is also the risk that they may become involved in antisocial behaviour.

Did you know?

Research has shown that many children and young people who engage in antisocial behaviour have had unhappy home lives.

Link Up!

Unit TDA 2.2 Safeguard the welfare of children and young people.

Ask Miranda!

Q Not all children live in their family home. Some are looked after by their local authority or have care status. I've heard that this can influence a child's development. Why is this?

A Attachments to primary carers are important to children and young people as they have a deep emotional need to be loved and nurtured by someone they are special to. Children who are looked after by their local authority or have care status are most likely to be lacking this stable, consistent, secure person in their life. They may also be experiencing the effects of disability, family breakdown, youth offending or unsatisfactory parental care. They may live in residential care or foster care and will perhaps be moved around throughout their childhood, which may also result in them changing schools frequently. Any of these unsettling influences can affect development, and when several are combined the effects may be significant.

Personal choices

Part of growing up is having increasing independence and the opportunity to make more and bigger decisions. Some of these can impact on development. For instance, young people make personal choices about:

- taking physical risks

- having sex

- drinking alcohol

- skipping school

- smoking

- taking drugs.

The implications of these can be serious and long term. For instance, taking drugs can damage the development of young brains as well as causing health and mental health problems. However, children and young people can also make positive choices that impact on development, such as choosing to apply themselves at school.

Education and learning

Children and young people spend a lot of their time in education. Of course, schools are where:

- a vast amount of learning that can impact on development is done

- socialising with large numbers of peers takes place.

Children and young people also learn throughout their lives in a range of other places. For example, at home and at groups they may belong to – everything from church, to Brownies, youth club, ice-skating or street dance. In terms of all sorts of education, the key to learning and development are the quality of the opportunity and how engaged children are. This is why our schools are regulated and inspected.

Children who are living in poverty are less likely to experience learning in the types of groups mentioned above as there is usually a cost. This can limit their opportunities.

Have a go!

Talk to the children or young people at your current workplace about groups that they belong to. You may be surprised by how and what they are learning outside of the setting.

Play, stimulation and interaction

Children's development benefits hugely from good play opportunities. This requires safe places to play indoors and outdoors, and access to a range of stimulating play resources, both at home and at the settings that children and young people attend. Children who aren't taken to early years settings can be at a considerable disadvantage in terms of play and learning experiences.

Continual exposure to interaction with others is also extremely important to development. Children who do not have parents and siblings who consistently talk and play with them throughout each and every day will also be at a disadvantage.

Concerns about development

Although children develop at different rates, significant delays in one area of development or many delays in several areas are a reason for concern. Formally observing and assessing children and young people's development helps practitioners to notice when children are not progressing as expected. (You'll learn how observation and assessment is carried out in Unit MU 2.2.)

Link Up!

MU 2.2 Contribute to the support of child and young person development.

Checks should be made as soon as possible to see if there are underlying causes for the delay/s, such as an impairment. If this is the case, a child may need support from a specialist such as a speech and language therapist, or they may need medical treatment. When concerns arise, practitioners should always act quickly to get support for the child, as this can limit the effect on long-term development.

When practitioners and professionals take action to support a child, it is referred to as 'intervention'. Many interventions are short term. Consider these examples:

■ A child has an operation for glue ear (a common childhood condition where fluid builds up in the middle ear), and this resolves their hearing problem.

■ A child has speech therapy for a short period, then they overcome their speech difficulty.

Interventions such as medical treatment may be short or long term

Unit MU 2.2 Contribute to the support of child and young person development.

Unit TDA 2.15 Support children and young people with disabilities and special educational needs.

For other children or young people, interventions are necessary in the long term. For example:

■ A child with cystic fibrosis (which affects the lungs and digestive system by clogging them with thick sticky mucus, making it hard to breathe and digest food) receives ongoing medical treatment.

■ A child with learning difficulties receives ongoing support.

(You'll learn more about these issues in Unit TDA 2.15.)

LEARNING OUTCOME 3

FOCUS ON

... understanding the potential effects of transitions on the development of children and young people

In this section you'll learn about the transitions experienced by most children and young people, and those that are experienced by some children and young people. You'll also learn about the effects of transitions on children's behaviour and development. This links with **Assessment Criteria 3.1, 3.2, 3.3**.

Transitions

Transitions are times of change that occur in the lives of children and young people. All children and young people will experience a range of transitions of different types as they grow up, and these have the potential to be unsettling times. This makes learning to cope with transitions an important life skill. Broadly speaking, there are four types of transition:

■ **Physical transitions:**
These occur when a child or young person moves from one physical place or setting to another, for example when starting with a new childminder. Transitions that involve moving on to the next phase of education can also be referred to as 'intellectual transitions'.

■ **Physiological transitions**:

These occur when changes happen to the body, for example at puberty.

■ **Emotional transitions**:

These occur when children and young people are deeply affected by a personal experience, for example a family break-up. It's important not to be misled by the title of this category. Children and young people can also be deeply affected emotionally by transitions that fall into the physical or physiological category. For instance, a young person can be expected to be deeply affected emotionally by becoming physically disabled.

■ **Smaller transitions**:

These minor changes happen during the course of a day, for example transitions between lessons in primary school. Younger children are generally affected the most by these smaller everyday changes. They can also prove challenging for some children and young people with learning difficulties. For example, it's not uncommon for children with autism to find changes to their present situation or usual routine emotionally challenging.

Further examples of transitions for each category are given in the table on page 144.

Did you know?

It's important to remember that, despite a few reservations or nerves, some transitions – such as starting secondary school – can be experienced as mainly positive and exciting by some children and young people.

THE LIBRARY
NORTH WEST KENT COLLEGE
DERING WAY, GRAVESEND

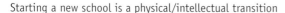

Starting a new school is a physical/intellectual transition

▶▶▶ Link Up! ◀◀◀

Unit TDA 2.2 Safeguard the welfare of children and young people.

Who experiences transitions?

Some transitions are experienced by most children and young people. The transition of leaving primary school and starting secondary school is a good example of this. But other transitions – such as entering care – are only experienced by some children and young people. Table TDA2.1.2 below shows which group is likely to experience the transitions you have learnt about.

Table TDA2.1.2: Transition table

Type of transition	Transitions experienced by most children and young people	Transitions experienced by some children and young people
Physical transitions	<ul><li>Children attending a setting for the first time, for example a nursery, pre-school, crèche, childminder's home, primary school, out-of-school club or secondary school.</li><li>Children moving within a setting, for example from the baby room to the toddler room, or from class to class.</li><li>Young people leaving school and preparing for work/college.</li></ul>	<ul><li>Children have new living arrangements, for example moving house, a stay in hospital, young people preparing to leave home.</li></ul>
Physiological transitions	<ul><li>Puberty.</li></ul>	<ul><li>Long-term medical conditions.</li><li>Experiencing an impairment.</li></ul>
Emotional transitions	<ul><li>Being separated from parents/carers (for example the first time with a babysitter).</li></ul>	<ul><li>Bereavement.</li><li>Entering care.</li><li>Leaving care.</li><li>The breakdown of the family unit.</li><li>New people living within the family home (such as a step-parent).</li><li>Family members leaving the family home (for example a parent or sibling).</li><li>A long-term medical condition affecting a family member.</li><li>An impairment affecting a family member.</li><li>The end of a close relationship, for example a split with a friend, boyfriend or girlfriend.</li><li>Experiencing abuse/bullying.</li></ul>
Smaller transitions	<ul><li>The daily handover of care from a parent to a practitioner within a day-care or educational setting.</li><li>Transitions between lessons in primary school.</li><li>Transitions between lessons, rooms and teachers in secondary schools.</li></ul>	<ul><li>The changeover of staff who work shifts in a residential home.</li></ul>

As you read through the transition in Table TDA2.1.2, consider how many of the transitions can be described as periods of change that involve the loss of a familiar person/familiar people in the life of a child or young person. This loss may be temporary or permanent. For instance, when a child leaves nursery to start school they will be permanently leaving behind their key person and other staff as well as many of their peers. When a child goes into hospital, they will be temporarily separated from family members.

The effects of transitions

As an adult you may be familiar with feeling unsettled and under pressure at a time of transition – perhaps when starting a new job or living somewhere new. Children and young people experience the same feelings, and they may find them hard to cope with. This can affect behaviour and development.

Different children respond differently to transitions. The scale of the transition is certainly a significant factor in how it will be experienced. A child who is bereaved would certainly be expected to experience more emotional difficulty than a child who is moving home, for example. However, individual children's responses will be influenced by their previous experience of change, their age, abilities and their personality. In most cases, the effect of transitions is short term.

Behaviour

All children and young people are different, and there can be huge variation in terms of the effects of transitions on behaviour. For instance, feeling stressed or worried may cause one child or young person to become short tempered and argumentative, while another may become quiet and withdrawn.

The key is to get to know well the individual children and young people who you work with, so that you are familiar with their usual behaviour. Then, by paying special attention during times of transition in their lives, you can spot if their usual behaviour changes. This is important because there are a number of strategies that you can implement to help children through the transitional period if support is needed. You'll learn about these strategies, and about how

Good practice

Practitioners must understand how transitions can affect a child or young person's behaviour and/ or development, as explained below. This understanding enables practitioners to give the children and young people in their care appropriate support should they be affected by the transitions they experience.

Think back to a major transition that occurred in your life when you were a child or young person. How did you feel both before and during this life event? How intense were the emotions that you experienced? How long did they last?

145

Unit MU 2.2 Contribute to the support of child and young person development.

you can prepare children and young people for transitions in their lives in Unit MU 2.2.

Examples of effects of transitions on behaviour include children and young people:

■ seeming generally unhappy or tearful

■ crying

■ being reluctant to do activities that they have previously enjoyed

■ becoming withdrawn

■ becoming emotional or upset more easily

■ being unreasonably snappy, argumentative or defiant

■ having outbursts of anger or tantrums

■ showing signs of ongoing anger

■ becoming clingy with parents or carers

■ having difficulty concentrating

■ refusing to talk about or acknowledge future plans

■ having unsettled sleep patterns

■ having a change in appetite – going off food or overeating for comfort

■ regressing (behaving in ways usually associated with a child younger than their own age, for example sucking their thumb, wanting a parent to feed them or hold their hand when they had previously outgrown this, bedwetting, using babyish language, playing with babyish toys).

Tempers may flare more easily during times of transition

Development

Transitions can also affect the development of children and young people. This usually occurs when the effects of transitions have been experienced over a longer period. For instance, if an older child misses school for a significant period due to the onset of a long-term illness, it may be difficult for them to catch up. This can impact on their intellectual development. Moving schools frequently can also disrupt children's learning and have a similar effect.

Transitions may also cause some children to miss out on the everyday play and life experiences that normally enable certain types of development. For example, if a toddler is confined to a hospital bed for a significant period, their large motor development may be delayed due to a lack of experience in moving around on the floor.

We have discussed the fact that transitions can cause children to feel unhappy and worried. Many experts agree that children who are unhappy and worried cannot concentrate or learn as effectively in the classroom as they might otherwise. They are less likely to feel engaged and more likely to be reluctant to participate in activities and opportunities. So if children feel unhappy or worried for an extended period of time, their intellectual and social development can be affected.

Spending a significant period in hospital can affect development

Losing familiar people

We have also discussed that many transitions involve the loss of a familiar person or people from the child or young person's life. In some cases – such as going into care or the death of a parent – this upheaval can affect social and emotional development. Children may experience difficulties with trust and relationships into their adulthood and perhaps throughout their life. This can put a strain on their relationships with adults (including their parents) and their peers, and they may find it difficult to make or keep friends. Confidence and self-esteem may also be affected, and unwanted behaviour may cause further social and emotional difficulties. Withdrawing from others can also impact on the development of social and communication skills.

It is a sad fact that some children and young people may experience effects on their physical development and health because their response to a transition is to drink alcohol, smoke, take drugs, self harm, become promiscuous (have casual sexual partners) or to eat unhealthily (both under- and overeating). Lack of rest and sleep may also affect health and ultimately growth.

For information on strategies to help children and young people experiencing the effects of transitions, see Unit MU 2.2.

Did you know?

Impairments themselves can also affect development. For instance, if a child becomes a wheelchair user, physical development may be affected in several ways.

Link Up!

Unit MU 2.2 Contribute to the support of child and young person development.

How are things going?

▶ Progress Check

1. What are the following?
   a Gross motor skills.
   b Locomotive skills.
   c Fine motor skills. (1.1)
2. At what approximate age are children expected to do the following?
   a Sit up.
   b Start to walk.
   c Start to run. (1.1)
3. At what approximate age are children expected to do the following?
   a Start to babble.
   b Say single words.
   c Say full sentences. (1.1)
4. What are reflexes? (1.1)
5. Children learn and develop holistically. Explain what this means. (1.2)
6. Give examples of how the following influences can affect children and young people's development:
   a Background.
   b Health.
   c Environment. (2.1)
7. Explain the term 'transitions'. (3.1)
8. Identify three transitions that most children and young people will experience during their lives. (3.2)
9. Identify three transitions that only some children and young people will experience during their lives. (3.2)
10. Give an example of how a transition may affect a child or young person's behaviour. (3.3)
11. Give an example of how a transition may affect a child or young person's development. (3.3)

Are you ready for assessment?

CACHE

Set tasks:

■ You are asked to produce a detailed display including a timeline that describes the expected pattern of development from birth to 19 years, examples of influences that affect development, the importance of recognising and responding to concerns about development. You must also produce a poster that identifies different sorts of transitions and gives examples how they may affect behaviour and development.

You can prepare by reading the unit and making relevant notes.

City & Guilds

You must complete the mandatory Assignment 5. This has three tasks, each one relating to one of the three Learning Outcomes. It entails completing the tables provided about stages of development, influences on development and transitions.

Edexcel

You may like to reflect on a time when you have noticed the effects of one of the influences on development, making notes in your reflective diary (e.g. you may have noticed that a child with physical impairment achieves certain development milestones later than usually expected). You can prepare by reading the unit and making relevant notes.

UNIT 2.2

Contribute to the support of child and young person development

LEARNING OUTCOMES

The learning outcomes you will meet in this unit are:

1 Be able to contribute to assessments of the development needs of children and young people

2 Be able to support the development of children and young people

3 Know how to support children and young people experiencing transitions

4 Be able to support children and young people's positive behaviour

5 Be able to use reflective practice to improve own contribution to child and young person development

INTRODUCTION

Many aspects of a practitioner's role are connected to promoting the development of children and young people. So your learning in this unit is central to your qualification. You may find it helpful to return to this information from time to time as you work through other related units.

LEARNING OUTCOME 1

FOCUS ON

... being able to contribute to assessments of the development needs of children and young people

In this section you'll learn about observing and recording aspects of development using different assessment methods. You'll also learn about supporting assessments of children's development needs and the ways in which these can be met within the work setting. This links with **Assessment Criteria 1.1, 1.2, 1.3, 1.4.**

Did you know?

Using a selection of methods over a period of time helps to build up a differentiated (varied) picture of a child's learning and development.

Observing and recording aspects of development

As you learnt in Unit TDA 2.1, it's important for practitioners to get to know children well and to be aware of their individual development. An important way to achieve this is by regularly observing children and using the information gathered to assess and track their development. This enables practitioners to promote development by supporting and challenging children appropriately on an ongoing basis.

Practitioners need to observe and assess children and young people's development in the following areas:

- Physical.
- Communication.
- Intellectual/cognitive.
- Social, emotional and behavioural.

Observation methods

A range of observation methods are described below. An important part of a practitioner's role is to always select an observation method that suits:

- the type of information that they want to collect
- the purpose for which the information will be used.

Assessment enables us to challenge children appropriately

Diary

Some settings use a diary system to briefly record what children do on a daily basis. Often, the diary is shared with parents and carers, and goes back and forth between home and the setting each day. This is especially useful for the parents of children when the children cannot tell them about their experiences themselves, for example babies, younger children and those with learning or communication difficulties. The diary is generally completed by a child's key person. Parents may also write in the diary to inform practitioners about the child's experiences at home and to comment on the practitioner's diary entries. This makes the diary a useful way to build positive relationships and work in partnership with parents and carers.

You will need:

- a diary

- a pen.

What to do

At the end of a session, make a note of the key things the child did, and of anything else you think is important. For example, for a baby you would record:

- when they slept and for how long

- when they had a nappy changed and whether they were wet or dirty

- when they were fed and how much feed they took

- a note or two on experiences they enjoyed, for example 'clapped hands when we had a sing-song'.

As young children grow up, the diary will begin to focus more on the activities they have taken part in and less on how their care needs were met.

Narrative

The observer focuses on the activity of the child, writing down everything seen during the allotted time. Observations are generally short, lasting for perhaps five minutes or less. They are helpful for

Did you know?

Some practitioners call the diary that is passed between the home and the setting a 'contact book'. Some settings include photos within the diary.

A diary may go back and forth between home and the setting

focusing on areas of difficulty for children, for instance working out exactly what is happening when a child struggles to feed themselves. These observations are often recorded in a notebook and written up afterwards.

You will need:

■ a notepad

■ a pen.

What to do

Write a detailed description of how the child carries out the activity being observed.

Note their actions and behaviour, including their facial expressions. Record what the child says and any non-verbal communication such as gestures. This is intensive work, which is why this type of observation is usually used for just a few minutes. Observations are usually recorded in the present tense.

Did you know?

Some practitioners call the narrative observation method by the name 'free description'.

Practical example

Narrative

Ben is sitting at the painting table next to Jessica. He picks up his paintbrush and looks at her. She looks back. He smiles and holds his brush out to her. Jessica takes it and smiles back. Ben says, 'Thank you'.

Running records

Running records are a variation of narrative records. Practitioners record all that they see as before, but the timing is flexible. For example, you may just record a short 'snapshot' of something interesting that a child is doing, or you may decide to observe them over an extended period – for as long as they are playing creatively perhaps.

Running records can also be used to observe an activity rather than a particular child. For example, you may observe everything that takes place at the water tray for a set amount of time. This type of

Running records can be used to observe an activity

observation is important because it enables practitioners to assess how effective their activities are by focusing closely on how children experience them.

Time sampling

The observer decides on a period of time for the observation, perhaps two hours or the length of a session. The child's activity is recorded on a form at set intervals – perhaps every 10 or 15 minutes. This tracks the child's activity over the period of time. However, significant behaviours may occur between the intervals and these will not be recorded.

You will need:

- a pre-prepared form giving the times for the observations

- a pen

- a watch.

What to do

Keep an eye on the time to ensure you observe at regular intervals. At each allotted time, observe the child and record their activity in the same way as in the 'narrative' method.

Practical example

Time sampling

10.00am
Ben is sitting at the painting table next to Jessica. He picks up his paintbrush and looks at her. She looks back. He smiles and holds his brush out to her. Jessica takes it and smiles back. Ben says, 'Thank you'.

10.15am
Ben gets down from the table. He goes to the nursery nurse. He looks at her and says, 'Wash hands'.

Event recording

This method is used when practitioners have reason to record how often an aspect of a child's behaviour or development occurs. A form is prepared identifying the aspect being tracked. Each time the behaviour or development occurs, a note of the time and circumstance is recorded. Samples may take place over a session, a week or in some circumstances longer. Practitioners may want to observe how frequently a child is physically aggressive for instance, as shown in the example below.

You will need:

■ a pre-prepared form adapted for the objective of the observation

■ a pen.

Practical example

Event recording

Event no.	Time	Event	Circumstances
1	2.30pm	Joshua pushed Daisy over	Joshua had left his teddy on the floor. He watched Daisy pick it up. He went over to Daisy and tried to take the teddy. She did not let go. Joshua pushed her over. Daisy gave Joshua the toy and started to cry. Joshua walked away quickly with the teddy

What to do

Watch a child, and each time the aspect of behaviour or development being observed occurs, record the circumstances along with the time.

Checklist

A form prompts the observer to look for particular skills or reflexes that a child has. The observer ticks them off as they are seen. This method is frequently used for assessing a child's stage of development. It is well suited to the observation of babies, whose physical development will typically progress rapidly. The observations may be done over time, or babies and children may be asked to carry out specific tasks.

A participant observer can encourage children to carry out the necessary tasks

You will need:

- a pre-prepared checklist (these can be purchased or developed by practitioners)

- a pen.

What to do

The checklist tells you what to observe and record. As a **participant observer**, encourage children to carry out the necessary tasks, ticking the relevant boxes to record the child's response – generally whether they could carry out the task competently. As a **non-participant observer**, tick the boxes as you see evidence of children's competence occurring naturally. (You'll learn more about participant/non-participant learners on pages 157 and 158).

key terms

Participant observer an observer who interacts with a child during the observation. They may ask or encourage a child to do things.

Non-participant observer someone who observes unobtrusively, without interacting with children.

Practical example

Checklist

Activity	Yes	No	Date	Observer's comments
Rolls from back to front				
Rolls from front to back				

Did you know?

Some practitioners call the checklist observation method the 'tick list'.

Target child

The observer will record a child's activity over a long period of time, but unlike the time sampling method, the aim is not to have any gaps in the duration of the observation. To achieve this the observer uses a range of codes to record, in shorthand on a pre-prepared form, what is happening.

You will need:

- a pre-prepared form with a key to the abbreviations that will be used

- a pen

- a watch.

What to do

With this type of observation the observer has to make decisions about which things are significant and should be recorded because it is impossible to record every detail over a long period. (It is interesting for two people to observe the same target child over the same period and then compare their forms. They are likely to have recorded different things.) Language and activity are recorded in separate columns for ease. It takes practice to get used to using the codes.

Have a go!

Why not find out more about target child codes and all observation methods by reading the following book:

Christine Hobart and Jill Frankel, *A Practical Guide to Observation and Assessment* (Cheltenham, Nelson Thornes Ltd, 1999).

Practical example

Target child

Time	Activity	Language	Social grouping	Involvement level
11.30	TC goes to the box of blocks. Uses both hands to tip the box up and get the blocks out	_TC_ 'Out'	SOL	1
11.31	TC sits down. Using right hand he places one block on top of another. He repeats this, building a tower of four blocks		SOL	1

Key:
TC = target child
_TC_ = target child talking to self
SOL = solitary grouping

1 = target child absorbed in their activity

Additional codes will be used, and codes vary within settings.

Anecdotal records

Anecdotal records are made when a practitioner is told by someone else about something important or interesting the child has done, rather than observing it for themselves. For example, a child's parent or another practitioner may tell you that they have seen a child crawl for the first time, or that they have said their first sentence. This anecdotal information can be added in note form to a child's development records. The date and the name of the person who observed the occurrence should also be recorded.

Observation with or without adults

When children play on their own or just with their peers, they may behave quite differently to when there is an adult joining in with them. So observers need to decide whether they want to observe a child with or without direct interaction from other adults. Ideally, children will be observed both with and without adults over a period of time.

During observations, the behaviour of children can change. If they are aware that they are being watched, some children may feel anxious or excited, or they may try harder than usual. To counteract this, the practitioner may decide to be a non-participant observer.

Non-participant observer

This means that the practitioner will be unobtrusive. They will settle themselves somewhere suitable to watch the child without alerting them to the fact that they are being observed. The practitioner will not interact with the children during this time. They will not speak and so there will be no need to make a record of their own actions or words during the observation.

It's easier to be objective and to record what is happening when you are not involved in events. However, it can be hard to find somewhere unobtrusive that still allows you to see and hear everything that occurs. Although you can use any method of observation as a non-participant observer, if you are looking to observe certain aspects of development or behaviour, you may not see them if you do not encourage children to carry out particular activities or tasks. However, this technique is well suited to the 'narrative' and 'target child' methods of observation, which are explained on pages 151–2 and 156.

A non-participant observer

Being a participant observer

Alternatively, the practitioner can be a participant observer. The participant observer can directly ask or encourage children to do things. This technique works well with the 'checklist method' of observation described on page 155, which is often used with babies and young children. Participant observers can ask questions to find out the reason for a child's behaviour, for example: 'Why are you doing that?'

Support assessment of children's development needs

Once information has been collected via observation, practitioners need to think about the picture that this builds of an individual child. Reviewing and assessing the information enables practitioners to draw conclusions about the child's development and to identify a child's individual development needs.

We'll look at each factor in turn.

Good practice

All settings have their own systems and procedures in place for assessment, and you will need to follow these as you play a part in supporting the assessment process. However, the main factors to consider are shown on the diagram below.

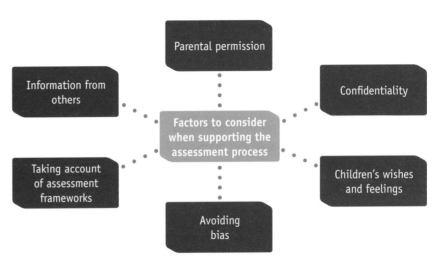

Factors to consider when supporting the assessment process

Parental permission

Parents and carers have the right to decide what personal information is collected and recorded about their child. It is essential that practitioners obtain written permission from parents authorising them to:

- carry out observations and assessment

- keep relevant documentation on record.

Good practice

It's essential that students also gain permission from workplace supervisors before carrying out observations. Supervisors will probably ask to see your completed observation and the child's family may also want to have a copy. You must also protect the child's identity. This may be done by changing the name, or using another way of identifying them, for example 'target child' or 'child A' or 'child 1'.

Confidentiality

You learnt about confidentiality in Unit SHC 21. The details of observation should be kept confidential unless withholding information would affect the well-being of the child. So it's important that you handle and store assessment documents and notes in line with the setting's confidentiality policy.

Children's wishes and feelings

Practitioners should respect children's wishes and feelings throughout the assessment process. They should not be made to feel under pressure to 'perform' or get things right. If they become reluctant or upset, it's often best to delay an observation to another time.

Good practice

Practitioners should also be respectful in terms of the tone and language used when recording observations or writing up assessment records. It can help to think about how the parent is likely to feel when they read it. However, this is not intended to prevent you from making accurate assessments.

Did you know?

Many settings ask for parental permission on the registration form that parents complete prior to their child attending the setting. This must be signed and dated.

Link Up!

Unit SHC 21 Introduction to communication in children and young people's settings.

Avoiding bias

Assessments should be accurate and fair, otherwise there's little point in doing them. So when practitioners carry out observations, they aim to be objective. In other words, they aim to record exactly what is happening at the time of the assessment. This means putting everything else they know about a child aside for a period of time, and focusing on what the child actually says and does now. Otherwise the observation is not valid and reliable.

Ask Miranda!

Q But what if a child is close to doing something but doesn't quite manage it ... can't I write it in?

A Practitioners may sometimes be tempted to record that a child can do something, perhaps because the child can nearly do it, and the practitioner wants them to have a favourable outcome. Or, perhaps the practitioner thinks they might have seen the child do something before, and so they want to give them the benefit of the doubt. However, once again the practitioner must only record what they see. It's important to remember that we use the assessments to plan what children should learn next and how they should be supported, so we will not be helping them by recording anything that is less than truthful and accurate.

Taking account of assessment frameworks

Many settings follow curriculum frameworks, such as the Early Years Foundation Stage which is followed by early years settings in England. These frameworks will include guidance on how children should be assessed. Settings must interpret this, and ensure that their own assessment procedures meet the guidance. There will be a requirement to assess each child's progress in terms of the curriculum. For instance, a nursery in England will consider which of the 'early learning goals' expressed in the Early Years Foundation Stage have been met. Meanwhile, the school nearby will be assessing children's progress in terms of the National Curriculum followed by all schools in England.

You'll learn more about curriculum frameworks in Unit MU 2.8.

Link Up!

Unit MU 2.8 Contribute to the support of positive enviornments for children and young people.

Information from others

It's good practice to collect information from a range of sources during the assessment process. This is because children behave differently and have different experiences when they are with various people and in various situations. For instance:

An only child who generally plays quietly and steadily at home and concentrates for long periods may love to rush around the setting, interacting with peers and trying lots of things.

As well as attending the setting, a child may regularly go swimming or attend dance classes.

A young person may tell you something interesting – what they learnt from a book for instance, or how they felt when they saw a film or a play.

A child may be working with a speech and language therapist who is building up a picture of their communication development.

Children have different experiences when they are with their families

Information may be collected from:

parents and carers

children and young people

colleagues

other professionals.

Ways that identified development needs can be met

Once children's development needs have been identified, practitioners must plan how the needs will be met through a programme of:

activities

experiences

support.

There are some important factors to consider, as described on pages 162–3.

Reflecting children's interests and views

The activities and experiences planned to promote a child's development should appeal to them. We can reflect individual children's interests by:

- planning activities they enjoy, for example painting, playground games, dance

- choosing topics or themes they are interested in, for example dinosaurs, farmyard animals, trains

- providing resources they enjoy for free play, for example musical instruments, sand, recycled objects.

We can reflect children's views by:

- asking them what they'd like to do

- asking them how they'd like to do something

- giving them choices as often as possible.

Play for children in the early years

Play and learning are intrinsically linked, and for young children play is the primary way of learning. This is wonderful because children love to play. When we provide high-quality, fun play experiences children learn naturally *and* have a great time. This helps to establish a love of learning and discovering new things, which stands children in very good stead when they move on to more formal learning in the school classroom.

Providing challenge

Activities and experiences must provide children with sufficient challenge. If this is not the case, then children will:

- not have much fun

- not become properly engaged

- soon lose interest and become bored

- learn little

- benefit little in terms of their development.

Did you know?

The foundations for all future learning are established through play in a child's early years. We must make those foundations as strong as possible.

Link Up!

Unit TDA 2.16 Support children and young people's play and leisure.

Good practice

It's important to strike the right balance, because if activities and experiences are too challenging, children are likely to become frustrated, and once again the bullet points at the bottom of page 162 will apply. The key is a good understanding of what children can currently do and what they are likely to do next. Ideally, practitioners will provide a blend of activities and experiences that both consolidate children's existing learning and promote the next step in their development. Or in other words, a blend of activities that children have already mastered on some level and activities that promote the skills they are likely to acquire next.

Flexible plans

Plans are important, but they should also be flexible, working documents that can be changed in response to what is happening. For instance, it may be necessary to change plans if:

- an activity or experience doesn't go well and you want to cut it short

- an activity or experience goes so well that you want to extend it

- children are so engaged in their current activity that you want to dedicate more time to that instead

- the weather is unsuitable (for example you've planned a bike ride but it's icy outside)

- something unexpected happens and you want to make the most of it (for example it has snowed and you want the children to explore the snowy garden)

- a colleague is off sick and there's no longer enough staff to supervise an activity that requires extra adult support (for example woodwork, a trip off the premises)

- a piece of vital equipment or some materials are faulty or missing

- it transpires that the activity will not meet the needs of all the children attending (see page 164).

You may want to change your plans if something unexpected happens

Good practice

It's quite common for settings to take last-minute bookings when a parent needs their child to attend for an extra session. Flexibility is important here, as it may be necessary for plans to be changed with little warning if they do not meet a child's needs. In particular, flexibility is crucial for drop-in settings, because it's not known who will come.

Meeting individual needs

Activities, experiences and the adult support given to children must meet their individual needs. Children's individual needs will fall into the categories shown in the diagram below.

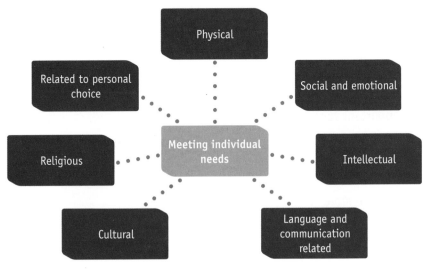

Meeting individual needs

You'll learn more about this in Unit MU 2.8.

▶▶ Link Up! ◀◀

Unit MU 2.8 Contribute to the support of positive environments for children and young people.

Unit SHC 23 Introduction to equality and inclusion in children and young people's settings.

Unit TDA 2.15 Support children and young people with disabilities and special educational needs.

FOCUS ON

... being able to support the development of children and young people

In this section you'll learn about carrying out activities with a child or young person to support their holistic development. You'll also learn about recording observations of children's participation in the activities. Lastly, you'll learn about contributing to the evaluation of the activities meeting the child or young person's identified development needs. This links with **Assessment Criteria 2.1, 2.2, 2.3**.

Activities to support holistic development

In Unit TDA 2.1 you learnt that children learn and develop holistically. It's important for practitioners to support this by providing activities that promote more than one area of a child's development. You may like to revisit the diagram in TDA 2.1 (page 132), which shows how one activity can promote several aspects of development. You'll also find information on providing a range of activities in Unit MU 2.8.

Recording observation of participation in the activities

In Learning outcome 1 you learnt how child observation enables practitioners to assess a child's development. But it also has another important benefit. You can use observations of children taking part in activities that you have provided to collect feedback about that activity.

When planning the observation, you should:

■ think carefully about the purpose of the observation (or in other words, what you want to find out)

■ select an observation method that suits the purpose.

Link Up!

Unit TDA 2.1 Child and young person development.

Unit MU 2.8 Contribute to the support of positive environments for children and young people.

Did you know?

Settings are busy places with lots of activities happening at the same time, especially during free play session. But it's important to take the time to focus on the quality of individual activities from time to time.

For instance:

- If you want to see how well the activity meets a particular child's development needs, you may select the narrative observation method (see pages 151–2), and record everything the child does while engaged in the activity. You will not observe the other children.

- If you want to see how effective the activity is generally, you may do a running record observation on the activity itself for a set amount of time (see pages 152–3), recording how all children participate in the activity within the time frame selected.

Practical example

Marissa observes an activity

Marissa is a supervisor at a pre-school. Recently, she's been thinking about how presenting familiar activities in new ways seems to motivate children to participate more than usual. She wants to see if she can measure this in some way. Marissa decides to observe the water tray for 15 minutes at the start of a free play session. The water tray is set up as usual, with a waterwheel and various pots and small buckets for children to play with. Marissa records:

1. how many children come to play at the water tray
2. how engaged they are
3. how long they play.

The next day, Marissa presents the water tray in a new way. She pours some washing-up liquid into the water. She then adds the crockery and cutlery from the home corner, along with two dish mops and two dish cloths. Again, Marissa records how many children come to play at the water tray, how they play, and how engaged they are. She finds that the water tray is much more popular today – so many children want to have a go at 'washing the dishes' that a member of staff comes to organise whose turn it is next. Children also play for longer and seem more engaged.

At the next pre-school meeting, Marissa shares her observation findings with her team. She encourages the team to come up with ways to vary more of the setting's familiar activities, to promote levels of participation and engagement.

In a busy setting, lots of activities take place at the same time

Contributing to evaluation of the activities

Evaluations of activities can be informed by written observations, as described on page 166. But even when you aren't formally evaluating, you should get into the habit of paying attention to how effective the activities offered within the setting are – both the ones you have personally provided and those planned by colleagues. This is important because:

- any information you pick up about what works well and what doesn't will help you to make your own activities better

- you will learn a great deal from the activity plans of experienced practitioners

- you will gain creative inspiration for your own activities

- you will be able to contribute to evaluations of a range of activities, not just those activities you have planned yourself.

When reviewing information about how children participated in an activity, it helps to consider:

- how engaged children were

- whether children were having fun

- what skills children were using or learning

> **Did you know?**
>
> Many settings discuss in staff meetings how activities are going, and they welcome feedback from everyone.

- what new discoveries children were making

- what existing learning the children were consolidating (reinforcing)

- which areas of development were being promoted

- whether the activity was pitched appropriately – was it challenging, but not overly so?

- whether the level of adult support available was appropriate (for example some activities may be supervised directly by a participating adult, others may have low-level supervision with no adult directly present)

- what the children's level of concentration was (for example high, medium, low)

- how long children spent at the activity

- what questions children were asking

- what viewpoints or opinions children were expressing

- how many children participated

- whether the activity reflected children's interests

- whether the activity looked appealing

- whether children played alone or socially.

When these questions have been considered, there's another big question to ask:

- Did the activity effectively meet its planned objectives, and what is the reason for this?

Finally, it's time to make that information useful in practice, by considering the following:

- Should the activity be repeated?

- If so, are there ways in which it can be improved?

- Should an extension activity be planned?

Or:

- Is it best not to repeat the activity?

- If so, what other activity could be planned to fulfil successfully the original planned objectives?

Sometimes it's best not to repeat an activity

LEARNING OUTCOME 3

FOCUS ON

... knowing how to support children and young people experiencing transitions

In this section you'll learn about the different transitions that children may experience. You'll also learn how to give adult support through each of these transitions. This links with **Assessment Criteria 3.1, 3.2**.

Types of transition

In Unit TDA 2.1 you learnt about transitions of the following types:

- Physical transitions.
- Physiological transitions.
- Emotional transitions.
- Smaller transitions.

You also learnt about the effects of transitions on behaviour and development. It's a good idea to recap this information as part of your study of this unit.

Link Up!

Unit TDA 2.1 Child and young person development.

Supporting children and young people through transitions

As you learnt in Unit TDA 2.1, periods of transition can be challenging for children and young people. So it's important for you to learn about strategies for supporting them through transitional periods.

The effect of positive relationships during periods of transition

Because children and young people can be expected to feel the effects of stress and anxiety during transitional periods, the care and support of those closest to them is always very important. These relationships are especially needed when the transition in question will mean the loss of one or more other familiar people in the child's life.

The transition to school will mean leaving early years practitioners behind

Existing relationships

Close, positive existing relationships will support children and young people by:

- providing them with security – some things might be changing, but they'll always have some key, stable relationships to rely on and to return to emotionally

- giving them someone to talk to and express their feelings with

- bolstering their confidence in advance of the transition, especially if strategies to help prepare the child or young person are carried out together, for example a visit to a new setting

- providing them with moral support at the actual time of transition, for example taking them to school on the first day, staying overnight at the hospital with them.

New relationships

Forming new positive relationships connected with the transition (for example making new friends, getting to know their new key person or teacher) will also be hugely beneficial, because:

- fear of 'not knowing anyone' and being isolated or lonely is often a big concern for children and young people

- it's reassuring to feel they have people they can turn to for help and support in the new situation

- once they have a friend, some transitions can start to feel fun, or like an adventure.

Preparing children and young people for transitions

Some transitions are entirely unexpected. A child suddenly becoming ill and going into hospital is a good example of this. Other transitions – such as starting school – are known about in advance. Whenever a transition is known about, we have the opportunity to devise strategies to help prepare the child or young person for what lies ahead. This can help them to feel less apprehensive and better able to cope.

The following strategies can be used to prepare children for a variety of transitions.

Did you know?

Adults need to think carefully about when to tell children and young people about future transitions. If this is done too early, children may be distressed for a needlessly long period. If it is done too late, children may not feel prepared, which can lead to feelings of panic and being unable to cope. Knowledge of the individual child and the nature of the transition need to be considered in each case.

Communicating with children about the transition

This means talking about what will happen, but also listening to children's concerns. It is important for practitioners to be honest and open as well as reassuring.

Arranging visits to a new setting prior to the transition

Depending on the child's age this may be in the company of parents or carers or with a current practitioner. For example, young children will generally visit an early years setting with their family. Children in their last year of primary school will often spend a day at secondary school escorted by their current teachers. If children are moving, visits to the new home and surrounding area are helpful. Adults from new settings may also visit the current setting, for example a reception teacher may visit their local pre-schools and nurseries in the term before children start school.

Young children will generally visit an early years setting with a family member

Arranging visits from others

Sometimes, practitioners from settings will also visit a child at home, for example many reception teachers carry out home visits.

In can also be helpful for other adults entering the lives of children and young people to spend time with them before the actual transition. For example, it's good practice for a new babysitter or nanny to visit and get to know a child before they begin working with the family. It's also advisable for anyone who will be moving into the home – such as a parent's partner – to become a regular visitor first.

Resources that deal with the subject

Practitioners can help to minimise children and young people's fear of the unknown by helping them to become more familiar with the process of change ahead of them. This can be done by exploring materials that deal with the subject of the future transition. For example, the practitioner and child/young person may explore books (stories and non-fiction), leaflets/brochures, DVDs or CD-ROMs together. There are many excellent resources that deal with subjects such as starting school, puberty, going into hospital, etc.

Opportunities for children to express their feelings

Allow plenty of opportunities for children to express their feelings through conversations, imaginative and expressive play/arts. These

Good practice

When younger children first start at a setting, it's usual for them to stay for just a short period. This helps them to get used to the environment and the people gradually, with minimum distress. Over a series of visits, the amount of time spent is increased, until the child is staying for a whole session. At the first visit (possibly the first couple of visits) a parent or carer will usually stay with the child to help them settle in.

opportunities should continue during and after the transition, as children and young people may be dealing with the emotions connected to it for some time afterwards.

Opportunities for increasing independence equip young people to handle change

Did you know?

It can be helpful to teach children strategies to deal with their biggest concerns. For instance, if a child is worried about getting lost at secondary school you can talk to the child about what they should do if they actually become lost.

Promoting independence

This means giving children and young people opportunities to experience increasing independence in line with their needs and abilities, as this better equips them to handle change and the transitions that relate to maturing. It also bolsters self-esteem and confidence. For instance, a young person due to leave home may start to do their own laundry or cook for themselves regularly. A young child due to start pre-school may be encouraged to do more personal-care tasks for themselves, such as those involved in toileting and washing their hands.

Specialist support for emotional transitions

When children or young people have experienced an intensely emotional transition such as a bereavement, they're likely to benefit from support given by a specially trained counsellor. The counsellor may devise a structured programme of activities to help the child explore and cope with the situation. This may include attending a support group with peers who are experiencing similar trauma in their own lives.

Table MU2.2.1 shows which strategies are generally used to support children and young people experiencing transitions of different types.

Table MU2.2.1: Transition strategy table

Type of transition	Transitions experienced by most children and young people	Transitions experienced by some children and young people	Suggested strategies to support children and young people
Physical transitions	■ Children attending a setting for the first time, for example a nursery, pre-school, crèche, childminder's home, primary school, out-of-school club or secondary school. ■ Children moving within a setting, for example from the baby room to the toddler room, or from class to class. ■ Young people leaving school and preparing for work/college.	■ Children have new living arrangements, for example moving house, a stay in hospital, young people preparing to leave home.	■ Communicating about the transitions. ■ Exploring resources together that deal with the subject. ■ Arranging visits to the new setting/room or home. ■ Opportunities for children to express their feelings. ■ Promoting independence.
Physiological transitions	■ Puberty.	■ Long-term medical conditions. ■ Experiencing an impairment.	■ Communicating about the transitions. ■ Exploring resources that deal with the subject together. ■ Opportunities for children to express their feelings. ■ Promoting independence (when children are unwell or become disabled, it's particularly important to empower them to have as much independence as possible, as overall, independence in some areas of their life may be affected in the short or long term).
Emotional transitions	■ Being separated from parents/carers (for example the first time with a babysitter).	■ Bereavement. ■ Entering care. ■ Leaving care. ■ The breakdown of the family unit. ■ New people living within the family home (such as a step parent). ■ Family members leaving the family home (for example a parent or sibling). ■ A long-term medical condition affecting a family member. ■ An impairment affecting a family member. ■ The end of a close relationship, for example a split with a friend, boyfriend or girlfriend. ■ Experiencing abuse/bullying.	■ Communicating about the transitions. ■ Exploring resources together that deal with the subject. ■ Arranging visits from others. ■ Opportunities for children to express their feelings. ■ Promoting independence. ■ Specialist support for emotional transitions.

Type of transition	Transitions experienced by most children and young people	Transitions experienced by some children and young people	Suggested strategies to support children and young people
Smaller transitions	■ The daily handover of care from a parent to a practitioner within a day-care or educational setting. ■ Transitions between lessons in primary school. ■ Transitions between lessons, rooms and teachers in secondary schools.	■ The changeover of staff who work shifts in a residential home.	■ When smaller transitions (which tend to affect younger children) will occur throughout the day, be ready to offer physical and emotional support where needed – for example you may take a child's hand and verbally reassure them. ■ It can help to remind children ahead of time that a transition will be happening, for example: '10 more minutes, and Carol will be here. Then it will soon be time for me to go home, and I'll see you again next time.'

Have a go!

You've learnt that when children are due to experience a transition, it can be really helpful for you to explore together books, leaflets/brochures, stories, DVDs or CD-ROMs that deal with the subject of their future transition.

Pick a transition most children or young people will experience, such as starting school or entering puberty. Now pay a visit to your local library and find out what resources they have to support children through your chosen transition. There is likely to be a range of books, leaflets/brochures, and perhaps DVDs or CD-ROMs. Have a good look at the resources that you find, and think about how you would use them in practice. You may like to write some notes in your reflective journal.

When a new child or young person starts at your setting

For many of us our first experience of supporting someone at a time of transition occurs when a new child or young person starts at our setting, as this is something that happens quite regularly.

The guidelines shown in the following diagram can help practitioners to support the child on the day.

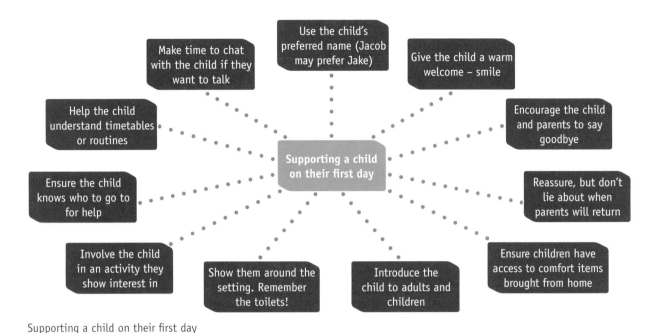

Make time to chat with the child if they want to talk

Use the child's preferred name (Jacob may prefer Jake)

Give the child a warm welcome – smile

Help the child understand timetables or routines

Encourage the child and parents to say goodbye

Supporting a child on their first day

Ensure the child knows who to go to for help

Reassure, but don't lie about when parents will return

Involve the child in an activity they show interest in

Show them around the setting. Remember the toilets!

Introduce the child to adults and children

Ensure children have access to comfort items brought from home

Supporting a child on their first day

LEARNING OUTCOME 4

FOCUS ON

... being able to support children and young people's positive behaviour

In this section you'll learn about how work settings can encourage positive behaviour. You'll also learn how children and young people are encouraged to engage in positive behaviour. Lastly, you'll reflect on your own role in promoting positive behaviour. This links with **Assessment Criteria 4.1, 4.2, 4.3**.

What is positive behaviour?

Positive behaviour is the type of socially accepted behaviour that you would like children and young people to repeat. Examples are shown in the diagram on page 176.

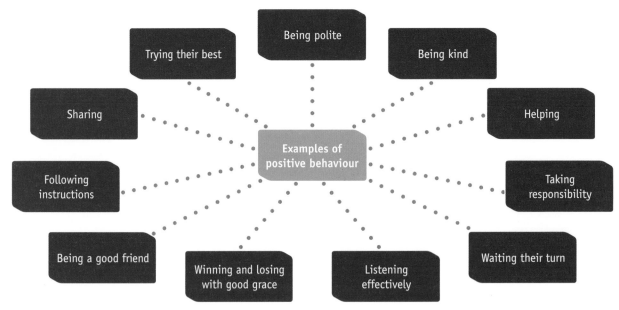

Examples of positive behaviour

See how many other examples of positive behaviour you can think of.

Unit TDA 2.9 Support children and young people's positive behaviour.

How work settings encourage positive behaviour

It takes children and young people time to:

- learn how to behave in the many different situations they encounter

- develop self-control.

As a practitioner, it's your role to work in partnership with your colleagues to support and promote children's positive behaviour. A range of techniques used by settings to promote positive behaviour are outlined on the following pages. This information links closely to Unit TDA 2.9. You're advised to read Unit TDA 2.9 as part of your study of this unit.

Developing positive relationships

Children want to receive attention from those who look after them. When a good relationship exists between children and adults, children will receive lots of pleasant attention when they are behaving positively. This encourages them to repeat the positive behaviour. If a child with good adult relationships receives negative feedback to an aspect of their behaviour, they are generally keen to alter their behaviour and go back to receiving positive attention. Children who experience good relationships are also more likely to turn to adults for support at times when they are upset, frustrated or overwhelmed, instead of behaving inappropriately, or 'acting up'.

However, if good relationships with adults are lacking in a child's life, they may receive very little attention when they are behaving positively. It may only be their inappropriate behaviour that gets a reaction. Children in this position often learn that negative attention is better than no attention at all, and they may well begin to behave inappropriately in order to be noticed. This behaviour can soon become ingrained.

In a good relationship, children will receive lots of pleasant attention

Listening to children and valuing their opinions

Listening to children and valuing their opinions demonstrates that you respect the children in your care, and it contributes to building positive relationships. Asking children what they want to do and finding out how they feel about things also helps to avoid frustration building. This is important because inappropriate behaviour is often fuelled by frustration and anger.

If a child has been in trouble and/or they are upset, frustrated or angry, it helps to talk to them about their feelings and opinions.

There are several benefits to this:

- It gives them a positive outlet for their emotions and opinions.

- It's a starting point for a conversation about how to resolve things positively.

- It helps you to understand more about the reasons for their behaviour.

- It helps you to identify ways to meet the child's needs more effectively.

Providing a stimulating and challenging environment

Providing a positive environment in which children can thrive is an important part of the practitioner's role. You will no doubt have felt the wonderful, happy atmosphere that exists in a setting when children are engaged by stimulating activities within a challenging environment. When children attend high-quality settings that provide these things for them, behaviour is generally more positive overall.

This is because children are more likely to behave inappropriately when they're bored, and if they aren't provided with an environment that holds their interest, boredom is likely to set in. But it's also important to remember that children's behaviour can also be affected if they become over-excited in a hyped-up environment.

The key to a stimulating, challenging environment is to provide balance. There should be good range of activities to promote all areas of development, and a routine that provides times for being active and times for more restful pursuits. A wide variety of resources will support this and help to keep children and young people's attention. Well-planned experiences are also essential. See below for further information.

Well-planned experiences

As you've learnt, boredom and insufficient challenge can lead to inappropriate behaviour. When planning play and learning experiences, you should ensure that the activities offered meet children's needs. To do this it's important to consider children's:

■ age and stage of development

■ interests

■ individual needs.

Activities should promote learning and development in line with any curriculums followed by the setting. But to engage children the activities should also be fun and playful.

Giving children choices

Giving children choices is a great way to encourage positive behaviour. Children are more likely to be in a positive frame of mind when they are able to have a say in what they do and how they do it. This promotes positive behaviour and decision-making skills. It also encourages responsibility.

Choices can be big or small. For example, a child may have a choice of drinking their juice from a small carton with a straw or pouring it into a beaker. They may decide whether to play inside or outside. Or they may decide whether to go to the park or the playground. Providing choices can be particularly helpful in breaking a cycle of inappropriate behaviour, as the Practical example on page 181 shows.

the Practical example on page 181 shows.

Choices can be big or small

Meeting individual needs

There's been much debate over the years about the best way to promote positive behaviour and to manage inappropriate behaviour.

Good practice

If you find planning activities a chore, check you have remembered to make them playful. Think about how much fun the children and young people will have taking part. This should fire up your own enthusiasm!

Your setting's SENCO can advise you on how you can promote positive behaviour in ways that meet the individual needs of the children and young people who you work with.

This is likely to always be the case. But in recent years, there's been something of a shift in focus. This began when debate turned to the fact that children's behaviour is linked directly to their needs.

In the past, the focus was on children who presented challenging behaviour, who were seen as the 'problem'. The action taken to manage them by an adult was seen as the 'solution'. However, the spotlight has now turned to the adult, and if children's behaviour is challenging, we're encouraged to think about whether we are responding to the child's individual needs in the most effective way.

Adult role modelling

It's important that adults model positive behaviour, as children naturally learn some of their own behaviour from what they see happening around them. Treating people with respect, being polite, not raising voices in anger, showing patience, being kind and considerate – these are the types of behaviour children should see from their role models. If adults behave in this way, it sets the tone for a positive culture within the group.

Clear boundaries

Boundaries set appropriate limits for children's behaviour and help children to learn how to behave in safe and acceptable ways. In other words, children are not permitted to behave in certain ways because to do so would be unsafe or socially unacceptable. For instance:

- Children are not allowed climb up on tables to play because it would be unsafe.

- They are not allowed to tease one other because this is socially unacceptable.

What children know and understand about boundaries will depend on their age, abilities and experience. Younger children may be just starting to learn about boundaries through repetition. They will need to be reminded of boundaries frequently. Children of school age are likely to have a good understanding of them.

Many out-of-school clubs involve the children in establishing a simple set of ground rules that are agreed by everyone. This helps children to accept the boundaries and appreciate their purpose. Young people may be involved in agreeing behaviour contracts in settings such as youth groups. Boundaries are most effective when they're set with children and young people as opposed to without them.

It is up to practitioners to help children understand boundaries whilst communicating to them that the boundaries are firm. This is known as defining boundaries. It is done through a consistent approach. When children are about to overstep a boundary, practitioners can take the opportunity to remind them of the boundary and why it exists, as shown in the Practical example below. Children learn from this, and often it is enough to stop them in their tracks and deter them from inappropriate behaviour.

Many out-of-school clubs involve children in establishing rules

Practical example

Defining boundaries

Pre-school practitioner Ashley is playing a simple board game with a small group of three- and four-year-olds. Four-year-old Chloe is impatient for her turn. When she puts out her hand to take the dice before it is her go, Ashley says, 'Remember that we all need to wait our turn. That way the game is fair, and everyone has fun'. Chloe changes her mind about taking the dice, and puts her hands in her lap.

Inclusive practice

Treating all children fairly and meeting each child's individual needs should always be a priority. Getting to know individual children well will help you to have realistic expectations for their behaviour. Some children may need to be reminded of the boundaries more often than others. This should always be done with patience. It's also important for you to consider the reasons for an individual child's behaviour. (You'll learn more about this on pages 183–5.) For example, behaviour expectations for a nine-year-old child with a learning difficulty may be consistent with those usually associated with a younger child.

Knowing individual children well will also help you to pinpoint when a child may need support with their behaviour to help them participate fully within the setting. A pre-school child with autism may need support to take turns during a game for instance.

Good practice

Remember that if a child's behaviour is consistently challenging, you should reflect on the way you are meeting their needs, as this may not be effective. Some children may have an individual behaviour plan for you to follow – you'll learn more about this on page 186.

Can you think of any other ways in which you could give positive attention to a child to reinforce their positive behaviour?

Positive behaviour reinforced

Practitioners can promote positive behaviour by rewarding children with positive attention when they behave in acceptable ways. Positive attention includes verbal praise such as, 'Well done', 'What a lovely thank you', or 'Great job!' It also includes smiling, eye contact, a nod, clapping, a pat on the back, a high five, a hug, etc.

Children enjoy being rewarded, so they are encouraged to behave in the same way again. When children repeat behaviours, over time they become an ingrained, natural part of what the child does. The more a child is given positive attention for behaving appropriately, the less inappropriate behaviour they are likely to display. There's further information about rewards in Unit TDA 2.9. You're advised to read Unit TDA 2.9 as part of your study of this unit.

Unit TDA 2.9 Support children and young people's positive behaviour.

Did you know?

Research has found that when it comes to reducing inappropriate behaviour and increasing appropriate behaviour, rewards are much more effective than punishments in terms of a long-term behaviour change.

Encouraging children to resolve conflict

All children will have problems with other children at some time. Learning to get along and cooperate with other people is an important life skill for everyone. Practitioners can help children to learn how to handle disagreements and disputes positively. The extent to which children are able to do this will depend on their age, needs and abilities. When working with younger children, practitioners can ask questions to prompt them to identify their problems and to come up with their own solutions. This is important as there will not always be adults on hand to step in as children grow and become more independent.

When working with older children, practitioners need to resist the temptation to intervene in children's problems right away. They should give the children the opportunity to resolve things for themselves as long their behaviour is not dangerous or so inappropriate that it should be stopped immediately (in the case of bullying for example).

Practical example

Encouraging children to solve conflict

Four-year-olds Caleb and Gracie are playing in the imaginary corner. Caleb is wearing the police hat from the dressing-up box. Gracie also wants to wear it, and she's trying to take it from Caleb's head. Caleb is protesting loudly and hanging on to it.

This is a familiar scene in any setting. By the time they are four, most children will have had plenty of experience of an adult settling this type of dispute for them. These children are likely to know how this is done.

Practitioner Lindsey intervenes. She asks the children what's wrong. Both say they want to wear the hat. Lindsey says, 'I see, there's only one police hat, and Caleb's wearing it at the moment. So what can we do?' Caleb suggests that Gracie has it next. Lindsey says, 'That sounds like a good idea. What do you think Gracie?' Gracie agrees. Lindsey says, 'So what can Gracie do while she's waiting?' Gracie suggests that she could wear a different hat. Caleb goes to the dressing-up box to help her find one.

Looking for reasons to explain inappropriate behaviour

Challenging behaviour is often a response to a child's immediate feelings and emotions or an event in their life. Finding the reason helps practitioners to approach the behaviour in the best way. Sometimes causes are easy to spot and short lived. Examples include:

■ When a child is tired or unwell, they may feel fractious and irritable. They may fall out with their friends easily as a result.

■ If children are bored, or if they feel they are not being supervised, they may behave inappropriately.

■ Jealousy may prompt a child to take a friend's toy away, or to hurt them.

■ Frustration/anger at not being able to have what they want may cause a child to have a tantrum, for example in the supermarket.

- Frustration/anger at not being able to achieve something may prompt a child to behave inappropriately. A child who is 'out' during a game may protest verbally, get cross and cry.

- Anxiety/stress at being in unfamiliar circumstances, such as the first day at a new school. A child may become frustrated and cling to their parent in an attempt to be taken home again.

- Tiredness when due for a nap, after an unsettled night or at the end of a busy day, may lead to challenging behaviour.

- A heightened sense of excitement. A lively activity or special event may make normal behaviour hard for a child to maintain.

- Changes in routine (different timings or layout of environment, for instance). A child may find it difficult to settle down, for example running around instead of sitting down for story time.

- Lack of opportunity for physical play and exercise, leading to pent up energy. A child may find it hard to sit still and focus, for example getting up from the table repeatedly at lunchtime, or fidgeting through circle time.

Boredom can lead to inappropriate behaviour

More serious factors may lead to prolonged periods of challenging behaviour. Such factors include:

- Bereavement.

- The child becoming disabled or seriously/chronically ill.

- A close family member becoming disabled or seriously/chronically ill.

- Parents' relationship breaking down.

- Parents becoming separated or divorced.

- Parent/s beginning new serious relationships.

- Becoming part of a stepfamily.

- Changes at home (living circumstances within the home or moving home).

- Having new carers.

Sometimes reasons for inappropriate behaviour are hidden, unconscious or in the past. This is complicated further by the fact that different children may respond to the same events or the same feelings by behaving in very different ways. For instance, one child who has been abused may become very quiet and withdrawn as a result, whilst another may become aggressive or violent. In these cases, challenging behaviour may be presented over a longer period of time, and professionals such as counsellors or psychologists may also work with the child.

Have a go!

Imagine you work in an after-school club. Eight-year-old Ali begins to display some challenging behaviour when he is 'out' of a game of musical statues. First of all he argues that he was not out and refuses to leave the dance floor area. When another child becomes frustrated with this behaviour and tells Ali he's 'being a baby', Ali shouts, 'It's not fair! I hate you!' He then runs to the edge of the room and starts to cry.

How would you respond to the situation?

Link Up!

Unit TDA 2.9 Support children and young people's positive behaviour.

You'll learn a range of strategies to deal with inappropriate behaviour in Unit TDA 2.9.

Following behaviour policy

All registered early years settings are required to have a clear behaviour policy. The document should be tailored to meet the needs of the setting, and promote the overall values, ethics and aims of the organisation. You must be familiar with your setting's policy, and work in line with it at all times.

A good policy will explain the setting's philosophy and strategies for promoting positive behaviour and dealing with inappropriate behaviour when it occurs. These must be in line with legislation.

Practices that physically hurt, frighten, threaten or humiliate children must *never* be used. Practitioners must *never* use physical punishments such as smacking. It is *illegal*.

Also see Unit TDA 2.9.

Have a go!

If you have not yet seen it, ask your workplace setting for a copy of their behaviour policy. Read it carefully, and if there's anything you're unclear about, ask your supervisor to explain.

Following plans for individual behaviour

Sometimes, in consultation with parents, it's necessary to plan a behaviour programme for an individual child. This is in line with, but in addition to, the behaviour policy that applies to all.

Particular behaviour goals are identified to suit the individual child, and strategies are planned to help them to achieve the goals. The practitioner (usually the key person), the child/young person and parent/carer should work together to devise the plan.

Individual behaviour programmes may be necessary if:

- a child frequently/persistently displays challenging behaviour
- a child's behaviour is inconsistent with their age
- a child's behaviour has changed recently
- a child has been identified as in need of specialist help and practitioners are asked to work in partnership with parents, carers and specialists. This could be due to an impairment such as a learning difficulty, communication difficulty or attention deficit.

Over time, practitioners will be able to monitor the impact of the programme. If the measures taken seem to be working, they can be continued until the child reaches their goal or until their behaviour is effectively managed. If the measures are not successful, new strategies may need to be introduced. Once a child has adopted a new behaviour and it has become ingrained, it may be appropriate to end the programme or to focus on a new goal.

Encouraging engagement in positive behaviour

By using the strategies outlined above, you can demonstrate how you encourage children and young people to engage in positive behaviour. It's a good idea to record some details of your actions in your reflective journal.

Did you know?

Thinking about what you can do differently next time is extremely valuable, and it helps you to feel more equipped to cope with future challenging behaviour. This improves confidence.

Reflecting on your own role

New practitioners often worry about promoting positive behaviour, and in particular whether they will be able to handle any challenging behaviour they're presented with. It does take time and experience to build confidence in this area. One of the best ways to build up your skills is to reflect on your own role in promoting positive behaviour.

Using the reflective practice methods you've learnt, consider what action you have taken and how effective this has been. This will involve thinking about how situations turn out. For example, was that child successfully distracted from the situation in which they were likely to get into trouble? Or was that conflict between two young people successfully resolved with your input? Or did your actions have little effect?

Another very important way to learn is to watch and reflect on how experienced practitioners successfully promote positive behaviour. You may like to ask them about this afterwards.

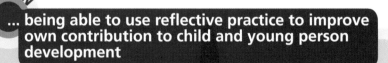

LEARNING OUTCOME 5

FOCUS ON

... being able to use reflective practice to improve own contribution to child and young person development

In this section you'll learn about reviewing the effectiveness of your contributions to the assessment of the development needs of children and young people. You'll also learn about reviewing the effectiveness of your own role in supporting development, and then identifying changes that you can make to your own practice. This links with **Assessment Criteria 5.1, 5.2, 5.3**.

How effectively do you contribute to assessments?

As you learnt in Unit SHC 22, it's good practice for you to reflect on all aspects of your practice. This includes:

■ How well you contribute to assessments.

■ How well you support children and young people's development.

Good practice

At the beginning of your career, it's always very helpful to spend some time thinking about how effectively you've conducted each observation that you do. Although observing will eventually feel very natural to you, it takes time to build observation skills and to get used to using the various observation methods. Reflection helps you to see how you can improve.

Link Up!

Unit SHC 22 Introduction to personal development in children and young people's settings.

You can reflect using the methods you learnt in Unit SHC 22, pages 63–4. As part of your reflection process, it will be useful for you to focus on the following questions:

■ Did you choose the right observation method for your purpose?

■ How well did you get on with using the observation method? (For example remembering the codes, finding the right column to write in, etc.)

■ Were you able to note down everything that happened?

■ If you had to choose what to record, did you manage to get everything that was significant?

■ Did you manage to keep to the timings you had set for the observation?

■ Did you position yourself in the right place? (For example could you see/hear everything without being obtrusive?)

■ How confident did you feel during the process?

Ask an experienced colleague to look at your work and give you feedback

Good practice

You also need to reflect on how well you have evaluated the observation. You can assess this by asking an experienced colleague to look at your work and to give you feedback. Focus on whether they agree with the conclusions you have drawn. If not, ask them what happened in the observation that made them draw different conclusions. It's one of the best ways to learn.

Reviewing how well you support development

In your role as a practitioner, you support children and young people's development in many ways, such as:

- providing challenging, interesting activities and experiences

- providing a range of activities and experiences to promote all aspects of development

- providing interesting resources and equipment

- supporting children when they need help and encouragement

- demonstrating skills

- the way you interact and communicate

- giving information

- answering questions/explaining things

- asking children questions

- providing a safe and healthy environment

- meeting children's care needs

- meeting individual needs and noticing when development isn't progressing as expected

- working in partnership with families and outside professionals.

Have a go!

Can you add to the list of the ways in which practitioners support children and young people's development?

Good practice

Over time, it's good practice to use the range of reflection methods you have learnt about to reflect on how well you fulfil each of the ways to support development. It's very important to get feedback from others and to consider this carefully in order to identify where you can improve your practice. Good sources of feedback include experienced colleagues, supervisors, tutors, assessors and mentors.

Identifying changes to make to your own practice

So, you've identified where you can improve your practice in supporting children and young people's development. The next stage is to plan the changes you can make. You may decide that you need more experience in certain areas, or more knowledge. Or perhaps you simply need to try a different approach.

Here are some examples of common changes that a practitioner may make to improve their practice:

- Ask children more questions to encourage them to think.

- Get down to the child's level when communicating with them.

- Gather more interesting ideas for children's activities by borrowing books and searching online.

- Practise reading stories to individual children (to build confidence for when it's the practitioner's turn to lead the whole group story time).

- Practise singing with a small group of children (to build confidence for when it's the practitioner's turn to lead the whole group music time).

- Improve knowledge of child development by reading a book dedicated to the subject.

- Carry out observations more often.

- Attend staff planning meetings to learn how the session plans are created.

- Go to a training day to learn more about the curriculum that applies to the setting (for example the Early Years Foundation Stage).

Once you have decided how to change your practice, you can use the information on setting SMART objectives in Unit SHC 22 to help you update your personal development plan.

Link Up!

Unit SHC 22 Introduction to personal development in children and young people's settings.

Good practice

Remember that you should monitor and review the effectiveness of any changes you make to your practice.

How are things going?

▶ Progress Check

1. What are the advantages of the checklist observation method? (1.2)

2. What observation method would you use to record each time a certain behaviour (such as aggression) occurred? (1.2)

3. Give an example of how you can support a child's holistic development. (2.1)

4. What would you do to evaluate whether an activity met a child's identified development need/s? (2.3)

5. Name six transitions that children/young people are likely to experience. (3.1)

6. Give three examples of how you could support a child due to make the transition from an early years setting to primary school. (3.2)

7. Explain how children and young people's positive behaviour can be encouraged by:
   a work settings and
   b individual practitioners. (4.1, 4.2)

8. Give an example of how you would review the effectiveness of your own contribution to the assessment of children's development needs. (5.1)

9. Give an example of how you would review the effectiveness of your own role in supporting a child's development. (5.2)

Are you ready for assessment?

Learning Outcomes 1, 2, 4 and 5 must be assessed in a real work environment.

CACHE

Set task:

■ You are asked to describe the different transitions children and young people may experience, and to explain how to give adults support for each of these transitions.

City & Guilds

In preparation for assessment of this Unit, you may like to discuss with an experienced colleague the strategies used by your workplace setting to support children who will shortly begin attending a new setting (e.g. children leaving preschool to start school).

Edexcel

You may like to gather evidence of times when you have contributed to supporting a child experiencing a transition (e.g. activity plans or evaluations of a relevant story, visit or imaginary play session).

UNIT 2.2

TDA

Safeguard the welfare of children and young people

LEARNING OUTCOMES

The learning outcomes you will meet in this unit are:

1 Know about the legislation, guidelines, policies and procedures for safeguarding the welfare of children and young people, including e-safety

2 Know what to do when children and young people are ill or injured, including emergency procedures

3 Know how to respond to evidence or concerns that a child or young person has been abused, harmed or bullied

INTRODUCTION

It's extremely important for you to learn the information in this unit as practitioners have a duty to safeguard the children and young people in their care.

'Safeguarding' is an umbrella term used to describe measures taken to keep children and young people safe from a wide range of dangers. In this unit it refers to children and young people's safety in relation to childhood illness, injuries, emergencies, use of technology and child protection. The term 'child protection' refers to the measures taken to keep children and young people safe from abuse and harm from others.

LEARNING OUTCOME 1

FOCUS ON

... know about the legislation, guidelines, policies and procedures for safeguarding the welfare of children and young people, including e-safety

In this section you'll learn about legal requirements for **safeguarding** the welfare of children and young people, and the policies and procedures devised by settings. You'll also learn about the roles of different agencies involved in safeguarding children and young people. This links with **Assessment Criteria 1.1, 1.2.**

key terms

Safeguarding an umbrella term used here to describe measures taken to keep children and young people safe from a wide range of dangers.

Child protection the measures taken to keep children and young people safe from abuse and harm from others.

Everyone who works with children has a duty to keep them safe from harm and abuse. There are laws, guidelines, policies and procedures in place that make this a legal requirement. You need to understand those relevant to your own home country.

Legislation

Children Act 1989

This Act set out people's duties to children. When it was introduced this law enforced a big change in the way parents' roles were regarded. The emphasis is now on parents having a responsibility to their children rather than rights over them. It recognises that children themselves have rights, and that they should be treated with respect. It also simplified existing **child protection** laws. The Children Act 1989 applies in England and Wales. In Northern Ireland, the Children (Northern Ireland) Order 1995 set out duties to children.

Protection of Children Act 1999

This Act includes clauses that set out the child protection duties of local authorities. It also defines the legal term 'significant harm'. It applies in England and Wales.

Everyone who works with young children has a duty to keep them safe

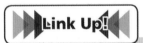

Unit SHC 23 Introduction to equality and inclusion in children and young people's settings.

Ask Miranda!

Q I've heard there are different sorts of CRB checks – Standard and Enhanced. Which one will I need?

A **Enhanced checks are for posts that involve working directly with children, young people or vulnerable adults.**

Children Bill 2004

Prior to this bill, there had been concerns that children's services were not working together effectively to protect vulnerable children from abuse. This was highlighted by an independent inquiry into the death of Victoria Climbié, who died tragically at the hands of her carers. The inquiry and subsequent report by Lord Laming led to Every Child Matters (a green paper) and then to the introduction of the Children Bill. (This Bill applies in England. Equivalent legislation was also established in the other home countries.) The Bill was passed to improve child protection for children and to ensure better coordination of services.

Working Together to Safeguard Children 2006

This applies to England and Wales. It provides statutory guidance on how organisations and individuals should work together to safeguard and promote the welfare of children and young people in accordance with the Children Act 1989 and the Children Act 2004 (see Unit SHC23, page 94 for details of the Children Act 2004).

Did you know?

Settings need to meet the additional requirements of the regulatory body in their home country. For example, early years settings in England that are registered with Ofsted must meet the Early Years Foundation Stage Welfare Requirements for Safeguarding and Promoting Children's Welfare.

Vetting and Barring Scheme

The new Vetting and Barring Scheme applies to England, Wales and Northern Ireland. Scotland is bringing in its own equivalent. It's law for anyone wanting to work or volunteer with children or young people to register with the Independent Safeguarding Authority (ISA). Everyone who applies will be vetted by the Criminal Record Bureau (CRB), who will check to see if there is information held that indicates the person may pose a risk to children and young people. This will include searching police databases and checking whether other organisations have reported concerns about the person. If no information is found, a CRB Disclosure can be issued. This is a document that proves to employers that the person has been fully approved to work with children or young people.

Safeguarding policies and procedures

Settings must have the following policies and procedures:

- Child protection.

- Health and safety (see Unit MU 2.4).

- Risk assessment (see Unit MU 2.4).

Child protection policies and procedures

A child protection policy and procedures will set out the setting's **safe working practices**. This term refers to the way practitioners work to protect children and to protect themselves from allegations of abuse. Your setting's guidelines will be based on the requirements of your home country, and they will be reviewed annually. Make sure you fully understand your setting's policies and procedures, and always work in accordance with them.

Key responsibilities of settings include:

- Appointing a named senior member of staff to be in charge of safeguarding.

- Ensuring all adults who have regular and unsupervised access to children are registered with the ISA and have a CRB check.

- Keeping a record of all checks carried out on staff and volunteers.

- Informing the ISA if they believe any person who has had involvement with a setting is a threat to the safety of children or young people.

- Ensuring all staff and volunteers have regular safeguarding training.

- Ensuring the minimum requirement for the ratio of staff to children is met.

- In group settings, ensuring there are always at least two staff present – even if one child is late being collected, two staff must stay on.

There must always be a trained first-aider present

Unit MU 2.4 Contribute to children and young people's health and safety.

key terms

Safe working practices the ways in which practitioners work to protect children and to protect themselves from allegations of abuse.

■ Ensuring there is always a qualified first-aider present.

■ Carrying out risk assessments (see page 237).

■ Having missing child procedures in place.

■ Keeping a registration document for each child or young person, with details of their full name, address and contact details of their parents and carers.

■ Taking out public liability insurance and employer's liability insurance where relevant.

E-safety

Most children and young people use computers and have access to a mobile phone. They may also use a game console that connects to the internet. Advances in technology have changed the lives of children and young people in many positive ways. But being online, playing video games and using a mobile phone do present some risks, and these are outlined below.

Risks and possible consequences of using technology

■ Physical danger/contact with paedophiles. Paedophiles may pose as a child or young person online. They may target a child by pretending to have similar interests, and use this to establish an online 'friendship'. When trust has developed, they may entice the child to meet up with them in person. This is known as 'child grooming' or 'child procurement'. Studies have shown that this threat is parents' biggest online worry.

■ Exposure to inappropriate material. Material may be pornographic, violent or hateful (for example promoting extreme political, racist or sexist views). It may promote dangerous or illegal behaviour, or it may simply be age inappropriate.

■ Divulging personal details. Children and young people may unintentionally disclose personal details which may be used to facilitate identity theft or cons. The details may also fall into the hands of people who may harm them.

Illegal behaviour. Users may become caught up in behaviour that is illegal, antisocial or otherwise inappropriate. This includes downloading copyright material illegally.

Bullying. Cyber bullying may occur via the internet, video games or mobile phones. It can leave victims extremely upset, scared and humiliated. See pages 199 and 218 for further details.

Online gambling. The internet gives easy access to gambling sites.

Wrong information. Children and young people may believe incorrect information that they come across online.

The Byron Review
In 2007 the government ordered a review to look at the risks to children from exposure to potentially harmful or inappropriate material on the internet and in video games. This was carried out by Professor Tanya Byron, who went on to outline objectives for e-safety.

Ways of reducing risk to children and young people
In response to the Byron Review, the government issued advice to parents and carers on reducing the risk. Here's a summary:

Parental controls
Use the parental controls available on computers and other digital technologies like games consoles and mobile phones. These allow adults to:

- block websites and email addresses by adding them to a filter list

- set time limits for use

- prevent children from searching certain words.

Rules
Parents are advised to create rules with the child. Examples of acceptable use include:

- The internet-connected computer must be in a family room with the screen facing outwards so the parent can see what is going on.

Mobile phones have both advantages and risks

Did you know?

In 2009 the government set a target for every home in Britain to have access to a broadband internet connection by 2012.

Have a go!

Visit www.education.gov.uk and search for Byron Review to read the review in full.

- If the child accidentally goes to an unsuitable website, they should tell the parent. The parent can delete it from the 'history' folder and add the address to the parental control filter list.

- It's never all right to use abusive or threatening language in any online communication.

- The child should take breaks from the computer every 30 minutes for health and safety reasons.

- The child shouldn't download unknown files from the internet without the parent's agreement. It's best to never download unknown files.

- Children should not download or share files illegally (for example music, films).

- Children should not attempt to buy or order things online.

Personal safety online

Parents are advised to explain to children that people online might not be who they say they are and could be dangerous, and that any personal information they give out can be used in financial scams or for bullying. Children should be told not to:

- give out personal information to people they only know online – this includes name, home address, landline and mobile numbers, bank details, PINs and passwords

- supply details for registration without asking for permission and help from their parent

- visit chat websites that aren't fully moderated/supervised

- sign up to social networking sites without asking for permission and help from their parent

- arrange to meet an online friend in person without parental knowledge and permission (if a parent agrees to let them, they should always go along with them)

- give any indication of their age or sex in a personal email address or screen name

- keep anything that worries or upsets them online secret from the parent

- respond to unwanted emails or other messages.

It's advisable to monitor children's internet use by checking the history folder on the browser, which contains a list of previously visited sites. Children should be made aware of child-friendly search engines, which filter out inappropriate internet sites. Or safe search settings can be turned on to allow safe use of traditional search engines.

Children should ask for permission and help before signing up to social networking sites

Cyber bullying

Ensure children understand that they should never be afraid to tell parents about frightening or bullying emails or messages they get with unacceptable content. It's not their fault that they have received them and the addresses of the senders can be added to the parental control filter list.

If there's a problem

If there's a problem, parents are advised to:

- contact their internet service provider if a child comes across inappropriate content or is subjected to any inappropriate contact while online

- install and regularly update filtering software to protect against inappropriate internet access.

Good practice

All children and young people's settings must take adequate steps to ensure that access to technology within the environment is safe. This means following the strategies you learnt about above. It's also important for practitioners to be vigilant about the appropriate use of the resources that children and young people bring into the setting from home. This includes mobile phones, hand-held game consoles and laptops.

If practitioners or parents are worried about illegal materials or suspicious online behaviour, they should report this to the Child Exploitation and Online Protection Centre. This is a police unit dedicated to ending the sexual abuse of children. You can find out more at http://ceop.police.uk.

Did you know?

Many parents say they are less able to understand and use technology than their children. So educating parents must not be overlooked in ensuring children's safety online.

Roles of agencies involved in safeguarding

All children and young people are known to a number of organisations and agencies who may potentially be involved in partnership working to support the child or young person and/or their family.

The initial role of practitioners and settings is to be vigilant in terms of safeguarding, and to report any concerns appropriately. You'll learn about this in Learning outcome 3. The roles and responsibilities of the other organisations are explained in Table TDA2.2.1 below.

Table TDA2.2.1: Roles and responsibilities of agencies involved in safeguarding

Organisation	Roles and responsibilities
GP or hospital	GPs are usually the first port of call for their patients, and as such they are often the first to pick up possible abuse when examining a child or young person at their surgery. In emergency situations, children and young people may be taken or may go to the accident and emergency unit at a local hospital. Hospitals keep a record of patients' visits, and if a child or young person is seen repeatedly with certain sorts of injuries, staff may identify possible abuse.
Social Services	Social Services have a statutory duty to support vulnerable families. They must also respond appropriately to referrals regarding concerns that a child or young person is suffering or likely to suffer significant harm, and work within the legal framework and local procedures to safeguard children and young people. Social workers must work sensitively with parents whilst ensuring their children are protected.
Health visiting	Health visitors have responsibilities relating to the health and development of children under the age of five. They also provide guidance and support to their families. This means that parents who are not coping may turn to them for help. As health visitors go into the family home, they are well placed to notice environmental causes for concern – for example if a child is being neglected or is otherwise living in unacceptable circumstances.
Police	The harm or abuse of children or young people may lead to criminal proceedings, which the police will have responsibility for. It is not uncommon for police officers to identify possible abuse when called to attend a domestic disturbance. Police officers may also be involved with social workers should a child or young person be removed from the family home as a safeguarding measure.

Organisation	Roles and responsibilities
Probation services	Probation services are involved when someone is found guilty of harming or abusing a child or young person. Probation officers have a number of duties, including making assessments to advise courts, managing and enforcing community orders, and working with prisoners during and after sentencing. In an effort to rehabilitate offenders, they also have a duty to enforce the conditions of court orders and release licences. In an effort to protect the public, they conduct offender risk assessments and ensure that offenders are aware of the impact of their crime on their victims and the public.
NSPCC	The NSPCC provide advice services for adults worried that a child or young person may be being harmed. Parents, professionals and members of the general public can call to help protect children. They also provide a free, online, specialised child protection resource for practitioners and other professionals working to protect children. They provide direct services to children and families, concentrating on important issues and groups of children most at risk. The NSPCC also support ChildLine, where trained volunteers are on hand to provide advice and support 24 hours a day to children who make contact by phone or online. A primary schools service is also being developed. It aims to teach children aged 5–11 in every community: ■ what abuse and bullying are ■ how to protect themselves ■ where to get help if they need it.
Psychology services	Child psychologists support children or young people who have been harmed or abused. Clinical or forensic psychologists are often asked to contribute to child risk assessments, which assess the level of risk that a parent may pose to a child or young person. This risk must be considered carefully when decisions are to be made about where a child or young person will live, and under what circumstances they will be able to see a parent who has caused them harm or abuse.

Good practice

Professionals are also there to support you. If you are feeling distressed after or during involvement in a case of suspected or actual abuse, you will need the opportunity to talk through your feelings. But because of strict confidentiality, you must not talk to anyone who does not 'need to know'. However, it's appropriate for you to talk to your supervisor, or to ask your supervisor for the name of the outside professional who you should contact to talk things over. This is generally a social worker or a worker from the NSPCC.

... knowing what to do when children and young people are ill or injured, including emergency procedures

In this section you'll learn about the signs and symptoms of common childhood illnesses, and the actions to take when children or young people are ill or injured. You'll also learn about the circumstances when urgent medical attention may be required and the actions to take in a range of emergency situations. This links with **Assessment Criteria 2.1, 2.2, 2.3, 2.4.**

Common signs and symptoms of illness

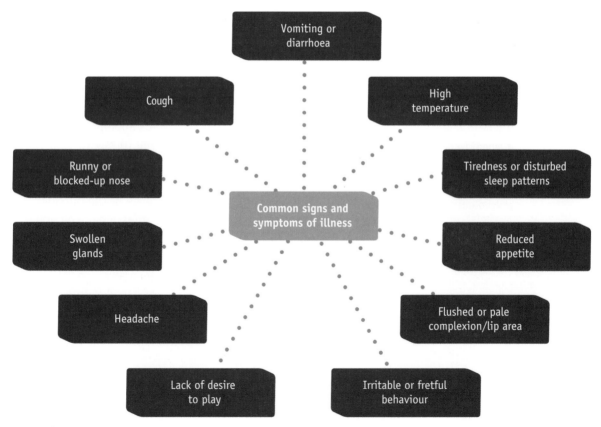

Common signs and symptoms of illness

All children and young people are unwell from time to time, so you need to be able recognise the signs and symptoms of illness. These are shown on the diagram on page 202.

Common childhood illnesses

Common childhood illnesses are infections that many children and young people experience. Table TDA2.2.2 tells you about these. The **incubation periods** are given. This is the amount of time between the infection and the onset of signs and symptoms.

Table TDA2.2.2: Common childhood illnesses

Disease and cause	Spread	Incubation	Signs and symptoms	Rash or specific sign	Treatment	Complications
Common cold (coryza) Virus	Airborne/ droplet, hand-to-hand contact	1–3 days	Sneezing, sore throat, running nose, headache, slight fever, irritable, partial deafness		Treat symptoms. Vaseline to nostrils	Bronchitis, sinusitis, laryngitis
Chickenpox (varicella) Virus	Airborne/ droplet, direct contact	10–14 days	Slight fever, itchy rash, mild onset, child feels ill, often with severe headache	Red spots with white centre on trunk and limbs at first; blisters and pustules	Rest, fluids, calamine to rash, cut child's nails to prevent secondary infection	Impetigo, scarring, secondary infection from scratching
Dysentery Bacillus or amoeba	Indirect: flies, infected food, poor hygiene	1–7 days	Vomiting, diarrhoea, blood, mucus in stool, abdominal pain, fever, headache		Replace fluids, rest, medical aid, strict hygiene measures	Dehydration from loss of body salts, shock; can be fatal
Food poisoning Bacteria or virus	Indirect: infected food or drink	30 mins–36 hours	Vomiting, diarrhoea, abdominal pain		Fluids only for 24 hours; medical aid if no better	Dehydration – can be fatal
Gastro-enteritis Bacteria or virus	Direct contact. Indirect: infected food/ drink	Bacterial: 7–14 days Viral: 30 mins–36 hours	Vomiting, diarrhoea, signs of dehydration		Replace fluids – water or Dioralyte; medical aid urgently	Dehydration, weight loss – can be fatal

Disease and cause	Spread	Incubation	Signs and symptoms	Rash or specific sign	Treatment	Complications
Measles (morbilli) Virus	Airborne/droplet	7–15 days	High fever; fretful, heavy cold – running nose and discharge from eyes; later cough	Day 1: Koplik's spots, white inside mouth. Day 4: blotchy rash starts on face and spreads down to body	Rest, fluids, tepid sponging; shade room if photophobic	Otitis media, eye infection, pneumonia, encephalitis (rare)
Mumps (epidemic parotitis) Virus	Airborne/droplet	14–21 days	Pain, swelling of jaw in front of ears, fever; eating and drinking painful	Swollen face	Fluids: give via straw, hot compresses, oral hygiene	Meningitis (1 in 400), orchitis (infection of testes) in young men
Pertussis (whooping cough) Bacteria	Airborne/droplet, direct contact	7–21 days	Starts with a snuffly cold, slight cough, mild fever	Spasmodic cough with whoop sound, vomiting	Rest and assurance; feed after coughing attack; support during attack; inhalations	Convulsions, pneumonia, brain damage, hernia, debility
Rubella (German measles) Virus	Airborne/droplet	14–21 days	Slight cold, sore throat, mild fever, swollen glands behind ears, pain in small joints	Slight pink rash starts behind ears and on forehead. Not itchy	Rest if necessary. Treat symptoms	Only if contracted by woman in first 3 months of pregnancy – can cause serious defects in unborn
Scarlet fever (or Scarlatina) Bacteria	Droplet	2–4 days	Sudden fever, loss of appetite, sore throat, pallor around mouth, 'strawberry tongue'	Bright red pinpoint rash over face and body – may peel	Rest, fluids, observe for complications, antibiotics	Kidney infection, otitis media, rheumatic fever (rare)
Tonsillitis Bacteria or virus	Direct infection, droplet		Very sore throat, fever; headache, pain on swallowing, aches and pains in back and limbs		Rest, fluids, medical aid – antibiotics, iced drinks relieve pain	Quinsy (abscess on tonsils), otitis media, kidney infection, temporary deafness

When a child or young person is unwell

It's a legal requirement that all registered settings have written guidelines for the management of illness within the setting. When you notice that a child or young person is feeling unwell, you should promptly take the action outlined in your setting's policies and procedures.

Good practice

Practitioners working as assistants will normally be required to alert a more senior member of staff about an illness or injury straight away. They will then take control. So while the procedures for caring for children who are ill are given below, in many settings it's likely that, in practice, you will not take responsibility for carrying them out. So you must take care not to overstep the boundaries of your role.

What practitioners should do

If a child or young person is unwell, practitioners should:

- **respond to symptoms if appropriate, in line with policies**:
  Cooling down a child with a temperature for instance
  (see page 206), or administering a child's asthma inhaler.

- **monitor the condition in case it becomes worse**:
  Also record appropriate details such as temperature readings or inhalers given.

- **arrange for the child or young person to be collected as soon as possible in the case of minor illness. Call the child's parent, carer or alternative contact person (as stated on the registration form)**:
  They may understandably be worried. Practitioners should be calm and supply the facts.

- **get emergency assistance urgently if necessary, and know which signs and symptoms indicate that immediate medical help is needed (see page 207)**:

Link Up!

Unit MU 2.4 Contribute to children and young people's health and safety.

Practitioners should not wait for parents or carers if it's an emergency. They should dial 999 and request an ambulance. If the child or young person needs to go to hospital before a parent or carer arrives, a practitioner should accompany them and meet the parents at the hospital. Practitioners should do everything possible to make a child or young person comfortable until they leave their care. Those who are ill may be upset or embarrassed. Practitioners should be sensitive and caring to soothe them, staying with a child in a quiet area and carrying out a quiet activity, such as sharing a book, if the child is interested.

- **record the illness**:
  See Unit MU 2.4, Learning outcome 5.

- **do what they can to stop the spread of infection**:
  See Unit MU 2.4, Learning outcome 6.

High temperatures

The normal temperature reading for a child is between 36.5 °C and 37.4 °C. Children may have a higher temperature when they are ill. Taking a child's temperature with a thermometer helps you to monitor their illness. Most settings will use a fever scan thermometer (placed on the forehead) or a digital thermometer (either placed in the mouth or the ear). These come with directions for use. They are safer than clinical thermometers, which are made of glass and contain mercury.

Practitioners should take steps to lower a temperature by:

- seeing that warm clothing is removed so that just a cool layer is worn

- providing a cool drink of either water or squash diluted with water

- cooling the environment (opening windows, turning off heat sources, using a fan, etc.)

- providing a cool wipe for the face and forehead.

Some children may be given paracetamol syrup by parents or carers or with parental consent, but this depends on the circumstances and the policy of the setting. For instance, a child may be prone to febrile convulsions brought on by a high temperature. Parents may therefore bring paracetamol syrup to the setting, giving written permission for it to be administered in the hope that convulsions may be avoided if their child gets a temperature.

Providing a cool drink of water

Note that children may also have a high or higher temperature after physical activity, such as running around, or after they have had hot food or fluids.

Action to take when children or young people are injured
This information is given in Unit MU 2.4, Learning outcome 4.

Taking a child's temperature with a digital thermometer

Signs that urgent medical attention may be needed

The following signs and symptoms of illness indicate that you may need to call for urgent medical attention:

- Breathing difficulties.

- Convulsions.

- Child/young person seems to be in significant pain.

- Child/young person cannot easily or fully be roused from sleep or a state of drowsiness.

- Baby becomes unresponsive and/or their body seems to be floppy.

- Severe headache which may be accompanied by a stiff neck or a dislike of light.

- Rash that remains (it does not fade) when pressed with a glass.

- Vomiting that persists for more than 24 hours.

- Unusual, high-pitched crying in babies.

- High temperature that cannot be lowered.

- Will not drink fluids – this is most worrying in babies.

Responding to emergency situations

All practitioners need to know how to respond in emergency situations including:

- fires

- security incidents

- missing children or young people.

For full details, see Unit MU 2.4, Learning outcome 3.

Link Up!

Unit MU 2.4 Contribute to children and young people's health and safety.

... knowing how to respond to evidence or concerns that a child or young person has been abused, harmed or bullied

In this section you'll learn about the transitions experienced by most children and young people, and those that are experienced by some children and young people. You'll also learn about the effects of transitions on children's behaviour and development. This links with **Assessment Criteria 3.1, 3.2, 3.3, 3.4, 3.5.**

The characteristics of different types of abuse

It's a sad fact of life that some people harm children and young people. The effects of abuse are serious and far reaching. Once experienced, a child or young person may suffer the impact of them for many years to come. For children's welfare, it is important that you learn how to recognise the possible signs, symptoms and behaviour that can indicate abuse. Practitioners learn this so that if they come across them they will realise that abuse could be taking place, and they will take the appropriate action. Experts sometimes use more categories to describe the specifics of abuse, but essentially there are four main types:

- Physical abuse.

- Emotional abuse.

- Sexual abuse.

- Neglect.

Physical abuse

Physical abuse occurs when someone deliberately causes physical harm to a child or young person. It includes the actions of hitting, kicking, shaking, biting, squeezing, burning, scalding, throwing, attempting suffocation or drowning, giving children poisonous substances or inappropriate drugs or alcohol.

Signs

Signs of physical abuse include bruises, cuts and abrasions. Since children frequently have minor accidents and therefore have bumps and bruises, it is important to take into account where on the body bruising or marking occurs. See the diagram below for parts of the body that are likely to become bruised or marked when abuse is taking place – this is called a 'body map'. In addition, consider how often a child has bruises and marks. If frequency is a concern, you can keep a dated record of the marks you observe to see if a pattern emerges.

Bruises made by abuse may be in the shape of hands, fingers or other implements. A torn frenulum (the web of skin inside the upper lip) is often a sign of abuse. The injury may occur if a child has something forced into their mouth, for instance if they are forcibly fed with a bottle or spoon. Injuries to this area rarely occur accidentally.

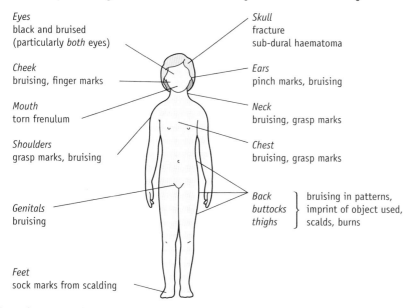

Eyes
black and bruised
(particularly *both* eyes)

Cheek
bruising, finger marks

Mouth
torn frenulum

Shoulders
grasp marks, bruising

Genitals
bruising

Feet
sock marks from scalding

Skull
fracture
sub-dural haematoma

Ears
pinch marks, bruising

Neck
bruising, grasp marks

Chest
bruising, grasp marks

Back
buttocks
thighs
bruising in patterns, imprint of object used, scalds, burns

Sites of common physical abuse injuries

Blank body maps are often used to record the marks actually seen on a child. Remember that physical signs are not always left by physical abuse. Common sites for bruising that occurs as a result of play and/or accident include marks to the legs and arms, particularly below the knees and elbows. Mongolian spots (or blue spots) are birthmarks that may occur on the lower spine or buttocks of children of southern European, African or Asian descent. They are smooth, with the bluish-grey tone of a bruise, and can be quite large. They should not be confused with a bruise or a sign of abuse.

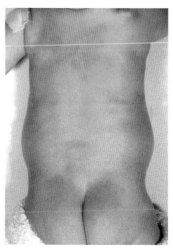

Mongolian (or blue) spot

Behavioural/emotional signs

Children or young people who are being physically abused may show signs of changed behaviour in addition to, or in the absence of, physical signs. They may include:

■ Being withdrawn.

■ Avoiding physical contact.

■ Lack of trust.

■ Afraid to go home or go with the abuser.

■ Aggressive behaviour.

■ Acting out aggression in play.

■ Signs of stress such as bedwetting.

■ Seeming sad/preoccupied/unable to have fun.

■ Lack of confidence.

■ Watches others carefully but does not participate (sometimes called 'frozen watchfulness').

Frozen watchfulness

Emotional abuse

Emotional abuse occurs when children and young people are harmed emotionally. When children's emotional needs, which include love and affection, are not met, then children's development is seriously damaged. They are likely to experience difficulties with social and emotional development, finding it particularly hard to relate to adults and to make friends with children. This can have the effect of putting the child at further risk of bullying.

Children often have low self-esteem and may develop poor emotional health (mental health). Children who are emotionally abused may live with constant threats, shouting, ridiculing, criticism, taunting and repeated rejection. The signs of emotional abuse are listed on page 211.

However, when children experience an emotional upheaval in their life, such as bereavement, divorce or a new baby in the family, they can also show some of those signs of stress for a period of time. You're advised to record instances and share the information with parents and carers. You will have notes in case the signs persist.

Emotional abuse may put a child at further risk of bullying

Signs

Children or young people who are being emotionally abused may show signs of changed behaviour. They may include:

- Low self-esteem and lack of confidence.

- Difficulty making friends.

- Being very wary of their parent's mood.

- Behaviour difficulties – aggression (may be towards self, for example head banging, biting), attention seeking, demanding, stealing, lying, tantrums (in children over five).

- Indiscriminately affectionate – may cuddle or sit on lap of any adult, even if they do not know them.

- Poor concentration leading to learning difficulties.

- Inability to have fun.

- Toileting problems after previously being dry.

- Overly upset by making a mistake.

- Behaviour associated with comfort seeking in children over five – sucking thumb, rocking, masturbation.

Sexual abuse

Sexual abuse is defined as the involvement of dependent and developmentally immature children/young people in sexual activities. It also includes behaviour that may not involve any physical contact, such as exposing them to pornography via any media, for instance photographs, videos, DVDs and the internet, or making them witness the sexual acts of others.

Sexual abuse happens to both girls and boys and to babies. Both men and women sexually abuse children. The majority of children who are sexually abused are abused by someone they know who is in a position of trust, such as a family member or family friend. A *minority* of sexually abused children go on to become abusers. Sexual abuse frequently causes lifelong emotional damage and serious difficulties in forming relationships. Sometimes children do not show signs of abuse until much later, when they have reached puberty for instance. It may be that the child had not previously realised that what was happening to them was wrong and abusive.

Signs

The following diagrams give the possible physical signs and behaviour indicators of sexual abuse. There are few physical signs that are likely to be noticed after a child is independent in terms of caring for their own body, so the behaviour signs are particularly important. Over-sexualised behaviour is when children act in sexual ways that are inappropriate for their age. For example, they may say things or know things that you would not expect them to know, or they may role-play or act out sexual situations.

Neglect

Neglect occurs when a family does not provide for a child's basic, everyday, essential needs. This can include a lack of supervision (such as leaving the child alone inappropriately), a parent being under the influence of alcohol or drugs while supervising a child, not protecting a child from danger and not providing stimulation. Children who have

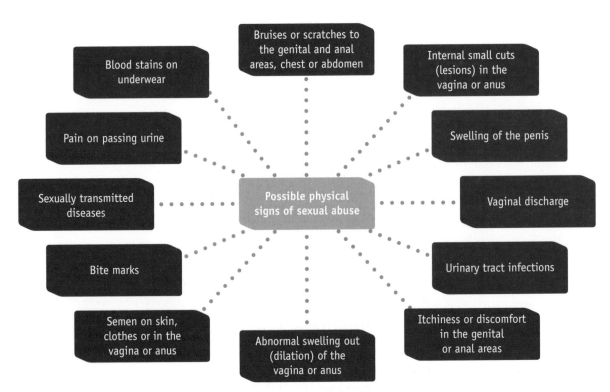

Possible physical signs of sexual abuse

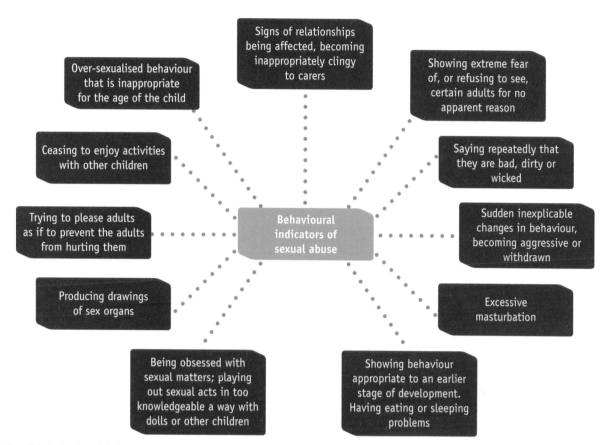

Possible behavioural indicators of sexual abuse

been neglected are often said to be 'failing to thrive'. Because of a lack of care and attention to their most basic needs, they may not be able to grow and develop as they should. These children are deprived.

Signs

Signs may include:

- Lack of food, or lack of healthy food leading to malnourishment, obesity (being overweight), hunger.

- Clothes uncared for. They may be dirty, smelly or worn, or the child may have clothes that are not suitable for the weather. These things can lead to bullying.

- There may not be adequate heating at home. They may be cold and uncomfortable, and in severe cases this can lead to hypothermia, especially in babies and younger children.

- The child's hygiene needs may not be cared for. They may be dirty and they may smell. They may have skin infections and infestations that go untreated (such as head lice). This is also likely to lead to bullying. The child may live in an unhygienic environment and frequently be unwell. Food poisoning is common.

- Inadequate supervision and lack of safety features at home may lead to frequent accidents, the child having too much freedom (they may be out alone in the street or garden late at night for instance, or a younger child may be out unsupervised). The child may play truant from school, leading to a lack of stimulation and education. There may not be a child's safety seat in the car.

- Poor medical care. Illnesses and injuries may go untreated, impairments may go unchecked. Developmental checkups, immunisations and dental appointments may be missed. These things can lead to serious or prolonged health problems and disability.

- Lack of love, care, affection and moral guidance leading to isolation and possible early smoking, drinking and substance abuse.

Children may appear to be:

- nervous, attention seeking or clingy

- sad, unpopular with peers

- caring for siblings or other family members, including parents

- angry, and may tell lies

- streetwise – they look after themselves.

Neglected children may be out alone in the street or garden late at night

Responding to evidence or concerns of abuse or harm

By recognising signs of abuse, practitioners can take the first steps that may ultimately stop the abuse happening to a child. Having a good knowledge of children's expected development and behaviour is key, since you will then be more likely to spot behaviour that is inappropriate for a child's age. For example tantrums or wetting themselves in children generally too old for this.

This knowledge is informed by the regular observations and assessment that practitioners make on children in their care. Observations can reveal and record how the child forms relationships, how their behaviour or mood may change over time, and recurring themes in their play or conversation.

If you have evidence or concerns about abuse or harm

If you suspect that a child may be being abused or harmed, you should:

- note down all of the information as soon as you can while it's still fresh in your memory. It is easy to forget details later, particularly those that don't seem to have much significance at the time but may prove to be important

- follow your setting's child protection policy, which will set out how you should report concerns, and what will happen next.

Usually you will need to speak privately to the named person in your setting who is responsible for safeguarding. In their absence, you may need to speak to another senior colleague. This person will then take responsibility for the situation. It will be their job to take the appropriate steps, which may include reporting the concerns to the appropriate outside agency (for example Social Services).

Actions to take if a child or young person alleges harm or abuse

Your setting will have clear policies in place to tell you what to do if a child or young person alleges harm or abuse, and it's extremely important that you follow these. However, general guidelines are given below.

Disclosure

'**Disclosure**' is the term that is used to refer to a child revealing to an adult that they have been abused. This may include:

- A **full disclosure**. When the child says who has abused them and goes into the history and nature of the abuse.

- A **partial disclosure**. A child may begin to tell of abuse, and then shy away and not continue. Or they may reveal only some details, leaving out what exactly has happened or the name of the abuser.

Good practice

Always date your observations. This is good practice in any case, but it is also important if the information is required as evidence.

Did you know?

If you notice signs and symptoms that cause you to suspect abuse, it's very important that you remain objective. You must follow procedures closely without making judgements. Remember that there could be other reasons for the child's behaviour or physical signs.

key terms

Disclosure when a child reveals to an adult that they have been abused.

Full disclosure when a child says who abused them and goes into the history and nature of the abuse.

Partial disclosure when a child begins to tell of abuse but does not continue, or when they do not give full details, such as the name of the abuser or the nature of the abuse.

Did you know?

Children sometimes disclose unintentionally. They may not be aware that what is happening to them is wrong, or they may have tried to block out or disguise the abuse, but they have unintentionally revealed it in their play or conversation.

- An **indirect disclosure**. This occurs when a child indicates abuse indirectly, through their play (often in a role play or imaginary situation), their artwork or, in the case of older children, through letters, stories or school work. Children may choose to disclose in this way if they are too afraid to tell directly, too embarrassed or ashamed, or if they find it too painful to discuss. They may fear that they will not be believed, or fear they will be punished or sent away from home. They may not know the right words to explain what has happened to them.

Ask Miranda!

Q I don't know how I'd handle it if a child told me they'd been abused. I'd be so shocked.

A When a child discloses abuse, it can be quite a shocking experience for a practitioner. However, your response is very important in terms of the welfare of the child, so you must stay calm, let the child see you are in control of yourself, and follow the guidelines below for dealing with the situation.

When the child is disclosing

- Look at the child, maintaining eye contact if the child is choosing to look directly at you. Aim to be on the same level as the child. Do not look away from the child – this can be interpreted by them as disapproval. Do not show any signs of disgust on your face whatever the child says, or they are likely to feel that they disgust you because they were involved in the abuse.

- Let the child do the talking, allow them to tell you spontaneously and in their own way.

- Listen and follow carefully. Try to remember exactly what the child is saying and the language they are using rather than interpreting what it all means.

- Do not ask the child questions or prompt them for more information. This may lead to confused information. It is not helpful for the child to have been 'led' should evidence be needed legally later on. If appropriate, a trained specialist will interview the child at another time.

What to say to the child

Let the child know that telling you was the right thing to do ('I'm so glad you've told me').

Tell them the abuse was not their fault.

Praise them for having told you, and for surviving their ordeal.

If the child asks if you believe them, say yes.

All allegations of abuse must be reported and taken seriously. It has been shown that children do not often lie about abuse. Even if the story seems confused or improbable, you must let the child see that you accept it. Your role is not to investigate, but to record and report. Never ask questions such as, 'Are you telling me the truth?' or, 'Are you sure that's what happened?'

If the child asks you to comment on the abuser, tread carefully. You should not be judgemental. Remember the child may love the abuser. It is acceptable to say that the abuser was wrong to do the things they have done.

If a child asks you what will happen to the abuser, say they will need some help.

Tell them that you have to tell someone else. You should never promise not to tell. It's your duty to report suspicions and disclosures of abuse, and the child will lose their trust in you when you do report it if you have not explained this.

Tell them what you are going to do next (for example talk to your supervisor in private).

Say you will talk to them again to let them know what has happened.

Reassure them that they can speak to you again about the abuse if they want to talk about it.

Bullying

Sadly, many children and young people are affected by bullying to some extent in their lives, and the fear of being bullied affects many more.

Excluding is a form of emotional bullying

Types of bullying

Bullying usually falls into one or more of the following types:

■ Physical: pushing, kicking, hitting, pinching and other forms of violence or threats.

■ Verbal: name calling, insults, sarcasm, spreading rumours, persistent teasing.

■ Emotional: excluding, ignoring, tormenting, ridicule, humiliation.

■ Cyber bullying: using information and communication technology deliberately to upset someone else, particularly mobile phones (upsetting texts, taking humiliating photos or video clips and circulating them) and the internet (often via social networking sites and email, and can include setting up 'hate websites').

Kidscape has carried out research into bullying. They define bullying as usually including:

■ deliberate hostility and aggression

■ a victim who is less powerful than the bully or bullies

■ an outcome that is always painful and/or distressing.

Their identified potential effects of bullying are shown on the diagram on page 219.

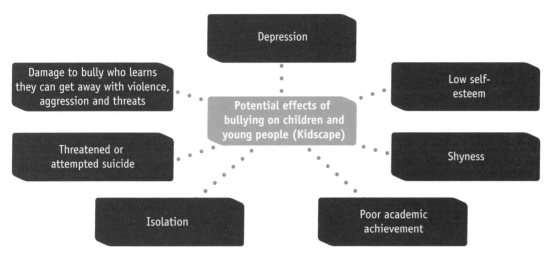

Potential effects of bullying

Did you know?

Research for ChildLine found that just over half of both primary- and secondary-school children thought that bullying was 'a big problem' or 'quite a big problem' in their school. Just over half of Year 5 students (aged 9–10) reported that they had been bullied during the preceding term compared with just over a quarter of Year 8 students (aged 12–13).

Reasons for bullying

There are numerous reasons why victims are bullied, but bullies tend to target children or young people who are different to them in some way. The bullying could be homophobic or gender based, racist, relating to special educational needs or disabilities. It could also be based on other physical characteristics, such as being short, or even being classed as pretty. It could relate to socio-economic factors, such as being perceived as a 'snob', or as coming from a 'poor' family. Being perceived as a 'swot' can also be a factor. Children or young people with low self-esteem and self-confidence are particularly at risk of bullying.

Have a go!

ChildLine provides information on bullying for children. You can view this online at www.childline.org. uk/explore/bullying/Pages/ Bullyinginfo.aspx.

Policies and procedures

It's a legal requirement for all schools to have an effective policy in place to prevent bullying. This must include consequences for bullying behaviour. Other settings may incorporate the policies and procedures on bullying into their behaviour policy, child protection policy or safeguarding policy.

Good practice

All settings should have clear procedures that tell practitioners what to do in response to concerns or evidence of bullying. These will enable practitioners to act swiftly and appropriately to prevent potential or ongoing bullying. They will also be able to support the victim and take action to tackle the bully's behaviour. Written procedures also ensure that a consistent approach is taken, and that a single, clear stance on bullying is promoted at all times.

Have a go!

You can view advice for children and young people at www.kidscape.org.uk

What children and young people should do if they are bullied

The anti-bullying policy should also address what children and young people should do if they are bullied, and it's important that the setting regularly communicates this to children and young people.

- They should know who to tell, and to tell them immediately.

- They should resist at the time of bullying, saying firmly or shouting 'NO!'

- Friends should stick together as there is safety in numbers.

See page 221 for the advice that Kidscape issue to professionals.

Bullies may send upsetting text messages or emails

Supporting children and young people

If a child or young person tells you they are being bullied, it's important to respond appropriately. Most will be upset and worried that telling will result in even more bullying as punishment for getting the bully into trouble. It may be that you are concerned about bullying that has not been reported to you by the victim. In this case, you will need to raise your concerns with the victim with extreme sensitivity, as they have decided for themselves not to challenge what the bully is doing to them. However, the bullying should still be addressed. Some children have committed suicide rather than tell anyone, so you should not wait for the victim to come to you.

Have a go!

You can view a sample anti-bullying policy online at www.kidscape.org.uk. Click on 'downloads' and select 'Anti-Bullying Policy Guidelines' from the download menu.

Kidscape: dealing with bullying and bullies

■ Tell the children from Day One that bullying (verbal or physical) is *not* tolerated in the school. Everyone is expected to ensure that it does not happen and has the responsibility to tell – this is not telling tales.

■ In class, have the children discuss bullying; what it is, what can be done, etc.

■ Have the children do a school survey to find out what children, teachers and staff think about bullying. Is it a problem, should it go on, should children tell if they are being bullied?

■ Have the children compile the survey and allow them to call a school assembly to announce the results.

■ Have the classes make up rules for behaviour. Agree a class/school set of rules.

■ Agree possible solutions (or consequences if necessary).

■ Have the children discuss ways to help the bullies become part of the group.

■ If bullying is happening, find out the facts, talk to the bullies and victims individually. If the bullying is about a particular issue (e.g. death, divorce, disfigurement), mount an education programme about the problem, but not focused on a particular child. Call in parents, ask their suggestions and solicit their support.

■ If necessary, break up the group dynamics by assigning places, keeping bullies at school at the end of the day, etc. Most bullying groups have a leader with other children being frightened of not bullying. Turn peer pressure against bullying and break up groups.

■ Teach children to be assertive using programmes such as Kidscape. Differences should be acceptable and never a cause for bullying. Reward and encourage children for individuality.

Dealing with bullying and bullies

Remember that many children and young people feel humiliated when they are bullied. They are embarrassed that they are disliked to such an extent, and may think it's their own fault for being 'unlikeable' or for having 'something wrong with them'. They may not want their teachers or parents to know that they are 'unpopular' at school or at the setting.

When bullying has taken place, the process of supporting the child or young person who has been the victim is similar to the process of handling a disclosure, which you learnt about on pages 216–17.

Concerns should be reported in private as soon as possible

Good practice

You should write down what has happened/what you have been told without delay. Make a note of who was there as there may be a group dynamic to the incident. Witnesses to the bullying may be important if different accounts of the event are given by those involved. Then report your concerns as soon as possible.

Action to take if you are concerned about a colleague

'Whistle-blowing' is the term used when a practitioner alerts superiors or outside professionals to their concerns relating to their own setting. All practitioners have a duty to safeguard children, so you must take action to blow the whistle if necessary, even though it may be uncomfortable.

You must report concerns about colleagues to superiors if you suspect them of:

- abuse (including bullying)

- causing harm

- failing to comply with safeguarding procedures.

If you have reported an incident or concerns to superiors but you feel they have not taken your concerns seriously or have failed to take the appropriate action, you must report this.

- If the concern relates to abuse or harm, you should call Social Services without delay.

- If the concern relates to failing to comply with safeguarding procedures, you can call the appropriate inspectorate (in England this is Ofsted).

Good practice

If you need to whistle-blow, write down as much information as possible about your area of concern. Include specific information where possible – names, places, dates, times, etc. Think through your concerns and make notes to help you explain them clearly. Managers must support whistle-blowers under the UK Public Interest Disclose Act 1998. While the matter is being investigated there is also a duty to protect those who have had allegations made about them.

Examples of failing to comply with safeguarding procedures include:

■ If you feel there has been a lack of action in response to suspicions you have raised about a child or young person being harmed or abused outside of the setting.

■ If you feel there has been a lack of action in response to suspicions you have raised about a colleague you suspect of abuse or harm.

■ If you suspect the CRB check processes are not being followed.

Did you know?

In 2009 there was a case involving a nursery worker in Plymouth who sexually abused toddlers in her care within the workplace. She took over 100 photos of her victims, which she shared with other paedophiles via the internet. It serves as a reminder that we must act if we are concerned about a colleague's practice.

Ask Miranda!

Q Does whistle-blowing only apply to concerns about deliberate harm or abuse of children or young people within the setting?

A No, it applies to any safeguarding issue. For example, you may need to report concerns about risk assessments being disregarded, or about a lack of care being taken with procedures to ensure that children and young people are collected by authorised people only.

Risks of using technologies

Full information is given in Learning outcome 1.

Confidentiality

Full information is given in Unit SHC 21, Learning outcome 5.

Link Up!

Unit SHC 21 Introduction to communication in children and young people's settings.

223

How are things going?

▶ Progress Check

1. What is the role of the following agencies in safeguarding the welfare of children and young people?
   a GPs.   b Social Services. (1.2)

2. Give five signs/symptoms of common childhood illnesses. (2.1)

3. What signs/symptoms indicate that children may need urgent medical attention? (2.3)

4. Define the following types of abuse:
   a Physical abuse.   b Sexual abuse.
   c Emotional abuse. d Neglect. (3.1)

5. Identify three key risks/possible consequences for children using the internet, mobile phones and other technology. (3.2)

6. What should you do if you are concerned that a young child who attends your setting may have been abused? (3.3)

7. What should you do if you are concerned that a colleague may be abusing a child or young person? (3.3)

8. What should you do if you are concerned that a colleague may be failing to comply with safeguarding procedures? (3.3)

9. Explain what is meant by the confidentiality term 'need to know basis'. (3.4)

Are you ready for assessment?

CACHE

Set tasks:

■ An in-depth task with two sections in which you must collect information and gather evidence that shows that you have developed an awareness of safeguardng the welfare of children and young people. This covers a broad range of knowledge, including the characteristics of child abuse and what to do in emergency situations.

You can prepare by reviewing your own setting's safeguarding policies and procedures (including child protection policies, emergency procedures and care of sick children).

City & Guilds

You must complete the mandatory Assignment 8, which has three tasks. It entails answering questions and completing tables about safeguarding requirements/procedure, responding to evidence/concerns about harm and emergency procedures (including illness). You can prepare by finding out about local current policies, procedures and guidance on the safeguarding of children and young people. (Your workplace setting will hold information about this.)

Edexcel

You may like to gather information about local current policies, procedures and guidance on the safeguarding of children and young people. (Your workplace setting will hold informaton about this.)

UNIT 2.4

Contribute to children and young people's health and safety

LEARNING OUTCOMES

The learning outcomes you will meet in this unit are:

1. Know the health and safety policies and procedures of the work setting

2. Be able to recognise risks and hazards in the work setting and during off-site visits

3. Know what to do in the event of a non-medical incident or emergency

4. Know what to do in the event of a child or young person becoming ill or injured

5. Be able to follow the work setting's procedures for reporting and recording accidents, incidents, emergencies and illnesses

6. Be able to follow infection control procedures

7. Know the work setting's procedures for receiving, storing and administering medicines

INTRODUCTION

The health and safety of children is of great importance to all practitioners. It's essential for you to learn how to establish and maintain healthy and safe services and environments for children, both indoors and outdoors.

LEARNING OUTCOME **1**

... knowing the health and safety policies and procedures of the work setting

In this section you'll learn about health and safety policies and procedures and the lines of responsibility and reporting within the setting. You'll also learn what risk assessment is and how this is managed. This links with **Assessment Criteria 1.1, 1.2, 1.3.**

Health and safety policies and procedures

Health and safety legislation and guidance is interpreted by settings in their own policies and procedures. It's important that you know about the legal requirements, and that you fully understand and follow your own setting's policies and procedures.

Health and safety legislation and guidance

Settings and practitioners must comply with the laws and regulations relevant to their home country. All of the laws and regulations referred to in this unit apply in England. However, health and safety legislation is fairly universal. You can find out more about the specifics for your home country online:

- Scotland: www.scotland.gov.uk
- Wales: www.wales.gov.uk
- Northern Ireland: www.deni.gov.uk
- England: www.direct.gov.uk

Key health and safety regulations and requirements that settings must meet
Health and Safety at Work Act 1974 and 1992

This Act is relevant to all places of employment. Employers have a duty of care to ensure that the workplace and equipment within it are in a safe condition that does not pose a **risk** to health. Employees (and volunteers) also have a responsibility to take care of themselves

key terms

Risk the likelihood of a hazard actually causing harm.

and others in cooperation with the employer. The Act also requires employers to use the basic principles of risk management – which are risk assessment, balanced control measures and training. You'll learn more about these in Learning outcome 2.

Workplace equipment must not pose a risk to health

Health and Safety (First Aid) Regulations 1981

While most settings will have several members of staff qualified to carry out first aid (and they must have at least one trained first-aider), these regulations set a minimum standard that applies to all workplaces. Employers must appoint at least one person to be a designated first-aider and keep a stocked first-aid box.

Food Safety Act 1990, and Food Handling Regulations 1995

This Act and the regulations cover how food should be prepared and stored, how food areas must be maintained, and how staff who prepare food must be trained. See Learning outcome 6 for further details.

The Control of Substances Hazardous to Health Regulations 1994 (COSHH)

Under these regulations, settings must assess which substances used on the premises are potentially hazardous to health. Practices to manage and store these safely must be devised and recorded.

Fire Precautions (Workplace) Regulations 1997

These regulations apply to all workplaces. Under the regulations, settings must carry out a fire risk assessment addressing seven key areas:

Did you know?

All settings have substances on their premises that are potentially hazardous, for example cleaning fluids that contain chemicals.

1) Fire ignition sources and risk from the spread of fire.

2) Escape routes and exits.

3) Fire detection and early warning of fire.

4) Fire-fighting equipment.

5) Fire routine training for staff.

6) Emergency plans and arrangements for calling the fire service.

7) General maintenance and testing of fire protection equipment.

You will learn more about this in Learning outcome 3.

Reporting of Injuries, Diseases and Dangerous Occurrences Regulations 1995 (RIDDOR)

Under RIDDOR regulations, workplaces must have an accident book. In addition, some types of accidents, injuries and illnesses that occur at work must be reported to the Health and Safety Executive (HSE). You will learn about this in Learning outcome 5.

Personal Protective Equipment at Work Regulations 1992

Under these regulations, employers must provide all protective equipment that their employees need in order to do their job safely. For instance, settings will provide disposable gloves and aprons to be used when dealing with bodily fluids and waste. See Learning outcome 6 for details.

Employers must provide all protective equipment needed

Protection of Children Act 1999
This law covers child protection. See Unit TDA 2.2 for details.

Children's Act 1989
This law covers equality of access and opportunity for all children, in addition to health and safety. Further details are included in Unit TDA 2.2.

Children Bill 2004
The Bill was passed to improve child protection for children and to ensure better coordination of services. You will learn more about this in Unit TDA 2.2.

Health and Safety (Young Persons) Regulations 1997
These regulations require employers to conduct special risk assessments for employees or volunteers under the age of 18, as they may be less aware of health and safety issues than more experienced workers.

Every Child Matters
Every Child Matters is the government agenda that sets out five major outcomes for all children:

1) Being healthy.
2) Staying safe.
3) Enjoying and achieving.
4) Making a positive contribution.
5) Economic well-being.

The Early Years Foundation Stage (see below) aims to meet the Every Child Matters outcomes.

The Early Years Foundation Stage Safeguarding and Welfare Requirements
Settings to which the Early Years Foundation Stage applies (see pages 297 and 301–2) must meet the EYFS safeguarding and welfare requirements. These fall into the five categories shown in Table MU2.4.1 on page 230.

▶▶Link Up!◀◀

Unit TDA 2.2 Safeguard the welfare of children and young people.

Good practice

You should note that all requirements are updated over time, and it's important that you remain well informed. This can generally be done effectively by subscribing to industry magazines and journals and regularly visiting government websites.

Did you know?

The Childcare Act 2006 was passed to introduce the Early Years Foundation Stage and to support settings in providing high-quality, integrated care and education for children aged 0–5 years. It also gave local authorities responsibility for improving outcomes for all children under five.

The Safeguarding and welfare requirements explain what providers must do to:

■ Safeguard Children.

■ Ensure the suitability of adults who have contact with children.

■ Promote good health.

■ Manage behaviour

In the introduction to the Safeguarding and welfare requirements, the EYFS tells us that children learn best:

■ When they are healthy, safe and secure.

■ When their individual needs are met.

■ When they have positive relationships with the adults caring for them.

Did you know?

It's important to remember that the Safeguarding and welfare requirements only set out the minimum standards that providers must not fall below. High quality providers will often exceed the minimum standards. For example, a da nursery may exceed the minimum staff to child ratio.

Have a go!

As part of your study towards this Unit, you are advised to read the Safeguarding and welfare requirements in full. You'll find them in Section 3 of The Statutory Framework for the EYFS, which you can download at www.foundationyears.org.uk/early-years-foundation-stage-2012.

Health and safety policies and procedures

As you have learnt, you must follow the policies and procedures at your setting, which will reflect the legal requirements.

Ask Miranda!

Q Why do settings need their own policies and procedures? Isn't knowing about the law enough?

A Regulations and requirements tell settings what standards they must meet. But generally they are not *prescriptive* – they don't tell practitioners how things should be done. It's up to settings to interpret this by devising policies that explain how they will work in line with the law and the regulations. Take the Health and Safety at Work Act for example. It says that employers must ensure that the workplace and equipment within it are in a safe condition. It doesn't tell settings how to achieve this. But the setting's health and safety policy will explain when and how equipment should be cleaned, what to do if equipment becomes damaged, etc. Sometimes, extra information is needed to explain how areas of a policy will work in action, so settings may devise additional written procedures that explain what to do in more detail.

Practical example

Stars Out of School Club interprets legislation

Stars Out of School Club mentions in its health and safety policy that suitable toys are sterilised once a month. This is one of the ways in which the club complies with legislation about health and hygiene.

A separate set of procedures gives practitioners a four-week timetable of sterilising – some of the toys get sterilised each week. The practical steps of sterilising are explained, including where to carry out the task and how to make up the sterilising solution.

Good practice

Good, clear policies and procedures are important because they communicate how the staff must work. Policies also let other professionals, parents, carers and children know how the setting operates. You must make sure that you understand all of your setting's policies, and you must work within them.

231

Key issues covered in health and safety policies

Table MU2.4.2 shows some of the key issues that will be covered within a setting's health and safety policy:

Table MU2.4.2: Key health and safety issues

Key health and safety issues likely to be covered within a health and safety policy	General details likely to be given
Registration	**Registration forms** All families must complete forms, giving children and young people's personal and medical details, before children can attend the setting. **Daily registers** All children, young people and adults attending a session must be registered on arrival and signed out on their departure.
Safeguarding procedures	What the setting does to safeguard children and young people, for instance, the use of safety equipment such as high-chair harnesses, and procedures for ensuring that young children cannot wander off the premises/older children cannot leave undetected.
Risk assessment	When risk assessment will be carried out and how often assessments will be reviewed. What staff training is given on risk assessment.
Emergency procedures	**Drills** Where the details of drills are displayed on the premises (who does what, where the meeting points are, who will call 999, etc.), and how often drills are carried out. **Maintenance of equipment** When equipment such as fire extinguishers and alarms are tested, and by whom. Where records/certificates of testing are displayed. **First aid** Who the qualified first-aider is, how they were trained, and where their certificate is displayed. How first-aid supplies are checked and replenished. The procedures for calling an ambulance and the family should a child need medical treatment urgently. **Care of sick children and young people** How sick children and young people cannot be cared for at a group setting. How arrangements will be made for the collection of sick children and young people. The procedure for calling an ambulance and the family should a child need medical treatment urgently.
Substances harmful to health	How the setting will identify substances harmful to health, and ensure their safe use and storage.
Food and drink	**Drinking water** How the setting makes water constantly available to children and young people. **Dietary requirements** How dietary requirements are met with regard to families' beliefs/religions/preferences, and regard to individual children and young people's allergies or medical requirements. **Healthy foods** How the setting will provide healthy meals and/or snacks. **Hygiene** How hygiene will be ensured with regards to food and drink preparation areas. How staff preparing food will have a Food Hygiene Certificate.
Hygiene	**Cleaning arrangements** How the setting will be kept clean and hygienic. Procedures for each room and the outdoor space may be referenced. Waste disposal. How all waste is handled and disposed of safely.
Child protection	Settings will have a separate Child and Young Person Protection Policy, but it may be referenced in the Health and Safety Policy.

Reviewing policies and procedures

Have a go!

Information and guidelines on aspects of health and safety that affect schools, including the medical needs of children, emergencies and school security, can be found at www.direct.gov.uk/en/Parents/Schoolslearninganddevelopment/YourChildsWelfareAtSchool/index.htm

Good practice

All settings and services will have established lines of responsibility and accountability. It's good practice to be familiar with the responsibilities and accountability of your colleagues as well as yourself. You'll then be clear who to go to should you have a health and safety issue to resolve.

Lines of responsibility and reporting

To ensure that no important jobs are left undone, it's crucial for all practitioners to be clear about their own responsibilities relating to health and safety in the setting. Practitioners should also have a firm understanding of their accountability in these matters. Or to put it another way, they should know who within the setting they are answerable to in relation to their responsibilities.

Risk assessment

The process of risk assessment makes settings safer places for children and young people. You'll learn about this is detail in Learning outcome 2.

FOCUS ON

... being able to recognise risks and hazards in the work setting and during off-site visits

In this section you'll learn why a safe but challenging setting is important, and the differences between risks and hazards. You'll also learn about potential hazards to health, safety and security and about contributing to risk assessments of the work setting and for off-site visits. This links with **Assessment Criteria 2.1, 2.2, 2.3, 2.4.**

Why a safe but challenging environment is important

Part of providing children with adequate challenge is permitting them to take appropriate risks. With physically active play there is always a risk of children getting hurt – most settings' accident books are likely to show regular minor playground injuries such as grazed knees and hands from children's falls while simply running. However, it would be inappropriate of practitioners not to allow children to run in case they fall and hurt themselves. In fact *not* running *would* potentially harm children, affecting their physical development, fitness, confidence and general well-being. In this case, the benefits justify the risk – and the risk is not significant. There may be a high incidence of playground injuries, but they are generally only very minor.

But it's sensible to minimise risk by making sure children have sufficient space to run around in without bumping into each other for instance. The use of apparatus such as a climbing frame is another example of an activity that has an element of risk. But practitioners take a number of steps to minimise the risk by, for instance, providing a safety surface underneath and around the apparatus, and restricting the number of children permitted on it at any one time.

Good practice

The risks that are appropriate for children and young people to take increase in intensity as they develop and grow up, and practitioners must allow for that. Remember, if children and young people are not allowed to take age-appropriate risks, they will not be sufficiently challenged.

A balanced approach to risk management

Sometimes children and young people may want to take risks that are inappropriate for safety reasons, or inappropriate for a child or young person of their age, needs or abilities. While practitioners should not be **excessively risk adverse** (prone to avoiding risk altogether), practitioners should not allow children and young people to do things that are dangerous and likely to hurt them. There's a difference between allowing children and young people to take appropriate risks that are worthwhile in terms of development when compared to the likelihood of injury, and allowing children and young people to do things that are likely to seriously hurt them or injure them without a justifiable developmental gain or experience. This is known as **excessive risk taking**.

The dilemma between rights and choices of children and young people and the health and safety requirement of a setting is explored in Unit TDA 2.16.

Young person taking an acceptable age-appropriate risk by skateboarding in full safety gear

Did you know?

If a child or young person is attracted to an activity that you consider to be too dangerous, you should consider if there's a safer, alternative way to give them a similar experience. This will be a good compromise.

key terms

Excessively risk adverse prone to avoiding risk altogether.

Excessive risk taking taking inappropriate risks.

Good practice

To decide what risks are acceptable and unacceptable and to see what can be done to minimise risk, practitioners should carry out risk assessments, as outlined on page 236. It's important that you know and understand your own setting's policies and procedures for risk assessment and that you follow them closely.

Link Up!

Unit TDA 2.16 Support children and young people's play and leisure.

Risk assessment

The process of risk assessment makes settings safer places for children and young people. However, no setting or activity can be completely safe, and as you've learnt, children and young people need to be able to take acceptable levels of risk in their play and activities, or their development will be stifled.

First steps

Good practice

Think of a child who is just starting to walk. They will fall down many times before they master the skill, and they might hurt themselves on occasion. But we wouldn't dream of stopping them from walking. It would be overreacting. The risk of injury from a fall is acceptable when a child is learning to walk. But we may decide to take some steps to reduce the chance of injury. Perhaps we will move the rug that they might slip on, and make sure there is plenty of clear floor space for example. Risk assessment is simply a formal version of this process.

What needs to be risk assessed?

Settings need to risk assess:

- premises both indoors and outdoors

- the activities that they plan

- any off-site visits planned.

What are hazards and risks?

Hazards

A **hazard** is the actual item or situation that may cause harm. Potential hazards are all around us in the world, and include the following:

- Physical hazards, for example unsafe objects, things that may be tripped over.

- Security hazards, for example insecure exits and windows.

- Fire hazards, for example heaters, electrical appliances.

key terms

Hazard an item or situation that may cause harm.

- Food safety hazards, for example faulty refrigerator, unsafe produce.

- Personal safety hazards, for example stranger danger, busy roads.

Risks

A risk is *likelihood* of the hazard actually causing harm. For example, whenever we walk along the pavement, road traffic (a significant potential hazard) is very close to us. But the likelihood of being harmed by traffic in this situation is low.

Identify potential hazards to health, safety and security and contribute to risk assessments

An older child preparing for the thrill of the zip wire

Part of your role is to contribute to the risk assessment process at your setting. This will soon become a very routine part of your role.

How to risk assess

There are six key risk assessment steps to follow:

1) **Identify hazards**. Remember that a *hazard* is the actual item or situation that may cause harm – a stack of chairs for instance.

2) **Decide on the level of risk posed by the hazards – low, medium or high**. The *risk* is the likelihood of the hazard causing harm. How 'risky' would you rate the stack of chairs? It would all depend on the circumstances. A stack of chairs in a baby and toddler room would be high risk. It's likely that a child will pull themselves up on the chairs, causing the chairs to tumble. A young child could be badly injured.

3) **Evaluate the risks**. What measures, if any, could/should be taken to minimise or remove the risk? Are there any safety precautions already in place? If so, are they adequate? Is the risk acceptable given the ages, needs and abilities of the children? What levels of supervision will be required? Consider the benefits of activities against the potential for harm. Finally, decide if the risk can be taken.

4) **If measures are to be taken to minimise or remove the risk, they should be carried out at this stage.** In our example, we can either remove the chairs from the room altogether, or simply unstack them. The risk is then removed.

5) **Record your assessment**. You should record the whole process and note your findings. Detail any measures you have taken, and enter the date. You should also set a date on which the risk assessment should be reviewed.

6) **Monitor the risk assessment and review it at a later date**. Monitoring the risk assessment means paying attention to how effective your measures are in practice. If the level of risk is still unacceptable, you should revise the assessment immediately (see below).

Also see the information on monitoring changing levels of risk in Unit TDA 2.16 on page 502.

Unit TDA 2.16 Support children and young people's play and leisure.

Risk assessments must be done on the premises

Good practice

Practitioners review risk assessments regularly in line with the setting's policies. They must also reassess if there are significant changes to premises or activities that impact on the original assessment. All reviews must be signed and dated.

Considering stages of development

A sound knowledge of child development will help you when you are carrying out risk assessments and planning security arrangements. You will be able to consider how aware children are of danger at various ages, their skill levels, and the things they are likely to do – pulling themselves up on a chair for example. Examples of this are given in Table MU2.4.3.

Unit TDA 2.1 Child and young person development.

Table MU2.4.3: Development indicators for planning health, safety and security arrangements

Approximate age	Development indicator	Implications for health, safety and security arrangements	Measures to be taken
4–5 months	Will roll from their back to their side	May roll when on a high changing unit	Use units with side bars and anticipate that baby may roll
6 months	Fascinated by small toys within reaching distance, grabbing them with the whole hand	Will pick up objects within their reach independently. This could include safety hazards such as sharp objects, unsafe substances and small objects which present a choking hazard	Ensure that nothing unsuitable is left in the vicinity of the baby
9 months	Starts to crawl and pull itself up to standing position	Crawling means a baby may independently move anywhere – to the stairs for instance. Standing up gives access to a whole new level – may be able to reach heaters, etc.	Install safety equipment such as stair gates, socket covers, cupboard locks, heater guards. Assess safety of the objects now on the baby's new level. Baby may pull objects on to themselves, and push less sturdy items of furniture over
15 months	Walking alone. Explores objects using trial and error	May want to walk alone instead of riding in a buggy when out and about. May wander off to explore	Use reins for safety. Supervise carefully on the stairs
2 years	Runs safely. Starting to understand consequences of own behaviour	May disappear from sight quickly	Keep a close eye on child's whereabouts. Be prepared to deal with more minor grazes and bumps
3 years	Walks upstairs, one foot on each step. Rides tricycle. Children are impulsive. May resent adults limiting their behaviour. Asks lots of questions	Learning to use stairs without supervision. May suddenly do something dangerous on impulse, like jump from a slide. May be reluctant to heed safety warnings	Ensure there is a handrail of appropriate height on stairs. Give child safety information as appropriate. Be prepared to be firm on matters of safety. ('No means no')
4 years	Climbs play equipment. May confuse fantasy and reality	Uses bigger, higher equipment. May become engrossed in fantasy play and forget the safety limits of the real world. (We cannot fly, even if we jump from somewhere high)	Ensure safety playground covering is suitable for the higher equipment. Gently remind about safety limits if necessary, but try not to disturb imaginary play unnecessarily
5 years	Balances on beam. Greater levels of independence achieved	Will want less adult support	Encourage child to think about their own safety for themselves
6–7 years	Rides a bicycle, makes running jumps. Increasingly mature	Spends more time alone at home, playing in the bedroom or garden perhaps, or riding bike on own street if it is in a residential area	Continue to support awareness of safety. Ensure cycle helmet is worn

Approximate age	Development indicator	Implications for health, safety and security arrangements	Measures to be taken
8–11 years	Rides scooters, bigger bicycles and skateboards/skates. May play sports. Increasingly independent	May ride a bicycle on the road. Goes out to play with friends without adult supervision. Children become more aware of risks, but may misjudge their abilities. May cross local roads alone	Continue to support awareness of safety. Ensure that helmets and padding designed for safety are used with skateboards, etc. Ensure that children have access to safe, good-quality sports equipment, and encourage them to warm up/cool down before/after sports. Ensure that children learn road safety (and cycle safety if appropriate)
11 onwards	Independence grows as children enter teenage years, and time spent unsupervised by adults increases greatly. Peer pressure may affect young people, and they may experiment with new experiences	Often, young people will not have an accompanying adult to point out risks to them, and they may not have an adult to turn to if they are in an unsafe or difficult situation. Children may try alcohol, drugs (including cigarettes) and engage in sexual behaviour	Ensure that children/young people can recognise risks for themselves. Teach them what to do when hazards occur (role plays, quizzes and moral dilemma games can all be used for this purpose). Teach children/young people about the dangers of alcohol and drugs. Support young people who ask questions about relationships and sex

Cupboard safety locks

Unit TDA 2.16 Support children and young people's play and leisure.

Levels of supervision

For information about safe levels of supervision and appropriate deployment of staff, see Unit TDA 2.16, pages 501–2.

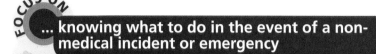

FOCUS ON

... knowing what to do in the event of a non-medical incident or emergency

In this section you'll learn about non-medical incidents and emergencies that may occur in the work setting, and how to respond to certain emergency situations. This links with **Assessment Criteria 3.1, 3.2.**

Non-medical incidents and emergencies

Non-medical incidents and emergencies can occur in the work setting at any time, and the policies and procedures for responding to them are hugely important. They can literally mean the difference between life and death should a serious situation occur.

Good practice

It's crucial that you spend plenty of time familiarising yourself with the emergency procedures of your setting or service, as this will help you to recall how to respond should an emergency occur. It's reassuring to know procedures inside out, and it will help you to think clearly if you suddenly find yourself under pressure to take the appropriate action.

Types of non-medical incident and emergency

A range of incidents and emergencies may occur in the setting, some of which require an emergency evacuation of the setting. Key examples are shown on the diagram on page 242.

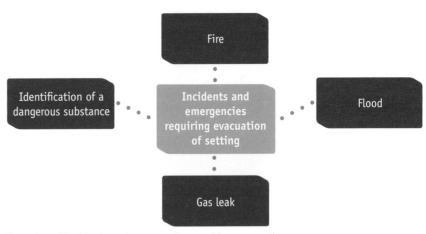

Examples of incidents and emergencies requiring evacuation

Responding to incidents and emergencies

To ensure that premises can be evacuated effectively in an emergency, it's essential that:

- **all staff know how to raise the alarm, where the exit points are, and where the assembly point is**

- **all staff are aware of their individual roles**, such as taking the register, dialling 999, checking rooms are empty

- **there are regular opportunities to practise evacuation drills.** These should be taken seriously, and any difficulties should be resolved. The sound of the alarm may upset some children or young people, so be sensitive, and help them to settle after the drill

- **evacuation drill notices are displayed for visitors to refer to.** These should give details of where the fire extinguishing equipment is kept

- **fire alarms, smoke detectors and emergency lighting should be checked regularly and maintained. Staff should know where they are and be trained in their use.** Details of checks should be recorded in the setting's evacuation log

- **emergency exits are not obstructed.**

How to call for help

For details of how to call for help and calling the emergency services, see Learning outcome 2 of Unit PEFAP 001.

Unit PEFAP 001 Paediatric emergency first aid.

Security

Settings must make suitable security arrangements in the interests of the children's safety. There should be clear procedures for children's arrival at the setting, their departure from the setting, and their security when on outings.

Arrivals and departures

All settings must keep a record of the children and adults who are in attendance at each session. This is known as keeping a register. In addition, a record of when children arrive and leave must also be kept. Some settings may keep a signing in/out book for this purpose, while others may include this information on their register document. Whatever the arrangement at your setting, it is essential that children are signed in as soon as they arrive, and marked out as soon as they leave. Otherwise there may be serious consequences in an emergency situation, as the Practical examples below show.

Did you know?

One person often takes responsibility for overseeing evacuation procedures and fire safety.

Fire drill at a school

Practical example

The importance of registers

Scenario 1

There is a fire at an out-of-school club and the building is evacuated. Outside in the playground, the register is taken. All children seem to be present. However, a practitioner forgot to mark a child in on the register when the child arrived. They are unaccounted for, and when the fire crew arrives no one knows to alert them that a child is missing and presumed to be inside.

Scenario 2

There is a fire at an out-of-school club and the building is evacuated. Outside in the playground, the register is taken. One child is found to be missing. The fire crew that arrives is alerted that a child is missing and presumed to be inside. A firefighter goes into the burning building to search for them. But in fact, the child has already been collected, and a practitioner has forgotten to mark the child out on the register on their departure.

If a child fails to arrive

For many settings, if a child does not arrive, then it is generally no cause for concern. The child is not the responsibility of the provider until their parent or carer brings them along. However, this is different for after-school clubs. If a child who has been booked in does not turn up, practitioners must quickly find out their whereabouts. It is helpful to bear in mind that a club may be:

■ based within a school, or

■ based elsewhere, in which case club escorts will be collecting children from school and then taking them to the club premises. The escorts will need to deal with the situation if children they are expecting to collect do not appear.

Staff should contact the parent or carer to find out if other arrangements have been made for the child's care. Frequently in these events, parents have forgotten to cancel a place that they no longer need. It often helps the situation if a practitioner can talk with the child's teacher to find out if the child was absent from school or if they saw who collected the child. It may be the case that a parent has rung the school to let them know that their child is off sick, but they have forgotten to let the club know. If a child did not attend school and a parent has not called either the school or the club, it may mean that the child went missing early in the morning on their way to school, and so contacting parents is still a matter of urgency to confirm the child's whereabouts.

Good practice

Written procedures for non-arrival are helpful for out-of-school club practitioners to refer to in these often complicated circumstances. It is also important that practitioners at all settings are aware who is authorised to collect each child. This information must be held on the registration form.

Do not forget to mark children's arrival and departure on the register

Security during sessions

During sessions practitioners must ensure that children do not leave the setting unattended, and that visitors cannot gain entry without detection. The indoor and outdoor premises must be secure. The way in which this is achieved depends entirely on the building and the age and stage of development of the children. However, fire exits must always be unobstructed, and the method of opening the door to escape must be quick and easy. Many settings fit an alarm to fire doors so that practitioners are alerted immediately if a child opens an outside door.

Off-site visits

On off-site visits (or in other words, outings or trips), settings need to take extra care with regard to safety and security. The lead practitioner on the trip will carry out a detailed risk assessment as part of their preparation.

It's important to ensure that the staff-to-child ratio is sufficiently high to enable the increased supervision that's necessary. Practitioners must take the children's ages, needs and abilities into consideration, as well as regulations. It is usual practice to split the children into small groups or pairs, and assign one or more adults to take care of each group/pair. This is particularly useful when children are walking around in a public place, from one location to another, even though the whole group may join in activities together on arrival. Whenever you change location, enter a building, or get on or

> **Did you know?**
>
> Before embarking on a trip, the lead practitioner will talk with children and staff about safety and security. The risk assessment made will inform this. It's reassuring to know that the safety information is fresh in everyone's minds.

Off-site visits need extra care

off transport, count the children *twice* in case of a miscount. It's good practice for more than one practitioner to count, so that you have double-checked that everyone is present before you move off.

Missing child procedures

All registered settings must have written procedures addressing what practitioners should do if a child is missing. You should know and understand these procedures as in such an emergency it is important to act quickly.

In most situations it would be appropriate to organise a full initial search of the setting, including outdoor areas, and to check when the child was last seen. If the child cannot be found, the search should be widened to the local area. The person in charge should raise the alarm, contacting police and the missing child's parents or carers. Later, if the setting or service is registered, the regulatory body of the home country (for example Ofsted in England) should also be informed. Sufficient staff must stay on the premises to care for the remaining children, but surplus staff may join the search. Police will take charge of the search when they arrive.

Good practice

Practitioners should log events in the setting's incident book while they are fresh in their mind. There will need to be an urgent review of the setting's security.

Ask Miranda!

Q I'm worried about how I'd cope in an emergency. What if my mind just goes blank?

A No one can be 100 per cent sure how they'd cope should one of the emergency situations we've been discussing happens in real life. But it helps to know you are well prepared. Read your setting's policies and procedures carefully, and ask questions if you are unsure of your role. Regular drills are also an enormous help. The procedures you need to follow will become second nature, so it's unlikely that you would forget them. If you are still worried, you may like to look for a course on managing incidents and emergencies as part of your personal development. The more you understand the issues, the more confident you're likely to feel.

FOCUS ON

... knowing what to do in the event of a child or young person becoming ill or injured

In this section you'll learn about the signs and symptoms that may indicate that a child or young person is injured or unwell, and about circumstances when children or young people may need urgent medical attention. You'll also learn about your own roles and responsibilities in the event of a child or young person requiring urgent medical attention. This links with **Assessment Criteria 4.1, 4.2, 4.3.**

Signs and symptoms of injury or illness

For common signs and symptoms, see Learning outcome 2 of Unit TDA 2.2.

When medical attention is needed

Some minor conditions can be effectively managed by a first-aider. But sometimes when a child or young person is ill or injured, they need emergency or urgent medical attention. Getting this for them in time can literally make the difference between life and death. So it's crucial that all practitioners know the signs and symptoms that indicate when emergency or urgent medical attention is needed, and how to get it.

Link Up!

Unit TDA 2.2 Safeguard the welfare of children and young people.

Did you know?

Babies and young children will not have the language to tell you when they are unwell, so you will need to rely on your ability to recognise the signs. Older children and young people will normally explain what's wrong, but remember that they may be so unwell that they are unable to do so, or the nature of the problem may prevent them.

Emergency medical attention

Any of the following signs and symptoms of illness indicate that an ambulance should be called for emergency medical attention:

- Breathing difficulties including an asthma attack that doesn't respond to the use of inhaler.

- Child/young person is unconscious or cannot easily or fully be roused from sleep or a state of drowsiness.

- Baby becomes unresponsive and/or their body seems to be floppy.

- Significant change in the usual level of alertness or in behaviour (for example withdrawn, agitated, confused).

- Child/young person seems to be in severe pain (especially if it's worsening).

- Seizures/convulsions/fits (including if a child or young person who is known to have epilepsy becomes unconscious).

- Meningitis symptoms: severe headache that may be accompanied by a stiff neck or a dislike of light, a purple or red rash that remains (does not fade) when pressed with a glass, fever/high temperature, unusual, high-pitched crying in babies.

- After a head injury: confusion, vomiting, headache, problems with vision, wobbling/unsteadiness.

- Wounds that won't stop bleeding.

- Burns and scalds.

- Grey, blue or purple appearance to skin/lips.

- Vomiting blood or coughing up blood.

- Eating or drinking any poisonous substance.

- Swelling of mouth/throat and itchy raised lumps on skin.

- Dehydration symptoms: passing little urine, sunken features, lethargic (babies in particular can become very ill).

Signs of frostbite (this develops especially quickly in babies; see page 398).

Signs of heat exhaustion (this develops especially quickly in babies; see page 400).

Any other condition that gives rise to serious concern that an ambulance may be needed – *if in doubt, dial 999*.

Urgent medical attention

The following signs and symptoms of illness indicate that urgent medical attention is needed:

Severe vomiting or diarrhoea.

Vomiting or diarrhoea that persists for over 24 hours.

Very high temperature or temperature that cannot be lowered.

Will not drink fluids – this is most worrying in babies.

Cuts that may need stitches.

Severe bruising.

Animal/human bites where the skin has been broken.

Bites or stings in which swelling or redness spreads, or which cause a child to feel unwell.

Puncture wounds if caused by an object that gives cause for concern (for example a rusty nail or needle).

Difficulty using arms or legs, especially after a fall.

Any other condition that gives rise to serious concern that urgent medical attention may be needed – *if in doubt, get help*.

Information on how to call for help is given in Learning outcome 2 of Unit PEFAP 001. Information on when to call for help in responding to first-aid incidents such as choking or fractures is given throughout Units PEFAP 001 and MPII 002.

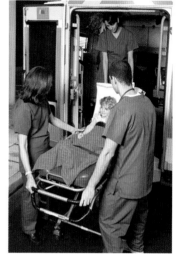

An ambulance may need to be called

Unit PEFAP 001 Paediatric emergency first aid.

Unit MPII 002 Managing paediatric illness and injury.

Your roles and responsibilities

What you need to do if a child or young person becomes ill or injured depends on both the setting's policies and procedures and the individual circumstances. Usually, a person qualified to Level 3 or above will take responsibility for managing the situation when a child or young person becomes ill or injured. This includes administering first aid.

But you still need to be confident that you know what to do because:

- you will need to recognise the signs and symptoms so that you know when to call for the appropriate person in the setting to help

- you will need to know how to assist and follow instructions. This may include calling for emergency or urgent medical attention, or contacting parents/carers

- you may be in a situation where you have to take lead responsibility yourself (for example if the qualified practitioner is ill or injured themselves, if you and some of the children are separated from others during an emergency such as a fire, or if you are babysitting and in sole charge of children).

After the event

When the situation has ended, you should make notes about it in preparation for contributing to recording and reporting procedures. You'll learn about these in Learning outcome 5.

LEARNING OUTCOME 5

FOCUS ON

... being able to follow the work setting's procedures for reporting and recording accidents, incidents, emergencies and illnesses

In this section you'll learn about the reporting procedures in work settings. You'll also learn about completing the associated workplace documentation. This links with **Assessment Criteria 5.1, 5.2.**

Reporting procedures

Settings must have clear written procedures for recording and reporting all:

- accidents
- injuries
- incidents
- emergencies
- illnesses.

Injuries, accidents and illnesses

The Health and Safety Executive

Settings have a duty to report some injuries and accidents and certain illnesses (diseases) to the Health and Safety Executive (HSE). This applies to injuries and illnesses affecting staff as well as the children and young people. Major injuries must be reported, such as:

- fractures, other than to fingers, thumbs and toes
- dislocation of the shoulder, hip, knee or spine
- loss of sight (temporary or permanent).

Reportable diseases include some skin diseases and infections such as:

- hepatitis
- tuberculosis
- tetanus.

Settings must also report any 'over-three-day injuries'. An over-three-day injury is one that occurs at the setting and is not major but results in the injured person being unable to attend the setting as normal for more than three days. Any deaths that occur at a setting must also be reported.

Regulatory body

Settings must follow the requirements of their home country's regulatory body (for example Ofsted), who will also need to be notified of deaths or serious accidents, injuries or illnesses. There may

Have a go!

You can find out more about the reporting requirements by visiting www.hse.gov.uk/riddor/what-must-i-report.htm

be an investigation in certain circumstances, and guidance to follow may be issued to the setting.

Child protection agencies

In accordance with local guidelines, child protection agencies will also be informed of deaths or serious accidents or injuries to children and young people. Guidance that should be followed may be issued to the setting.

Incidents

Your setting will have a policy on what types of incident that occur in the setting must be reported. This is likely to include:

- bullying

- fighting

- children physically harming others (for example biting, which in the case of an early years setting will not usually be regarded as 'bullying')

- other aspects of socially inappropriate behaviour (for example racist comments)

- incidents that give rise to concern for a child's welfare

- significant damage to property or premises

- security breaches

- any other emergencies that occur.

The key areas covered in the report are shown in the diagram below:

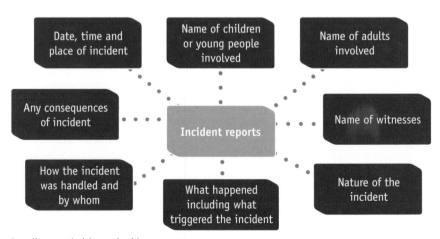

Details recorded in an incident report

Emergency equipment and evacuation drills

Also required is a log of when checks are carried out to ensure that the fire safety features of the setting are in good working order. This includes fire alarms and smoke detectors. A log of when emergency evacuation drills are carried out is also required.

If you are required to contribute to a report

Your setting will ask you to contribute to a report if you are involved in or you witness an accident, incident or emergency. So as soon as possible after the event you should make your own notes, while events are fresh in your mind. You will then have all of the information you'll need ready to contribute to a report. You should note:

■ what you saw, including what triggered the incident or accident. If you didn't see the trigger, note how you became involved, for example: 'The team leader came into the kitchen where I was preparing lunches and asked me to come and help her in the playground urgently'

■ what you did

■ who else was involved and what they did

■ who witnessed what you have described.

Regular checks are carried out to ensure safety features are in good working order

Completing workplace documentation

Settings must keep a record of illness, accidents and incidents that occur.

Illnesses

When a child or young person becomes ill at a setting, the practitioner should record the time and date, and describe the signs and symptoms of illness. They should record their response to the child or young person's condition, making a note of details such as temperature readings, if appropriate. The parent or carer should be asked to sign the record.

Incidents, accidents and emergencies

Practitioners must record the time, date, location and circumstances. Details of any injuries must also be recorded along any action taken, including first-aid treatment. The parent or carer and the practitioner who dealt with incident/accident must sign the log.

Medication log

A medication log must also be kept (see page 261).

Did you know?

Your setting may also have additional procedures for practitioners to report illnesses, accidents and incidents to managers or to the setting's committee. If so, you should follow your organisational policies

LEARNING OUTCOME 6

FOCUS ON

... being able to follow infection control procedures

In this section you'll learn about the procedures for infection control. You'll also learn about the personal protective clothing for preventing the spread of infection, and how to use it. Lastly, you'll learn how to wash and dry hands to avoid the spread of infection, and you'll find out about safe waste disposal. This links with **Assessment Criteria 6.1, 6.2, 6.3, 6.4, 6.5**.

Procedures for infection control

Routine cleaning

All areas of settings must be kept clean and hygienic at all times. Jobs such as hoovering, sweeping and mopping floors should be carried out at the end of each day, before the setting up of activities and resources for the following day. It's also important to dust regularly – this is often done with a damp cloth to prevent dust flying around as it is a common allergen for those with asthma. Attention should be paid to skirting boards, which can be dust traps and are in the reach of children.

You should follow your setting's full procedures for keeping the environment clean and hygienic. However, some special considerations for key areas are outlined in Table MU2.4.4 below.

Table MU2.4.4: Special considerations for keeping key areas clean and hygienic

Area	Special considerations
Kitchen	<ul><li>Food storage, preparation and cooking facilities, equipment and utensils must be kept scrupulously clean – this includes cookers, microwaves and fridges.</li><li>Work surfaces to be wiped with a disinfectant spray before and after each use.</li><li>Cloths to be kept scrupulously clean and to be replaced as necessary.</li><li>Separate equipment and utensils to be used for raw meat (e.g. dedicated chopping board and knife).</li><li>See also 'safe waste disposal' on pages 259–60.</li></ul>
Toilet/bathroom areas	<ul><li>To be cleaned daily with a disinfectant agent, which should be rinsed/wiped off after use in areas accessible to children.</li><li>In-between times, areas should be cleaned as necessary – toilets and sinks may both need attention during the day.</li><li>See also 'safe waste disposal' on pages 259–60.</li></ul>
Play rooms	<ul><li>A cover should be used for floors and tables to protect them during messy play and activities, and to make cleaning up afterwards easier. All traces of paint, modelling clay, cooking ingredients, etc. should be cleaned away without delay when play/activities are finished.</li><li>Tables, etc. should be wiped daily at the end of the session before resources are set up again for the next play session.</li><li>See also 'safe waste disposal' on pages 259–60.</li></ul>
Eating areas	<ul><li>Tables should be wiped with a disinfectant spray before and after each use. The floor should be cleaned as appropriate after each meal/snack, to remove food remains.</li></ul>

Area	Special considerations
Sleep rooms	■ Cots, beds, mattresses and bedding should be kept clean and hygienic at all times, with bedding changed in-between each child. If a child wets or soils a cot or bed, it must be fully cleaned with disinfectant, which should then be wiped/rinsed off.
Outside areas	■ Playgrounds and paths should be swept regularly, and hosed down as necessary. Lawns should be well cared for. Following a daily visual check, any inappropriate matter (e.g. animal faeces, berries dropped by birds, litter) must be disposed of safely and the area cleaned with disinfectant if appropriate.

Keeping equipment and materials safe and hygienic

You should carefully check and evaluate the condition of materials and equipment as you set it out and as it is tidied away. Worn or broken equipment or materials can pose a hazard to safety. When plastic breaks there may be sharp edges, or wood may splinter. Remove any worn or broken items from the play space, and report the condition to the appropriate person within your setting.

You should also check that resources are in a hygienic condition. Settings will have established a schedule for washing or sterilising appropriate materials and equipment. However, you may notice that resources need cleaning in interim periods. (Feeding equipment, nappy-changing equipment and baby toys will need cleaning every time they are used.) The process of cleaning gives practitioners a further opportunity to check that equipment is in a safe condition.

Good practice

Remember to check the condition of large pieces of equipment and furniture, which may stay in one place within the setting. This includes swings, slides, tables, chairs, bookcases and cots.

Preventing cross-infection

Good standards of hygiene are the key to preventing disease and the spread of infection. Cross-infection occurs when germs are passed from one affected person or material to another previously unaffected person or material. Settings should have written guidelines covering the prevention of cross-infection through the safe handling of body fluids (blood, urine, faeces and saliva) and other waste. This is necessary because waste products are a source of germs. An example of this is the risk of infection from blood-borne viruses. This includes hepatitis B, hepatitis C and HIV (human immunodeficiency virus).

Many practitioners get immunised against hepatitis B

Good practice

It's recommended that practitioners become immunised against hepatitis B. You can talk to your GP about this. This involves three injections given in the arm. There is currently no vaccine against HIV or hepatitis C. However, the viruses can only be transmitted through an exchange of body fluids. Such an exchange could happen within a setting if an affected person's blood makes contact with a practitioner's blood, through a cut or graze on the practitioner's hand for example. But if you follow good-practice guidelines and take sensible precautions, you will not need to be overly anxious.

Food hygiene

Food hygiene is essential for the prevention of food poisoning. Food must be stored safely, prepared and cooked safely, and food areas must be kept hygienically. See the basic food safety section of Unit MU 2.8, Learning outcome 4 for further information.

Personal protective clothing

Your setting will provide the personal protective clothing that you need for your role. It's your responsibility to wear it. This will include two very important items that are worn frequently:

- Disposable vinyl gloves.
- Disposable plastic aprons.

Use of personal protective clothing

You must wear personal protective clothing when:

- changing nappies
- toileting children
- giving first aid or when in contact with a child who is vomiting
- cleaning up any bodily fluids
- handling soiled items such as children's clothes or used plasters.

For information on the use of personal protective clothing in a first-aid situation, see Learning outcome 1 in Unit PEFAP 001.

Link Up!

Unit MU 2.8 Contribute to the support of positive environments for children and young people.

Did you know?

In settings, a separate dedicated laundry facility must be provided. Any soiled linen must be washed on its own on the hottest wash suitable for the fabric. Gloves and an apron should be worn when handling it. Soiled children's clothing should be placed in a sealed plastic bag and sent home. It should not be rinsed through at the setting.

Link Up!

Unit PEFAP 001 Paediatric emergency first aid.

Washing and drying hands

We wash our hands regularly as part of cross-infection control. One of the most effective measures you can take is to ensure that you wash them thoroughly each time, and teach children and young people to do the same. The following diagram is from the NHS 'Clean your hands' campaign.

NHS

Hand-washing technique with soap and water

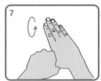

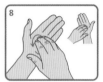

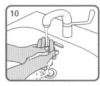
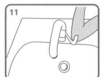

1 Wet hands with water	2 Apply enough soap to cover all hand surfaces
3 Rub hands palm to palm	4 Rub back of each hand with palm of other hand with fingers interlaced
5 Rub palm to palm with fingers interlaced	6 Rub with back of fingers to opposing palms with fingers interlocked
7 Rub each thumb clasped in opposite hand using a rotational movement	8 Rub tips of fingers in opposite palm in a circular motion
9 Rub each wrist with opposite hand	10 Rinse hands with water
11 Use elbow to turn off tap	12 Dry thoroughly with a single-use towel

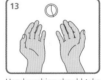

13 Hand washing should take 15–30 seconds

cleanyour**hands**®
campaign

NHS
National Patient Safety Agency

© Crown copyright 2007 283373 1p 1k Sep07

Adapted from World Health Organization *Guidelines on Hand Hygiene in Health Care*

Hand-washing guide from the NHS 'Clean your hands' campaign

If the taps cannot be turned off with the arm, it's advised that if possible you cover your hand with a paper towel when turning them off, to avoid recontamination from germs.

Personal hygiene checklist

You must always remember to do the following:

Wash your hands as directed on page 258 before and after handling or eating food, before and after first aid or caring for a sick child, after going to the toilet/toileting children/changing nappies, after coming into contact with bodily fluids (including wiping children's noses) and after handling animals.

Cover the mouth and nose with a tissue when coughing or sneezing and encourage children to do the same. Wash hands afterwards.

Safe waste disposal

When dealing with waste you should ensure that:

there are designated areas for covered bins

there are covered bins kept specifically for different types of waste, including domestic waste and clinical waste items containing body fluids

items containing body waste, such as nappies, dressings and used gloves, are disposed of in a sealed bag, which is placed into a sealed bin for disposal

sharps must be discarded straight away in a sharps bin that conforms to safety standards. This will normally be wall mounted and must be out of the reach of the children

bins are emptied daily

you always put on disposable vinyl gloves before dealing with any body fluids and before you begin first-aid treatment. You may also wear a disposable apron. Wash your hands well with antiseptic soap afterwards (and before you approach a first-aid casualty if possible)

you cover any cuts or grazes on your hands with a waterproof dressing

you cover blood with a one per cent hypochlorite solution before wiping it up

■ you teach children and young people good hygiene procedures. Make sure they wash their hands after going to the toilet and before eating or preparing food. Teach them to cover their mouths and noses when they cough and sneeze, and make sure they dispose of tissues in the bin. Adults must do these things too! Make sure you wash your hands with antiseptic soap after wiping a child's nose.

LEARNING OUTCOME 7

FOCUS ON

... knowing the work setting's procedures for receiving, storing and administering medicines

In this section you'll learn about the procedures of the work setting governing the receipt, storage and administration of medicines. You'll also learn how these procedures protect children, young people and practitioners. This links with **Assessment Criteria 7.1, 7.2.**

Medicines

Some children and young people may take medication regularly to treat conditions they have. For instance:

■ A baby with asthma may use inhalers.

■ A child with ADHD may take tablets.

■ A young person with eczema may use creams.

■ Other children and young people may need to take medication that was prescribed to treat an illness that they have now recovered from. For instance, a child may have been ill for several days and absent from the setting. But when there are well enough to return, they may still need to finish a course of antibiotics.

A baby with asthma may use inhalers

Did you know?

Some medicine needs to be kept in a refrigerator.

Receipt and storage of medicines

Parents need to give written consent for the medication belonging to their child or young person to be administered by the setting. The name of the medication, the dosage, when medication should be given and by whom, should all be recorded in the setting's medication log. The medication should be clearly labelled with the child or young person's name, and it should be kept in a safe, appropriate place. The member of staff who receives the medication will sign the log to confirm it was handed over to them.

Administration of medicines

Settings will have strict but differing policies about the way in which medicine is stored and administered, and these must be followed. You should be shown how to administer medication such as inhalers if you are required to administer them. Make sure you are confident about how to administer the particular type of medicine. If you are in any doubt at all, ask for help or clarification rather than make an error. In some settings, older children and young people may keep their own inhalers close at hand – this will depend on the policy of individual settings.

Record keeping

The member of staff who administers medication (and, if applicable, their supervising colleague) will sign the medication log, confirming the time and the dosage administered to the child. When the child is collected, the parent will be asked to inspect the log and sign it. Any remaining medicine will be returned, and the parent and member of staff will confirm in the log that it has changed hands.

How procedures protect children, young people and practitioners

The procedures we've discussed protect children, young people and practitioners by helping to ensure that:

- no medication is given without parental consent
- medication is not given without serious regard to health and safety
- the right medication is given to the right child
- the right dose is administered at the right time
- medication is stored appropriately, which prevents it from perishing
- there is a record of medication taken should it be needed for medical purposes (for example if a child is taken ill)
- there are no allegations of missing medication because there is a record of when medication changes hands between the parent and the setting.

Did you know?

Often, one practitioner will administer medication under the supervision of a colleague. This ensures that two people check the dosage, etc.

Good practice

Your setting will have a policy about who is authorised to administer medication. This may be limited to Level 3 qualified staff and/ or trained first-aiders. So you may not be authorised to administer medication in your role.

How are things going?

▶ Progress Check

1. What are 'lines of responsibility'? (1.2)

2. Why is a safe but challenging environment important? (2.1)

3. Explain the stages to follow when carrying out a risk assessment. (2.2, 2.4)

4. What non-medical incidents and emergencies may occur within a setting? (3.1)

5. Explain how to respond to emergencies in your setting. (3.2)

6. Give five signs/symptoms that indicate that:
   a a child needs emergency medical attention
   b a child needs urgent medical attention. (4.1, 4.2)

7. What workplace documents need to be completed when there is an accident, illness, emergency or incident? (5.2)

8. In what circumstances should you wear personal protective clothing to prevent the spread of infection? (6.1, 6.2, 6.3)

9. What are the usual procedures for the following?
   a The receipt of medication.
   b The storage of medication.
   c The administration of medication. (7.1)

Are you ready for assessment?

Learning Outcomes 2, 5 and 6 must be assessed in real a work environment.

CACHE

Set tasks:

■ An in-depth task with four sections in which you produce information that shows that you understand your role in contributing to children and young people's health and safety.

You can prepare by ensuring that you fully understand the duty of care requirements of your specific job role. It will be helpful to refer to a job description and the setting's health and safeguarding policies.

City & Guilds

You can prepare for assessment by reviewing your workplace setting's health and safety and safeguarding policies, to ensure you fully understand the role of practitioners.

Edexcel

You may like to collect together risk assessment documents that you have completed in the workplace, to use as evidence.

TDA 2.9

Support children and young people's positive behaviour

LEARNING OUTCOMES

The learning outcomes you will meet in this unit are:

1 Know the policies and procedures of the setting for promoting children and young people's positive behaviour

2 Be able to support positive behaviour

3 Be able to respond to inappropriate behaviour

INTRODUCTION

This unit has close links to Learning outcome 4 of Unit MU 2.2 Contribute to the support of child and young person development. You are advised to reread this information as part of your study of this unit.

FOCUS ON

... knowing the policies and procedures of the setting for promoting children and young people's positive behaviour

In this section you'll learn about the relevant policies and procedures of settings. You'll also learn about the importance of all staff applying boundaries and rules consistently and fairly, in accordance with the policies and procedures of settings. This links with **Assessment Criteria 1.1, 1.2.**

Link Up!

Unit MU 2.2 Contribute to the support of child and young person development.

Policies and procedures

You were introduced to behaviour policies in Unit MU 2.2, Learning outcome 4. Clear behaviour policies and procedures – which may include codes of conduct – are beneficial to a range of people, as shown on the diagram below.

Policies and procedures should promote the setting's overall:

■ values

■ ethics

■ aims.

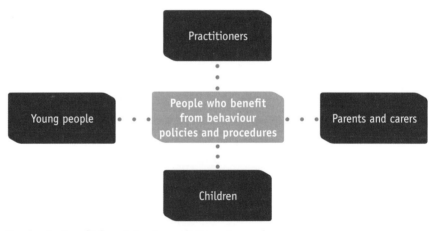

People who benefit from behaviour policies and procedures

Staff code of conduct

A staff code of conduct outlines how practitioners should conduct themselves as they go about their general duties. Conduct is particularly relevant when it comes to the issue of behaviour:

- Practitioners are behaviour role models for children and young people. It's important for adults to model the behaviour they'd like to see, for example showing respect for others, being kind and considerate.

- Fairness is important. When it comes to rewarding positive behaviour and dealing with inappropriate behaviour, all children must be treated equally.

- Consistency is important. If a consistent approach to dealing with **inappropriate behaviour** is lacking, children will become confused and behaviour development will be affected.

- Inappropriate behaviour sometimes tries adult's patience, causes frustration or offends. Practitioners need to stay calm and professional. Inappropriate behaviour sometimes calls for a firm approach, but getting angry or annoyed is inappropriate and it will make the situation worse.

- Practitioners must be careful to only ever use strategies and sanctions accepted by the setting to deal with inappropriate behaviour. This helps to promote fairness and consistency. It also ensures that inappropriate strategies and sanctions (including those that are illegal because they hurt, humiliate or frighten children) are never used.

Child/young person code of conduct

Schools and other settings may also draw up a code of conduct for older children and young people who attend. This clearly sets out how they are expected to behave within the setting. Many schools ask young people to sign the code of conduct, making it into a contract for behaviour.

key terms

Inappropriate behaviour actions that conflict with the accepted values and beliefs of the setting and society. Inappropriate behaviour may be demonstrated through speech, writing, non-verbal behaviour or physical abuse.

Did you know?

New practitioners should be introduced to the behaviour policy and procedures as part of the induction process, and all practitioners must work in accordance with it at all times. Behaviour policies should also be shared with parents and carers when their child is registered with the setting.

265

Your conduct should be calm and professional at all times

All of the following information should be set out clearly in a setting's behaviour policies and procedures.

The boundaries of the setting

You were introduced to boundaries in Unit MU 2.2, Learning outcome 4. It's a good idea to look at page 180 now. The boundaries (ground rules) of the setting should be clearly expressed. This is important because a common understanding of the boundaries enables practitioners to be consistent in terms of the behaviour they promote and the behaviour they discourage.

When parents and carers are familiar with the boundaries of the setting from the outset, it helps to prevent or resolve disagreements about a child's behaviour that may arise in the future. For example, if a young person makes a negative comment about another child's religion, the setting and the young person's parents may disagree about whether it is inappropriate. Referring to the boundaries set out in the behaviour policy will help the setting to clarify that this behaviour is not acceptable within the setting, even if the parents would allow it at home.

Ages and stages of development

Our expectations for children's behaviour depend greatly on their age and stage of development. This should be reflected in the boundaries set for children of different ages and abilities. Table TDA2.9.1 opposite gives examples of this.

As you learnt in Unit MU 2.2, older children and young people may be involved in setting their boundaries. These will need to be recapped and revised regularly. For example, a holiday club may recap and revise the rules at the start of each new school holiday.

Did you know?

Younger children learn through repetition. They come to understand boundaries when practitioners explain to them why the way they are behaving is unacceptable. Practitioners also define boundaries regularly to remind children to keep their behaviour within acceptable limits. You can read more about defining boundaries on page 180.

Table TDA2.9.1: Age-related boundaries

Age of child	Example boundary issue	Response of practitioner
1–2 years	Children do not yet understand the dangers that exist around them and may repeatedly do something potentially dangerous.	Continue to say a firm 'No' and explain why the behaviour is inappropriate. Be patient and remember that children learn through repetition.
2–3 years	May swing between being independent and dependent, becoming frustrated when they don't have the skills to perform the tasks they want to do or themselves.	Support the child by praising them for trying things for themselves, ignoring the frustrated behaviour as much as possible and offering the practical assistance needed.
3–4 years	Now the child is playing more independently with peers, they will quarrel at times and experiment with behaviour as they learn to get along with others.	Be understanding of the fact that children are still learning about relationships with peers. Encourage them to resolve their own conflicts with your support – see page 182.
4–5 years	The school transition may unsettle children, and this may affect behaviour.	Be understanding of the fact that children have a lot to adjust to in their life at this time. Be patient and support children emotionally if they regress to behaviours they had previously given up. Usually this doesn't last long. Also see page 169.
5–6 years	Friends are becoming increasingly important, and children may show off in front of their peers.	Always seek to avoid embarrassing or humiliating children in front of their friends. If necessary, take them to one side for a quiet word about their behaviour.
6–8 years	Children are susceptible to peer pressure.	Help children to develop their own 'moral compass' by talking to them about what to do in situations they encounter. Provide activities that promote self-reliance and self-esteem. These help children to do what they think is right rather than blindly following their peers.
8–12 years	The secondary-school transition may unsettle children, and this may affect behaviour.	Children may have big concerns that result in frustrated, irrational behaviour at times. You may choose to ignore some of this at the time to allow them to calm down, and talk about the reason for their outburst later.
12–19 years	Puberty leads to the young person experiencing mood swings	Remember that the mood swings are unpleasant for the young person as well as those around them. Staying in good humour can help young people to 'swing back round' to more desirable social behaviour.

Rewards encourage more positive behaviour

How the setting will promote positive behaviour, including use of rewards

■ Policies and procedures should set out how the setting promotes positive behaviour. This will include the use of rewards. It's important that everyone is clear about this to ensure that all children are treated fairly.

■ Responding to positive behaviour with praise and other rewards is the most effective way to encourage more positive behaviour and to discourage inappropriate behaviour. You'll learn more about this in Learning outcome 2. Also see Unit MU 2.2, Learning outcome 4.

Strategies and sanctions to deal with conflict and inappropriate behaviour

As well as knowing how to promote positive behaviour, practitioners need to understand how to deal with conflict and inappropriate behaviour within the setting. The strategies and sanctions used should be carefully explained in the policy and procedures. When inappropriate behaviour occurs, it's up to practitioners to select a response that suits the individual circumstances. But it's important to remember that there should be a consistent approach. We'll look at a range of strategies and sanctions for dealing with inappropriate behaviour in Learning outcome 3.

Anti-bullying strategies

Bullying can make children's lives miserable, and bullying behaviour negatively affects both the bully and their victim. This makes anti-bullying strategies an extremely important part of the behaviour policy. See Learning outcome 3 of Unit TDA 2.2 for further details.

Attendance

Attendance generally isn't mentioned in the behaviour documents of early years settings. But in school settings where attendance is mandatory, it will be included. The strategies and sanctions used to encourage attendance and deal with truancy will be outlined. The code of conduct for pupils is also likely to set out the school's expectations for attendance and inform pupils that being truant from school will incur a sanction.

Good practice

Settings generally share their behaviour policy with new parents when they are registering their child. This gives parents the opportunity, before their child attends, to check they are happy with the way the setting handles inappropriate behaviour.

Individual behaviour plans

Behaviour policies and procedures should explain the circumstances in which individual behaviour plans are devised for children, and how they are followed through. This links with your learning in Unit MU 2.2.

Ask Miranda!

Q What if parents say they disagree with something in the behaviour policy?

A Some parents may feel that the setting's expectations of behaviour are either too high or too low, or perhaps they would deal with inappropriate behaviour differently themselves at home. Or, at times, a parent may be unhappy with the way a situation has been handled. In these circumstances it's important that issues are discussed openly. Practitioners should explain the thinking or reasoning that underpins a policy statement, an action or approach. But it's important for practitioners to listen carefully to what parents and carers have to say, and to monitor and adapt their procedures when it's appropriate to do so.

Link Up!

Unit MU 2.2 Contribute to the support of child and young person development.

Unit TDA 2.2 Safeguard the welfare of children and young people.

Consistency and fairness

You were introduced to the importance of consistency in Unit MU 2.2, Learning outcome 4.

When all practitioners understand their setting's policies and procedures and interpret them in the same way, they will share the same approach to:

■ promoting positive behaviour

■ dealing with inappropriate behaviour.

This is crucial because when boundaries and sanctions are consistently applied, children can learn what is expected of them. This also:

■ gives children a sense of security

■ helps children to see that they are being treated fairly.

If consistency is lacking, children will become confused. For instance, if some practitioners let children have extra turns during a board game to keep the peace, a child will learn that it is worth trying to get an extra turn because sometimes they are rewarded. The same applies if one practitioner varies their approach, sometimes allowing certain behaviour and sometimes not allowing it. This can make children feel insecure – they are not sure what is required of them, and they never know what reaction their behaviour will get.

Practical example

Supermarket sweets

Tallulah is three years old. When she goes to the supermarket with her mum each week, she repeatedly asks for a big packet of sweets. Her mum generally says no eight or nine times as they progress around the supermarket. Tallulah gets increasingly annoyed and upset with this answer. Her asking soon turns to whining and eventually there are angry tears and shouting. By the time they get to the sweet aisle, Tallulah's mum has been worn down, and she allows Tallulah to choose some sweets. Her mum has noticed recently that Tallulah has started to progress to crying a lot more quickly.

Today, Tallulah and her mum pop into the newsagents. Tallulah sees a box of chocolates on the shelf behind the counter, and tells her mum that she wants it. Her mum says no, explaining that it's more the sort of thing they might buy as a special present for a grown up. As soon as she hears 'No', Tallulah bursts into angry tears.

Tallulah's mum realises that her daughter has learnt that this behaviour is the most effective way to get her to change her mind and buy Tallulah the item she wants. Tallulah's mum knows it would be ridiculous to buy her the chocolates, and she resolves to break this cycle of behaviour. From now on, no will mean no. There will be a difficult but necessary period of adaptation for both Tallulah and her mum.

Good practice

To make sure that all members of a staff team approach behaviour consistently, settings will regularly spend time talking about and reviewing their behaviour policies and procedures, assessing how consistently they are put into practice. Staff teams will also undertake behaviour-related training together on a regular basis.

FOCUS ON

... being able to support positive behaviour

In this section you'll learn about the benefits of encouraging and supporting positive behaviour, and how to apply skills and techniques for doing so. You'll also learn about realistic, consistent and supportive responses to behaviour. Lastly, you'll learn about providing an effective role model for the standards of behaviour expected of the children, young people and adults within the setting. This links with **Assessment Criteria 2.1, 2.2, 2.3, 2.4.**

The benefits of encouraging and rewarding positive behaviour

Practitioners promote positive behaviour by rewarding children when they behave in acceptable ways. This is a very positive way for children to learn about the behaviour we want from them.

Children enjoy being rewarded, so they are encouraged to behave in the same way again. When children repeat behaviours, over time they become an ingrained, natural part of what the child does. So the more a child is given positive attention for behaving appropriately, the less inappropriate behaviour they are likely to display.

Rewarding positive behaviour also has a strong effect on children and young people's well-being because it increases their self-esteem and self-confidence.

Skills and techniques for encouraging behaviour

You were introduced to ways in which you can support and encourage positive behaviour in Unit MU 2.2. You should reread pages 175–186 as part of your study of this section.

Did you know?

Children who regularly receive positive attention from the adults who care for them have higher expectations for their own lives.

Rewarding positive behaviour increases self-esteem and self-confidence

Rewards

The rewards that can be given to children fall into two categories: tangible and intangible.

Tangible rewards are real items that physically exist and can be seen. Intangible rewards are not physical items, but something that children can experience. Some examples are shown in Table TDA2.9.2 below.

Table TDA2.9.2: Rewards

Tangible rewards	Intangible rewards
Prizes	Praise
Stickers	Smiles
Certificates	Cuddles
Stars/ink stamps	Round of applause/cheers
Trophies/awards	A 'thank you'
Toys	Public acknowledgement (praise given in front of other people to draw their attention to an achievement)
Money	Pats on the back
Allowed to choose something tangible from a shop	Opportunities to pick a game or story for the group
Work displayed/published (in a newsletter for instance)	Special trips or the provision of favourite activities (e.g. going to the park or baking cakes)

Intangible rewards

Practitioners use mainly intangible rewards. These are extremely valuable because they can be used to encourage children throughout an activity or task, showing them that they are behaving correctly and giving them the confidence to continue. You can give children warm praise, thanks and smiles frequently throughout every day, but it would be impractical to do the same with tangible rewards.

Tangible rewards

Tangible rewards do have their place. Stickers in particular seem to work well, as children can wear them with pride and they don't break the bank! Tangible items are often used in individual behaviour plans/ programmes to reward individual children who are working towards specified behaviour goals that have been identified for them (see

Unit MU 2.2, page 186). They are also effective for rewarding and celebrating occasional achievements that are out of the ordinary, and they can be kept as a reminder of that time. Some tangible rewards, such as money, may be given by parents and carers, but in most settings it would be considered inappropriate to use these.

Certificate of Achievement

Awarded to: .... On: ....

For: Helping a friend

Signed .... **Well done!**

A certificate rewarding achievement

The effect of rewards on others

Take care to consider how children feel about the rewards being given to others. Tangible rewards in particular may lead to jealousy or a feeling of being treated unfairly if they are not handled carefully. For instance, if one child is given a sticker for sitting quietly at story time because this is one of their individual behaviour goals, children who generally sit quietly at story time and are not rewarded may feel unsettled by this.

Good practice

Remember, a reward is only a reward when a child likes it! It is important to reward children in a way that values them as an individual. For instance, some children feel uncomfortable with public acknowledgement or being physically touched – they may not appreciate a pat on the back. Also, while it is natural for a practitioner to cuddle a young child, it is not considered to be appropriate in all environments (such as the classroom) or with all children, particularly as they get older. You must follow the accepted policies and procedures of your setting.

Good practice

Generally speaking, rewards should be given quickly soon after the behaviour occurs, when they have relevance and meaning. You should always say why the reward is being given – children can't repeat the positive behaviour if they don't know what it was! Research shows that intermittent rewarding works best. This means that children don't need a reward every time in order to repeat behaviour. However, if a behaviour you haven't rewarded for a while begins to slide, you may like to try increasing the frequency of reward for a short period. Make sure tangible rewards are small, appropriate and not over-used. However, lots of intangible praise and positive attention given at the right time is never a bad thing.

Realistic expectations

The goals set for children's behaviour should be realistic. They should take into consideration children's age, needs and abilities.

When expectations are too high

If expectations are too high and children can't achieve them, they are likely to be in trouble frequently. This is not good for a child's self-esteem and long term it isn't good for their behavioural prospects. Children who are often in trouble may start to feel they are incapable of being good, and they may stop trying to reach behaviour goals. This attracts further negative feedback from adults, which confirms their beliefs. In these cases, it's important to break the cycle and find reasons to praise a child or young person's behaviour. See the Practical example on page 275.

When expectations are too low

If expectations aren't high enough, children won't learn how to behave appropriately, and this is also likely to affect their progress. For instance, a school-aged child who has not learnt how to take turns, share fairly and handle winning and losing is likely to have difficulties with their peers and they may dislike and avoid group activities such as playground games.

Consistency and supportive responses

Behaviour is an area of development. Children and young people need you to give them just as much support with this area of their development as you'd give them with any other.

For example, if a child was having difficulty with a physical skill such as pedalling a tricycle, you would be understanding and supportive. You'd think of ways to help them achieve the skill, and you'd find reasons to praise them to encourage them to keep trying. You certainly wouldn't be annoyed with them or take it personally!

Children who are often in trouble may feel they are incapable of being good

Practical example

Jasmine breaks a behaviour cycle

Jasmine is the nursery key person for four-year-old Felix. His story-time behaviour pattern tends to go something like this.

Jasmine has difficulty persuading Felix to go to the book corner. He eventually sits on the carpet with her and his peers, but he soon loses interest in the story. He then lies down and rolls about, causing a distraction. Jasmine ends up removing him from the book corner. The more Felix gets into trouble at story time, the more reluctant he is to go to the book corner. Jasmine realises she needs to look again at how she's meeting Felix's needs at story time.

She borrows some story books that feature Felix's favourite thing – trains. When Felix arrives, she tells him about the special books, and asks if he'd like to see. She and Felix go to the book corner together and enjoy some informal one-to-one time looking at them. Felix responds well to the positive attention. Jasmine asks if he'd like everyone to hear a train story later. Felix is keen. He then goes off to play.

When story time is approaching, Jasmine asks Felix if he'd like to choose a train book. When the practitioner who is reading the story arrives, Felix is eagerly waiting to hand over the book. Jasmine then gives Felix another choice – he can stand with the practitioner and turn the pages for her, or he can sit on the carpet. Felix chooses to turn the pages. He's engaged throughout the story, and enjoys the responsibility. Jasmine praises Felix for listening well and being helpful. This breaks the cycle of Felix expecting to get into trouble at story time. He now has a positive experience to build on when the next story time arrives.

Always take the same approach to children's behaviour. Find ways for them to practise the skills they need to develop (such as taking turns) and praise them frequently when they work towards them. If a child is displaying challenging behaviour, stay calm and support them to end it using appropriate strategies (see Learning outcome 3).

Consistency is also important, as you learnt in Unit MU 2.2, Learning outcome 4.

▶▶▶ Link Up! ◀◀◀

Unit MU 2.2 Contribute to the support of child and young person development.

Being a good role model

It's important that adults model positive behaviour, as children naturally learn some of their own behaviour from what they see happening around them. You learnt about this in Unit MU 2.2, Learning outcome 4. Also see the Practical example below.

Practical example

Ruth's role modelling

Ruth works at a holiday club for older children. They have been playing playground games outside. Now it's time to go in, everyone is putting away the resources. But 12-year-old Oscar is refusing to help. He tells Ruth angrily, 'I didn't play with that stuff, and I'm not helping!'

Ruth has already dealt with two other instances of inappropriate behaviour from Oscar this morning. She says to him firmly, 'Yes, you did, you played tennis with Chris. So I'd like you to come and help please.' Oscar kicks a ball across the playground and says, 'You're lying. I didn't!' Ruth says, 'Yes, you did! I saw you.' Oscar shouts, 'I didn't!' Ruth says loudly, 'Yes, you did!' Oscar then shouts, 'You're making it up!'

Ruth realises that her response is inappropriate. She isn't being a good role model and she's causing the situation to escalate. She takes a breath, and regains her composure. She says calmly, 'Oscar, I am not going to argue with you. Everyone is tidying up, so I'd like you to do your fair share please. If you decide not to help, you won't be allowed to choose which resources we get out when we go inside. It's up to you.'

LEARNING OUTCOME 3

FOCUS ON

... being able to respond to inappropriate behaviour

In this section you'll learn about selecting and applying agreed strategies for dealing with inappropriate behaviour. You'll also learn about the sorts of behaviour problems that should be referred to others. This links with **Assessment Criteria 3.1, 3.2**.

What is inappropriate behaviour?

Inappropriate behaviour should be clearly defined in a setting's behaviour policy. But generally, it's behaviour that conflicts with the accepted values and beliefs of the setting and society. For example, both in settings and society, acts of violence (such a hitting someone) are unacceptable. Inappropriate behaviour may be demonstrated through:

Spreading rumours about a peer can be a form of inappropriate behaviour

- speech, for example teasing, racist comments, swearing, spreading rumours

- writing, for example upsetting notes, inappropriate texts or emails, graffiti (also see cyber bulling in Unit TDA 2.2, on page 218)

- physical abuse, for example hitting, kicking, pushing, hair pulling

- other non-verbal behaviour, for example taking people's property, playing truant, damaging equipment, rude gestures.

Read on to learn about dealing with inappropriate behaviour.

Being respectful

Whatever strategy you use to deal with an instance of inappropriate behaviour, you must always maintain a respectful approach when you are interacting with children and young people. Even if they are in trouble, the well-being of children is paramount. You should always try to intervene sensitively.

Link Up!

Unit TDA 2.2 Safeguard the welfare of children and young people.

Did you know?

You must never try to control a child by intimidating or scaring them.

Being clear

When it comes to defining boundaries and dealing with inappropriate behaviour, ensure that you communicate information in a way that children can understand. You must take their age, needs and abilities into consideration.

Unclear directions can confuse children. If they do not do what is required of them due to a misunderstanding, they may get into further trouble. Rather than saying to a young child, 'You upset Callum so you should go and make friends again', a practitioner could say, 'Callum was upset when you took his toy away. Please go and say sorry to him'. This is a clear instruction, and the child will know what to do.

Strategies for dealing with inappropriate behaviour

We'll look at a range of strategies for dealing with inappropriate behaviour. Different strategies are best suited to different circumstances. When deciding how to respond to an instance of inappropriate behaviour, you must take children's age, needs and abilities into consideration, as well as the nature of the behaviour.

Facial expressions

A disapproving look (maintaining a few seconds of eye contact if need be) is an effective way of showing children that they are overstepping a boundary and diverting them. It can be used in conjunction with other strategies. When a child is already aware of a boundary, a look may be enough on its own to prompt them to think about what they are doing, causing them to alter their behaviour accordingly.

No

A firm, simple 'No' is an appropriate way to make even very young children aware of a boundary. It's also useful to quickly halt a child's behaviour – it can stop them from doing something dangerous for instance (the consequences of their action can be discussed once they are safe). If 'No' is to have this effect, it should not be used all the time, so that children take notice when they do hear it. Phrase your instructions positively whenever possible. Instead of 'No running in the corridor!' try the more pleasant, 'Please walk in the corridor'. This also helps you to avoid nagging the children.

Consequences/sanctions

We've established that children may not understand why their behaviour is unacceptable unless they are told. The next step is to make them aware of the consequences of their actions. Sometimes it's necessary to point out that if a child continues to behave in a certain way, a sanction (such as limiting children's choices) will have to be applied as a consequence. This helps children to learn why boundaries are in place and to accept them.

For instance, a practitioner may say, 'You must not run up the slide because the children coming down will bang into you, and people will get hurt. Please go up the steps instead'. If the child continues to run up the slide, a practitioner might say, 'I have asked you to stop running up the slide. If you carry on doing it you will have to go and play with something else, otherwise someone will get hurt'.

Limiting children's choices

As in the example above, if a child continues to behave inappropriately, it may be necessary to limit the choices available to them by:

- redirecting them to another activity (perhaps something calmer)

- taking away the resource or equipment they are using.

This course of action can be effective and called for, but it should be used sparingly as it limits the opportunities for play and learning that are available to that child.

The best way to learn about the practicalities of dealing with inappropriate behaviour is to observe skilled, experienced colleagues putting the strategies outlined opposite into action. Pay close attention to their approach, and ask them questions afterwards if necessary.

Did you know?

No must mean no. If you say no and then give in to children, it teaches them that it's worth not complying because they may get their way if they resist you for long enough. Also, you should never say you will carry out a consequence unless you mean it.

Sometimes a sanction needs to be applied as a consequence

key terms

Compliance children cooperating with requests (National Occupational Standards).

Rewarding compliance

When a child complies by altering their behaviour, practitioners should respond immediately by demonstrating their approval. A smile, nod or a thank you would all be appropriate. It's important to acknowledge **compliance** so that a child can see that they are valued as an individual – it was only their behaviour that was disapproved of, and now they have altered it they can feel acceptance once again. This protects children's self-esteem. Children will also be more likely to comply again in the future.

Selective ignoring

If an adult does not notice or reward positive behaviour, but does take notice of inappropriate behaviour, children may start to behave inappropriately to seek attention. They may feel that even negative attention is better than no attention at all. If this occurs, practitioners can try rewarding children with plenty of attention when they are behaving appropriately, whilst ignoring inappropriate behaviour as much as possible unless it is dangerous or upsetting for other children.

De-escalating and diversion

Diversionary tactics are particularly helpful when working with young children whose behaviour tends to be very 'of the moment' and reactionary. Diverting their attention, finding a way to avoid a likely flashpoint or a way to take the heat out of a situation (de-escalation), helps to keep a calm, pleasant environment. Once this is achieved, you can praise the positive behaviour.

Time out

Time out should not be used as a punishment. The purpose is to allow children and young people the chance to calm down and take stock of a situation by removing them from the source of conflict or temptation. Children should feel that this is the purpose of time out – they should not be made to feel that they are being rejected from the group. Time out is not recommended for young children who cannot yet understand this.

Time out removes children from the source of conflict or temptation

Practical example

Diverting and de-escalating the behaviour of toddlers

Kayleigh is a childminder for 20-month-old Leila and 24-month-old Mattie. Leila has left her comfort blanket from home on Kayleigh's sofa, and is happily playing with some building blocks.

But when Mattie picks up her blanket, Leila immediately protests vocally and tries to grab it. Mattie looks at her angrily and doesn't let go. Mattie brought his own special toy car from home today, so Kayleigh finds it and offers it to him as a distraction. Mattie takes it and lets go of the blanket, which he is no longer interested in. Leila sits down and rubs the silky edge of the blanket soothingly against her face. Kayleigh has successfully diverted Mattie and de-escalated Leila's reaction.

Good practice

The time-out strategy is particularly effective with older children and for handling aggression. In the case of aggression, it's best to take children somewhere quiet away from others if possible, and to stay with the child until they calm down. You must remain calm and in control yourself. This is particularly important when children have lost control of themselves as this can be frightening for them and for you. After a period of time out, practitioners should talk to children, resolving any remaining issues if necessary and smoothing their transition back into the activities of the group.

Use of physical intervention

Rarely, in extreme circumstances, it may be necessary to physically restrain a child to prevent them from hurting themselves or somebody else. If such an event occurs, you must use the *minimum force possible*. If possible, have someone else with you to protect yourself from allegations of abuse. You should record the incident in the setting's incident book and report it to your superiors as soon as possible. They will need to report it to the child's parents.

Good practice

Practices that physically hurt, frighten, threaten or humiliate children must never be used. This means that practitioners must never use physical punishments such as smacking. It is illegal. Reins and harnesses must only be used to keep young children safe – when they are in a high chair for instance. Children should never be restrained for punishment, either physically or by reins or harnesses.

Common inappropriate behaviour

Table TDA2.9.3 gives tips on dealing with four common instances of inappropriate behaviour.

Table TDA2.9.3: Dealing with common inappropriate behaviour

Type of behaviour	Description of behaviour	Strategy
Attention seeking	Children may throw tantrums, cry frequently or refuse to settle at activities for long unless an adult is beside them. Children may be hostile or jealous towards another person receiving attention. Children displaying this type of behaviour may be feeling insecure and in need of adult reassurance. However, they may simply be used to lots of adult attention.	Go out of your way to praise positive behaviour, and try to ignore inappropriate behaviour when possible. Otherwise, you reward the inappropriate behaviour with the attention the child is seeking.
Aggressive/destructive behaviour	Children may hurt others by hitting or kicking. They may throw or kick over equipment or furniture. Children may be experiencing frustration, and may have been feeling unhappy for some time. With older children often this behaviour has been building up, but it may be more spontaneous in younger children.	Be firm and in control to stop the child getting out of control. Calm the child quickly in a quiet place if possible. Children who have lost control may be quite scared and eventually tearful. When the child is ready, find out the source of the upset and resolve the issue. Talk with children about the consequences of their behaviour.

Type of behaviour	Description of behaviour	Strategy
Offensive comments	Children swear or use offensive words or comments that they have heard. They may not understand what they are saying.	Tell children why their words are unacceptable within the setting, making it clear that they cause hurt and upset. This also applies to name-calling, which should also be regarded as completely unacceptable and should be taken seriously. In all cases it is important to encourage children to acknowledge that they have hurt the feelings of other people, and for them to apologise. They can also do what they can to make up for it if appropriate.
Arguments between children	Arguments may range in intensity from low-level bickering to loud, full-scale rows.	Learning to get along and cooperate with other people is an important life skill for everyone. Practitioners can help children to learn how to handle disagreements and disputes positively. The extent to which children are able to do this will depend on their age, needs and abilities. When working with younger children, practitioners can ask questions to prompt them to identify their problems and to come up with their own solutions. This is important as there will not always be adults on hand to step in as children grow and become more independent. When working with older children, practitioners need to resist the temptation to intervene in children's problems right away, giving them the opportunity to resolve things for themselves, as long their behaviour is not dangerous or so inappropriate that it should be stopped immediately (in the case of bullying for example).

Behaviour referrals

As you've learnt, all children and young people behave inappropriately at times, and this is to be expected. But sometimes, inappropriate behaviour is a sign that a child is experiencing the kind of difficulty which needs additional support. In these situations, you will need to refer the behaviour.

You should follow your setting's guidelines for referring. But generally speaking, an assistant would normally refer the behaviour to a more senior colleague or to the setting's SENCO. They will then consult with the family and make a referral to outside professionals if necessary. An individual behaviour plan may be drawn up, putting strategies in place for supporting the child.

Settings will usually try a few different strategies to deal with the behaviour before outside professionals are contacted. They may also conduct some extra observations of the child during this period, to help them to understand the behaviour better. Serious behaviour (which you'll learn about on page 285) is the exception, and in this case outside support may well be sought sooner.

A range of outside professionals may work with children and young people following a referral, as shown in the following diagram.

Example of outside professionals who may work with children and young people following a behaviour referral

Behaviour problems that should be referred

Behaviour that needs to be referred often falls into the categories described below.

Behaviour at odds with expected behaviour patterns

To recognise when behaviour problems should be referred, you need a good understanding of behaviour development patterns. This is because a behaviour problem that should be referred is often at odds with the behaviour you would expect from a child of that age. Some examples follow.

Biting

Young children often go through a phase of biting. It's particularly common in toddlers, who don't yet have the language to express themselves when they are frustrated. Their behaviour is very 'of the moment' (reactionary), and they do not yet have sophisticated self-control. Biting is unpleasant, but this common behaviour usually stops by the age of three. If a child continues to bite or begins to bite after this age, the behaviour should be referred.

Physical aggression

All children fall out with their peers from time to time, and some find getting along in a group more challenging than others. Young children are the most likely to show physical aggression because, as described above, they have difficulty expressing themselves and controlling their impulses. Hitting and pushing are particularly common. But as children mature they are expected to gain more control. Physical aggression needs referring if:

- ◼ it occurs randomly for no apparent reason

- ◼ it is frequent (see page 286)

- ◼ the seriousness of impact on others concerns you (see page 287).

Bullying

Bullying is harmful to the bully as well as their victims, and this behaviour should always be referred. For further details, see Learning outcome 3 in Unit TDA 2.2.

Attention seeking

Attention seeking through inappropriate behaviour usually declines as children mature and find more sophisticated ways to get the attention they want. It's perfectly normal for some older children and young people to do plenty of good-natured 'showing off' – this has much to do with individual personalities. But challenging behaviour such as frequently being uncooperative for no apparent reason, deliberately breaking things or dropping things on the floor, or shouting to cause a disruption should be referred, as there may be an underlying issue that needs to be explored.

Inappropriate behaviour that occurs frequently

In some cases, an element of behaviour may be consistent with the age of a child or young person, but the frequency of the behaviour causes concern. For example, very frequent aggression shown by young children may still need to be referred.

Good practice

It takes experience to judge whether the frequency of an aspect of behaviour is cause for concern. If you are at all unsure, check with an experienced colleague.

Behaviour that changes

We all have good days and bad days, but if a child or young person's behaviour changes noticeably for a period of time or they do something significantly out of character, this may be an indication that help and support is needed. For instance, if a child who is usually keen to talk to adults and to participate in activities becomes withdrawn and reluctant to join in, something specific could be wrong. Sometimes a child may behave differently on certain days of the week, at specific times of the day or when in the company of particular people (both adults and peers). Sometimes practitioners say they 'have a sense' that a previously happy child is now frequently sad, worried or distant.

The cause of a change of behaviour is often emotional distress triggered by an event happening in the child's life. This could be a number of things, for example a transition such as a bereavement or family break-up, or an experience such as child abuse.

Serious behaviour

You will also need to refer any serious behaviour, even if it has only occurred once. Serious behaviour can include:

- Self-harming (for example cutting skin, pulling out hair, biting arms and hands, head banging).

- Drug use.

- Sexual assault.

- Physical aggression that causes serious damage to property or leaves people injured.

- Carrying or use of weapons.

- Playing with fire.

Possible causes of behaviour problems

The types of behaviour problems we've been discussing may be caused by:

- an emotional difficulty or experience in the child or young person's life

- an impairment, such as a learning difficulty

- a medical condition.

You can recap on the expected behaviour development patterns by following the row coloured orange in the development tables in Unit TDA 2.1, pages 113–31.

Unit TDA 2.1 Child and young person development.

Unit TDA 2.2 Safeguard the welfare of children and young people.

How are things going?

▶ Progress Check

1. What is a staff code of conduct? (1.1)

2. Why is it important to apply your setting's boundaries consistently? (1.2)

3. What are the two main benefits of encouraging and rewarding positive behaviour? (2.1)

4. What are the following?
   a Tangible rewards.   b Intangible rewards. (2.2)

5. Explain the possible negative effects when children experience expectations that are:
   a too high   b too low. (2.3)

6. How must you conduct yourself to become an effective role model for children and young people's behaviour? (2.4)

7. Explain the purpose of time out. (3.1)

8. What immediate strategy would you use to respond to an older child who has just hit out at a peer? (3.1)

9. Give four examples of behaviour problems that should be referred. (3.2)

Are you ready for assessment?

Learning Outcomes 2 and 3 must be assessed in a real work environment.

CACHE

Set task:

■ You are asked to describe your setting's policies and procedures on promoting positive behaviour, and to explain with examples the importance of staff consistently and fairly applying rules and boundaries for children in line with policies and procedure.

You can prepare by reviewing your setting's policies and procedures on promoting positive behaviour. You can also use your reflective diary to think through how staff work in line with the policies and procedure to promote consistency and fairness.

City & Guilds

In preparation for assessment of this Unit, you may like to review your setting's policies and procedures on promoting positive behaviour. You can also reflect on times when you have promoted positive behaviour using your reflective diary.

Edexcel

In preparation for assessment of this Unit, you may like to review your setting's policies and procedures on promoting positive behaviour. You can also reflect on times when you have promoted positive behaviour using your reflective diary.

UNIT 2.8

Contribute to the support of positive environments for children and young people

LEARNING OUTCOMES

The learning outcomes you will meet in this unit are:

1 Know the regulatory requirements for a positive environment for children and young people

2 Be able to support a positive environment that meets the individual needs of children and young people

3 Be able to support the personal-care needs of children and young people within a positive environment

4 Understand how to support the nutritional and dietary needs of children and young people

INTRODUCTION

Children and young people should be provided with safe, positive environments that meet their learning, development and welfare needs. These include personal and nutritional care requirements that must be met sensitively, so children can thrive in terms of both health and development.

LEARNING OUTCOME 1

FOCUS ON

... knowing the regulatory requirements for a positive environment for children and young people

In this section you'll learn what is meant by a positive environment. You'll also learn about the regulatory requirements that underpin a positive environment for children and young people. This links with **Assessment Criteria 1.1, 1.2.**

What is a positive environment?

All children and young people should be provided with a positive environment. This is an environment that:

- is safe

- promotes children and young people's welfare

- supports children and young people's learning and development.

Different kinds of environments

Did you know?

Whatever building or room is provided, it's up to the practitioners working within it to organise the space in a way that will meet children and young people's needs.

There's a huge range of very different environments offered by different types of children and young people's settings. Even within each type of setting, the range of environments will differ greatly. For example, some day nurseries are purpose-built early years settings. Other day nurseries convert existing buildings that have previously been houses, industrial buildings or even churches or barns. Likewise, some pre-schools and out-of-school clubs meet in their own building, while others hire a suitable space for the duration of sessions. This might be in a school or a village hall for example, in which case staff will set out all equipment on their arrival and clear it away again at the end of the day, so the space is ready for the next user.

A nursery setting

Use of space

The use of space has a huge impact on the quality of the overall experience that children receive while at the setting, and this in turn impacts on the quality of their learning and development. Settings manage their space by dividing it up into areas for:

- playing and learning

- resting and sleeping

- mealtimes.

Playing and learning

There are so many possibilities for wonderful play and learning activities. But because settings only have a limited amount of space, most will vary the use of their premises throughout each session. For instance, at the start of the day there may be an area dedicated to construction during **free play**, which is set up with wooden blocks. But this area may later be tidied away and used for circle time, when children will come together as a group to talk about their news. By the afternoon, the same area may be set up with musical instruments.

key terms

Free play a period of time in which children freely choose what resources to play with and how to play with them. Practitioners usually set the room up with a range of resources to choose from. Children will also be able to select additional resources if they prefer.

Most settings vary the use of their premises throughout each session

A balanced approach to areas

Taking a balanced approach to providing play and learning areas is about findings ways to meet the diverse range of children's environmental needs. This includes areas for the following:

- Child-initiated free play of different types. For example, a range of free-play areas may be set up in advance of each session (see the section on common dedicated areas on page 294).

- Taking part in a range of adult-initiated activities of different types. This might include story time, planting seeds, circle games, etc.

- Playing and learning alone, with peers and with adults. Including opportunities to engage in all stages of play (see Unit TDA 2.16 for information on stages of play).

- Taking part in play and activities that are appropriate to the age and stage of development of the children in the group. This can vary greatly. For example, when considering physical play in a room for under threes, practitioners must ensure that the areas provided meet the needs of babies who are not yet mobile, babies who crawl, those who are beginning to walk and those confident walkers who move around quickly.

■ Taking part in play and activities that are personalised. This means that individual children's abilities, needs, preferences and interests should be considered in the provision of areas.

■ Rest and quieter activities. This may be achieved through the provision of large floor cushions/children's beanbags/upholstered children's furniture such as sofas. In the case of settings caring for young children, these areas will be in addition to the sleeping area, which will feature cots/beds.

■ Physical activity and exercise. Enough clear space for this is important. While it's best to have an outdoor area of a good size, opportunities for physical activity and exercise can also be offered successfully inside. In practice, most settings will use a combination of approaches. For example, playground games and riding tricycles and bikes may take place outside, whilst dancing and music and movement may take place inside.

■ Time both indoors and outdoors. Outdoors should not be seen as simply for physical activities. The majority of activities that may have been thought of traditionally as 'indoor' pursuits can also take place effectively outside. There are also many unique experiences and opportunities that can only be had outside – collecting and measuring rainfall for instance.

More information about rest and physical activity and exercise is included in Learning outcome 3.

Ideally there will be a good-sized outdoor space

Over time imaginary areas may be a home corner, a shop, a hospital, etc.

Common dedicated areas

Settings often have a number of dedicated areas within the setting that stay the same, although the individual play and learning activities offered in those areas are rotated. Common examples of dedicated areas that feature in settings include:

■ The imaginary area. Over time this may be a home corner, a shop, a hospital, etc.

■ The construction area. Rotated resources may include blocks, bricks and natural objects such as small logs, etc.

■ The messy play area. Including sand and water trays which have their own sets of equipment that are also rotated (for example buckets, spades, etc.). Malleable materials such as play dough, cornflour paste, earth and plasticine, also with rotated equipment (such as cutters, rolling pins, etc.).

■ The arts and crafts area. Equipped with resources such as paint, glue, paper, collage materials, mark-making resources, etc.

■ The book corner. A comfortable area with bean bags/cushions/child-sized soft furnishings, stocked with books.

■ Displays. Displays fall into three categories: paper-based artwork or writing that is displayed on the wall, craft work displayed on shelves or tables (for example models made from recycled materials), and interest tables displaying three-dimensional objects linked together by type or a common theme (for example an autumn table, featuring leaves of different colours, conkers and acorns).

Location of areas

Once practitioners have decided on the areas they will provide for play and learning activities within a session, thought must be given to where they should be located. The following guidelines are helpful:

■ Hygiene and cleanliness: Set up messy activities in areas that have furniture and flooring which can be cleaned easily. Make sure there's easy access to sinks for hand-washing too – you don't want children trailing paint over carpeted areas on their way to the bathroom!

■ Restful, quiet activities and noisy, busy activities: Locate quiet pursuits away from noisy or busy ones. This ensures that children don't disturb each other or have to be told to keep the noise down.

■ Sufficient space: Give activities the space they need. Overcrowded areas or equipment can not only affect the quality of the experience, they can be dangerous and/or difficult to supervise.

Locate noisy activities away from quiet ones

Factors affected by room layout

Room layout can affect a number of factors, as shown in the diagram below.

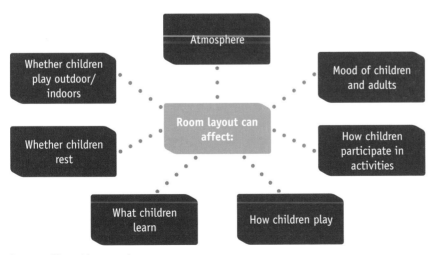
Factors affected by room layout

Good practice

Restrict the number of children permitted in an area/at equipment at one time if necessary. Ensure that equipment is located safely (for example a slide should be placed on level ground) and that resources do not obstruct fire exits at any time. Considering the needs of all the children, leave sufficient room for children to move around the play space, between the activities, furniture and equipment. Also ensure that activities, furniture and equipment are accessible.

Good practice

When presenting resources and activities, try to vary things. It is easy to always put the same things out in the same way without thinking about it, so you may find it helpful to record how an activity will be presented on your activity plans.

Vary the way you set out activities in your setting by trying one of the following:

- Combining resources that do not usually go out together. For example put interlocking bricks out with cars, and children may create garages. Or put cars out with long lengths of paper and they may draw roads.
- Changing the position of items. Try a train set on the table instead of setting it up on the floor, and move the chairs away. Take craft resources such as paper, cellophane, fabric, tissue, etc. and put them on the floor instead of the table.

Ask Miranda!

Q Can you give me any tips for setting up areas for free play?

A Set activities up attractively, so they look welcoming, interesting and inviting. When setting up the home corner, set the table and sit a teddy there ready for play, for instance. Start off an activity as a play cue for children – set out the blocks with a partially built tower, or begin a puzzle. Ask yourself if the activities look flat, because when resources are just placed on a table, they often look static and uninspiring. A table of pipe cleaners that has two or three bright pipe-cleaner structures standing upright is far more interesting than just the raw materials lying there.

Supporting learning and development

Positive environments support learning and development by meeting the requirements of the curriculum framework that applies to the setting. For example, in early years settings in England (including reception classes), this will be the Early Years Foundation Stage. In primary and secondary schools, this will be the National Curriculum.

All early years curriculum frameworks are divided into categories. In England, Wales and Northern Ireland these are referred to as 'areas of learning'. In Scotland, the term 'areas of experience' is used. For clarity in this unit, we will use the term 'areas of learning'. Table MU2.8.1 below shows the areas of learning for each home country.

Table MU2.8.1: Areas of learning

England	Wales
Communication and language. Physical development. Personal, social and emotional development. Literacy. Mathematics. Understanding the world. Expressive arts and design.	Personal and social development, well-being and cultural diversity. Language, literacy and communication skills. Mathematical development. Welsh-language development. Knowledge and understanding of the world. Physical development. Creative development.
Scotland	**Northern Ireland**
Expressive arts. Health and well-being. Languages. Mathematics. Religious and moral education. Sciences. Social studies. Technologies.	Physical development and movement. Language and literacy. The world around us. Mathematics and numeracy. The arts.

Good practice

When planning the provision of areas for both child-initiated and adult-initiated opportunities within the setting, practitioners must make sure that there is a balance across all of the areas of learning included in the curriculum framework of their home country. You'll learn how to promote the areas of learning through activities and resources in Learning outcome 2.

The effective practice of practitioners is crucial to the provision of a positive environment

In the bullet list below, can you add some more key duties that impact on the provision of a positive environment?

Did you know?

Even the very best building, equipment and resources cannot create a positive environment if the practice of practitioners is second rate.

Unit MU 2.4 Contribute to children and young people's health and safety.

For full information about the Welfare requirements that apply in England, visit www.education. gov.uk/publications/ eOrderingDownload/eyfs_ practiceguid_0026608.pdf and read section 3 of the Practice Guidance for the EYFS.

Effective practice of practitioners

The effective practice of practitioners is crucial to the provision of a positive environment. We've discussed the importance of creating a good layout and providing high-quality activities to support learning and development. But practitioners must also fulfil a number of other key duties well, such as:

- establishing good relationships with children, young people, families and colleagues

- establishing an effective key-worker system

- working in partnership with outside professionals as necessary

- working in partnership with parents and carers

- keeping their own knowledge and skills up to date

- promoting children and young people's independence and choice

- embracing diversity and differences

- meeting children and young people's individual needs

- keeping children and young people safe.

Regulatory requirements

Each home country in the UK has set out welfare requirements or standards. These are the minimum standards that settings must meet in order to ensure children's health, safety and well-being. These include strict guidelines about the physical environment.

It's important that you know and understand the welfare requirements for your own home country. In England, the Safeguarding and welfare requirements are part of the Early Years Foundation Stage. You'll find further details in Learning outcome 1, Unit MU 2.4. You are advised to reread this as part of your study of this unit.

LEARNING OUTCOME 2

... being able to support a positive environment that meets the individual needs of children and young people

In this section you'll learn about greeting children and young people and providing opportunities for them to engage in activities of choice. You'll also learn about providing activities and resources to meet individual needs and to promote the use of senses. Lastly, you'll learn about giving praise and encouragement. This links with **Assessment Criteria 2.1, 2.2, 2.3, 2.4, 2.5.**

Meeting and greeting children and young people

It's good practice to ensure that children and young people start the day on a positive note by meeting and greeting them appropriately. Practitioners should:

- smile and say hello warmly to children and their parents or carers

- use the child's name when greeting them

- find out how the child is

- have a brief chat with parents or carers if appropriate, and include the child in the conversation

- tell the child about some of the activities available today

- encourage the child to say goodbye – in some settings children may also wave goodbye at the window

- take children to hang up their coat and put any belongings away

- encourage the child to choose an activity or friend to play with, and support them to settle in.

Did you know?

Informing older children and young people which of their friends are expected to come can help them to settle in, particularly if they are one of the first to arrive at a session.

Unit TDA 2.7 Maintain and support relationships with children and young people.

Unit TDA 2.16 Support children and young people's play and leisure.

Also see the section on developing a rapport with children and young people in Learning outcome 2, Unit TDA 2.7. For information about settling in children who are new to the setting, see page 175.

Encourage children to say goodbye to their parents or carers

Opportunities to engage in activities of choice

Children and young people need a balance of activities. This should include opportunities to engage in activities that they choose for themselves. An important way in which settings promote this is through providing plenty of free-play time. You were introduced to this in Learning outcome 1. You can also find information on freely chosen play in Unit TDA 2.16. Another way to ensure choice is to

Children need opportunities to select resources independently

involve children and young people in the planning of activities through a consultation process. For more information, see the ideas and suggestions section (and the Practical example that follows this) in Unit TDA 2.7, Learning outcome 2 pages 426–7.

Activities and resources to meet individual needs

The environment and the activities and experiences offered must meet the individual needs of children. Depending on the needs of the children, practitioners may have to consider some of the following:

- Using bright lighting/diffused lighting in some areas.

- Using colour to indicate certain areas.

- Using scents to indicate areas or activities.

- Having tactile wall borders or floor runners.

- Changing the height of tables.

- Increasing the space between activities.

- Taking some activities to children instead of children going to them, for example having individual trays of sand or bowls of water to play with.

- Installing hearing loops.

- Making the environment quieter by having carpet and rubber cushioning under furniture.

- Having non-slip rubber matting on meal tables so that plates and bowls do not move around.

Link Up!

Unit SHC 23 Introduction to equality and inclusion in children and young people's settings.

Unit TDA 2.15 Support children and young people with disabilities and special educational needs.

Activities and resources to promote areas of learning

In Learning outcome 1 you learnt that positive environments support learning and development by meeting the requirements of the curriculum framework that applies to the setting. Table MU2.8.2 on pages 302–3 gives examples of activities and resources that can be used to promote each area of learning of the EYFS, which applies in England. (The activities and resources listed can also be used to promote the areas of learning/areas of experience of other home countries.)

Table MU2.8.2: Activities and resources to promote the EYFS areas of learning

Area of learning	Resources/equipment	Activities
Personal, social and emotional development	Puppets, dolls and soft toys (with expressions for exploring feelings), table-top games, dressing-up clothes, cultural artefacts, a range of dolls showing a representation of people in the world (in terms of ethnicity, age, gender, ability), well-resourced imaginary areas including a home corner, comfortable quiet areas for resting and talking	New activities to build confidence, excitement, motivation to learn: leaves in the water tray, or earth to dig instead of sand, games for rules and turn-taking, celebrating festivals for awareness and respect of the wider world, handling living things for sensitivity, pouring drinks for independence, circle time for talking about home
Communication and language	Comforable book area/corner, books (fiction and non-fiction, picture books, poetry etc), story tapes, talking books, musical recordings, sequencing cards, pictures, telephones, walkie-talkies, audio recorders	Understanding elements of stories, feely bags to promote descriptive language, role play for negotiation, participating in and making up stories, rhymes, songs and poems, circle time for talking and listening, interest tables for promoting new language and asking questions
Literacy	Wide range of mark making materials and paper, letter frieze, cards/tiles/magnetic letters, comfortable book area/corner, books (fiction and non-fiction) word processor, communication boards, signs notices, labels, lists	Story time for understanding how print carries meaning, mark making opportunities in role play areas for writing with purpose, opportunities to write alongside adults, creating word banks for learning how to write and correctly spell) new words
Mathematics	Counting beads, sorting trays, diverse objects to sort, scales, weights, rulers, measures, height chart, number cards/tiles/magnetic numbers, number and shape friezes/posters, number line, numbers signs/notices/symbols and labels, shape sorters, shape puzzles, different-shaped construction resources, clocks, cash till, money	Counting how many they need (cups, for example), sharing out for calculating, singing number songs/rhymes for number operations (e.g. 'How many speckled frogs are left now?'), tidying up for sorting objects/positioning (e.g. 'That goes on the shelf'), finding numbers we see on our own front doors for number recognition, weighing cooking ingredients
Understanding of the world	ICT resources (e.g. computers, programmable toys, tape recorders), magnifying glasses, binoculars, money, books and CD-ROMs, water and sand tray/water and sand resources (e.g. funnels, wheels, rakes) living plants, manufactured construction materials (e.g. interlocking bricks), natural resources (e.g. fir cones, wooden logs)	Bark rubbings for observing closely, looking up information for asking questions and investigation, growing plants from seeds for observing change, patterns, similarities and differences, going for a walk and discussing ICT (e.g. traffic lights to identify technology, making recycled models from junk for building and joining)
Physical development	Tools – scissors, brushes, rolling pins, cutters, computer mouse, etc. – threading beads, modelling clay/cornflour paste/jelly, different-sized balls, hoops and quoits, large-wheeled toys (ride-on toys), tunnels, carts to push and pull, low stilts, skittles, hoopla, bats, parachutes, slide, climbing frame, balance beam, swing, stepping stones	Playground games (e.g. 'What's the time Mr Wolf?') for movement – creeping, running etc., negotiating a chalk-drawn 'road' on wheeled toys for awareness of space (themselves and others), obstacle courses for travelling around, under, over and through, pretending to go 'on a bear hunt' for moving with confidence/imagination

Area of learning	Resources/equipment	Activities
Expressive arts and design	Diverse range of art and craft resources including different colours and textures (e.g. paper, card, tissue, cellophane, paint, glue, felt tips, crayons, craft feathers, lollipop sticks, sequins, buttons, pipe cleaners, etc.), musical recordings, musical instruments, equipped role-play areas, dolls	Painting anywhere outside with water and large brushes for expression and imagination, making tactile collages for responding to what they see, touch and feel, music and movement for using imagination in movement and dance, singing time with musical instruments for play with expression

Remember: children's learning is not compartmentalised – all of these activities and resources can be used in many ways to promote different aspects/areas of learning, even at the same time

Sensory activities

Sensory experiences are those that stimulate children's senses (that is, their sight, hearing, touch, smell and taste). Examples of sensory activities include the following:

■ **Feely bags**:
Practitioners hide items of different textures inside a drawstring bag. Without looking inside, children take turns to delve their hands in. They describe the item they can feel. Older children may enjoy playing this game in teams, scoring points when they can guess the identity of an item.

■ **Tasting fruit**:
Children have the opportunity to taste a range of different fruits, from sour lemon to sweet pineapple. They can compare the different tastes, textures and the visual appearance of the fruit.

■ **Sound lotto**:
This game is played similarly to ordinary lotto, but instead of matching picture cards to their playing boards, children listen to familiar sounds on a compact disc or audio tape, matching the sounds to the pictures on their boards.

■ **Many everyday toys that have sensory features**:
Including rattles, teething rings, battery-operated toys such as cars with lights and sirens, play telephones, textured play mats, etc.

Many everyday toys have sensory features

303

Good practice

Sensory experiences are valuable for all children as part of the general learning and play that is offered within a setting. They may also be used in specific ways to stimulate the senses of some disabled children. Practitioners must consider the needs of all children in their care when planning sensory activities, making adaptations where necessary.

Practical example

Shelly's sensory activity

Pre-school assistant Shelly has organised a fruit-tasting activity for the children. She's pleased with how much the children enjoy it, and with the language they use to describe the tastes and textures. Just as the activity is about to end, one of the children says, 'The pineapple smells sweet.' This gives Shelly an idea.

Shelly asks the Pre-school Leader if she can organise a similar activity this afternoon, as she has plenty of fresh fruit left over. But this time she'd like to ask children to close their eyes and smell dishes of different fruits, to see if they can identify them from smell alone. The Pre-School Leader thinks it's a great idea, and she's keen for Shelly to try it out.

Praise and encouragement

It's important to celebrate children and young people's individual achievements through praise. This encourages them to feel proud of themselves, which impacts positively on their self-esteem and self-confidence. However, it's also very important to encourage trying by praising the effort that children and young people make, even if they haven't achieved their goal. This motivates them to try again and helps them to learn perseverance. It also promotes their resilience (or, in other words, their ability to cope when things don't go as they would wish). You might encourage and praise children and young people:

- verbally
- by displaying children's work
- by sharing positive feedback (for example by telling a child's parents how well they've done)
- non-verbally (for example by clapping or giving a thumbs up)
- by sharing time (for example talking about the achievement at circle time).

Further details of these strategies are given in Unit TDA 2.9, Learning outcome 2.

Link Up!

Unit TDA 2.9 Support children and young people's positive behaviour.

LEARNING OUTCOME 3

FOCUS ON

... being able to support the personal-care needs of children and young people within a positive environment

In this section you'll learn about caring for skin, hair and teeth, and about how to support personal-care routines that meet individual needs. You'll also learn about how routines meet the needs of children and families. Lastly, you'll learn about the importance of balancing physical activity with rest. This links with **Assessment Criteria 3.1, 3.2, 3.3, 3.4.**

Skin and hair care

The skin and hair needs to be kept clean to prevent disease and the spread of infection. If they are not washed regularly, dead skin cells and bacteria on sweat cause an unpleasant smell, and sore areas develop on the skin and scalp. Good hygiene practices include:

- A daily bath or shower. If this is not possible, a thorough wash instead. Care should be taken to ensure that children are properly washed and dried in their skin creases and between their toes (to prevent dryness and skin cracks). Children must learn to wash their bottoms last for hygiene reasons. For younger children, these showers/baths/washes should ideally be taken at the end of the day, as children become dirty during play. The skin should be observed for soreness/rashes.

- Washing hair three times a week or more frequently if families prefer. Shampoo should be thoroughly rinsed out with clean water, until the water runs clear. Wet hair should be combed not brushed, to prevent hair shafts from breaking.

- Hands and face should be washed each morning.

Did you know?

Some families make bath time part of the routine for getting ready for bed. Others prefer to wash babies in the morning so that they start the day feeling fresh.

Some families will give their baby a full bath each day

- Hands should be washed after toileting, after messy play and before eating, drinking or touching food.

- Nails should be kept short by cutting straight across. This should be done as necessary, and nails should be kept clean.

Bathing and washing babies

Parents and carers will have differing preferences about the way their babies are bathed. Some families will give their baby a bath each day. Others may bath their baby less often, but 'top and tail' the baby daily. This term describes the process of washing a baby's face, neck, hands and bottom without putting them in a bath of water.

Care of the nappy area

Wet and dirty nappies are uncomfortable for babies and they can cause a baby's skin to become sore and inflamed. To avoid this, practitioners should change a baby's nappy as often as necessary. It's usual to change nappies every three to four hours to coincide with mealtimes and in-between if the baby is awake and uncomfortable. Babies should always have a clean nappy when they are settled down to sleep. It is essential for key persons to talk with parents and carers about their child's individual nappy-changing requirements and the family's preferences.

Personal care that meets individual needs

Families will have differing preferences about how their children's care needs are met, from the timings of the daily routine to which toiletries are selected. Care needs should be met in a way that reflects the requirements of individual children as long this does not compromise the welfare of children.

Differences based on culture/religious practices

Some of the different preferences may be based on cultural/religious practices or ethnicity.

- Muslim children and some Hindu and Sikh children may be taught to use the right hand for eating and the left hand for matters of personal hygiene. They may also learn to wash their hands before prayer.

Some Jewish boys may wear a skull cap (known as a kippah).

Muslim girls may be required to keep their heads, hair and legs covered.

Rastafarian girls may wear a headscarf, and boys may wear a hat (a tam) over dreadlocks.

Some Jewish and Christian groups require girls to wear headscarves.

Sikh boys may not have their hair cut when they are young, but have it plaited around their head. Next they may put their hair in a jura (similar to a bun) covered by cloth. When they become teenagers they may wear a turban.

Jewish boys may wear a kippah

Differences based on ethnicity

Children will also require different care depending on their skin colour or type and the type and texture of their hair. For instance:

Dry skin needs to be moisturised with lotions or oils. These may be massaged in or added to bath water. Black skin may have a tendency to be dry.

Very curly hair or thick hair that is difficult to comb out may need to be treated with conditioners after shampooing. A wide-toothed comb with rounded ends should be used for combing out.

■ Curly black hair may need to be treated daily with oil that is massaged in. This prevents dryness and reduces breakage of the hair shafts. A wide-toothed comb with rounded ends should be used for combing out. This type of hair can have a tendency to pull out from the root. Care must be taken when combing or when styling the hair into braids, bunches, etc.

Sun protection

Sun damage can cause the skin to become painful, to peel and blister. But long-term damage to health may also occur, as some skin cancers that develop in later life are believed to be caused by

Did you know?

It is important to note that all skin types need to be protected from the sun. It is sometimes thought that black skin does not need protection – but this is not the case.

Did you know?

It is strongly advised that on hot days children stay out of the sun during the hottest part of the day – between 11am and 3pm. There's still plenty of fun to be had in the shade!

sun damage in childhood. To prevent this, sun block or high-factor sunscreen should be applied to skin (according to the directions) when necessary. Children should also wear a hat – legionnaire-style caps or wide-brimmed sun hats cover the neck as well as the head. Children should also remain covered in the sun, so leave T-shirts, etc. on. This is particularly important for babies and younger children who have highly vulnerable skin. It's also important to keep babies and young children cool to prevent them from becoming ill during spells of very hot weather. Their health can be seriously affected not only by sunburn and heatstroke but by dehydration and heat exhaustion.

Dressing and undressing

Clothing needs to be the right size for the child and suitable for the weather conditions and the activity that the children will be engaged in. Layers are generally better than one thick item of clothing as they can be removed as necessary. Most settings try to encourage parents and carers to dress children in play clothes rather than their best clothes, so that they can play freely without undue concern for their outfit. It's important for practitioners to provide protective clothing (aprons, etc.) when children will be engaging in messy play or water play, or arts and crafts involving paint, glue, etc.

Children need clothes that are suitable for the weather

Toileting

Children can only become clean and dry, or 'toilet trained', when they have control over their bowels and bladder. Bowel and bladder control develops at different times in different children. It often occurs between the age of about 18 months and three years. Most children are dry and clean during the daytime by the time they are three.

Frequent accidents can be expected at first as children may not notice until the last minute that they need to go to the toilet. Or children may wait too long to go, particularly if they are absorbed in an activity. Initially adults generally need to remind children to go to the toilet. The best way to do this is to build visits to the toilet into the day-to-day routine. It makes sense to ask children to go to the toilet before meals and snacks as they will be going to the bathroom to wash their hands in any case. You should also take them to the toilet before and after naps.

Build visits to the toilet into the daytime routine

Ask Miranda!

Q What about night-time/sleep-time bladder control?

A This takes longer to develop. Many children still have accidents at night until the age of six or seven, and some beyond this age. Some disabled children may develop bowel and bladder control much later and may continue to use nappies. Some may never develop control.

Caring for teeth

A child's first set of teeth, known as milk teeth, usually start to appear during the first year. Cleaning the teeth should become a habit from the time a baby has their very first tooth. Most children have all 20 of their milk teeth by the time they are three. From the age of five or six, children's milk teeth begin to fall out as their permanent teeth grow from inside the gum and eventually push them out. Thirty-two permanent teeth are expected in all. As the name suggests, these teeth should be kept as long as possible – hopefully a lifetime – so it is very important to look after them from the outset. Children should be encouraged to:

■ begin brushing their own teeth as soon as they are able

■ brush at least twice a day: after breakfast and after the last time they eat or drink before bedtime

■ brush after all meals if possible. Some settings facilitate this and minimise cross-infection from toothbrushes by providing safe individual storage for each child's own brush

■ visit the dentist regularly. It is a good idea to read the children stories about going to the dentist to familiarise them with this process. Role play can also be helpful

■ eat a healthy diet that is high in calcium (which is good for teeth) and low in sugar (which encourages decay). Avoid giving children sugary snacks between meals. Sugary drinks should also be avoided. Never give sweet drinks from a bottle as this helps to coat the teeth with sugar. Sugar can even pass through the gums and cause decay in teeth that have yet to come through

■ eat foods that are hard and crunchy to chew as they are good for teeth and gums. Apples, raw carrot and celery are good options.

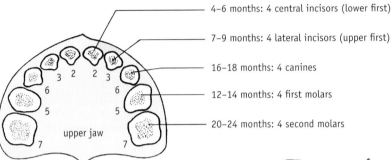

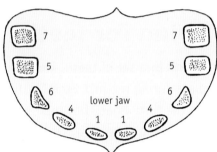

4–6 months: 4 central incisors (lower first)

7–9 months: 4 lateral incisors (upper first)

16–18 months: 4 canines

12–14 months: 4 first molars

20–24 months: 4 second molars

The first teeth normally come through in this order

Tooth development

Showing respect when meeting personal needs

You must always take the greatest care to touch children respectfully when carrying out physical care. It's also important to ensure that all children are allowed their dignity and their privacy when appropriate. You should remain professional and you should be sensitive to children's preferences, which will vary partly in relation to their age and stage of development. For instance, some children may prefer privacy when they are undressing to go swimming, whilst others may be happy to get changed alongside their peers in a communal room.

Supporting independence and self care

Most children will eventually take care of their bodies independently. The skills required to do this are learnt gradually. When attending to a child's care needs, practitioners can:

■ show children how to carry out tasks such as washing, dressing and cleaning their teeth

■ encourage children to help the adult as the child is washed, dressed, etc. The extent of help will depend on the child's age and ability

■ encourage children to take care of the environment as they care for themselves by keeping areas tidy and safe. For example, by avoiding or cleaning up spillages of water in the bathroom

■ praise children for their attempts at self care

■ have high expectations of what children can achieve whilst ensuring they are properly supported.

Practical example

Gail adjusts her approach

Practitioner Gail adjusts her approach when washing the hands of different children. She knows that one-year-old Daniel still needs lots of help from her, but he will hold out his hand ready for some liquid soap. Eighteen-month-old May will press the nozzle on the soap bottle herself, and rub her hands together – but she still needs Gail's help to rinse and dry her hands. Two-and-a-half-year-old Kayleigh can manage everything but turning the tap on and off. Gail assists her with this.

Good practice

Practitioners should appreciate which aspects of self care children are comfortable with and respect their wishes when it comes to the level and type of assistance they require. However, sometimes practitioners may need to step in. For example, in preparation for lunch a child may have washed their own hands after painting, but they may still be covered in paint. In this situation the practitioner should gently point out the missed paint and direct the child back to the sink, offering help if it is needed. This must be done sensitively so that the child's confidence in hand washing is not undermined. It is part of having high expectations whilst ensuring that proper support is available.

Routines that promote independence

Everyday routines such as personal hygiene, washing and dressing give opportunities for children to learn about independent self care, as we have discussed. But there are also many opportunities for children to learn and develop in other areas. The list is extensive, but here are some examples of learning opportunities:

Most children will eventually take care of their body independently

- When dressing, children can practise the fine motor skills required to fasten buttons, Velcro, toggles and zips.

- Children can help each other with putting on outside clothes, thus developing their social skills.

- When eating, children can practise the hand–eye coordination needed to pick up food with cutlery.

- When pouring out their own drinks from a jug children can learn about capacity and volume.

- While sitting at the table at mealtimes, children can learn about manners and social skills as they interact with one another.

- Children can count out the right number of cups or plates at snack time, learning about numbers.

- Children can communicate with their carers, practising their language skills. Adults and children may also share rhymes or songs, such as 'This is the way we wash our hands'.

Balancing physical activity and rest

For physical and mental well-being, it's important that children and young people have a balance of:

- physical activity and exercise. Physical activity and exercise is essential for all humans. It helps to keep the heart healthy and strengthens the lungs, muscles and bones, while helping children to learn and consolidate physical skills

- stimulation. Children need stimulation in order for their brains to develop and for learning to take place. Free play, activities, experiences and interactions with adults and with other children all provide stimulation

- sleep, rest and quiet times. Rest and sleep is extremely important for all humans, whatever their age. A good balance of restful, quiet activities is needed throughout the day, alongside sufficient night-time sleep and daytime naps if required.

The importance of sleep

Neural connections are being made in the brain while children sleep. Sleep aids the brain to process information and it also aids concentration and memory function, all of which is important to learning and development. Sleep supports a healthy immune system and the repair of damage to the body's cells. In children, the human growth hormone is released during a deep sleep, and a chronic lack of sleep can affect this hormone release and therefore disrupt growth patterns.

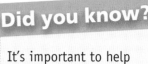

Did you know?

It's important to help children to wind down ready for sleep. Quiet activities such as sharing a book together help children to settle.

Help children to wind down ready for sleep

Ask Miranda!

Q Apart from tiredness, does lack of sleep cause any short-term problems?

A Lack of sleep can lead to lethargy, irritability and emotional outbursts that all affect behaviour. Children who are suffering from lack of sleep are less able to control their behaviour and their impulses. Concentration and memory are affected, and creativity and problem-solving skills can also be reduced.

How positive routines meet the needs of children and families

When caring for babies and young children, there's a lot to do! Well-planned routines are essential. Not only do they help the practitioner to ensure that they fit in everything that needs to be done, they provide an important structure to each day for the babies and young children. Most are happier and feel more emotionally secure when they have settled into a good routine, and in particular their sleep pattern is generally much improved. Routines need to take into account the individual needs of the babies and young children you work with. Activities such as play and going for a walk in the fresh air will be fitted around a core structure of repetitive everyday physical needs such as:

- nappy changes/toileting

- bathing and washing

- dressing

- rest, naps and night-time sleep

- feeding/mealtimes/snacks (see Learning outcome 4).

LEARNING OUTCOME 4

FOCUS ON

... understanding how to support the nutritional and dietary needs of children and young people

In this section you'll learn about the basic nutritional requirements of children and young people. You'll also learn how to establish their different dietary requirements. Lastly, you'll learn about basic food safety. This links with **Assessment Criteria 4.1, 4.2, 4.3.**

Basic nutritional requirements

Food and water is the body's fuel. Without it, humans literally cannot keep going – they die. The body must have a combination of different nutrients to be healthy. This is especially important during childhood when the body is growing and developing. Large quantities of the four nutrients listed below are found in our food and drink:

Protein.

Fat.

Carbohydrates.

Water.

But only small quantities of the following are present:

Vitamins.

Minerals.

Fibre.

Proteins provide material for:
• growth of the body
• repair of the body.

Types of proteins:
• **Animal** – first-class or complete proteins, supply all 10 of the essential amino acids.
• **Vegetable** – second-class or incomplete proteins, supply some of the 10 essential amino acids.

FOODS CONTAINING PROTEINS

Examples of protein foods include:
• **animal proteins** – meat, fish, chicken, eggs, dairy foods
• **vegetable proteins** – nuts, seeds, pulses, cereals.

Protein foods are made up of amino acids. There are 10 essential amino acids.

Foods containing proteins

Carbohydrates provide:

- energy
- warmth.

Types of carbohydrates:

- Sugars.
- Starches.

**FOODS CONTAINING
CARBOHYDRATES**

Examples of carbohydrate foods include:

- **sugars** – fruit, honey, sweets, beet sugar, cane sugar
- **starches** – potatoes, cereals, beans, pasta.

Carbohydrates are broken down into glucose before the body can use them.
Sugars are quickly converted and are a quick source of energy.
Starches take longer to convert so they provide a longer-lasting supply of energy.

Foods containing carbohydrates

Fats:

- provide energy and warmth
- store fat-soluble vitamins
- make food pleasant to eat.

Types of fats:

- Saturated.
- Unsaturated.
- Polyunsaturates.

**FOODS
CONTAINING FATS**

Examples of foods containing fats include:

- **saturated fat** – butter, cheese, meat, palm oil
- **unsaturated** – olive oil, peanut oil
- **polyunsaturated** – oily fish, corn oil, sunflower oil.

Saturated fats are solid at room temperature and come mainly from animal fats.
Unsaturated and polyunsaturated fats are liquid at room temperature and come mainly from vegetable and fish oils.

Foods containing fats

So it's most common for vitamins, minerals and fibre to be missing from children's diets. Vitamins and minerals are needed for healthy growth, development and normal functioning of the body. Water contains some minerals, but primarily it maintains fluid in the cells of the body and in the bloodstream. Fibre adds roughage to food. This stimulates the bowel muscles and encourages the body to pass out the waste products of food after it has been digested. The diagrams on page 316 and the tables below and on page 318 explain the sources and functions of nutrients.

A regular supply of water-soluble vitamins is needed as these cannot be stored in the body. Fat-soluble vitamins can be stored in the body, but intake should still be regular.

Table MU2.8.3: The main vitamins

Vitamin	Purpose	Foods
A Fat-soluble. Pregnant women must avoid too much vitamin A.	Maintenance of good vision and healthy skin. Promotes normal growth and development. Deficiency may lead to skin and vision problems.	Carrots, tomatoes, eggs, butter, cheese
B Water-soluble. Very regular intake required.	Promotes healthy functioning of the nerves and the muscles. Deficiency may lead to anaemia and wasting of the muscles.	Meat, fish, green vegetables. Some breakfast cereals are fortified with vitamin B (it is added to them).
C Water-soluble. Daily intake required.	Maintenance of healthy tissue and skin. Deficiency leads to a decreased resistance to infection, and can result in scurvy.	Fruit. Oranges and blackcurrants have a high vitamin C content.
D Fat-soluble	Maintenance of bones and teeth. Assists body growth. Deficiency in children may lead to bones that do not harden sufficiently (skeletal condition known as rickets). Also leads to tooth decay.	Oily fish and fish oil, egg yolk, milk and margarines are fortified with vitamin D. Sunlight on the skin can cause the body to produce vitamin D.
E Fat-soluble	Promotes blood clotting, healing and metabolism. Deficiency may result in delayed blood clotting.	Cereals, egg yolk, seeds, nuts, vegetable oils
K Fat-soluble	Promotes healing. Necessary for blood clotting. Deficiency may lead to excessive bleeding due to delayed blood clotting. Vitamin K is normally given to babies after birth as deficiency is sometimes seen in newborns, although rare in adults.	Whole grains, green vegetables, liver

Table MU2.8.4: The main minerals

Mineral	Purpose	Foods
Calcium	Required for growth of teeth and bones. Also necessary for nerve and muscle function. Works with vitamin D. Deficiency may lead to rickets and tooth decay.	Milk, cheese, eggs, fish, pulses, whole grain cereals. White and brown flour are fortified with calcium.
Fluoride	Maintenance of healthy bones and protection from tooth decay.	Present in water in varying quantities. May be added to water. Many toothpastes contain fluoride.
Iodine	Used to make the thyroid hormone. Also required for normal neurological development. Deficiency may lead to thyroid problems.	Dairy products, sea foods, vegetables, water. Salt is fortified with iodine.
Iron	Essential for the formation of haemoglobin in the red blood cells, which transport oxygen around the body. Deficiency may lead to anaemia. Vitamin C helps the absorption of iron.	Meat, eggs, green vegetables, dried fruits.
Phosphorus Babies must not have a high intake as can be harmful.	Promotes the formation of teeth and bones.	Meat, fish, vegetables, eggs, fruit
Potassium	Essential for water balance in the body. Also promotes functioning of cells, including the nerves.	A wide range of foods
Sodium chloride Salt must not be added to food for babies or young children during food preparation or at the table.	Essential for water balance in the body. Involved in energy utilisation and nerve function.	Salt, meat, fish, bread, processed food

Salt

Too much salt can be bad for children. The *maximum* amount of salt that children should be having depends on their age:

- 1–3 years: 2 g a day (0.8 g sodium).
- 4–6 years: 3 g a day (1.2 g sodium).
- 7–10 years: 5 g a day (2 g sodium).
- 11 years upwards: 6 g a day (2.4 g sodium).

Link Up!

Unit TDA 2.14 Support children and young people at mealtimes and snack times.

How to establish dietary requirements

When a child is registered with a setting it is important for practitioners to find out whether the child has any specific dietary requirements so that they can meet the child's needs whilst still promoting a healthy diet.

Food has a spiritual significance within some cultures, religions and ethnic groups, which may mean that certain foods cannot be eaten or that food should be prepared in a particular way. Others make decisions about food based on personal beliefs. It is important that practitioners respect and comply with parental wishes. Individual people vary in terms of the dietary codes or restrictions that they follow. Practitioners should never assume that they will be able to tell from their religion what a child may or may not eat – they must always find out directly from the family. However, in general terms, Table MU2.8.5 below gives some helpful guidance.

Vegetarian diets

The lacto-ovo-vegetarian diet excludes meat but includes milk, milk products and eggs. The lacto-vegetarian diet excludes meat and eggs. The semi-vegetarian diet eliminates some meat, often red meat, but may include poultry and fish.

Good practice

You should never add salt to children's food during or after preparation, and if buying processed foods check the salt information on the labels and choose those with less salt content. Nuts are considered a choking hazard for young children, and they are a common cause of food allergy, so many settings have introduced a 'no nut policy'. They do not use nuts or nut products, and children may not bring them into the setting.

For information on government food guidance, see Unit TDA 2.14.

Table MU2.8.5: Cultural food

Group	Principles
Christians	May give up certain foods for Lent. May eat fish rather than meat on Fridays.
Jews	May not eat pork or shellfish. May not cook or eat milk and meat products together. May use different sets of crockery and cutlery for milk products and meat products. May only eat meat and poultry prepared by a kosher butcher. May fast for Yom Kippur (Day of Atonement).
Rastafarians	May be vegetarian. May not eat food from the vine. May only eat 'Ital' foods – those in a whole and natural state. May not eat processed or preserved foods.
Muslims	May not eat pork or pork products. Children may be breast-fed until the age of two years. Families may fast between sunrise and sunset during Ramadan, so they may rise early to eat at these times. Children under 12 do not generally fast. May drink no alcohol.
Sikhs	May be vegetarian or eat only chicken, lamb and fish. May fast regularly or just on the first day of Punjabi month.
Hindus	May eat no beef or be vegetarian. During festivals may eat only pure foods such as fruit and yoghurt. May drink no alcohol.

Vegan diets

These generally exclude all foods of animal origin including meat, milk and milk products, honey, and additives made from animal products, such as gelatine.

Food allergies, intolerances and medical conditions

Some children have food allergies, intolerances or medical conditions that may mean their diets have to be restricted. This can be caused by an allergic response, a medical condition such as diabetes, or an enzyme deficiency. It is very *important* to ensure that you fully understand children's dietary requirements so that you meet their needs without error.

Here are some key facts:

■ Practitioners should ensure that full details of diet restrictions are recorded on the registration form. They must also communicate children's requirements to everyone involved in caring for the child.

■ A list of children's requirements should be displayed in the kitchen and eating area to remind all staff. *Never give a child food or drink without checking that they can safely have it*. This also applies to raw cooking ingredients or food used in play that is not intended for consumption.

■ Common allergens include nuts and milk.

■ Some children (for example those with diabetes) may need to eat at certain times of the day.

■ Children might take medication daily (for example, those with diabetes may have insulin injections to manage the sugar levels in their body).

■ Children may have medication to take if they show symptoms of their condition or if you become aware that they have eaten, or in the case of some children even touched, a food they should not have. Often, time is of the essence in these situations. Practitioners must ensure they are absolutely clear about what to do for the individual child, and they must know how to recognise their symptoms. This can save a life.

Basic food safety

Food hygiene is essential for the prevention of food poisoning. Everyone handling or preparing food should attend a course about food hygiene to gain a Basic Food Hygiene certificate. But essentially, you should ensure that food is stored safely, prepared and cooked safely, and that food areas are kept hygienically. You should wash your hands with antiseptic soap before and after handling food. Food storage guidelines include:

- Keep the fridge and freezer cold enough. Use a thermometer to check. Fridges should be below 4 °C, and freezers should be −18 °C maximum. They must be cleaned/defrosted regularly.

- Cool food quickly before placing it in the fridge.

- Cover food that is stored, or wrap it with cling film.

- Label items with a correct use-by date if necessary.

- Separate raw and cooked food – store raw food at the bottom of the fridge and cooked food higher up, so that juices from raw food (should they spill) will not contaminate cooked food.

- If food has started to thaw, never refreeze it.

- Ensure food is fully thawed before cooking.

Food preparation guidelines include:

- Use waterproof dressings to cover any cuts or grazes on your hands.

- Do not cough or sneeze over food.

- Wear protective clothing (such as an apron) that is only used for food preparation.

- Cook food thoroughly – cook eggs until firm and cook meat all the way through.

- Test chicken to check it is cooked properly.

- Do not reheat food.

Never give a child food or drink without checking that they can safely have it

Link Up!

Unit TDA 2.14 Support children and young people at mealtimes and snack times.

Have a go!

Coeliac disease is triggered by gluten, which is contained in wheat, rye and barley. Children with coeliac disease must follow a gluten-free diet. You can learn more about the condition and access gluten-free recipes at www.coeliac.org.uk.

Cover food that is stored, or wrap it with cling film

How are things going?

▶ Progress Check

1. Describe what is meant by a 'positive environment'. (1.1)

2. Describe how you would greet a child and welcome them into the setting. (2.1)

3. Give three examples of activities you could provide to promote the use of children's senses. (2.4)

4. In what ways might you praise a child or young person for individual achievements? (2.5)

5. Explain how to:
   a care for children's teeth
   b protect children's skin from the sun. (3.1)

6. Why is it important to balance periods of physical activity with rest and quiet times? (3.4)

7. Name foods that contain the following:
   a Protein.
   b Carbohydrates.
   c Fat. (4.1)

8. What are dietary requirements? (4.2)

9. Describe five actions you would take to promote basic food safety when handling/storing/cooking food. (4.3)

Are you ready for assessment?

Learning Outcomes 2 and 3 must be assessed in a real work environment.

CACHE

Set tasks:

■ You're asked to produce an information leaflet which includes a description of what is meant by a positive environment and the regulatory requirements that underpin the provision of this. You're also asked to produce a poster about nutritional requirements, a poster about food safety and a leaflet about dietary requirements.

City & Guilds

You can prepare for assessment by rereading the information about the regulatory requirements that underpin the provision of a positive environment – these are on page 298. Follow the advice given to find out more.

Edexcel

You can prepare for assessment by rereading the information about the regulatory requirements that underpin the provision of a positive environment – these are on page 298. Follow the advice given to find out more.

UNIT 2.9

Understand partnership working in services for children and young people

LEARNING OUTCOMES

The learning outcomes you will meet in this unit are:

1 Understand partnership working within the context of services for children and young people

2 Understand the importance of effective communication and information sharing in services for children and young people

3 Understand the importance of partnerships with carers

INTRODUCTION

Practitioners work in partnership with parents and carers, their colleagues, and professionals from a range of agencies that provide support for children, young people and their families. Working together ensures that the needs of children, young people and their families are met in a holistic, coordinated way. Practitioners need to understand how these partnerships work and how to communicate effectively with others for professional purposes.

LEARNING OUTCOME 1

FOCUS ON

... understanding partnership working within the context of services for children and young people

In this section you'll learn about who the partners would be in your own work setting, and why partnership working with others is important for children and young people. You'll also learn about the characteristics of effective partnership working and the barriers to partnership working. This links with **Assessment Criteria 1.1, 1.2, 1.3, 1.4.**

The importance of working in partnership with others

Part of a practitioner's role is to work in partnership with:

■ parents and carers

■ multidisciplinary teams

■ colleagues

■ other professionals.

You'll learn more about working in partnership with parents and carers in Learning outcome 3.

Working with multidisciplinary teams and other professionals

There are a range of statutory, voluntary and private agencies and services both locally and nationally that provide support for children, young people and their families. Traditionally services were organised separately, through strictly separate health, education and social-care services. But it was found that families' needs could be met far more effectively by working together in a coordinated way. This is known as a holistic approach.

Every Child Matters (ECM) is an important government framework that supports working together to improve the following five major outcomes for all children and young people:

■ Being healthy.

■ Staying safe.

■ Enjoying and achieving.

■ Making a positive contribution.

■ Achieving economic well-being.

Multi-agency working

'Multi-agency working' is the term we use to describe what happens when a range of practitioners and professionals from different agencies, services and teams work together to meet the needs of children, young people and/or their families. Workers from health, education, childcare and social-care services will liaise with one another to enable them to meet a family's needs in a coordinated way. You'll learn how practitioners make referrals to other agencies in Learning outcome 2.

Integrated learning

'Integrated working' is the term we use when different services are offered in the same building. Sure Start Centres (or children's centres) are a good example of this, as under one roof there might be:

Professionals at a formal meeting

- a health visitor running in-house baby clinics and an outreach service

- a nursery providing early years education

- an out-of-school club providing child care

- a speech and language therapist working with children and young people.

There may even be career support and adult education classes with crèche facilities running alongside.

The diagram below shows the range of professionals who may work together to meet the needs of children, young people and their families.

Working in partnership with colleagues

You learnt about maintaining everyday relationships with colleagues in Unit SHC 21. You may like to reread this information as part of your study of this unit.

Link Up!

Unit SHC 21 Introduction to communication in children and young people's settings.

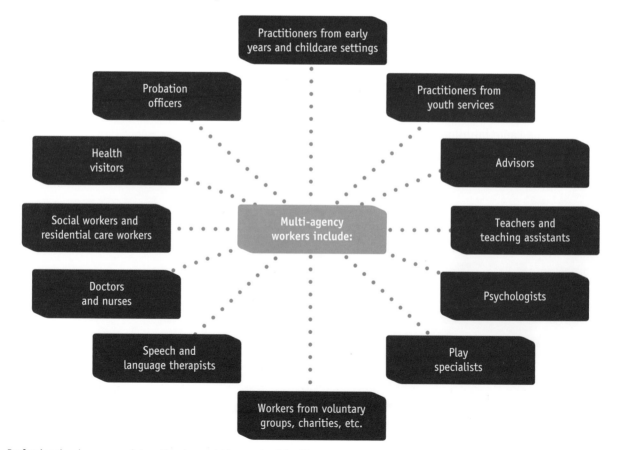

Professionals who may work together to meet the needs of families

Practical example

Meeting Jayden's needs

Three-year-old Jayden was taken to his GP by his parents, who were concerned that there may be something wrong with his mouth. The GP picks up a difficulty with speech/language, and refers Jayden to a speech and language therapist, who is based in the local Sure Start Centre. Jayden's parents say they haven't been to the centre before. Jayden does not currently access any early years care or education, as his parents prefer to have him at home with them.

When they meet the therapist, she recommends a number of strategies to help Jayden with his speech and language, including weaning him off his dummy, talking to him more and providing opportunities for him to socialise. She suggests that Jayden and his family could benefit from the support and social opportunities available within the building, including drop-in family play sessions and a pre-school. She says if they decide to use the other services, she will be happy to speak to the practitioners there about the strategies they are using to promote Jayden's speech and language development, so that everyone works with Jayden in a consistent way.

Partners in your own work setting

In early years settings you will always work in partnership with other practitioners (who are your colleagues) and the parents and carers of the children and young people who attend. Who else you work in partnership with will depend on:

■ the type of setting. If you work in an integrated setting such as a children's centre (as described above), you may work in partnership with a diverse range of professionals on a regular basis

■ the needs of the children and young people. If you don't work in an integrated setting, your involvement with a range of professionals will largely depend on the support needed by the individual children and young people attending the setting at any given time.

Did you know?

During your career you will also interact with a range of professionals who do not directly work with the children or young people themselves. This includes inspectors who visit the premises (such as Ofsted inspectors or environmental health inspectors) and assessors, trainers, advisers, students and visitors from other settings. These may come from the private, state, voluntary or independent sectors. They may also come from primary care trusts.

Characteristics of effective partnership working

Partnerships work most effectively when:

There may be visitors from other settings

- all partners respect one another's roles and treat each other as equals

- all partners listen to and value one another's opinions

- there's honest, open communication

- there are clear lines of communication

- there are policies and procedures for information sharing

- shared information is recorded clearly and accurately

- confidentiality is respected

- referrals are made appropriately.

You'll learn more about this in Learning outcome 2.

Barriers to effective partnership working

Multi-agency and integrated working is still relatively new to the early years sector. As it continues, the processes and procedures will become more familiar to everyone involved. The common barriers to effective integrated and multi-agency working include:

- Professionals from different backgrounds using specific terms or jargon that are not familiar to or understood by other professionals or practitioners.

- Professionals trained to work in very different ways finding it difficult to agree the best way to work together.

- Professionals from different backgrounds having differing priorities.

- Professionals not used to sharing their expertise, views or findings and having them questioned by other professionals.

Did you know?

Effective communication is at the heart of good partnership working.

- Professionals not used to taking the expertise, views or findings of others into consideration.

- Professionals having different ways of interacting with colleagues and other adults (such as parents).

- Professionals having different ways of interacting with children and young people.

- Professionals having different responsibilities in terms of documentation (such as the format of reports, etc.).

Overcoming barriers

Ongoing, open communication is the best way to overcome these barriers, along with a willingness to embrace new ways of working. If difficulties are expressed, the parties can work together to address them. For instance, an educational psychologist will not know that he needs to explain his use of terms unless a practitioner expresses the fact that they do not follow what he's saying.

Good organisation also helps immensely, and there should always be a lead professional who takes responsibility for the coordination of services for a family. They should also act as the point of contact for families when joint communication needs to take place. In the case of integrated working, it helps when professionals working under one roof have their own desk space, storage space, computer and telephone line.

Open communication is the best way to overcome barriers

Good practice

Everyone involved has a part to play in making the organisational aspects of the partnership work in practice. It should not be underestimated how much practicalities can help professionals to work together effectively, such as booking a room for a meeting at your setting as arranged, or ensuring that you forward the required documents in plenty of time.

LEARNING OUTCOME 2

FOCUS ON

... understanding the importance of effective communication and information sharing in services for children and young people

In this section you'll learn about effective communication between partners. You'll also learn about policies and procedures for sharing information, and conflicts or dilemmas in relation to sharing information. Lastly, you'll learn about recording information, storing data and how referrals are made to different agencies. This links with **Assessment Criteria 2.1, 2.2, 2.3, 2.4, 2.5, 2.6.**

Clear and effective communication

As you've learnt in other units, practitioners should always aim to communicate clearly and effectively to ensure that:

- the practitioner's own messages are understood by others

- the practitioner understands the messages that others communicate to them.

Practitioners need to pay particular attention to clear and effective communication when they are working together with partners to support a child or young person. Effective communication enables a number of partners to work together by:

- sharing and discussing information

- learning from one another

- understanding each other's opinions

- agreeing methods of working together, for example how to record information

- planning how to meet children and young people's needs

- reviewing the progress made by children and young people

- evaluating the effectiveness of partnership working.

You learnt about effective communication in Unit SHC 21. You may like to recap your previous learning by rereading the information as part of your study of this unit.

Link Up!

Unit SHC 21 Introduction to communication in children and young people's settings.

Good practice

When working in partnership, the following aspects of communication are particularly important:

- Active listening to understand information given and to demonstrate respect and interest.
- Asking questions when necessary to ensure understanding and to gain further information.
- Consulting with others to ensure all opinions are heard and considered.
- Explaining your own point of view/opinion to ensure you contribute.
- Sharing information to ensure all partners are kept up to date (in line with confidentiality procedures – see page 334).
- Negotiating to develop plans or solutions that all partners agree with.
- Summarising to ensure everyone understands what has been agreed or what will happen next.

Did you know?

Partners should always keep children, young people and their families at the centre of any communications about them. Even if they're not present at meetings or involved in discussions, they should still be at the heart of everything the partnership does. Information should also be shared with them as appropriate.

Active listening is important

Policies and procedures for information sharing

Your setting will have a policy and procedures in place about the way in which information is shared with partners, including the colleagues you work with on a daily basis. The policy and procedures will set out how the setting works to comply with:

- relevant legislation (Data Protection Act 1998, Children Act 2004, Children Plan 2007)
- Every Child Matters
- curriculum frameworks that apply to the setting (for example the Early Years Foundation Stage).

Policies and procedures of settings will cover how information is shared:

- between colleagues within the setting
- with parents and carers
- with outside professionals.

This will include the following types of information:

- Details relating to children and young people's assessment and development (for example observations shared with outside professionals).
- Details needed for the continuity of care between settings and carers (for example information shared with a parent about when a child slept, fed, etc.).
- Particulars that are needed for transition from one setting to another (for example when a child leaves nursery to start school).

Good practice

It's important that you understand and follow these procedures. Failing to do so is unprofessional. It can promote a lot of confusion (the first Practical example on page 333 demonstrates this) and sometimes has serious consequences (as demonstrated in the second Practical example).

Practical example

Eddie's note

Eddie is an assistant working the morning shift at a pre-school. At the end of the session, he writes a useful note for Jane, the assistant working the afternoon shift, about the activities carried out so far by the children who are staying all day. He pins the piece of paper to the noticeboard in the staff room where he thinks she'll see it, and leaves for the day.

However, Jane expects any handover information to be left in her pigeon hole in the staff room, in line with the pre-school's procedures. When she arrives, she checks her pigeon hole and finds nothing. She doesn't look at the noticeboard at all.

Practical example

Rebecca's message

Nursery practitioner Rebecca is having a busy day, but she's on the early shift and will soon be finished. She's returning some files to the office when the phone rings. It's the mother of three-year-old Asher calling to say that she's not feeling well, so her neighbour will collect Asher today. The neighbour is already noted on the registration form as having permission to collect him, just as long as Asher's mother gives advance warning. Rebecca says she'll pass the message on. Just after she hangs up the phone, Rebecca is called to help a child who has fallen over outside and needs some first aid. By the time she's seen to this, it's time for her to go home. She's forgotten all about the message.

At the end of the session, the neighbour arrives to collect Asher. But as none of the practitioners know about his mother giving permission for her to collect Asher today, they can't let him go. The supervisor tries to ring Asher's mother but there's no answer. The neighbour says she was going to the doctors, so she has probably switched off her mobile phone. Asher is now the only child left, and he's starting to get upset.

Follow your setting's procedures for sharing information

Confidentiality conflicts or dilemmas

When working with partners, it's important to remember that not everyone may have access to the same information. You should be clear about what information you can share, and what should remain confidential. If you are at all unsure, always check with your supervisor. You learnt about the principles and practices relating to confidentiality in Unit SHC 21, Learning outcome 5. These apply to information that is verbal, paper based and electronic. You may want to read that section again to refresh your memory as part of your study of this unit.

Link Up!

Unit SHC 21 Introduction to communication in children and young people's settings.

Recording information

In your setting, systems will be in place for recording a great deal of information, as shown by the diagram below.

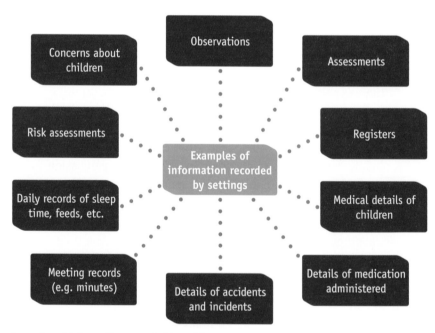

Examples of information recorded by settings

Contributing to the recording of information

All practitioners contribute to the recording of information, and it's important that this is done in the following ways:

- Legibly. Other people must be able to read the information easily, and it should be free from errors. If you need help with spelling, punctuation or grammar, it's absolutely fine to ask a colleague for help with this as you go or to ask them to check your work when you've finished. But make sure that the colleague you ask is permitted to have access to the information.

- Clearly. If you are at all vague, others may misunderstand your meaning. This is likely to affect the quality of partnership working, and could lead to mistakes being made. It's also useful to consider who will be accessing the information. This will help you to avoid using jargon or terms that others (including parents) may not be familiar with. Ensure that you record sufficient detail so that everything makes sense.

- Concisely. While sufficient detail is needed, your records should also be concise (or to the point). If your records are long and rambling, time and effort is wasted by you and those who read the information. In addition, key pieces of information can be lost or buried. Using bullet points can be very effective.

- Accurately. Obviously all records should be accurate. Check facts carefully where appropriate. If you are recording the opinion of yourself or another partner rather than a hard fact, make that clear in your report.

- In a way that meets legal requirements. For instance, if you are recording details of an accident that has occurred in the setting, you are required to record certain facts, such as how the accident occurred and the extent of any injuries sustained. In addition, all of your records must be made and stored in line with the data protection legislation (see page 336).

It takes time to become familiar with how to record different types of information

Did you know?

It's particularly important to make sure that information recorded by hand is legible. Child observations are a good example of this because we often share them with partners. But with certain observation methods we need to record a lot of detail, so we have to write very quickly during the observation period. This may mean that you need to write or type up your notes afterwards so that others can read them.

Good practice

It takes time to become familiar with how to record all of the different types of information in the right way. So when you are required to formally record a type of information for the first time, you should consult your supervisor. They will help you to use the right format and the right sort of language. For instance, in a factual report such as an accident report, you should only record the specific facts rather than your interpretation of events. So you would write, 'Patrick was sitting under the table. He bumped his left cheek on the table leg as he crawled out' rather than, 'Patrick was sitting under the table. He was so keen to crawl after his friend that he wasn't thinking about where he was going, and unfortunately he bumped himself on the table leg.'

Meeting data protection requirements

Unit SHC 21 Introduction to communication in children and young people's settings.

As you learnt in Unit SHC 21, Learning outcome 5, you must ensure that all communications and records are made securely and held securely in line with data protection requirements.

The following checklist will help you to ensure that you are acting professionally when recording and storing information:

- Have you read and understood your setting's organisational procedures for recording, sharing and storing information?

- Have you followed those organisational procedures to the letter?

- Have you met the requirements of the Data Protection Act 1998?

- Have you made sure that confidentiality is maintained whilst you are using information? (For example checking that no one else can see your computer screen or paper document, and closing and securing files as soon as the information has been used.)

- Have you made backups of electronic files and stored them safely?

- Are computer security systems working properly, and are regular virus checks carried out to protect information?

- Have you made sure you won't be overheard if confidential information needs to be discussed?

Practical example

Nigel reports a problem

Nigel works for a childcare company that owns a day nursery and an out-of-school club. He works at the out-of-school club, which meets within the premises of a primary school.

The main office is at the nursery, and Nigel has a laptop that he keeps locked away in a filing cabinet at the club.

Today, Nigel has received an on-screen message to say there is an error and that the scheduled virus check cannot be completed. He tries to run the check again, but it still won't work. He calls the manager at the nursery to let her know. She asks him not to use the laptop today, and arranges to come up to have a look. She says that if she can't resolve the problem herself, she'll get the technical support person who the setting uses to visit and sort things out.

Did you know?

Some settings may ask you not to use children and young people's real names in some circumstances – when writing a report for instance, or when writing up the minutes (notes) of a staff meeting.

Referrals between agencies

When a practitioner or professional feels that additional support is needed by a child, young person or family, they must ensure that their needs are met by making a referral. Local procedures must be followed, and these do vary. But generally speaking, each local borough will have set up their own multi-agency referral panel, to whom referrals will be made. Information about the child, young person or family must be submitted, and that will include common assessment (see below). The panel will then consider the information that has been made available to them and decide what support will be offered and how this will be coordinated.

The common assessment framework (CAF)

Different practitioners and professionals have different ways of assessing the development and needs of children and young people. So a common assessment framework was introduced to help a range of practitioners to work together in the same way. The following shows what the Department for Children and Families tells us.

About CAF

The CAF is a key part of delivering frontline services that are integrated, and are focused around the needs of children and young people. The CAF is a standardised approach to conducting assessments of children's additional needs and deciding how these should be met. It can be used by practitioners across children's services in England.

The CAF aims to help early identification of need, promote coordinated service provision and reduce the number of assessments that some children and young people go through.

Why the CAF has been introduced

We all want better lives for children and young people. We have high aspirations for this to be the best place in the world for children and young people to grow up. Most children and young people do well. Most move in and out of difficulties through their lives, and some have important disadvantages that currently are only addressed when they become serious. Sometimes their parents know there is a problem but struggle to know how to get help. We want to identify these children and young people earlier and help them before things reach crisis point. The most important way of doing this is for everyone in the children and young people's workforce to pay attention to their progress and well-being, and be prepared to help if something is going wrong.

CAF

Did you know?

The common assessment covers three domains: development of the child or young person; parents and carers; and family and environment.

The main purpose of CAF is to:

- identify additional needs of children and young people

- ensure that additional needs of children and young people are met through multi-agency working.

The CAF consists of the following:

- A pre-assessment checklist to help practitioners decide who would benefit from a common assessment. (There's no need to do a common assessment for every child or young person. Children and young people who are progressing well, or have needs that have already been identified, do not need one.)

- A process to enable practitioners to undertake a common assessment where necessary, and then act on the result.

- A standard form to record the assessment.

- A delivery plan and review form.

- A standalone consent statement.

Practitioners must undertake a CAF training course before they can undertake common assessments

Undertaking common assessment

Practitioners must undertake a locally approved CAF training course before they are able to undertake common assessments. But it's important that all practitioners recognise when it may be needed so that they can arrange for a trained person to do the assessment. To enable this, any practitioner can use the short CAF pre-assessment checklist to help decide whether a common assessment should be undertaken. It guides practitioners by looking at the five Every Child Matters outcome areas and considering whether the child or young person is:

■ healthy

■ safe from harm

■ learning and developing

■ having a positive impact on others

■ free from the negative impact of poverty.

If the answer to any of these is no, and additional services might be required, this suggests that a common assessment would be an appropriate next step. The practitioner would then refer this to the person in their setting who is trained to complete common assessments.

To access the pre-assessment form and further information on completing it, visit: www.cwdcouncil.org.uk/caf and follow the links at the bottom of the screen.

Did you know?

The CAF is often the first assessment made of children and young people with special educational needs.

Link Up!

Unit TDA 2.15 Support children and young people with disabilities and special educational needs.

The diagram below shows the range of professionals likely to access the CAF.

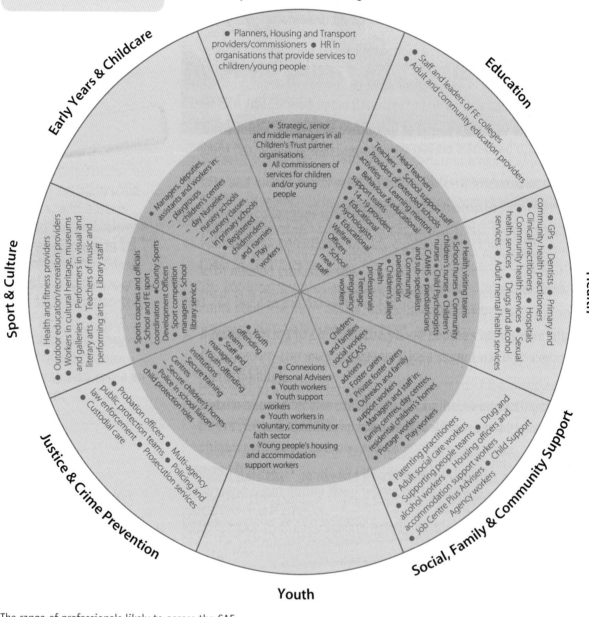

The range of professionals likely to access the CAF

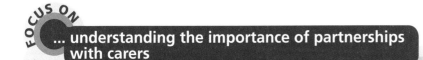

LEARNING OUTCOME 3

FOCUS ON

... understanding the importance of partnerships with carers

In this section you'll learn about the reasons for partnerships with carers, and how these are developed and sustained in your work setting. You'll also learn about circumstances when partnerships with carers may be difficult to develop and sustain. This links with **Assessment Criteria 3.1, 3.2, 3.3.**

Working in partnership with parents and carers

You must always respect and value the important role of family members in their children's lives. Although we may share the care of children and young people, parents are usually the primary carers. They usually:

- know their child best

- have the closest bond with them.

Good practice

Children generally feel a deep sense of love and connection with their parents and carers. They are usually the most consistent people in a child's life to provide them with love, affection and care. Children share experiences with family members that they will remember for the rest of their lives. Good relationships and sharing information is the key to effective shared care.

The reasons for partnerships with parents and carers

The diagram on page 342 shows the benefits of good relationships between families and practitioners. These benefits are the reason why good relationships are so important.

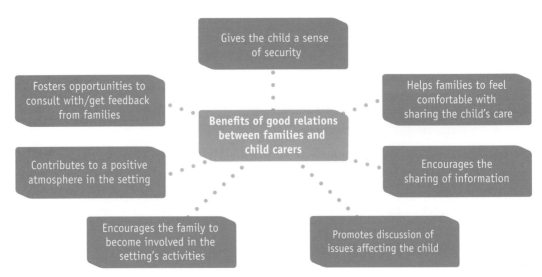

Benefits of good relationships between families and practitioners

Key person system

Babies begin to bond emotionally with their parents or primary carers soon after birth, and this gives them a sense of safety, security and love. In order for babies and young children to feel happy, settled and secure, they also need to make emotional attachments with other adults who care for them when their parents aren't there.

To ensure that each child within the setting has the opportunity to form a deeper relationship with an adult on a one-to-one basis, many settings operate a **key person** system. This means that a member of staff is appointed to take a special interest in the welfare of a particular child, and to get to know them and their parents or carers well. Most key persons will look after the interests of several children within a setting. They will also have the main responsibility for observing and assessing the development of their key children and for liaising with their key children's parents and carers.

key terms

Key person a person appointed to take a special interest in the welfare of a particular child.

Did you know?

It's particularly important for a key person to form solid partnerships with the parents of their key children. Good communication is essential to ensure that all relevant information is shared.

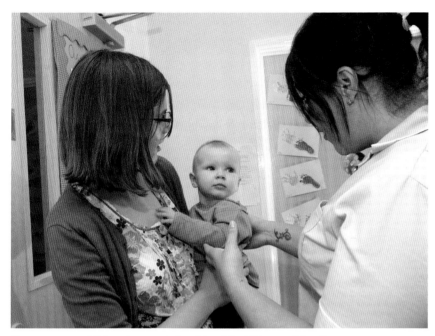

Key persons establish a deeper relationship with children and families

Developing and sustaining partnerships

The strategies outlined below help practitioners to develop and sustain partnerships with parents and carers.

Valuing diverse family backgrounds

Lots of different types of families love and care for children successfully. For example, backgrounds will reflect:

- different cultures, religions, beliefs, and relationships between adults

- that some children live with family members other than their parents

- that some children live with carers they are not related to by blood

- that some children divide their time between more than one home (for example if parents have separated)

- that some children may live within social-care facilities rather than a family home.

Some children live with family members other than their parents

Did you know?

The EYFS states that, 'Parents and practitioners have a lot to learn from each other.'

You should value and accept the diverse family backgrounds of all children and the homes in which they live, and work to form positive relationships with their primary carers.

Exchanging information with parents and carers

The relationship between a child's key person and their parents is particularly important as the key person will normally be the parents' chief point of contact within the setting. Parents and practitioners are much more likely to share important information and concerns when a positive relationship exists.

Practitioners must share information that can affect the care and well-being of children. In the case of babies and young children, it's particularly important that day-to-day information about the care routine is shared when they are handed back to parents and carers, as the Practical example below shows. Passing on this information allows parents and carers to continue the child's care appropriately.

Practical example

Barinder hands back

Barinder works in the baby room of a day nursery. It's nearly the end of the session, and her five-month-old key child, George, will soon be going home. During the day, Barinder has been keeping notes on a 'daily routine sheet' designed by the setting. She has recorded when George was fed and how much milk he took, when he slept and how long for, when his nappy was changed and whether it was wet or soiled. She checks that the record is up to date. She then adds a short message about some experiences that George has enjoyed today. She pops it into his bag.

Benefits of encouraging families to share information
Practitioners should also encourage families to share information they have about their baby or child that may affect their care and well-being. This information may include details about and changes to:

- medical conditions including allergies and details of any medication or treatment

- medical history

- dietary requirements

- likes and dislikes

- general routine – including details of eating and sleeping patterns

- events in the child's life that may impact on their emotions.

Good practice

Establishing a good partnership with parents and carers helps families to feel confident in approaching staff to discuss issues at home that may affect their child's emotional well-being. This allows practitioners to be aware of and understand children's feelings. It gives them the opportunity to plan how they can best offer appropriate support. This is important not only when big life events occur, but on a day-to-day basis. For instance, a baby or young child may be in an irritable mood if they are tired following a night of disturbed sleep at home. Or they may feel angry because they have been told off by a parent before coming to the setting.

Did you know?

The information should be documented on the registration form, in line with the setting's organisational policies and procedures. Some information, about feeding or allergies for example, will also be displayed in food preparation and eating areas. Practitioners must pass on relevant information to colleagues, such as a child's sleeping pattern. However, information of a confidential nature must only be shared on a need-to-know basis.

Methods of encouraging families to share information

Practitioners encourage families to share such information by:

- explaining the benefits of working in partnership when families first visit the setting

- making families aware of the setting's confidentiality policy

- making a private area available for confidential conversations

- ensuring that key persons are accessible to parents who wish to talk to them.

Did you know?

Settings are increasingly making use of technology to stay in touch with parents and carers and to pass on information to them about their child's time at the setting. Digital photos, video clips and audio clips may all be emailed home.

Unit MU 2.2 Contribute to the support of child and young person development.

Observations and assessments

Parents and carers should also be informed periodically about the developmental progress of children and young people. This process can really engage parents and carers, who will be able to contribute information about the children's learning and development away from the setting and the skills that this is helping children to develop.

Planning

After involving parents in the observation and assessment of their child's learning and development, it makes sense to progress on to involving them in planning future activities and experiences for the child. It's beneficial to consult parents about how they see the child's needs, and how they feel about how they are met. You may gain new insight into what the child might enjoy or be interested in based on popular activities at home, and parents may also have some great new ideas to try out.

Encouraging families to participate within the setting

Encouraging families to participate within a setting is another way to demonstrate that families are valued and respected. It also strengthens the partnership between practitioners, parents and carers, which is good for everyone concerned. There are many ways to encourage families to participate, such as:

- invitations to social activities, such as fundraising events or coffee mornings

- invitations to make a one-to-one appointment with the key person to discuss their child's progress

- written reports on the child's progress

Good practice

Some settings might also offer a parents group, which may organise their own events including some of those mentioned above. A parents room may be provided within the setting. Newsletters, blogs and noticeboards help families to feel involved and up to date with activities within the setting.

- home-to-setting diaries

- invitations to join the setting's committee

- invitations to annual general meetings (AGMs)

- collection of feedback via suggestion boxes and evaluations

- running family sessions, where adults can attend with their child and the child's siblings

- having training or information evenings on topics of interest, such as first aid or baby massage

- organising family trips out

- organising family festival celebrations, a Christmas party for instance

- inviting family members to volunteer during sessions, or to help by using their skills, for example making dressing-up clothes or story sacks, or demonstrating to the children how to cook a particular dish, or how to do woodwork

- holding exhibitions of children's art and craft work

- holding open days and/or evenings

- organising children's concerts or plays

- holding a toy library or book exchange.

Did you know?

Most settings devise their own policy and procedures that outline how practitioners should work in partnership with parents and carers. You must always work in line with these.

Have a go!

Have you seen your setting's policy on working in partnership with parents and carers? If not, ask your supervisor if you can see it. Read it through carefully, and ask questions if there's anything that you don't understand.

Parents and carers can be invited to open days

Where partnerships may be difficult to develop and sustain

There are some circumstances in which partnerships with parents or carers may be difficult to develop and sustain.

Barriers to participation

You learnt about barriers to participation in Unit SHC 23. These can prevent parents and carers from participating fully in a setting's activities or from accessing their services, in the same way that barriers can affect children and young people's rights to inclusion and equal opportunities. It's up to practitioners to put their setting's equal opportunities policy into practice by overcoming any barriers that are identified for individual parents and carers. Examples of barriers that may be identified and strategies that may be developed to overcome them are given in the following series of Practical examples.

Link Up!

Unit SHC 23 Introduction to equality and inclusion in children and young people's settings.

Practical example

Breaking down a language barrier

A Polish couple have booked a place for their new baby. They have just started to learn English as an additional language, and so there is a language barrier between the staff and the parents.

Using the computer, the setting's manager translates the setting's 'Welcome Pack' into Polish. This contains the information given to all new parents. She arranges for a Polish-speaking interpreter to come to a meeting with the family and the key person. They talk about ongoing strategies to meet the family's needs. At the meeting, the practitioners find out that the baby's uncle will soon be living locally. He speaks English and will be staying with the family. It's agreed that the uncle will act as an interpreter when necessary. The manager will carry on translating written material for as long as necessary.

Practical example

Literacy support

A dad meets his daughter's key person on her first visit to a holiday club. He tells the key person he has difficulties with literacy. He struggles to read and write without support. He's worried this will be a problem because there are registration forms to fill out and information to read.

The key person tells him there's no need to worry, she can talk him through the written information. She suggests she takes responsibility for verbally telling him about new information contained in newsletters, etc. They agree she should also give a copy to the child to take home as usual. When forms need to be completed, the key person invites the dad into the office. She asks him questions verbally and records the answers on the form.

Practical example

Staying in touch

The mum of Liam, a child at nursery, has become seriously ill. She doesn't leave her home very often, but she still wants to feel involved in her son's life at nursery. His gran will be bringing him in and collecting him from now on.

The setting makes really good use of a home-to-nursery diary, recording details of Liam's experiences. They take digital photos of nursery activities and displays, and email them to Liam's mum often. If she isn't well enough to visit the setting to discuss Liam's development from time to time, Liam's mum knows the setting will arrange for Liam's key person to visit her at home or talk to her on the phone. She also knows she can call the key person at any time.

Responses to partnership opportunities

Settings generally come across a range of responses from parents and carers to the partnership opportunities that they make available. Some of these are positive and some are negative. However, the job of practitioners is to handle all responses positively.

The following diagram shows the factors that may lead to a negative response.

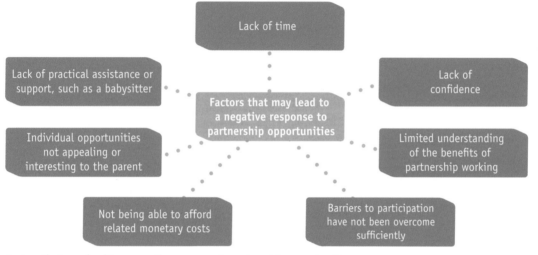

Factors that may lead to a negative response to partnership opportunities

Strategies to overcome a negative response

If a parent responds negatively to opportunities for partnership working, it's good practice for practitioners to find out why and to offer strategies to overcome a negative response. For instance:

■ **Lack of time:**
Appointments to discuss children's progress to be made in the evening as well as in the day. If parents don't have the time to attend group meetings etc., you can distribute information afterwards via newsletters or emails, which parents can read at a time that suits them.

■ **Lack of confidence:**
Don't push anyone to participate in a certain way if they are feeling insecure. Instead, find a way of engaging the parents that is within their comfort zone. For example, the parent who is reluctant to run a stall at the summer fair may be very happy to sell raffle tickets.

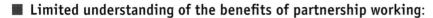

■ **Limited understanding of the benefits of partnership working**:
Most settings have a policy on partnerships with parents and carers
that explains the advantages. However, there's a lot for parents
new to a setting to take in, so if a family responds negatively to
opportunities for participation, it can be helpful for the key person
to discuss the benefits with them again.

■ **Barriers to participation have not been properly overcome**:
Check with families to see if there are any barriers that have not
already been identified, and to see if further action is necessary
to overcome barriers that have been identified previously. It may
be that previous strategies weren't adequate, or that they are no
longer effective.

■ **Not being able to afford related monetary costs**:
The majority of partnership opportunities should not incur any
expense. However, some events, such as a family day out, may
incur a charge. It's good practice to keep charges as low as
possible, and if a number of trips are available, to include some
that are free or require a nominal fee only.

■ **Lack of practical assistance or support**:
Find out what support is needed and see if the setting can offer
a solution. Two common problems are a lack of transport or no
babysitter, which makes attending events difficult. Settings
may be able to help by providing a crèche service alongside key
events such as the annual general meeting (AGM), or by letting
everyone know that any offers to share transport would be much
appreciated.

■ **Individual opportunities not appealing or interesting to the
parent**:
It would be unrealistic to expect all of the partnership working
opportunities to appeal to and interest all of the parents and
carers at the setting, and you must respect people's preferences for
involvement. A good range of opportunities will help a setting to
appeal to the widest range of parents. For example special events
that require attendance, as well as other ways to communicate (via
suggestion boxes and evaluations for instance). It's good practice
to collect feedback on the opportunities that are offered, so that
they can be developed and improved.

How are things going?

▶ Progress Check

1. Why is working in partnership with others important? (1.1)

2. Define the characteristics of effective partnership working. (1.3)

3. Identify three potential barriers to partnership working. (1.4)

4. What are the benefits of clear and effective communication between partners? (2.1)

5. Explain where there might be conflicts in respect of sharing information with partners and confidentiality. (2.3)

6. Explain how communications and records should be stored securely to meet data protection requirements. (2.5)

7. Explain the following:
    a Why referrals are made to different agencies.
    b How referrals are made to different agencies. (2.6)

8. What are the reasons for working in partnership with parents and carers? (3.1)

9. Describe circumstances where partnerships with parents and carers may be difficult to develop and sustain. (3.3)

Are you ready for assessment?

CACHE

Set tasks:

■ An in-depth task with three sections in which you produce information that shows that you understand what partnership working means in practice.

You can prepare by reviewing your setting's policies and procedures on confidentiality, sharing information and working with partners. You may like to ask an experienced colleague about their experience of working with outside partners (such as social workers, health visitors etc.)

City & Guilds

You must complete the mandatory Assignment 013, which has three tasks. It entails answering questions about partnership working, the importance of effective communication and information sharing, and the importance of working in partnersip with carers. You can prepare by reviewing your setting's policies and procedures on confidentiality, sharing information and working with partners.

Edexcel

You can prepare by reviewing your setting's policies and procedures on confidentiality, sharing information and working with partners. You may also like to ask an experienced colleague about their experience of working with outside partners (such as social workers, health visitors etc.).

UNIT 001

Paediatric emergency first aid

LEARNING OUTCOMES

The learning outcomes you will meet in this unit are:

1. Understand the role of the paediatric first-aider

2. Be able to assess an emergency situation and act safely and effectively

3. Be able to provide first aid for an infant and a child who is unresponsive and breathing normally

4. Be able to provide first aid for an infant and a child who is unresponsive and not breathing normally

5. Be able to provide first aid for an infant and a child who has a foreign body airway obstruction

6. Be able to provide first aid for an infant and a child who is wounded and bleeding

7. Know how to provide first aid for an infant and a child who is suffering from shock

INTRODUCTION

It is a fact of life that accidents, injuries and illnesses happen to all children on occasion, regardless of the precautions that you take. For this reason, all practitioners should undertake a paediatric first-aid course. The information in this unit by no means replaces first-aid training.

LEARNING OUTCOME 1

FOCUS ON

... understanding the role of the paediatric first-aider

In this section you'll learn about the responsibilities of the first-aider and how to minimise the risk of infection to self and others. You'll also learn about first-aid equipment, what information needs to be recorded in accident/incident records and the definition of a child and an infant for first-aid purposes. This links with **Assessment Criteria 1.1, 1.2, 1.3, 1.4, 1.5**.

The responsibilities of a paediatric first-aider

When a child (the casualty) has become ill or injured, the responsibilities of a paediatric first-aider are as follows:

1 Assess the situation calmly.

   a Protect yourself and others from any danger.

   b Prevent further harm to the casualty.

2 Comfort and reassure the casualty and others present.

3 Take care of the casualty until a medic or the child's parent/legal guardian takes over.

   a Assess the casualty.

   b Give early treatment to prevent the condition from worsening and to promote recovery.

   c Ensure emergency help is on the way if it is needed.

   d Pass on relevant information to medics/emergency services/parent/guardian.

Did you know?

Sometimes first aid is all that is necessary, and medical assistance is not required. For example, common minor injuries such as grazes can be sufficiently treated with first aid. However, it's important to recognise when urgent medical assistance is required.

First-aider responsibility in a setting

USUALLY A PERSON QUALIFIED TO LEVEL 3 OR ABOVE WILL TAKE RESPONSIBILITY FOR ADMINISTERING FIRST AID AT THE SETTING. SO EVEN IF YOU ARE FIRST AID TRAINED, YOU MAY JUST BE REQUIRED TO CALL THEM FOR HELP, DEPENDING ON THE CIRCUMSTANCES. YOU MUST FOLLOW YOUR OWN SETTING'S PROCEDURES.

Minimising the risk of infection to self and others

You learnt about following infection control procedures in Unit MU 2.4, Learning outcome 6. You are advised to reread this information, as minimising the risk of infection protects you, the casualty and others. Your personal protection from risk of infection must also be a priority.

Personal protection

When in a first-aid situation, you should:

- wash your hands well with antiseptic soap if possible

- ensure that any cuts or grazes on your hands are covered with a waterproof plaster – this is good practice in any case when working with children

- always put on disposable vinyl gloves before dealing with any body fluids and before you begin first-aid treatment. You may also wear a disposable apron

- cover blood or other bodily fluid spills with a 1 per cent hypochlorite solution before wiping it up

- ensure that all used items such as dressings and used gloves and aprons are disposed of in a sealed bag, which should be placed into the correct sealed bin for disposal

- wash your hands well with antiseptic soap immediately after coming into contact with bodily waste, including blood.

Link Up!

Unit MU 2.4 Contribute to children and young people's health and safety.

Did you know?

Whenever you are dealing with an accident, incident or illness, you must stay calm. You should reassure casualties and children or young people who are bystanders, as they may be very frightened.

Use of suitable first-aid equipment

Every setting must have a first-aid kit. Here's what you need to know:

- Kits should be stored somewhere accessible for staff but out of the reach of children, in a dry place so that items won't perish. They should always be returned to the correct place so that they can be found right away in an emergency.

- Kits now come with a list of contents inside, often on a sticker inside the lid. It's crucial that as items are used the box is replenished, and the sticker makes it easier to check that everything is present and correct. Systems should be devised to ensure that is the case. Often, one person takes responsibility for overseeing the first-aid kit, and checks it on a weekly basis.

- It's good practice to keep 'guidance cards' within a first-aid kit. These contain brief notes (reminders) on how to carry out life-saving procedures – many kits now come with guidance cards included.

- A notepad and pen should be kept in the kit so notes can be made on the casualty's condition.

All settings must have a first-aid kit

Medical contents of a first-aid kit

- Protective, disposable vinyl gloves and aprons.

- Plastic bags for the safe disposal of used items.

- Plasters for dressing small cuts and grazes.

- Sterile dressing pads for covering wounds.

- Sterile large combined dressings for large wounds (dressing pad attached to a roller bandage).

- Adhesive tape for securing pads.

- Scissors for cutting tape/dressings/the casualty's clothes if necessary.

- Crêpe roller bandages for securing dressings in place/supporting injured joints.

- Eye dressings for protecting injured eyes.

- Sling/triangular bandage to support injured arms or shoulders.

- Safety pins for securing slings.

Settings may also have alcohol-free cleansing wipes in the first-aid box for cleansing wounds.

Good practice

Only use items in the first-aid kit for first-aid purposes. For instance, don't borrow the notepad and pen for another reason. This helps to ensure that everything is present and correct at the time of an emergency, which could occur at any time.

Accident reports and incident records

Reports must be made in writing when there's an accident or incident at a setting. See Unit MU 2.4, Learning outcome 5 for full details.

Link Up!

Unit MU 2.4 Contribute to children and young people's health and safety.

Definition of an infant and a child

As you learn more about first aid, you'll find out that in several first-aid situations infants (babies) need to be treated differently to a child who has the same illness or injury. For the purposes of first aid, an infant is classed as being 12 months old or younger. A child is classed as being over 12 months old.

Good practice

You should be aware that the condition of a baby can deteriorate rapidly. They lose consciousness more quickly than children, and loss of body fluids causing dehydration can make them ill very fast.

LEARNING OUTCOME 2

... being able to assess an emergency situation and act safely and effectively

In this section you'll learn about conducting a scene survey and a primary survey. You'll also learn when and how to call for help. This links with **Assessment Criteria 2.1, 2.2, 2.3.**

How to conduct a scene survey

A scene survey will usually take only a few seconds, but it's one of the most vital factors in managing a first-aid situation. A scene survey is about *stopping and thinking calmly* before approaching a casualty or accident scene. It's the first thing a first-aider should do when they become aware of a first-aid situation. It stops them from rushing in and making a mistake in the heat of the moment. For example, if a child is lying on the ground because they've been electrocuted and a first-aider rushes in, they could also be electrocuted. Rushing in does not protect anyone present.

Process

The following things are considered in a scene survey:

1 Safety:
   a Are there any dangers? If so, can you make them safe? (See below.)
   b Are you wearing protective clothing?
   c Is it now safe to approach?

2 Scene:
   a What has happened? How did the incident occur? (For example, did a child on the ground fall, trip or collapse? Has an infant been involved in an accident or did they become ill?)

3 Situation:
   a Who is involved? How many children are casualties? How old are they?

4 Help:

  a Who is available to help you?

    i Ideally other practitioners will be on hand. But if not, older children or young people who are responsible can be asked to help.

  b What help do you need? What can you get people to do for you?

    i Fetch the first-aid kit.

    ii Fetch other adults (for example if an incident occurs in the playground an older child may be sent to fetch another member of staff).

    iii Call an ambulance if necessary.

    iv Call the casualty's parent or guardian.

Children who are bystanders should be removed from the scene as soon as possible. They'll need to be supervised and may also need some comfort and reassurance. Witnessing a first-aid incident can be frightening and children may also be worried about their friend.

Making dangers safe

On a first-aid course you will learn in detail about making dangers safe. A brief overview is given here. Potential dangers to check for include:

- Fire.
- Smoke and fumes.
- Live electricity.
- Water.
- Dangerous animals including dogs.
- Trip hazards.
- Sharp objects.
- Falling masonry (rubble) from a building.
- Chemical spills.

If dangers are present, the first-aider should do what they can to try and make the area safe. This might include turning off the supply of electricity, removing a trip hazard or moving a casualty out of danger if it's safe to do so.

> **Good practice**
>
> It's important for someone to ensure that all other children who should be present are there, as the incident may have separated the group or caused adults to focus on the casualty rather than on supervising the group as a whole.

Children who are bystanders may need reassurance

> **Did you know?**
>
> A first-aider *must* not approach until a scene is safe. If it cannot be made safe, emergency services must be called.

How to conduct a primary survey on an infant and child

Once the scene survey has been completed and it's safe to approach, the first-aider must conduct a primary survey. This is a quick survey to find out if any injuries or conditions are life threatening. It means the first-aider can find and treat any life-threatening conditions as a priority.

Response

The response of the casualty is observed to find out if they are conscious or unconscious. The first-aider observes the casualty as they approach – do they look normal? They talk to the casualty to see if they respond to their voice. A child can be asked questions that require answers, for example: 'Are you all right?' 'What happened?' If there's no immediate response, a command may be tried, for example: 'Open your eyes, Jack!' If there's still no response, a child's shoulder will be tapped, or an infant's foot will be tapped. If there's still no response, the casualty is unconscious and will need treating urgently.

Airway, breathing, circulation (ABC)

Next the first-aider will check the airway, breathing and circulation of the casualty, in that order. You can use the abbreviation 'ABC' to help you remember this.

Airway

The first-aider checks that the airway is open and clear of obstruction. If a casualty is unconscious and on their back, the first-aider will tilt their head by placing one hand on their forehead and gently lifting their chin to open the airway. This stops the tongue from rolling back and causing an obstruction. If the casualty is conscious, other conditions such as choking or suffocation may be blocking the airway and must be treated urgently.

When the airway is clear the first-aider can move on.

Breathing

The first-aider checks for signs that the casualty is breathing by looking for the rise and fall of the chest, listening for breathing and feeling for breath on their cheek. If a casualty is not breathing the heart will stop. In this case, 999 must be called and CPR must start (see page 367). If a casualty is breathing, difficulties breathing (such as asthma) may be found and treated.

Circulation

The first-aider observes the skin for signs of circulation problems. For example the skin may look very pale or very flushed (pink), or there may be a bluish tinge or blotches. Also, severe bleeding can affect the circulation system. If these signs are present, 999 must be called immediately.

How and when to call for help

As you learnt in Learning outcome 1, first aid in settings is usually carried out by members of staff qualified to Level 3 or above. So if you become concerned that a child is ill or injured, or that something isn't right, you should immediately call a qualified member of staff to help. If that isn't possible, call for an ambulance. The simple rule is: *if you are ever in doubt, get help*.

For signs and symptoms that indicate urgent medical attention is needed, see page 249.

Calling for an ambulance

All practitioners should know how to call the emergency services. Dial 999, and be prepared to give the following information:

- The nature of the injury.

- The age of the child.

- Your location.

Listen carefully and follow any instructions you are given. Stay on the phone until you are told to hang up.

Did you know?

If no life-threatening conditions are present or if those found have been managed, the first-aider will move on to a more detailed, secondary survey of the casualty to assess what is wrong and how to treat them.

Link Up!

Unit MU 2.4 Contribute to children and young people's health and safety.

Good practice

Many settings have a reminder of how to call the emergency services by the phone. They will also display the setting's full address, postcode and telephone number so that these can be given correctly.

LEARNING OUTCOME 3

FOCUS ON

... being able to provide first aid for an infant and a child who is unresponsive and breathing normally

In this section you'll learn about placing a casualty in the recovery position and how to continually assess and monitor a casualty whilst in your care. This links with **Assessment Criteria 3.1, 3.2.**

Priorities

If a child or infant is unconscious (not responding to your voice or touch) and breathing normally, a first-aider's priorities are to:

- keep the airway open

- put them in the recovery position to maintain breathing

- call an ambulance

- keep monitoring their condition.

The airway

A casualty's airway must be kept open so that they can breathe in the air they need to keep living. The circulation system transports the oxygen that we breathe around the body. Without it, the heart will stop beating and the casualty will die. The lives of many unconscious casualties are saved because someone opens and maintains the airway. As you learnt in Learning outcome 1, the tongue often rolls back and blocks the airway of an unconscious casualty, as does blood or vomit.

Opening the airway of a child

To open a child's airway, a first-aider will:

- place one hand on the forehead and tilt the head back gently. The casualty's mouth will open a little

place the fingertips of the other hand under the chin and gently lift.

Next, the first-aider should:

look, listen and feel for breathing for up to 10 seconds. (With their ear close to the casualty's chest the first-aider will look for movement of the chest, listen for breathing sounds and feel for breath on the face)

if they are breathing, check for any life-threatening conditions, such as severe bleeding (see the primary survey information in Learning outcome 1)

call for help

if there are no life-threatening conditions, or when life-threatening conditions have been treated, put the casualty in the recovery position.

A casualty's airway must be kept open

Opening the airway of an infant

When opening the airway of an infant, just one finger will be used on the point of the chin to tilt the head. Care will be taken not to push on the soft tissue under the chin as this could block the airway.

Placing a child in the recovery position

To place a child in the recovery position, a first-aider will:

kneel next to the casualty and remove the casualty's glasses if they are wearing them

turn the child on to their side, using the technique practised on first-aid courses and pictured below. (One of the child's arms will be at right angles to their body on the floor, with the elbow bent and palm upwards. The other will be placed across the body and held in place, with the back of the child's hand against their cheek. One knee will be bent and used to pull them over on to their side)

pull the uppermost knee forward to balance them in place

check the airway is still open. It may be necessary to reposition the head

Did you know?

The recovery position is different for children and infants.

The recovery position

■ stay with the child and monitor their breathing and pulse continuously until help arrives.

If a spinal injury is suspected

If a spinal injury is suspected, the first-aider will avoid placing the casualty in the recovery position as it could cause further damage. They will also avoid tilting the neck to open the airway. Instead, they will:

■ kneel behind the child and place steady hands on either side of their face

■ use fingertips to lift the jaw gently, opening the airway

■ stay with the child and monitor their breathing and pulse continuously.

Placing an infant in the recovery position

To place an infant in the recovery position, a first-aider will:

■ cradle the infant in their arms, tilting the head downwards to prevent choking on the tongue or vomit

■ monitor their breathing and pulse continuously until help arrives.

Good practice

If a first-aider is alone when an incident occurs and they need to call 999 themselves, they will take the infant with them to the phone.

Assessing and monitoring a child or an infant

To monitor and assess a child or infant, a first-aider will keep going through the ABC process (checking airway, breathing and circulation) until an ambulance arrives. They will also talk to the casualty to check for a response (as you learned in Learning outcome 2), and offer plenty of reassurance that everything will be fine, as even a child who is not responding may be able to hear.

LEARNING OUTCOME 4

FOCUS ON

... being able to provide first aid for an infant and a child who is unresponsive and not breathing normally

In this section you'll learn about when and how to administer CPR. You'll also learn about dealing with a seizure. This links with **Assessment Criteria 4.1, 4.2, 4.3**.

Rescue breaths

If an ABC check reveals that a child is unresponsive and not breathing, their life is in danger. A first-aider must act quickly by giving five 'rescue breaths' or they may die.

For a child

To give the five rescue breaths a first-aider will:

- check the airway is still open

- look in the mouth and pick out any obstruction that can be seen (rather than 'sweeping' the mouth with the finger)

- with the casualty's head still tilted back, use finger and thumb to pinch the soft part of the child's nose, closing the nostrils so that air will not escape

■ take a deep breath, then seal lips around the casualty's lips, making an airtight seal. (This is different for an infant)

■ steadily blow air into the mouth for a second. The chest should rise. Remove lips and watch for the chest to fall. If it doesn't rise and fall, the head may need to be adjusted and the first rescue breath should be given again. If it does rise and fall, four more rescue breaths will be given.

If the child is not breathing after five rescue breaths, CPR is needed.

For an infant

Instead of pinching the nose and forming a seal around the lips, for an infant the first-aider will seal their mouth around both the infant's nose and mouth.

How and when to administer CPR

If a casualty is not breathing after five rescue breaths, a first-aider must start CPR.

To do this on a child they will:

■ kneel alongside the casualty

■ put the heel of one hand in the centre of the chest with the arm straight. (This is different for an infant)

Five initial rescue breaths are given

A first-aider will alternate 30 compressions with two rescue breaths

press down to compress the chest by one-third of its depth. Then release the chest with the hand still in place and allow the chest to come up ready for the next compression. Thirty chest compressions should be given, followed by two more rescue breaths. This cycle should take one minute

continue alternating 30 compressions with two rescue breaths until the casualty starts breathing again or emergency help arrives or exhaustion stops them from continuing.

CPR on an infant

On an infant, just the first two fingers are used for compression rather than the hand.

Dealing with a seizure

In infants and children, seizures (also known as convulsions or fits) are most commonly due to epilepsy or fever. (Fever is a raised body temperature that is the result of an infection, for example an ear infection.) A first-aider recognises a seizure by the shaking/jerking/ violent twitching movements of the body.

There may also be:

rolling or fixed or squinting eyes

loss of consciousness or impaired consciousness

drooling

loss of bowel/bladder control

holding of breath

signs of fever – skin is hot and flushed, there may be sweating.

During a seizure

A first-aider will:

instruct someone to call for an ambulance

make sure the area around the casualty is safe, for example move chairs, etc. out of the way

Did you know?

A seizure caused by a fever is also known as a 'febrile convulsion'.

- place pillows or rolled up blankets or towels around the casualty so jerking movements don't cause them injury. The casualty will not be restrained. Nothing will be put in their mouth

- loosen tight clothing

- when a seizure has ended, put the casualty in the recovery position to keep their airway open. If a casualty is hot, they can be cooled by removing their top

- monitor the casualty's condition and reassure them.

LEARNING OUTCOME 5

FOCUS ON

... being able to provide first aid for an infant and a child who has a foreign body airway obstruction

In this section you'll learn about differentiating between a mild and a severe airway obstruction. You'll also learn about how to treat a casualty who is choking, and the procedure to be followed afterwards. This links with **Assessment Criteria 5.1, 5.2, 5.3.**

Airway obstruction

Did you know?

The obstruction in an airway is often referred to as a 'foreign body'.

Children and infants can choke to death on a small object that blocks their airway. This can be food or other items because, as you know, they will put other things in their mouths. That's why we have to be so careful about the objects that are within the reach of young children in particular. Choking on food can be caused in a number of ways, including laughing or gasping when eating, attempting to swallow a piece of food that is too large, or eating lying down.

Mild and severe airway obstruction

If an airway obstruction is mild, the casualty will still be breathing some air into their lungs, but breathing will be difficult. They will be able to cough and, with difficulty, talk, cry or make a noise.

If an airway obstruction is severe, the casualty will not be able to breathe, talk, cry or make a noise. They may instinctively hold their neck – a sign recognised as choking distress. The casualty will eventually lose consciousness, so immediate treatment is needed and an ambulance must be called.

Good practice

It's important that first-aiders pick visible obstructions from the mouth rather than doing a 'finger sweep' of the inside of the mouth, as a finger sweep can make matters worse by pushing objects into the throat.

How to treat a child who is choking

A first-aider will treat a child who is choking as follows:

- If they are breathing, they will encourage them to cough as this could clear the obstruction.

- If the obstruction is severe and the child can't breathe, or if coughing fails, the child will be bent forwards and given up to five sharp blows on the back between the shoulder blades with the heel of the hand.

- The mouth will be checked and any obvious obstruction will be picked out.

- If the child is still choking, abdominal thrusts will be administered. The first-aider will stand behind the child and put their fist between the navel and the lower breastbone, grasp the fist will the other hand and pull sharply in an upwards and inwards movement, up to five times.

- The mouth will be rechecked as before.

- If the child is still choking, the first-aider will alternate between back blows and abdominal thrusts until the airway is cleared or emergency help arrives or the child becomes unconscious.

How to treat an infant who is choking

A first-aider will treat an infant who is choking as follows:

- If an infant has a severe obstruction and cannot breath, cough or make a noise, they will be laid along the first-aider's forearm on their front, keeping the head low. Care will be taken to support the head. The infant will be given up to five sharp blows on the back between their shoulder blades with the heel of the hand.

- The infant will be turned on to its back along the first-aider's other arm. The mouth will be checked and any obvious obstruction picked out.

- If the infant is still choking, chest thrusts will be administered. With two fingertips, up to five sharp thrusts will be given on the lower part of the breastbone (a finger's breadth below the nipples), pressing inwards and upwards.

- The mouth will be rechecked as before.

- If the infant is still choking, the first-aider will alternate between back blows and chest thrusts until the airway is cleared or emergency help arrives or the infant becomes unconscious.

After administering treatment

A child or infant who has had abdominal chest thrusts administered will need to be seen by a doctor to ensure no injuries have been sustained.

FOCUS ON

... being able to provide first aid for an infant and a child who is wounded and bleeding

In this section you'll learn about common types of wounds and the types and severity of bleeding. You'll also learn about safe control of minor and major bleeding and about how to administer first aid for minor injuries. This links with **Assessment Criteria 6.1, 6.2, 6.3, 6.4.**

Common types of wounds

Wounds can be caused by many different accidents and incidents. They can be:

- open

- closed

- minor

- major.

Minor wounds

Minor wounds can be:

- abrasions (grazes): the top layer of skin is scraped off in this superficial wound. Little blood is lost but the area is raw and tender

- lacerations (small): the skin is torn with a gap between the edges

- puncture wounds (shallow): may be caused by a needle for example

- incised wound (small, shallow): a cut from an object with a sharp edge, for example a knife

- contusions (bruises): usually caused by a blunt blow.

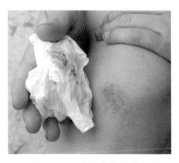

Abrasion: little blood is lost but the area is raw and tender

Major wounds

Major wounds can be:

- incised wounds (deep or large): a cut from an object with a sharp edge, for example a knife, glass, a razor blade

- avulsion wounds: where a piece or flap of skin has been torn away

- amputations: when a part of the body has been torn or cut off

- puncture wounds (deep): the object that caused the puncture may still be in the wound, for example a nail or needle that has been stepped on

- contusions (bruises): extensive bruising can indicate internal injury or a fracture.

Types and severity of bleeding

External bleeding occurs when the skin is broken and blood vessels are damaged. The type and severity of bleeding depends on the type of blood vessel.

Minor bleeding

Most minor wounds have some capillary bleeding (capillaries are small blood vessels throughout the body). With capillary bleeds there may be brisk bleeding at first but this is stopped easily with gentle pressure. Usually, there will only be a slight blood loss overall.

Major bleeding

Major bleeding (also called severe bleeding) does not stop easily with pressure and can cause a casualty to go into shock, which can cause death. Major bleeding can come from the following:

- Arteries. These carry blood away from the heart. If an artery is damaged, a lot of blood will be lost in spurts, in time with the heart beat of the casualty.

- Veins. These carry blood to the heart. Blood from veins is darker red. Veins can bleed heavily.

- Injuries to parts of the body such as the head where there is a larger number of blood vessels and therefore more blood loss.

Control of external bleeding and effect on casualty

Even with minor bleeding, an infant or child may be frightened by the blood, and the wound may be very sore. So empathy and reassurance are needed. An ambulance will need to be called for major bleeding.

A first-aider will treat bleeding in the following ways.

Minor bleeding

Clean the wound.

Apply a dressing (a plaster is often sufficient).

Major bleeding

Put a sterile dressing over the wound and apply firm pressure with the palm or fingers.

Raise and support the injured part to get it above the casualty's heart if possible.

Minimise risk of shock by getting the casualty to lie down and raising and supporting the legs.

Place a pad over the dressing, and use a bandage to secure it.

The circulation (beyond the bandage) will be checked regularly (the bandage may need to be reapplied).

If blood comes through the bandage, another pad can be placed on top.

Monitor and assess until emergency help arrives. The casualty may lose consciousness.

Good practice

Gentle pressure can be applied if necessary, and the injured part can sometimes be raised above the casualty's heart.

A plaster is often sufficient for a minor wound

Good practice

Usually a first-aider will apply direct pressure on a sterile pad. But if there's a foreign body in the wound, indirect pressure is needed. Pads should be placed around the wound and pressure applied. A first-aider will not attempt to remove the foreign body – the safest thing is to leave it for a medical professional to deal with.

FOCUS ON

... knowing how to provide first aid for an infant and a child who is suffering from shock

In this section you'll learn about recognising and managing shock. You'll also learn about recognising and managing anaphylactic shock. This links with **Assessment Criteria 7.1, 7.2**.

Shock

Shock is a life-threatening condition that requires urgent treatment. It occurs when there's a failure in the body's circulatory system. Vital organs (for example the heart and brain) are deprived of oxygen. Shock can be caused by a number of factors, such as:

■ blood loss (the most common cause)

■ severe loss of body fluids (can be caused by diarrhoea, vomiting, burns, especially in infants)

■ heart problems

■ severe allergic reaction (anaphylactic shock – see page 375)

■ hypothermia

■ hypoglycaemia (low blood sugar levels).

Recognising shock

First signs of shock are:

■ rapid pulse

■ skin is pale, cold and clammy

■ sweating.

When shock develops, the signs are:

■ weak pulse

■ grey skin especially around the lips

Good practice

A first-aider will always look out for signs of shock following bleeding and other conditions or injuries, as it can develop quickly and at any time.

Did you know?

Shock can become worse if a patient is frightened and/or in pain, so an important part of the first-aider's job is to keep them calm and reassured.

- feeling sick/vomiting
- dizziness and weakness.

The late-stage signs of shock are:

- restlessness/aggressiveness
- yawning and gulping/gasping for air
- unconsciousness.

Casualties should be kept calm and reassured

Managing shock

A first-aider will treat shock as follows:

- Treat any cause of shock that can be found, for example bleeding.
- Lay the casualty down with their head low.
- To improve blood supply to the vital organs, a child's legs will be raised and supported above the level of their heart. An infant will be cradled in the first-aider's arms with the head lower than the legs.
- Tight clothing will be loosened.
- The casualty will be kept warm with blankets.
- Call for an ambulance.
- Monitor and assess ABC (see page 360).

Anaphylactic shock

Anaphylactic shock is a severe allergic reaction and a life-threatening situation. An ambulance must be called immediately. Anaphylactic shock can be caused by any allergens, but common triggers include nuts, eggs, shellfish, and wasp and bee stings.

Recognising anaphylactic shock

Signs of anaphylactic shock are:

- red, itchy rash or blotchy skin that becomes raised
- swelling of face, hands, feet
- pale or flushed skin
- puffy/red/itchy/watery eyes

> **Did you know?**
>
> The casualty may lose consciousness and stop breathing, in which case CPR will be needed.

- wheezing/difficulty breathing

- swelling of tongue and throat

- abdominal pain

- vomiting/diarrhoea

- agitation/confusion

- signs of shock.

Managing anaphylactic shock

To treat shock a first-aider will:

- call for an ambulance

- check if the casualty has their own auto-injector of adrenaline and if so administer it (if trained to do so)

- help the casualty to sit in a position that helps breathing

- monitor and assess until help arrives

- if the casualty becomes pale with a weak pulse, treat for shock – lay them down and raise their legs.

Ask Miranda!

Q I'm worried I'll never remember it all when I'm a first-aider.

A First-aiders do have a lot to remember and it is a very important role. But the first-aid training reflects this. It's detailed and there's time to recap on things. There's also plenty of time devoted to hands-on, practical work – you'll practise everything from CPR to putting on a sling. First-aiders are required to update their training regularly, so you'll have opportunities to practise on an ongoing basis.

How are things going?

▶ Progress Check

1. Describe how to minimise risk of infection to self and others. (1.2)

2. Define an infant and a child for first-aid treatment purposes. (1.5)

3. Describe how to conduct a scene survey. (2.1)

4. Describe how to continually assess and monitor a child. (3.1)

5. Describe how to deal with an infant experiencing a seizure. (4.3)

6. Explain the difference between a mild and a severe airway obstruction. (5.1)

7. What procedure must be followed after administering treatment for choking? (5.3)

8. Describe how to control major bleeding. (6.3)

9. Describe how to recognise a child who is suffering from shock. (7.1)

10. Describe how to treat a child who is suffering from anaphylactic shock. (7.2)

Are you ready for assessment?

CACHE

Simulation is permitted for the Unit, but Learning Outcomes 2, 3, 4, 5 and 6 must be assessed in a realistic simulated environment.

Set tasks:

■ You are asked to produce a folder of information that you can refer to at work. This will include information about the responsibilities of the first aider, how to minimise infection, suitable first aid equipment, accident/incident reports, the ages of an "infant" and "child" for first aid purposes, recognising and managing shock and anaphylactic shock.

You can prepare by rereading pages 354–376 and making relavant notes.

City & Guilds

You can prepare for assessment by rereading pages 354–376 and making relevant notes.

Edexcel

You can prepare for assessment by rereading pages 354–376 and making relevant notes.

UNIT 002

Managing paediatric illness and injury

LEARNING OUTCOMES

The learning outcomes you will meet in this unit are:

1 Be able to provide first aid to an infant and a child with a suspected fracture and a dislocation

2 Be able to provide first aid to an infant and a child with a head, neck and back injury

3 Know how to provide first aid to an infant and a child with conditions affecting the eyes, ears and nose

4 Know how to provide first aid to an infant and a child with a chronic medical condition or sudden illness

5 Know how to provide first aid to an infant and a child who is experiencing the effects of extreme heat and cold

6 Know how to provide first aid to an infant and a child who has sustained an electric shock

7 Know how to provide first aid to an infant and a child with burns or scalds

8 Know how to provide first aid to an infant and a child who has been poisoned

9 Know how to provide first aid to an infant and a child who has been bitten or stung

INTRODUCTION

As you learnt in Unit PEFAP 001, all practitioners should undertake a paediatric first-aid course. The information in this unit by no means replaces first-aid training. There are several links to Unit PEFAP 001. You are advised to follow these as you work through this unit.

LEARNING OUTCOME 1

... being able to provide first aid to an infant and a child with a suspected fracture and a dislocation

In this section you'll learn about common types of fractures, and about managing both a fracture and a dislocation. You'll also learn about the application of a support sling and an elevation sling. This links with **Assessment Criteria 1.1, 1.2, 1.3, 1.4.**

Common types of fractures

The term 'fracture' means a broken bone. There are three types of fracture:

- Open. This occurs when the skin is broken at the site of the fracture, causing an open wound. The bone itself may or may not protrude (stick out). If the bone does protrude, there's risk of infection to the bone.

- Closed. The skin does not break so there isn't an open wound at the site of the fracture.

- Greenstick. Young children's bones are more flexible, and often a fracture doesn't break the whole bone. This is sometimes called a 'greenstick' fracture.

A closed fracture

Dislocations

Dislocations are injuries to a joint that occur when bones are partially or completely pulled out of their correct position. They're generally caused by wrenching or a violent muscle spasm. When there's a dislocation of a joint, the bones involved may also be fractured. It's hard for a first-aider to tell the difference between a dislocation and a closed fracture. But the first-aid priorities for both a dislocation and a closed fracture are the same – to immobilise and support the injured part until an ambulance arrives to take the casualty to hospital.

Did you know?

The nerves, muscles, blood vessels and even organs around a fracture may also be affected by the injury.

Good practice

Dislocation can occur easily in young children. To avoid causing dislocation, we need to be extremely careful not to pull on young children's arms, hands, feet or legs. Also, they should never be picked up by their hands or arms, or swung by their arms or legs.

Recognising a fracture or dislocation

Signs of a fracture or dislocation include:

- severe pain – the casualty may feel sick with pain

- deformity – the affected body part is in an unnatural position. It may look shorter than normal

- swelling

- bruising

- difficulty moving or using the body part

- in the case of an open fracture, broken skin

- the casualty hearing or feeling grating (from the ends of the broken bone).

On recognising these signs, a first-aider will call for an ambulance.

How to manage a fracture or a dislocation

A first-aider will:

- tell the casualty to keep as still as possible to minimise pain and prevent further damage

- support the injured body part to help keep it still. Padding may be placed around the injured part.

In the case of injury to an arm, shoulder or collar bone, a sling may be applied for support if the casualty is sitting up (see page 381).

Application of slings

There are two types of sling:

- Support sling. This gives support to injuries to the wrist, forearm or upper arm. The arm is held in position at a right angle to the body.

- Elevation sling. This gives support for a shoulder injury. The arm is in a raised position across the chest with the fingers touching the shoulder.

You will learn to do both types of slings on a first-aid course by watching a demonstration and practising on a partner who is not actually injured.

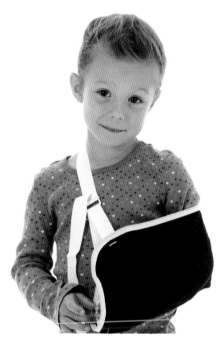

Support sling

Good practice

Once a sling has been applied, a first-aider will check the casualty's circulation every 10 minutes to ensure that the sling hasn't become too restrictive.

... being able to provide first aid to an infant and a child with a head, neck and back injury

In this section you'll learn about recognising and managing head injuries. You'll also learn about managing a suspected spinal injury. This links with **Assessment Criteria 2.1, 2.2.**

Recognising head injuries

It's important for first-aiders to recognise head injuries as they:

■ are relatively common

■ can be serious

■ can result in impaired consciousness or unconsciousness

■ may require emergency surgery.

What is a head injury?

Brains are wrapped in layers of tissue and encased within the hard, protective skull. The skull is made of bone. The following head injuries may occur:

■ Concussion: caused when the brain is shaken within the skull, usually by a blow to the head. Normal brain activity is disturbed temporarily, but this is usually followed by a complete recovery.

■ Cerebral compression: occurs when pressure builds up on the brain. This is usually a result of swelling of injured brain tissues or a build-up of blood within the skull, caused by a blow to the head. Surgery is generally required to relieve the pressure. Prolonged pressure can cause disability and death.

■ Skull fracture: this is a break in the skull caused by a blow to the head.

Did you know?

Cerebral compression is usually caused by a head injury, but it can also be caused by an infection, a brain tumour or a stroke.

Signs and symptoms of head injury

The casualty is known to have had a blow to the head. But you should note that cerebral compression can develop hours or days after a head injury. So it's possible that a child could become ill from the effects of a head injury that the practitioners caring for them are completely unaware of.

A bump or other swelling.

Bruising.

Headache.

Drowsiness.

Loss of consciousness (may only last seconds).

Vomiting or nausea.

Confusion/loss of memory (for example the casualty can't remember the accident or immediately before it).

Dizziness or loss of balance.

Seizures.

Problems with vision (for example blurred vision).

Pupils of the eyes are uneven in size.

Blood or clear fluid coming from the nose or ear.

Bleeding from the head.

Breathing problems.

Weakness or paralysis down one side of face or body (includes weakness in an arm or leg and difficulty walking).

Difficulty talking.

Change in behaviour (for example irritable, disorientated).

In babies

In babies there may also be:

a change in the sound of their cry

■ a swollen fontanelle (a soft spot on a baby's skull).

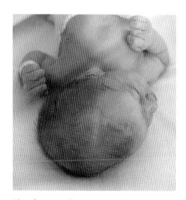

The fontanelle may swell

Protecting the spine

It's common for those with head injuries to also injure their neck (which is part of the spine). The spinal cord contains nerves that take messages from the brain to other parts of the body. If the spinal cord becomes damaged due to broken/dislocated bones in the spine, paralysis and other serious conditions may occur. So a first-aider will treat an unconscious casualty with a head injury as though they also have a spinal injury, to prevent them from causing further damage.

A fall from playground equipment can cause a head injury

Good practice

Even if a child has had a seemingly minor bang on the head which results in a bump but no other symptoms, it's important that practitioners/parents/carers:

■ watch them closely for at least six hours
■ remain alert to any signs and symptoms of a head injury for several days.

This is because a brain injury may become apparent over time. Many settings produce a fact sheet to be given to parents and carers when the child has received a bang to the head. This will tell them what to watch for and advise them to seek medical advice if they are at all worried.

Signs and symptoms of spinal injury

- Neck or back pain.
- Abnormal curve of the spine.
- Loss of sensation.
- Abnormal sensation.
- Weakness in or inability to move limbs.
- Skin feels tender.
- Loss of bladder/bowel control.
- Breathing difficulties.

Managing a brain injury

If a brain injury is suspected, a first-aider will do the following:

- Call for an ambulance.
- Apply a pad and direct pressure to any head wound. The pad may be secured in place with a bandage.
- Lay the casualty down. See below for details when spinal injury is suspected or when the casualty is unconscious and therefore treated as though there is a spinal injury.
- Monitor and record the level of consciousness, breathing and pulse until the ambulance arrives. Also record symptoms, including how long any loss of consciousness lasted, if blood or fluid has leaked from the nose or ear, pupil size, any vomiting, etc.

Managing a suspected spinal injury

If spinal injury is suspected or if the casualty is unconscious, a first-aider:

- will not move the casualty, and if the casualty is conscious they will tell them not to move
- will kneel behind the child and place steady hands on either side of their face. They will steady and support the neck and head, and keep holding it until the ambulance arrives.

If others are available to help, the first-aider should get them to place padding such as rolled up towels or blankets around the neck and shoulders (without moving them). This will provide extra support.

FOCUS ON

... knowing how to provide first aid to an infant and a child with conditions affecting the eyes, ears and nose

In this section you'll learn about managing foreign bodies in the eyes, ears and nose. You'll also learn about recognising and managing common eye injuries. This links with **Assessment Criteria 3.1, 3.2.**

Managing foreign bodies in the ears and nose

Young children sometimes put small objects in their ears or nose, where they are liable to become stuck. Objects such as beads and food seem to fit especially well. First-aiders should not try to remove these as it can make the obstruction worse rather than better. Children will normally be taken to their nearest hospital or walk-in clinic to have the item removed.

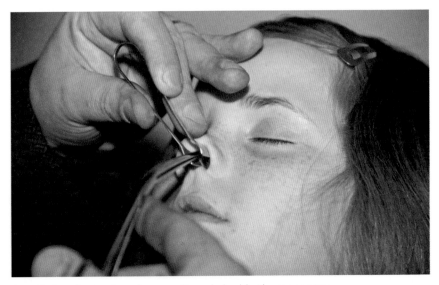

A medical professional must remove items lodged in the ear or nose

Good practice

Young children may become distressed when they realise an item can't be easily removed, and they may also experience discomfort or pain. It's important that they are comforted and reassured that the object will soon be removed. It's helpful for a first-aider to distract them from trying to touch the object as they may push it in further. If the object is in the nose, the first-aider will encourage the child to stay calm and breathe through their mouth at the normal rate.

Insect in the ear

Insects can crawl or fly into the ear. In this case, the first-aider will try the following:

- Sit the casualty down and get them to lean back over a sink or bowl.

- Tilt the head to one side and support it, with the affected ear facing upwards.

- Cover the casualty's clothes to protect them from water.

- Gently pour tepid water into the ear to flood it. Often, the insect will float out.

If this doesn't work, medical help is required to remove the insect safely.

Eye injuries

The eyes are delicate and can be damaged if:

- the inside of the eye is penetrated by a foreign object

- a foreign object damages the surface (cornea) of the eye.

Causes

Eye injuries can be caused in many ways including by:

- chemical splashes (these may come from products that are sprayed as well as those that are poured)

- fingernails

- toys

- sharp objects such as chipped metal, glass, china or grit

- sports injuries.

Signs and symptoms of eye injuries

- Foreign object may be visible.

- Pain/discomfort.

- Sensitivity to light.

Good practice

Insects in the ear can be particularly distressing as a child may be able to hear them or feel them moving, and they may begin to panic. It's important that the first-aider takes a calm approach and reassures them.

Did you know?

Even small grazes to the cornea are concerning as potential scarring or infection can affect the eyesight to some extent.

Did you know?

Injuries can also be caused by natural objects at eye level, such as bushes or low-hanging tree branches.

- Vision problems, for example blurred vision, double vision, loss of or reduced vision.

- Redness or swelling.

- Watering eyes.

- Blood in the eye.

- Eyelids in spasm.

- Numbness.

- Difficulty opening the eye.

Good practice

Chemical splashes can come from antibacterial sprays as well as substances such as cleaning fluids. These are frequently used in settings. You should *never* spray products when children are close by. Other sprays such as air freshener or hairspray can also cause an injury.

Managing foreign bodies in the eyes

A first-aider will not attempt to remove anything that is stuck to the eye or penetrates into the eye. The casualty will need urgent medical attention. In the meantime the first-aider will:

- get the casualty to lean back

- help them to hold a sterile dressing over the eye to prevent infection (this may be bandaged in place)

- encourage the casualty to keep both eyes still (moving the good eye also moves the bad eye, which can cause further damage).

In minor cases

Sometimes foreign bodies float on the surface of the white part of the eye. For instance:

- A speck of grit.

- An eyelash.

- A loose contact lens.

- A speck of eye make-up.

In this case, a first-aider would:

- sit the casualty facing the light (so the first-aider can see what they are doing) and gently tip their head back

- stand behind/beside the casualty, gently separating the casualty's eyelids with their thumbs

- tell the casualty to look up, down and to each side so the whole of the eye can be visually examined.

If the object can be seen on the *white part* of the casualty's eye, the first-aider will:

- cover the casualty's clothes with a towel

- help the casualty to lean back

- stand behind the casualty, hold their eye open and gently pour clean water or sterile eyewash into the eye from the inner corner (by the nose). The water will run on to the towel, hopefully flushing out the object. If this does not work, it may be possible to lift the object off with the corner of a damp, clean tissue or swab.

If unsuccessful, medical help will be needed.

If the object seems to be in the upper eyelid, a first-aider will try:

- holding the upper eyelashes and gently pulling the upper lid down over the lower lid, so the lower lashes can brush the object clear of the lid.

If unsuccessful, or if the object can be seen on the coloured part of the eye, medical help will be needed.

Did you know?

Even a speck of dirt in the eye can feel very large and cause a lot of irritation.

FOCUS ON

... knowing how to provide first aid to an infant and a child with a chronic medical condition or sudden illness

In this section you'll learn about recognising and managing chronic conditions. You'll also learn about recognising and managing serious sudden illnesses. This links with **Assessment Criteria 4.1, 4.2.**

Recognising and managing chronic conditions

In the vast majority of cases, practitioners will know about a child's chronic condition, which means they will be prepared to deal with it. They will have found out about the condition and how it affects the individual, and if necessary they will have been trained in administering any medication the child may require. There are many chronic conditions. Common conditions that practitioners are likely to come across are:

■ diabetes

■ asthma

■ sickle cell anaemia.

Diabetes

Insulin is a hormone. In children with diabetes, the body doesn't produce insulin, and this affects the body's ability to process the sugar or glucose found in food. To counteract this, most children with diabetes will need to have insulin injections at various times of the day. If they have either too much or too little insulin in their body, a child can experience one of the following serious conditions:

Young people are likely to manage their own insulin injections

■ Hypoglycaemia (often called a 'hypo'): this occurs when the blood sugar level falls below normal.

■ Hyperglycaemia (often called a 'hyper'): this occurs when the blood sugar level is higher than normal.

Signs and symptoms of a hypoglycaemic attack (hypo)

Signs and symptoms of entering a hypo include:

- Drowsiness with a deteriorating level of response.

- Feeling weak or faint.

- Feeling hungry.

- Confusion or irritability.

- Behaving irrationally.

- Palpitations.

- Muscle tremors (trembling).

- Sweating and cold, clammy, pale skin.

- Rapid pulse.

Managing a hypoglycaemic attack

The casualty needs to get sugar into their system to balance out the insulin level which is incorrect. This is often caused by more exercise than usual or lack of food at the right time. Children and young people with diabetes will have a care plan, and practitioners will know what to give them if they show signs of not having enough food. This may be a sugary drink such as orange juice, chocolate or a tube of special glucose gel. They will bring this to the setting with them.

If impaired consciousness has already occurred, the attack is in an advanced stage and an ambulance is needed. If the attack is at an earlier stage, a first-aider will:

- sit the casualty down

- give them their drink/gel, etc. as described above.

If the casualty responds, the first-aider will:

- give them more food and drink until they feel better

- encourage the casualty to rest.

Young people may have the equipment with them (a glucose testing kit) to check their own glucose levels.

A glucose testing kit

If the casualty doesn't respond, an ambulance is needed. The first-aider will monitor and record the level of response, breathing and pulse, and also remain alert to other reasons for the symptoms.

Signs and symptoms of a hyperglycaemic attack (hyper)

Signs and symptoms of entering a hyper include:

- Drowsiness resulting in impaired consciousness/unconsciousness if not treated.
- Feeling very thirsty.
- Rapid breathing.
- Warm, dry skin.
- Rapid pulse.
- Fruity, sweet-smelling breath.
- Passing urine frequently.

Managing a hyperglycaemic attack

A hyper develops slowly over a few days. It requires emergency medical treatment to prevent the casualty from falling into a diabetic coma (unconsciousness brought on by diabetes). A first-aider will:

- call for an ambulance
- monitor and record the level of response, breathing and pulse. If a casualty loses consciousness, the first-aider will open the airway, check breathing and be ready to start CPR if necessary.

Asthma

Asthma affects the airways. In people who have asthma, the airways are more sensitive. When their lungs become irritated by a trigger (see page 393), the lining becomes inflamed. There's an increase in the production of phlegm (sticky mucus). This causes:

- coughing
- wheezing
- shortness of breath
- tightening of the chest.

All of the above make it hard to breathe.

Asthma triggers

Asthma attacks may be triggered by:

- very cold air
- exercise
- air pollution including cigarette smoke
- living in damp conditions
- anxiety/stress.

Attacks can also be caused by allergens that affect the individual child. These commonly include:

- Pollen.
- Dust.
- Animal hair.

Managing asthma

Asthma can be managed but not cured. Children who have asthma will normally have a reliever inhaler (usually blue) to take if an asthma attack occurs. They may also take a preventer inhaler every day. Children may use a spacer device to take their inhalers. This is a plastic chamber through which the inhaler is administered. In the case of young children, a face mask will be fitted to the spacer. This will cover their mouth and nose. Older children will seal their lips around a mouthpiece. Children and young people may need to take their inhaler before sport or physical activity such as dancing. The reliever should always be nearby – older children and young people may carry this themselves. Practitioners should check they have it with them at all times.

If a casualty has an asthma attack

If a casualty has an asthma attack, a first-aider will:

- help the casualty to take their inhaler, or in the case of a younger child, administer it
- sit the casualty slightly forward, in a position that helps them to breathe comfortably. The casualty must not lie down

Children may use a spacer device to take their inhalers

- encourage the casualty to breathe slowly and deeply.

A mild attack will begin to ease a few minutes after the casualty has used the inhaler. If it does not, another dose can be taken.

- An ambulance must be called if the inhaler has no effect, if breathlessness is preventing talking, or the child becomes exhausted. The inhaler may be reused.

- The first-aider should monitor and record the level of response, breathing and pulse. If an attack worsens, the casualty may lose consciousness. In this case the first-aider will open the airway, check breathing and be ready to start CPR if necessary.

Sickle cell anaemia

Sickle cell anaemia is caused by a genetic mutation that affects haemoglobin, a substance found in red blood cells. The haemoglobin inside the red blood cells clumps together into solid structures, and the cells take on a rigid, sickle shape.

Sickle cell crisis

'Sickle cell crisis' is a common symptom of sickle cell anaemia. This is an episode of pain caused when abnormal blood cells block the blood vessels to the body's tissue. The cells in the affected tissue will start to die, and in doing so they will irritate the nearby nerve endings, where pain is felt. Pain can affect any body part, but it is most common in the:

- spine
- ribs
- pelvis
- abdomen
- chest bone (sternum)
- long bones in legs and arms.

In young children under 18 months, only the bones and joints in the hands and feet are usually affected by pain.

Did you know?

A casualty having an asthma attack should never be left alone. An attack can escalate in severity very quickly.

Did you know?

Children's hands or feet often swell during a sickle cell crisis.

Sickle cell anaemia triggers

There may be no apparent cause for a crisis, although it may be triggered by:

- dehydration

- the cold

- lack of oxygen due to physical exercise, exertion or stress

- infections, especially if there's a high temperature or breathing difficulties.

Managing sickle cell anaemia

Children with sickle cell anaemia will have a care plan that explains what should be done when a crisis occurs. Practitioners should work in line with this. If pain is severe, a child will need to go to hospital urgently.

Recognising and managing serious sudden illnesses

Meningitis

When someone has meningitis, the linings around the brain and spinal cord become inflamed.

Information from the Meningitis Trust

> There are many different causes of meningitis, but the two most common organisms are viruses and bacteria.
>
> - Viral meningitis is usually a mild disease, but it can make people very unwell. Many thousands of cases occur each year, mostly affecting babies and children. Although most people will make a full recovery, some are left with serious and debilitating after-effects.
>
> - Bacterial meningitis can be life-threatening and needs urgent medical attention. Most people who suffer from bacterial meningitis recover, but many can be left with a variety of after-effects and one in 10 will die.
>
> - The main bacteria that cause meningitis in the UK are Meningococcal, Pneumoccal, TB and Hib. Neonatal meningitis occurs in babies under one month old. Other causes of meningitis are all serious and need medical attention.

Did you know?

Children with sickle cell anaemia are vulnerable to complications including infection, and they often take antibiotics daily as a precaution.

Signs and symptoms of meningitis

In children/young people the symptoms of meningitis are:

- high temperature or fever

- cold hands and feet

- vomiting

- severe headache

- stiff neck

- drowsiness/difficult to wake

- confusion

- dislike of bright light

- seizures

- skin rash of red/purple 'pin prick' spots. If the spots spread, they can resemble fresh bruising, but this is difficult to see on black skin. The rash does not fade when the side of a glass is pressed against it (see the picture page 397)

- joint/muscle pain.

In babies there may also be:

- restlessness

- high-pitched crying or screaming

- limp or floppy body

- swelling of the soft fontanelle area of the skull

- refusal to feed

- fretful behaviour, dislike of being handled

- blank, staring eyes.

Managing meningitis

A child will need help urgently. If sure of the symptoms, a first-aider should call an ambulance. If at all unsure, a doctor should be called out urgently. If a doctor cannot be contacted or will be delayed, the first-aider should call for an ambulance. If the casualty has already seen a doctor but is becoming worse, the first-aider should dial 999. The first-aider will reassure the casualty and keep them cool until help arrives.

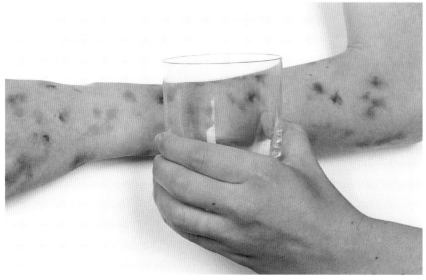

The glass test

Febrile convulsions

For information on febrile convulsions and other seizures, see Unit PEFAP 001, Learning outcome 4.

Link Up!

Unit PEFAP 001 Paediatric emergency first aid.

LEARNING OUTCOME 5

FOCUS ON

... knowing how to provide first aid to an infant and a child who is experiencing the effects of extreme heat and cold

In this section you'll learn about recognising and treating the effects of extreme cold and extreme heat in an infant and a child. This links with **Assessment Criteria 5.1, 5.2**.

Recognising the effects of extreme cold

Moderate hypothermia can set in when body temperature falls below 35 °C. It causes body functions to slow, but it can usually be reversed. If body temperature falls below 30 °C a casualty is likely to die. Hypothermia occurs as a result of prolonged exposure to the cold.

Indoors

Hypothermia can develop indoors if there is inadequate heating. Being chronically ill or fatigued increases the risk, as does lack of physical activity. Babies are particularly vulnerable because they are inactive and their mechanisms for regulating temperature are not yet fully developed. They can quickly develop hypothermia in a cold room.

Outdoors

Moving air cools bodies much faster than still air. So a high wind-chill factor during a spell of cold weather makes hypothermia more likely. Water also cools the body quickly, so getting wet in the rain or falling into cold water also increases the likelihood of hypothermia.

Signs and symptoms of extreme cold

- Low body temperature.

- Shivering.

- Pale, dry skin.

- Lethargy (sluggishness).

- Impaired consciousness.

- Disorientation.

- Irrational behaviour.

- Slow, shallow breathing.

- Slow, weakening pulse.

In infants signs may also include:

- Limp body.

- Unusually quiet.

- Refusal to feed.

- Healthy-looking skin that feels cold to the touch.

Treating effects of extreme cold

An ambulance must be called for casualties suffering from hypothermia. A first-aider will also attempt to reheat the casualty gradually by:

- bringing the casualty into a warm room. If they are outside and it is not possible to go inside, they will take the casualty to a sheltered spot to shield them from the wind

- taking off any wet clothes and replacing them with dry ones including a hat if possible

- wrapping the casualty in a blanket, coat or foil survival bag. If outside, the casualty will also be laid on an insulating blanket rather than the cold ground

- encouraging the casualty to drink warm drinks and eat high-energy food such as chocolate

- monitoring and recording levels of response, breathing and circulation. In severe cases the heart may stop.

In the case of an infant, the first-aider will:

- wrap the infant in blankets

- cradle the infant close to their own body

- warm the room.

Recognising effects of extreme heat

It is particularly dangerous for infants and young children to overheat. When the body reaches 40 °C, brain damage and death can occur.

During hot weather, practitioners should routinely encourage children to cool down if they begin to look quite hot when playing actively or when outside. You can achieve this by encouraging them to play a less-active game, to get out of the sun and to have a cool drink of water. This helps to prevent the adverse effects of extreme heat.

Overheating is also a contributing factor to sudden infant death syndrome, so it's important that babies and young children are not put in conditions that are too hot. This includes over-doing the blankets when putting them to bed and/or over-dressing them. Heat exhaustion is also common if children have been playing actively in hot weather.

Signs and symptoms of extreme heat

- Red, flushed face.

- High temperature.

- Rapid breathing.

- Feeling sick/unwell.

- Tiredness.

In babies and young children there may also be febrile convulsions (see Unit PEFAP 001, Learning outcome 4).

Treating the effects of extreme heat

A first-aider will:

- move the casualty away from the heat (for example bring them indoors) and sit them down

- remove excess clothing

- cool them by applying cool wet cloths to the body

- give them plenty of cool water to drink.

Even if a casualty recovers quickly they will need urgent medical attention. If they do not recover quickly or if symptoms worsen, an ambulance must be called. A first-aider will monitor and record levels of response, breathing and circulation until help arrives.

In this section you'll learn about safely managing an incident involving electricity. You'll also learn about first-aid treatments for electric shock incidents. This links with **Assessment Criteria 6.1, 6.2.**

Managing an incident involving electricity

Electricity can be extremely dangerous, and electric shocks can kill by stopping the heart. That is why it's so important for settings to fit socket covers that protect children from electric shocks caused by poking fingers or objects into electric sockets.

Isolating the source of electricity

If someone has been electrocuted, it's important to stop the flow of electricity urgently. This is known as 'isolating the source' of the electricity. The casualty must *not* be approached until this has been done, otherwise the first-aider is also likely to receive an electric shock.

To isolate the source, the power should be turned off at the mains or master switch. If this isn't possible, the casualty may be pushed or pulled well away from the source using material that won't conduct the electricity. A first-aider will learn how to do this safely on a first-aid course. Techniques may include using a thick towel looped around the feet to enable a child to be pulled, or using a wooden broom to push them away from the source.

Did you know?

When electricity enters the body it will travel along and then exit at another point. This can cause damage to a large area of the body.

The flow of electricity must be stopped urgently

First-aid treatments for electric shock incidents

Once the source of electricity has been isolated, the first-aider will approach the casualty. If their heart has stopped, an ambulance is needed. The first-aider will check the airway, breathing and circulation and commence CPR.

Electricity can cause burns at the entry and exit points which a first-aider will treat with cold water (see page 404). But note that the source of electricity must be turned off or the casualty must be well removed from it, as water and electricity is a very dangerous combination. Urgent or emergency medical attention will be needed, depending on the extent of the burns.

Good practice

Any child or young person should receive urgent medical attention to ensure they are not hurt, even if they seem to have recovered from an electric shock and have no burns.

Practical example

A worn wire

Michelle is 15 and lives in a care home. She's getting ready to go out and is drying her hair upstairs. The cord on her hairdryer has become worn, but she hasn't mentioned it to staff.

Practitioner Kelsey is downstairs working on the computer when she hears a bang. At the same time all of the lights go out and her computer loses power. She also hears a scream from upstairs. She runs up to Michelle's room, where she finds Michelle looking dazed. She has dropped the hairdryer on the floor.

LEARNING OUTCOME 7

FOCUS ON

... knowing how to provide first aid to an infant and a child with burns or scalds

In this section you'll learn about recognising the severity of burns and scalds and responding accordingly. You'll also learn about treating burns and scalds. This links with **Assessment Criteria 7.1, 7.2**.

Recognising the severity of burns and scalds

Causes

Burns can be caused by:

- fire
- hot materials (for example hot metal)
- chemicals
- electricity
- the sun.

Scalds are caused by liquids, most commonly hot drinks or hot water. This is why it's so important to keep hot drinks and boiling kettles or saucepans out of the reach of young children.

Severity of burns and scalds

Three factors are considered when assessing the severity of a burn or scald:

- **The size of the affected area**:
  This is expressed as a percentage of the skin, with the palm of the hand equalling 1 per cent. When describing a burn to the emergency services, a first-aider may compare the size to a commonly known object, for instance by saying the burn is the size of a postage stamp.

> **Did you know?**
>
> Hob guards and special curly kettle flex can be bought to prevent young children pulling the hot contents of saucepans and kettles over themselves. Kettles are often pulled over by the flex, but it's harder to pull over a kettle fitted with a curly flex because there isn't as much tension.

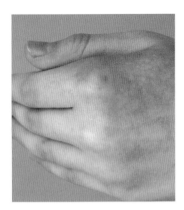

A scald injury

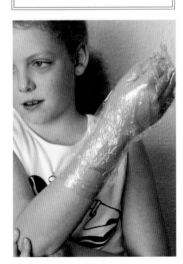

Cling film may be used to cover a burn or scald

■ **The depth of the burn or scald:**
'Superficial' burns or scalds affect just the top layer of the skin and redness occurs. 'Partial thickness' means blisters have been caused, 'full thickness' causes charred skin or 'ash whiteness' of the skin.

■ **The location of the burn or scald:**
The most serious locations for burns are the hands, feet, face and genital area.

Treating burns and scalds

Burns and scalds need immediate treatment as this can limit their effect. An infant or young child with any burn needs to go to hospital immediately. Older children and young people also need urgent medical attention if:

■ the injury is deep

■ there is blistering

■ there is severe pain

■ there is a chemical or electric burn

■ there's a burn to the hands, feet or face

■ the burn is larger than a postage stamp.

To treat a burn a first-aider will:

■ take action immediately

■ cool the area with water for at least 10 minutes, preferably by holding it under gently running tap water

■ remove any jewellery, watches, belts or restrictive clothing that isn't stuck to the burn/scald before swelling occurs

■ cover the burn/scald with clean cling film or place a clean plastic bag over a foot or hand. Cling film should be applied lengthways instead of being wrapped around a limb due to the risk of swelling. If cling film/bags aren't available, a sterile dressing may be used.

... knowing how to provide first aid to an infant and a child who has been poisoned

In this section you'll learn how poisons enter the body. You'll also learn about recognising and treating those affected by common poisonous substances including plants. This links with **Assessment Criteria 8.1, 8.2, 8.3**.

How poisons enter the body

A number of common household/workplace substances and plants can poison children. That is why it's so important for practitioners to take precautions to ensure that children do not come into contact with these. Poisons enter the body when:

- they are swallowed, for example medication, bleach or berries

- they come into contact with the skin, for example poison ivy

- they are breathed in, for example poisonous gas fumes or dust such as ant powder.

Common poisonous substances and plants

Common items that poison include:

- Cleaning fluids and sprays.

- Medication, including over-the-counter medication and prescription drugs. Medication prescribed for the actual child in question also has potential to harm if ingested in the wrong quantity.

- Personal-care products and make-up, including deodorants, perfumes, nail varnish, nail varnish remover, hairspray, etc.

- Pesticides (which should never be used around children).

> **Did you know?**
>
> Pesticides should never be used around children.

Poisonous plants

Poisonous plants include:

Daffodil bulbs are dangerous

- Delphinium.

- Mistletoe (including berries).

- Some mushrooms and other fungi.

- Foxglove.

- Daffodil bulbs.

- Poison ivy.

Berries from bushes and trees should all be regarded as poisonous as it's difficult to tell which are safe and which are not.

Good practice

Items with the potential to poison must be kept out of children's reach. In a setting, items such as cleaning fluids and medication should not be stored in any room to which the children have access. Cleaning fluids may be kept in a locked cupboard in the kitchen for example. Gas boilers must be serviced annually to help prevent them from becoming faulty and leaking gas. Plants must not be brought into the setting unless they can be identified as safe. If there is any doubt about what a plant is, it must not be introduced. Care must be taken about where the bags belonging to visitors are stored, as they may well have prescribed or over-the-counter medication in them. For instance, many women carry painkillers in their handbags.

Recognising poisoning

The signs and symptoms of poisoning vary according to what the poison is and how it has been ingested. But they include:

- Vomiting.

- Pain.

- Drowsiness or unconsciousness.

Burns to the mouth (if chemicals such as cleaning fluids have been swallowed).

Blisters on the skin.

Swelling.

Itchy skin and/or severe rash.

Breath that smells unusual.

Other evidence

Other evidence may also be present, such as:

smells, for example the smell of gas fumes or bleach

spilt poisonous liquids

open chemical containers such as bottles of cleaning fluid

open/empty medication blister packs or medicine/pill bottles

open medicine cabinet

open cleaning cupboard

berries or pieces of plant in the vicinity of the child.

Treating poisoning

As soon as it is discovered that poisoning has occurred, an ambulance must be caused. A first-aider will also try to find out:

what substance or plant the child has consumed or been in contact with

how much of the substance they have eaten or drunk and when.

This information will be passed on to the emergency services. If a substance or plant has been touched, the first-aider will rinse the skin under a running tap. They will monitor the child closely, and will be ready to act if they become unconscious. (The first-aider will check airway, breathing and circulation, place the child in the recovery position and continue to monitor them until help arrives.)

> ### Did you know?
>
> You should never try to get a child who has swallowed a poisonous substance to vomit. If chemicals have been swallowed they will have burnt the child on the way down and will burn again on the way up, causing further injury.

FOCUS ON

... knowing how to provide first aid to an infant and a child who has been bitten or stung

In this section you'll learn about recognising the severity of bites and stings and responding accordingly. You'll also learn about treating bites and stings. This links with **Assessment Criteria 9.1, 9.2.**

The severity of bites and stings

Insect bites and stings

In the UK most bites and stings are minor, although they can be painful and transmit infection. A first-aider will normally clean the area of the bite/sting and remove the sting if necessary (see page 409).

Animal bites and snake bites

Bites can become infected and there could be a risk of disease. So bites should always be checked by a doctor or staff at a walk-in centre if the skin is broken. In many countries (including Europe) rabies is a concern, but this is not the case in the UK. Snake bites are extremely rare in the UK. The only poisonous snake that is native to the UK is the adder. Bites can be extremely painful and unpleasant, and being bitten can be a very frightening experience.

Allergic reactions

An allergic reaction is dangerous, and many children are allergic to bites and stings, particularly from wasps and bees. If a child has had an allergic reaction before, they will have adrenaline that needs to be administered urgently. For signs and symptom of an allergic reaction and how it is treated, see Unit PEFAP 001, Learning outcome 7. (An ambulance must be called immediately.)

Did you know?

If one child bites another, the skin may be broken. The bite should be treated as described in the bites section on pages 410–11, and as with other sorts of bites, the injury should be checked by a medic.

Link Up!

Unit PEFAP 001 Paediatric emergency first aid.

Recognising and treating bites and stings

Insect bites and stings

Symptoms include:

- Pain.

- Itching.

- Redness.

- Mild swelling, often a small, single raised bump.

A bee sting

Treatment

A first-aider will:

- move a child away from the risk of further stings

- examine the sting area. If there's a sting or other insect body parts present, these can be scraped away with a finger nail or the edge of a credit card. (Tweezers must not be used)

- raise the affected area if possible, and cover with a cold compress or ice pack to reduce swelling

- watch for any signs of an allergic reaction (see page 375).

Stings to the mouth

If a child has been stung in the mouth, a first-aider will give them cold water to drink or an ice cube to suck to prevent swelling, as any inflammation could block the airway. They will watch for swelling closely and call for an ambulance immediately should it start to develop.

Bites

Symptoms include:

- Teeth marks or puncture wounds.
- Pain.
- Redness and slight swelling.
- Signs of a developing bruise.

If there's a cut, the edges are jagged.

Treatment

These are the steps that a first-aider will take to treat a bite:

- If there's severe bleeding (see page 372) an ambulance is required. The first-aider will treat the bleeding until help arrives.
- If the bite is less serious, it will be washed well with antiseptic soap and water, and patted dry carefully.

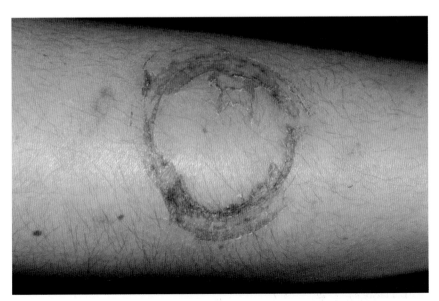

An animal bite

A dressing will be applied if the skin is broken.

A cold pack will be applied to reduce swelling.

Arrangements will be made for the child to see a doctor if the skin has been broken.

Snake bites

Symptoms include:

Small puncture wounds – one or two may be present.

Painful burning sensation at the bite site.

Rapid swelling.

Blisters filled with blood or discoloration.

A child may show signs of shock (see pages 374–5 for details).

Treatment

A first-aider will:

move the child well away from the snake to prevent further bites (a first-aider will never attempt to handle or otherwise move the snake)

keep the bitten body part lower than the heart (if the bite is on an arm or leg, as is usually the case) and keep the child calm, still and quiet, as this will help to slow the spread and effects of the venom

call for an ambulance

monitor the child's airway, breathing and circulation and watch for signs of shock until help arrives.

▶▶ **Link Up!** ◀◀

Unit PEFAP 001 Paediatric emergency first aid.

How are things going?

1. Describe the common types of fractures. (1.1)

2. Describe how to recognise and manage head injuries. (2.1)

3. Describe how to manage a child with a foreign body in their:
   a eye
   b ear or nose. (3.1, 3.2)

4. Describe how to recognise and manage:
   a sickle cell anaemia
   b diabetes
   c asthma. (4.1)

5. Describe how to recognise and deal with meningitis. (4.2)

6. Describe how to recognise and treat the effects of:
   a extreme heat
   b extreme cold. (5.1, 5.2)

7. Describe how to safely manage an incident involving electricity. (6.1)

8. Describe how to treat burns and scalds. (7.2)

9. Describe how to recognise and treat a child affected by common poisonous substances including plants. (8.2)

10. Describe how to recognise and treat bites and stings. (9.2)

Are you ready for assessment?

CACHE

Simulaton is permitted for the Unit, but Learning Outcomes 1 and 2 must be assessed in a realistic simulated environment.

Set task:

■ You are asked to produce a folder of information that you can refer to at work. (You can add to the folder produced for Unit PEFAP001 if you wish). This will include information on how the first aider should recognise and treat all of the conditions covered in this Unit.

You can prepare by rereading pages 379–411 and making relevant notes.

City & Guilds

You can prepare for assessment by rereading pages 379–411 and making relevant notes.

Edexcel

You can prepare for assessment by rereading pages 379–411 and making relevant notes.

UNIT 2.7

Maintain and support relationships with children and young people

LEARNING OUTCOMES

The learning outcomes you will meet in this unit are:

1 Be able to communicate with children and young people

2 Be able to develop and maintain relationships with children and young people

3 Be able to support relationships between children and young people and others in the setting

INTRODUCTION

Maintaining and supporting positive relationships with children and young people is a key part of a practitioner's role. The skills and knowledge required underpin much of your practical work. Because of that, this unit links closely with several other units. You are advised to follow the links given as part of your study.

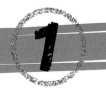

LEARNING OUTCOME 1

FOCUS ON

... being able to communicate with children and young people

In this section you'll learn why creative development is important to children's learning. You'll also learn how creative development links to other areas of learning and development within the framework related to your own work setting. This links with **Assessment Criteria 1.2, 1.3.**

Communicating appropriately with individuals

Link Up!

Unit SHC 21 Introduction to communication in children and young people's settings.

In Unit SHC 21, Learning outcomes 1–4 you learnt a great deal about communicating appropriately with individuals, using conventional language and body language. You are advised to reread this as part of your study of this unit.

For information on informal and formal interaction, and for tips on interacting with children of different ages, see Learning outcome 2.

Actively listening

For information on active listening, see Unit SHC 21, Learning outcome 1.

Checking communications are understood

There are two key reasons to check that children and young people have understood the communications we make:

■ To avoid misunderstandings that occur from time to time when people communicate.

■ To check their understanding and knowledge in a learning situation.

Avoiding misunderstandings

You can check that the message or information you have given has been understood by:

- asking a child or person if everything is clear

- inviting them to ask any questions.

If you think they may have misunderstood but they are not aware of this, you can always ask them to summarise as shown in the Practical example below.

Practical example

Rina checks understanding

Rina is a classroom assistant at a primary school. Every Friday afternoon the school has an extended play time. It's a reward for working hard all week. Each Friday, a different child is selected to be the playground monitor. They are given a few special responsibilities to carry out, such as helping the teacher on duty to get some equipment (footballs, etc.) out of the shed.

Eight-year-old Taylor is going to be the playground monitor for the first time. Rina has been explaining the special responsibilities to her. When she's finished, Rina says, 'Just to make sure we're both clear Taylor, can you tell me what you need to do when it's your turn to be the playground monitor this afternoon?'

Some children may avoid speaking out in group situations

Good practice

When communicating with groups of children or young people, you can still ask if everything has been understood and invite questions. But it's important to recognise that some children may avoid speaking out in group situations. To overcome this, it can be helpful to add something along the lines of, 'If you think of any questions later, you can come and ask me at any time.'

Checking understanding and knowledge

Checking understanding and knowledge in learning situations is one of the ways in which we meet the needs of individual children and young people. It allows us to pitch our communications at the appropriate level, and to identify any gaps in understanding and knowledge that we should address. This is done most effectively through asking open-ended questions that specifically relate to the learning we are focusing on. These questions often feature the words:

- how

- what

- why.

Here are some example questions:

- We had five balls, and we took one away. How many are left?

- It's time to water the plants. Can you remember why we need to water them?

- In our story about the weather, the character looked upwards and said, 'It looks like rain.' What sign of rain do you think she saw in the sky?

Did you know?

When communicating, you should also keep an eye on the responses of children and young people. Facial expressions and body language give helpful indications of whether your communication is being followed and understood.

... being able to develop and maintain relationships with children and young people

In this section you'll learn about the equipment and activities used to support creative development, and about setting out and implementing activities with children. You'll also learn about using clear language, encouragement and praise to support creative development. This links with **Assessment Criteria 2.1, 2.2, 2.3, 2.4, 2.5.**

Respectful, trusting relationships

It's impossible for you to work effectively with children and young people unless you can form respectful, trusting relationships with them. This is because positive relationships enable children and young people to feel happy and relaxed in our company, and to feel that they are being cared for. If children and young people don't feel comfortable with us and able to trust us to take care of them, any relationship established will be uneasy, and this will have a negative effect on their well-being. When you've established positive relationships, it's more likely that the children or young people that you work with will:

■ feel settled in the setting and as a result be more likely to leave their parents without getting upset

■ want to spend time talking with you, which enhances their language and social skills and presents opportunities for spontaneous learning

■ be keen to join in with play and learning activities alongside you

■ feel confident to play and learn independently

■ feel confident to make friends and interact with peers – your own relationship will also serve as a model for this

■ feel content and therefore less likely to become stressed or frustrated, which in turn leads to less inappropriate behaviour

■ be able to concentrate and learn effectively.

When good relationships exist, children will be keen to join in alongside you

Respect

You should always interact with children and young people with respect. This means:

■ Actively listening (see Unit SHC 21, Learning outcome 1)

■ Taking time to explain things and giving reasons for your actions (see page 428)

■ Giving children the attention they need in a way that is fair to everyone (see pages 423–4)

■ Valuing children's contributions and ideas (see page 426)

■ Giving supportive responses (see page 425)

■ Being polite and using good manners at all times (especially when asking someone to do something)

■ Never patronising or speaking down to children or young people

■ Using appropriate facial expressions, body language and tone of voice.

Trust

Children and young people develop a sense of trust over time when practitioners:

- develop a rapport with them

- show them respect

- take good physical and emotional care of them

- build a positive relationship with their parents or carers.

Ask Miranda!

Q How does building a positive relationship with parents and carers help a child to trust you?

A Children unconsciously pick up all sorts of emotional signs and signals from their parents and carers. If a child detects that a parent or carer trusts you and feels confident that you will take good care of them, the child is more likely to feel a sense of trust in you.

Developing a rapport with children and young people

When a rapport exists between people, they have a friendly, relaxed way of interacting, based on a special understanding of each other. Developing a rapport with a child or young person relies partly on good communication skills and partly on 'tuning in' to individuals – spending time with them and noticing how they like to relate to you and the world in general. For instance, on their arrival at a holiday club, some children love a big hello and an enthusiastic catch-up chat from a playworker they haven't seen since last term. Others like to slip more quietly back into the routine of the setting, and will prefer a quieter one-to-one talk later when they've settled in a bit. In addition to greeting children in the way they prefer, the following can help you to establish a rapport:

It's great to laugh together

Have a go!

Spend some time observing an experienced practitioner who has a good rapport with children or young people. Can you put your finger on how they are maintaining the rapport? Are they using strategies that you can incorporate into your own practice?

Did you know?

It is not good practice to pass a baby around from person to person within the setting.

■ Knowing what children's interests are.

■ Remembering things that are going on in their lives and asking about them or mentioning them, for example what their new puppy has been getting up to, or their upcoming holiday.

■ Knowing what amuses children and appealing to their sense of humour – it's great to laugh together.

■ Spending time playing with children and doing things with them so you have shared experiences.

Formality and informality

Practitioners interact with children and young people with differing levels of formality depending on the circumstances. When working with young children, an informal approach is always needed. But as children mature, much will depend on the setting. For example, a playworker will generally be expected to have a more informal rapport with the older children or young people who they work with than a practitioner working with the same children or young people in a school classroom. However, skilled practitioners will be able to achieve a warm rapport regardless of formality.

Key person systems

To ensure that each child within the setting has the opportunity to make a deeper relationship with an adult on a one-to-one basis, many settings operate a key person system. This is explained on pages 342–3.

Building relationships with babies and young children

It's particularly important for babies and young children to have the opportunity to form key attachments within the setting. Consistency is an important aspect of this, so it's good practice for key persons to spend plenty of time with their key babies, and to personally meet their care needs regularly (feeding, changing nappies, dressing, etc.), as these are ideal bonding opportunities. They give you a one-to-one opportunity to engage in eye contact, to talk to the baby, to touch them and to be close to them. Relationships with other staff should still also be encouraged to avoid upset if the key person is absent. Ideally, a small number of regular staff will work with babies and younger children.

All babies should have a special key person

Touch

Physical contact is extremely important, and along with the use of our voice (see below), it's the main way in which we reassure babies and let them know that they are valued and cared for. The way in which you touch, hold and cuddle a baby will have a huge impact on the quality of the relationship you develop with them. Babies must always be touched respectfully during the meeting of care needs, and these tasks should always feel unrushed.

Good practice

When talking to babies, the actual words you say will not be understood, but the message you convey will be received – think how easy it is to distinguish anger, playfulness and empathy just from the pitch and tone of your voice and the look on your face. You should always pay attention and respond to any interactions that a baby initiates with you – such as babbling, smiling, crying and making eye contact.

An age-appropriate approach to developing relationships

▶Link Up◀

Unit TDA 2.1 Child and young person development.

As you've learnt, in order to develop good relationships with children and young people you must respond and relate to them as individuals. However, a good knowledge of children's and young people's development patterns will help you in your approach. Table TDA2.7.1 below and on page 423 gives an example of this. You are advised to also refer to the development tables in Unit TDA 2.1, on pages 113–31.

Table TDA2.7.1: Developing relationships with babies, children and young people

Age	Approach
0–1 years	Babies are entirely dependent and need to form key attachments. Consistency in terms of staff should be promoted. Give babies sensitive physical contact to reassure them and meet their care needs. Make eye contact and talk with babies frequently, and value and respond to the interactions they make with you.
1–2 years	Key relationships continue to be extremely important. Children beginning a setting at this age may have difficulties settling and will need close support. They can be changeable emotionally, alternating between wanting to do things alone (which causes frustration if tasks cannot be managed) and being dependent, so an emotionally responsive approach is important to achieve a relationship that is supportive but not stifling. Children want to play and explore the world as long as carers are close by, providing security to which they can frequently return, so it's important to remain available to them, both emotionally and physically. Children begin to understand much of what is said to them and will develop an expanding vocabulary of single words, so talk with children often and encourage the learning of words as labels.
2–3 years	Children begin to be more responsive to the feelings of others and often relate to carers lovingly (for example initiating a cuddle). This paves the way for a deepening of relationships, as the child takes increasing notice of how the carer is responding to them – ensure that you demonstrate your approval of children and give plenty of praise and encouragement. Vocabulary increases and words are joined together. Children begin to understand their own feelings. Acknowledge feelings and give children words to express them – 'sad', 'happy', etc.
3–4 years	Children understand more about their own role in relationships. They can talk about their feelings and tell carers what they want, so it's important to take the time to listen. They can empathise with the feelings of others, and they enjoy the company of peers and friends as they become increasingly confident socially. Children need carers to support them in these friendships, helping to smooth things out when there are conflicts or disagreements. Children want adult approval and they are affected by the mood of carers. Providing consistency and stability is therefore extremely important.

Age	Approach
4–8 years	Children will have started school, and will need support during the transition. Children have an increasing sense of their own personality and they are keen to 'fit in' with others. Approval from adults and peers is desired. Show that you value and respect the child's individuality, and support the development of positive self-image and self-esteem. Adjust your level of physical support as children become increasingly able to meet most of their own care needs for themselves. Talk with children about the things they do independently when away from you – what they did at playtime or at a friend's house for instance. This will help to keep you connected to the child's world while allowing them to grow in independence and confidence.
8–12 years	Children may feel unsettled when making the transition to secondary school and as puberty approaches. A sensitive, responsive approach is needed, especially as this may result in some unsettled behaviour and reluctance. Stable friendships are relied upon, and children may develop stronger personal interests, some of which may result in a desire to learn out of school (for example dance class). Be sure to show an interest in things that matter to individual children, and informally check in with them about how the big things in their life are going – school, learning, relationships with friends, etc.
Young people	Young people develop a desire to express their individuality and yet also have a strong need to fit in with peers. They may worry about aspects of their appearance and experiment with their identity through appearance. Carers should aim to respect this process and the young person's choices as long as this is not inappropriate (for example you would not support someone under age getting a tattoo or doing something against the wishes of their parents). Young people are developing their own morals, beliefs and values, and these should be shown respect. They become interested in their own sexuality and feel attraction to others, and carers will need to establish boundaries around their development of such personal relationships. Young people may feel overwhelmed and anxious, particularly as exams loom. However, as they are now more likely to communicate their innermost thoughts and feelings to friends than to adults, you will need to remain vigilant in order to offer the emotional support that may be needed, while respecting that the young person may want to spend more time with friends than family and carers, and more time when at home on their own in their room.

Giving attention fairly

Every child and young person is unique, and they all have their own way of interacting with the world. Some are outgoing and frequently approach adults to strike up a conversation, ask a question or give their opinion. Others are less likely to do so. Likewise, some children will come for a cuddle, slip their hand in yours or sit down on your lap, while others are more reserved. This is partly to do with personality and personal preference, and partly to do with experience. As you've learnt in other units, some children come from noisy, busy households and others come from homes where things are generally much quieter. Some families show affection through cuddles while others are less demonstrative.

Your role

Your job as a practitioner is to give everyone some individual attention, and to ensure that everyone's voice is heard. A good strategy is to encourage those children who are more reserved by gently prompting them to talk, or by asking them a direct question. This should always be done sensitively to avoid them feeling under pressure to speak out, as this tends to be counterproductive.

Some children simply take longer than others to build up the trust needed to try and gain your attention, or to attract attention to themselves in group situations. In these cases, it can be helpful for you to spend some time playing casually alongside a child, ensuring that they can enjoy your company without always feeling under pressure to have a conversation with you. Meanwhile, activities and resources that promote interaction with adults and other children can be incorporated into the routine. For example:

■ Resources such as telephones and walkie-talkies.

■ Word games, for example I Spy, I went to market and I bought …

Puppets can be used to promote interaction

- Role play and imaginary areas.

- Puppets.

- Singing and rhymes.

- Circle time (sharing news, etc.).

- Mealtimes together at the table.

- Tabletop games.

- Playground games.

- Team games (for older children).

Supportive responses

We need to think carefully about how we respond to a child or young person's:

- Questions.

- Concerns.

- Ideas.

- Suggestions.

Our responses will impact on the relationships we have with the individual children and young people who we work with.

Questions

Asking questions is:

- a key way for people of all ages to learn

- an indication that children and young people are engaged and interested in events and activities

- important to the development of thinking and problem-solving skills (see Unit OP 2.17).

So it's important that we encourage children and young people to ask questions, by:

- listening patiently to the whole question, even if it is a little rambling

Have a go!

Spend a moment thinking about how you would feel if you:

- asked your tutor a question but they didn't answer it

- told a family member you were worried about something, but they didn't seem at all interested in hearing about it

- shared an idea for a fun day out with a friend, but they said it was a 'stupid idea'

- suggested some ideas at a thought storming session, but the group leader didn't write them down.

Link Up!

Unit OP 2.17 Contribute to the support of children's creative development.

- giving a full, *appropriate* answer

- remembering that children learn through repetition, so being patient when questions are asked frequently or repeatedly (for example 'Why?')

Concerns

When children or young people have concerns, their emotional well-being is at stake, so it's extremely important that we listen to what they have to tell us. Only then can we take action to put their mind at rest. No concern should ever be dismissed as silly. Occasionally the concerns that children and young people raise may be serious – a disclosure of abuse or bullying for example. For information on how to respond to this, see Unit TDA 2.2, Learning outcome 3.

▶▶▶ **Link Up!** ◀◀◀

Unit TDA 2.2 Safeguard the welfare of children and young people.

No concern should ever be dismissed as silly

Did you know?

Often we can put an end to a young child's worries by providing just a small amount of information. Young people often find that the process of talking over a concern lightens their emotional load – if they are worried about exams for instance.

Ideas and suggestions

It's up to the practitioner to find out about the ideas and suggestions of children and young people, as well as responding to them when they are given spontaneously. So practitioners should consult with children and young people about their ideas, opinions and preferences, and involve them in decisions about what happens in the setting. This becomes increasingly important as children grow up, and it enables practitioners to provide play activities and experiences that children and young people will enjoy participating in.

Consultation can also help children and young people to feel:

- **listened to:**
  Children and young people spend a lot of time listening to adults at school and perhaps in the home. Some children naturally initiate conversations with practitioners more frequently than others.

When practitioners are consulting and actively looking to seek out everyone's opinion, they have the opportunity to encourage everyone to have their say. That includes those children/young people who are less likely to put forward their opinion without it being asked for and those children who do not routinely approach adults and/or gain their attention easily.

■ **valued and worthwhile:**

We know as adults how good we feel if our employers ask for our opinions and ideas. It is good to feel that your thoughts are worthwhile and so your opinion is sought out and valued. The same is true for children/young people.

■ **included:**

This is particularly important for children belonging to groups that may be at risk of discrimination. It also gives children and young people the opportunity to make a positive contribution, which is one of the five Every Child Matters outcomes.

Practical example

Claire's consultation methods

Claire runs an out-of-school club for older children. One of the ways she ensures the setting is child centred is by offering lots of opportunities for consultation. Over time, she asks children for their suggestions, ideas and feedback on the setting's themes, activities, resources, equipment, boundaries, day trips, meals and routines. Recent methods have included:

■ Using a suggestion box.

■ Thought storming.

■ Voting.

■ Opinion polls.

■ Evaluation games.

■ A group meeting.

Using a suggestion box

Link Up!

Unit TDA 2.9 Support children and young people's positive behaviour.

Did you know?

You must always make sure that you give reasons for your actions if there is a consequence or sanction due to the inappropriate behaviour of a child or young person (if you are taking a toy away from them for instance). See Unit TDA 2.9, Learning outcome 3.

Did you know?

Children and young people need to understand how poor choices can affect the outcomes in life, for example, the effect of choosing to break the law, take drugs, play on a building site, or have unprotected sex. This starts at a young age when explaining to children *why* they mustn't behave in certain ways, and what the *consequences* are if they do. This must be age appropriate.

Giving reasons for actions

When appropriate, explaining your actions helps children and young people to see that they are being treated fairly, and it also helps them to learn from us. Here are some examples:

- Children are not permitted to have the ride-on toys in the playground because it's icy today and it wouldn't be safe.

- A child needs to give up a toy they've enjoyed playing with because it belongs to another child who is going home soon.

- An instance of inappropriate behaviour will have to be explained to the child's parent when they arrive, because parents need to know when there's been a difficulty. Everyone can talk about it together.

- Children have been divided into certain groups or teams because you'd like them to have a go at working with someone new or with someone who has different skills or opinions to their own.

Encouraging children to make choices for themselves

Children and young people need to be empowered to make personal choices about the things that they experience in their lives. This enables them to influence their own outcomes and life chances. So it's important for us to give children and young people a voice, and to listen to what they tell us. This is a key part of providing services that are child/young person centred.

Good practice

Children and young people have had the right to have their voices heard since the UN Convention on the Rights of the Child was ratified in 1989. Article 13 states that children must be consulted about matters and decisions that are important to them. Children and young people's voices also need to be sought and listened to on a day-to-day basis. This can be done effectively in settings through consultation about what children and young people would like to do and how they'd like to do it.

FOCUS ON

... being able to support relationships between children and young people and others in the setting

In this section you'll learn about reviewing how your own working practice has contributed to children's creative development. You'll also learn about adapting your practice to meet the needs of individual children. This links with **Assessment Criteria 3.1**, **3.2**, **3.3**, **3.4**, **3.5**.

Support communication with others

Part of the practitioner's role is to support children and young people to communicate effectively with their peers and other adults. As discussed in Learning outcome 2, children and young people are all unique. They will have their own various styles of communication, and ongoing interaction will be easier for some than others.

Young children

Young children usually need the most support because they have a lot to learn about how relationships work. They will not yet have learnt how to respond appropriately to the communications of others, so they may not give out the signals that encourage others to keep talking to them – making eye contact for example. When young children are communicating with each other, we can support them by encouraging and sensitively prompting them to:

- listen as well as talk
- let the other person finish rather than interrupting them
- ask each other questions
- tell one another about their experiences and ideas.

Did you know?

Young children have a tendency to say whatever they are thinking right away, so they are likely to interrupt one another frequently.

Also see the bullet points on pages 424–5 for information on how we can promote communication between children through the activities and resources we offer.

Older children and young people

Older children and young people have had much more experience of communicating, but there is still plenty for them to learn about the complex process of communicating effectively. It's important for practitioners to support older children and young people to do the following:

- Find the confidence to share their feelings and views with others. You can sensitively prompt this by asking them questions, such as what they think about the current topic of conversation.

- Explain what they mean clearly. You should give them time to express themselves. If their communications aren't clear, ask them to clarify what they mean.

- Work together in pairs or small groups. Discussion-based tasks and team games can be very effective to break the ice and get the conversation flowing.

- Respect other people's feelings and views and respond to them appropriately in conversation. See page 431.

- Respect individuality, diversity and differences. See below.

- Communicate calmly when there is disagreement or conflict. See page 432.

Individuality, diversity and differences

When communicating, children and young people should always be supported to understand and respect the individuality, diversity and differences that they come across. We can promote this in a number of ways, including:

- Answering their questions about individuality, diversity and differences in a sensitive way. A child may ask why someone reads and writes in Braille for instance.

Young children have a lot to learn about how relationships work

Giving them the means to communicate with those who have communication difficulties. This may involve teaching them a few Makaton or British Sign Language signs for example, or helping them to interpret what a child who uses a communication board is saying to them.

Encouraging them to learn a few words of someone else's home language. Words for greeting them and saying, 'Do you want to play?' are particularly useful.

Explaining to them that some children need a bit more time to respond when communications are made to them.

Planning activities that give children and young people with diverse ways of communicating opportunities to work or play together in a supportive atmosphere.

Respecting other people's feelings and views

Children who are learning about interacting with others need our support to respect other people's feelings and views. There will be many times when children simply don't realise that they could be upsetting someone else. We can help by stepping in. Sometimes, a gentle prompt to do or say the right or polite thing may be all that's needed. At other times, an explanation may be needed, or we may need to model the behaviour we wish children to emulate. Consider the following scenarios for instance:

Max asks his friend Sammie if she wants to play in the ball pool with him. Sammie doesn't want to play in the ball pool at the moment, so she just walks away.

Josh asks Becky – who is Jewish – what she had for Christmas. Becky replies, 'Nothing.' Josh says, 'You must be really naughty.'

Callum is heading off to play outside. On the way, he steps over Florence, who is lying on the floor on her side playing with the train set. Callum accidentally stands on her long hair. Florence starts to cry. Callum looks at her for a moment, then carries on outside.

Good practice

Children and young people will watch and learn from the way you respond to individuality, diversity and differences in your own communications. So use your own practice to role model the responses you would like children to emulate (or copy).

Have a go!

Spend a few moments thinking about the scenarios above. Decide how you would step in to sensitively support the children involved to respect one another's feelings and views.

Older children and young people will bicker, argue and fall out at times

Link Up!

Unit MU 2.2 Contribute to the support of child and young person development.

Unit TDA 2.9 Support children and young people's positive behaviour.

Did you know?

All adults frequently come across others who disagree with their own opinions and views. So learning to respect the views of others is an important skill that children and young people will need throughout their lives.

Older children and young people

Older children and young people may know that they should respect other people's feelings and views, but they are likely to find this challenging at times. This is especially true when they feel passionately about their own beliefs or viewpoints. For instance, a young person who is very environmentally conscientious may at times find it a challenge not to disrespect those who have strong opposing views. In addition, older children and young people will of course still bicker, argue and fall out at times, even with their closest friends, and feelings will be hurt in the process. We can support older children and young people by encouraging them to:

- express themselves calmly

- use language that avoids making the issue personal, for example 'I don't agree with that point of view myself' rather than, 'How can you believe that rubbish!'

- constructively try to understand other views, for example 'Can you tell me why you think that?'

- constructively put across their own view, for example 'I respect your opinion. But I think that ...'

- avoid blowing things out of proportion by generalising, for example 'You *never* listen to me!' or 'You *always* do that!'

Group agreements about interactions with others

As you learnt in Units TDA 2.9 and MU 2.2, older children and young people are often involved in setting the boundaries or rules for their own settings. In informal settings such as out-of-school clubs, this is often a simple list of behaviour guidelines that make it clear what is expected. These guidelines are generally displayed on the wall or noticeboard as a constant visual reminder.

In more formal settings such as schools, older children or young people may also be given a code of conduct to follow, which they may be required to sign. This then becomes a contract to stick to the rules. The group agreements made with children and young people both formally and informally will normally include guidelines on:

Showing respect for their peers

Showing respect for the adults

Having a positive attitude

Using acceptable language

Not hurting others physically or emotionally.

Supporting the development of agreement

If you have the opportunity to support children and young people to develop agreements about the way they interact with others, encourage a discussion about:

the ways in which children and young people want to be treated by others

the types of behaviour and actions that contribute to a pleasant, positive environment

the types of behaviour and actions that contribute to an unpleasant, negative environment

the types of behaviour and actions that hurt other people emotionally and physically

the types of behaviour and actions that help to avoid confrontation and to handle disagreements and conflict positively.

When a written agreement is drawn up, encourage children and young people to phrase the rules using positive language. Also see Unit MU 2.2, Learning outcome 4.

Dealing with conflict

For information on supporting children to deal with conflict themselves, see Unit MU 2.2, Learning outcome 4.

Did you know?

Codes of conduct will also tell children and young people how to handle conflict without retaliation, and what to do if they are bullied.

Link Up!

Unit MU 2.2 Contribute to the support of child and young person development.

How are things going?

▶ Progress Check

1. Describe how to actively listen to children. (1.2)

2. Describe how to check that children and young people understand what is communicated. (1.3)

3. What can you do to establish a rapport with children and young people? (2.1)

4. Why must you provide children and young people with reasons for your actions when appropriate? (2.4)

5. Why should you encourage children and young people to make choices for themselves? (2.5)

6. What strategies might you use to support children to communicate effectively with others? (3.1)

7. What strategies might you use to help children and young people to respect the feelings and points of view of others? (3.3)

8. How can you encourage children to deal with conflict for themselves? (3.5)

Are you ready for assessment?

All assessment criteria must be assessed in a real work environment.

CACHE

There is no set task. In preparation for assessment of this Unit, you may like to ask colleagues for feedback on how effectively you communicate with children and young people. You can then spend some time reflecting on this and make notes on how you can improve where necessary.

City & Guilds

In preparation for assessment of this Unit, you may like to ask colleagues for feedback on how effectively you communicate with children and young people. You can then spend some time reflecting on this and make notes on how you can improve where necessary.

Edexcel

In preparation for assessment of this Unit, you may like to ask colleagues for feedback on how effectively you communicate with children and young people. You can then spend some time reflecting on this and make notes on how you can improve where necessary.

UNIT 2.14

Support children and young people at mealtimes and snack times

The learning outcomes you will meet in this unit are:

1 Know the principles of healthy eating for children and young people

2 Know the benefits of healthy eating for children and young people

3 Know how to encourage children and young people to make healthier food choices

4 Be able to support hygiene during mealtimes or snack times

5 Be able to support the code of conduct and policies for mealtimes or snack times

INTRODUCTION

Children and young people need to eat healthily in order to stay physically fit and healthy. As a practitioner, you have the opportunity to support children and young people to make healthier food choices and to learn and follow hygiene guidelines that will stand them in good stead throughout their lives.

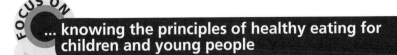
FOCUS ON

... knowing the principles of healthy eating for children and young people

In this section you'll learn about the nutritional requirements of a healthy diet, and healthy meals and snacks for children and young people. You'll also learn how culture, religion and health conditions impact on food choices. This links with **Assessment Criteria 1.1, 1.2, 1.3.**

Nutritional requirements of a healthy diet

A great deal of information on nutrition is provided in Unit MU 2.8, Learning outcome 4. You are advised to reread this as part of your study of this section.

Advice from the Food Standards Agency

The information on page 437 sets out the Food Standards Agency advice on providing children with a healthy balanced diet.

The nutrient-based standards

The School Food Trust is a specialist adviser to the government on school meals, children's food and related skills. In 2006 it led the implementation of the '14 nutrient-based standards for school lunches'. Schools must meet these standards. The Trust tells us that the standards:

> make sure that the average school lunch offers the right mix of energy and nutrients for growing children – about a third of their daily requirement. They also limit children's exposure to sugary, fatty, and salty foods, providing food and drinks that are packed with essential nutrients rather than those full of empty calories.
>
> www.schoolfoodtrust.org.uk/about-us/about-the-trust

Link Up!

Unit MU 2.8 Contribute to the support of positive environments for children and young people.

Have a go!

Read the 14 nutrient-based standards for yourself by visiting www.schoolfoodtrust. org.uk/the-standards.

Children need a healthy, balanced diet, which is rich in fruit, vegetables and starchy foods.

Encourage your child to choose a variety of foods to help ensure that they obtain the wide range of nutrients they need to stay healthy.

Remember to include these sorts of foods:

- Milk, cheese, yoghurt, soya beans, tofu and nuts are rich in calcium, which is needed for healthy bones and teeth.
- Fortified breakfast cereals, margarine and oily fish are good sources of dietary vitamin D, which helps ensure a good supply of calcium in the blood and therefore healthy bones. The main source of vitamin D is from the action of sunlight on skin, but avoid strong sun especially around midday when there is a risk of burning.
- Meat, particularly red meat, and fish are rich sources of iron. Pulses (beans and lentils), green vegetables and fortified breakfast cereals are also good sources of iron. Iron is needed for healthy blood and research has shown that some children have low intakes of iron, particularly older girls.
- At least two portions of fish a week, because fish are a good source of protein, vitamins and minerals and they are low in saturated fat. Oily fish, such as mackerel, salmon and sardines, also contain omega 3 fatty acids. You can give boys up to four portions of oily fish a week, but it's best to give girls no more than two portions of oily fish a week.
- Citrus fruit (such as oranges and lemons), tomatoes and potatoes, are all good sources of vitamin C, which is essential for health. Vitamin C may help the absorption of iron, so having fruit juice with an iron-rich meal could increase iron absorption.
- Milk, margarine with added vitamins, green vegetables and carrots are all good sources of vitamin A, which is important for good vision and healthy skin.

Avoid giving children shark, swordfish and marlin. This is because these fish contain relatively high levels of mercury, which might affect a child's developing nervous system.

Drinks

- Cartons of fruit juice are extremely convenient, but like dried fruit, are high in sugar and should be eaten at mealtimes.
- Sweet drinks also damage the teeth, especially if drunk frequently or sipped from a bottle over long periods between meals.
- So, keep drinks such as fruit juices or squashes to mealtimes, and try to encourage your child to drink water or milk in between.

Foods to limit
Sweets and snacks

Eating sweet and sticky foods frequently between meals causes dental decay. Snack foods such as cakes, biscuits, chocolate and sweets can be high in sugar and saturated fat, and low in certain vitamins and minerals. So if your child does eat these sorts of foods:

- try to make sure they eat them only occasionally or in small amounts, so they only make up a relatively small part of the overall diet
- help and encourage your child to clean their teeth every day
- try picking a weekly sweet day, or choose the weekends as a time when your child is allowed to eat sweets
- check the label and choose those options lower in fat, saturated fat, sugars and salt.

Advice from the Food Standards Agency

The importance of water

Children and young people should always have access to fresh drinking water because it's a vital part of a healthy diet. Water makes up about two-thirds of a healthy body weight. One of its functions is to enable blood to carry nutrients around the body. Water is lost when children urinate, sweat and breathe (through evaporation). This needs to be replaced so that children remain healthy. Plain water is the

Children and young people should always have access to fresh drinking water

healthiest choice. It doesn't contain sugar (which can damage teeth) and it is calorie free.

Examples of healthy meals and snacks

When planning menus, including snacks and drinks, it's important to consider:

- the nutritional balance needed by children for a healthy diet, including the required calorie intake. What have children eaten for their previous meal/snack, and what will they have next? Always consider this across the day, and ideally across the week

- the current government guidelines, including five servings of fruit/vegetables a day

- the time of day the food will be consumed

- children's individual dietary requirements and allergies

- children's preferences

- variety

- offering children new and interesting foods to try

Explore the nutritional advice on the NHS Choices website at www.nhs.uk/livewell/healthy-eating. Choose the from the child health menu options on the left-hand side of the screen to see advice that relates to children and young people of different ages.

Ask Miranda!

Q What should I do if a child is a picky eater?

A If children are reluctant to try something new, or they do not like new food, practitioners are advised to simply remove it and offer an alternative. But do present the food again at another time – some children change their mind once a food is familiar to them. If not, once again, don't make a fuss. Our tastes for food change throughout our lives – we go off things, or suddenly start to enjoy a taste. The child may enjoy the food at some point in the future. Not making a fuss about food is a good general rule. Battling with children over food is unproductive, and the child may come to dread mealtimes. If children regularly refuse food, not offering food outside of mealtimes is a good idea.

- involving children in food preparation (see page 449)

- how food will be presented to add interest (see 448)

- how families can be consulted about meals and snacks.

Suggestions for healthy meals

The government offers advice on all aspects of nutrition for babies, children, young people and adults on their NHS Choices website. Table TDA2.14.1 lists meal suggestions for children from the NHS Choices Guide.

Table TDA2.14.1: Meal suggestions for children aged two years and older, from the NHS Choices Guide

Breakfast
- Porridge or unsweetened cereal mixed with whole cows' milk (or your child's usual milk) with mashed ripe pear.
- Wholewheat biscuit cereal with milk and stewed fruit.
- Toast fingers with mashed banana.
- Toast fingers with boiled egg and slices of ripe peach.
- Stewed apple, yoghurt and unsweetened breakfast cereal.

Lunch or tea
- Cauliflower cheese with cooked pasta pieces.
- Plain fromage frais with stewed apple.
- Small pieces of soft ripe peeled pear or peach.
- Mashed pasta with broccoli and cheese.
- Baked beans (reduced salt and sugar) with toast.
- Stewed fruit and custard.
- Scrambled egg with toast, chapatti or pitta bread.
- Cottage cheese dip with pitta bread and cucumber and carrot sticks.

Dinner
- Mashed sweet potato with mashed chickpeas and cauliflower.
- Shepherd's pie with green vegetables.
- Rice and peas with courgette sticks.
- Mashed cooked lentils with rice.
- Minced chicken and vegetable casserole with mashed potato.
- Mashed canned salmon with cous cous and peas.
- Fish poached in milk with potato, broccoli and carrot.

Fruits and vegetables
Try these ways of increasing your child's intake of fruits and vegetables:
- Put their favourite vegetables or canned pineapple on top of pizza.
- Give carrot sticks, slices of pepper and peeled apple for snacks.
- Mix chopped or mashed vegetables with rice, mashed potatoes, meat sauces or dhal.
- Mix fruit (fresh, canned or stewed) with yoghurt or fromage frais for a tasty dessert.
- Chop prunes or dried apricots into cereal or yoghurt, or add them to a stew.

Healthy snacks

The government's Change 4 Life campaign aims to support families to 'eat well, move more, live longer'. It suggests the following healthy snacks for children:

- Dried fruit (for example mango, banana, pineapple, papaya, raisins).

- Chunks of fresh fruit.

- Low-fat fruit yoghurt.

- Raw chunks of low-sugar jelly.

- Pumpkin and sunflower seeds.

- Homemade popcorn (without sugar or salt).

- Oven-baked crisps.

- Rice and corn cakes.

- Breadsticks.

- A handful of dry, reduced-sugar cereal with some raisins or sultanas.

- Vegetable sticks – carrot, celery, baby sweetcorn, peppers and radishes with a reduced-fat hummus dip.

- Sliced apple and a lower-fat soft cheese to dip.

Good practice

Babies and toddlers following a weaning programme have very special dietary needs. The meals and snacks suggested here are not intended for this age range.

Have a go!

Why not try these snack suggestions on a hot day:

- Strawberries dipped in yoghurt – put them in the freezer for half an hour before you serve them so the yoghurt goes hard.
- A frozen banana – put it in the freezer in its skin and serve like an ice lolly.
- A glass of sorbet.

Traffic lights labelling system

The Food Standards Agency traffic lights system allows us to see the nutritional content of commercially produced foods. The aim is to help us make more healthy choices easily and quickly, for ourselves and for children. The amount of fat, sugar, saturates and salt per serving is shown in grams, and a corresponding traffic light colour lets us know if this amount is considered high (red), medium (amber) or low (green). The amount of calories will also be shown. The estimated average number of calories required each day is shown in Table TDA2.14.2.

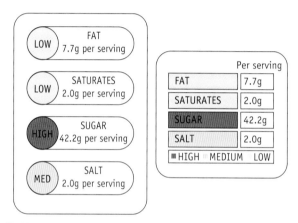

Example of traffic light food labelling from www.nhs.uk/Livewell/Goodfood/Pages/food-labelling.aspx

Table TDA2.14.2: The estimated average number of calories required each day

Age	Daily calorie intake for males	Daily calorie intake for females
1–3	1,230	1,165
4–6	1,715	1,545
7–10	1,970	1,740
11–14	2,220	1,845
15–18	2,755	2,110
Adults	2,550	1,940

The impact of culture, religion and health conditions

The impact of culture, religion and health conditions on food choices is described in Unit MU 2.8, Learning outcome 4.

Link Up!

Unit MU 2.8 Contribute to the support of positive environments for children and young people.

FOCUS ON

... knowing the benefits of healthy eating for children and young people

In this section you'll learn about the benefits of healthy eating and the possible consequences of an unhealthy diet. You'll also learn how to recognise and deal with allergic reactions to food, and where to get advice on dietary concerns. This links with **Assessment Criteria 2.1, 2.2, 2.3, 2.4.**

Did you know?

Childhood obesity is on the rise. This is worrying as it's linked to many health complications, some of them serious.

Benefits of healthy eating

Eating healthily helps children, young people and adults to:

- stay physically fit and healthy

- be less at risk of obesity

- be less at risk of some medical conditions/illnesses including Type 2 diabetes and heart disease.

Possible consequences of an unhealthy diet

Did you know?

It can be easy to forget about the calories that are contained in healthy drinks – juices and smoothies in particular – so remember to factor these in when estimating the number of calories in a child's meals and snacks.

It's important for both practitioners and parents to think about food management for the children in their care. It's not just what children and young people eat that matters, it's the portions that they have. Portion control is important because if children eat too much food they will become overweight/obese (even if the food they are eating is generally healthy) and this has health implications (including high blood pressure, high cholesterol, gall bladder problems and even headaches and drowsiness). However, if children eat portions that are not large enough, they will get insufficient nutrients from their food and they will become undernourished. Type 2 diabetes is also a common consequence of an unhealthy diet.

Good practice

If there are concerns about weight in the early years, children should not be made aware of them. If children become stressed or anxious or feel guilty about what they do or do not eat, psychological issues with food can develop or become apparent in later life. They may last throughout their life.

Allergic reactions to food

You were introduced to food allergies in Unit MU 2.8, Learning outcome 4. You're advised to reread the information now, before reading the rest of this section.

Common food allergies

Common food allergens include:

■ Nuts.

■ Dairy products.

■ Wheat.

■ Food additives.

Did you know?

Food allergies are most common in younger children, who may eventually grow out of them. But they can develop at any stage of life.

Signs and symptoms of an allergic reaction

As you've learnt, your setting will have systems in place to inform all staff about the known food allergies of the children or young people in your care. You will also be told about the signs and symptoms of a child's allergy, and what must be done should they have an allergic reaction. Common signs and symptoms of allergic reactions are shown on the diagram on page 444.

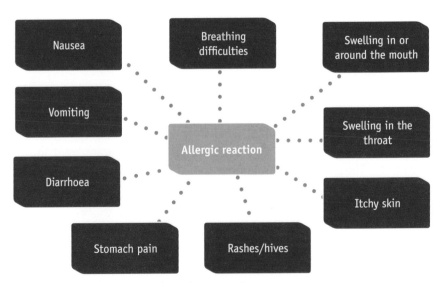

Nausea

Breathing difficulties

Swelling in or around the mouth

Vomiting

Allergic reaction

Swelling in the throat

Diarrhoea

Itchy skin

Stomach pain

Rashes/hives

Common signs and symptoms of an allergic reaction

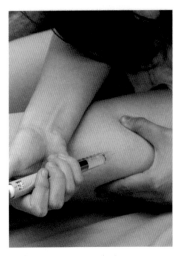

Children may have their own auto-injector

Link Up!

Unit PEFAP 001 Paediatric emergency first aid.

Anaphylaxis

Anaphylaxis is a severe allergic reaction that can be fatal. Symptoms include breathing difficulties, swelling in/around the mouth or throat and falling blood pressure. Casualties may go into shock and become unconscious. They need to be given an adrenaline injection urgently.

If a child or young person is known to be at risk of this kind of severe reaction, they will have their own auto-injector to be administered. Practitioners at the setting who have been trained in paediatric first aid will be given additional training from a member of the child's healthcare team on how to administer the injection in an emergency. They must act immediately. (Training is often given by a health visitor in the early years settings.) For information on treating shock, see pages 374–5. For resuscitation, see pages 365–6.

Advice on dietary concerns

Within your setting, your manager will be able to give you advice on supporting children for whom there are dietary concerns. The setting may also work in partnership with outside professionals who are supporting children, such as health visitors, GPs and dieticians. Health visitors are also a good source of general advice about dietary matters, and often advise individual settings on their menus for meals and snacks. They will also have a range of informative leaflets and posters, which settings may display and make available to staff and families.

You can access dietary advice from the following:

- NHS Choices (www.nhs.uk/livewell/healthy-eating): information on child nutrition and feeding/weaning babies and young children.

- Change 4 Life campaign (www.nhs.uk/change4life): information on making changes to the diets of families.

- NHS Healthy Start programme (www.healthystart.nhs.uk): information on the five-a-day fruit and vegetable programme.

- The Schools Food Trust (www.schoolfoodtrust.org.uk): information on nutrition for school children.

- Caroline Walker Trust (www.cwt.org.uk): this charity provides guides for early years practitioners on nutrition for babies and young children.

Have a go!

Visit the dietary advice websites to find out more about the extent of the advice available to you.

LEARNING OUTCOME 3

FOCUS ON

... knowing how to encourage children and young people to make healthier food choices

In this section you'll learn about food policies. You'll also learn about ways of encouraging children and young people to make healthier food choices and to eat the food provided for them. This links with **Assessment Criteria 3.1, 3.2.**

Food policies

Settings are required by their country's regulatory body to make healthy provision for children in the area of food. For example, in England, Ofsted will check to see that early years settings "promote good health" (one of the key considerations of the Early Years Foundation Stage safeguarding and welfare requirements). Schools are currently being encouraged to draw up a 'whole school food policy' in response to the school standards you learnt about in Unit MU 2.8. The document 'Food Policies in Schools'

Link Up!

Unit MU 2.8 Contribute to the support of positive environments for children and young people.

from the National Governors Association advises schools to cover the following key points in their policies:

■ School councils: how the school consults pupils and gives them responsibilities for aspects of the food policy.

■ School lunches: how the food provided meets the new standards for school lunch, is of a high quality and promotes health. How the choices provided address cultural, religious and special dietary needs.

■ Packed lunches brought from home: the agreement made with parents and carers about the content of packed lunches brought into school.

■ Breakfast clubs: how healthy breakfasts are provided, and how the provision is in line with the rest of the school.

■ After-school clubs: how healthy snacks and drinks are provided, and how the provision is in line with the rest of the school. How activities promote a healthy eating agenda, for example cookery clubs or gardening clubs.

■ Dining environment: how this is a desirable place with enough space to sit and eat, promoting sociable mealtimes.

■ Break-time snacks and drinks: how the food provided by the school meets the new standards, and the agreements made with parents and carers about bringing snacks and drink from home.

Vending machines are common in secondary schools

Tuck shops: how tuck shop provision is in line with food standards legislation and how healthier food and drink is available.

Vending: how healthier refreshments are providing both inside and outside of school catering hours, how vending is in line with legislation and whole school policy, how branding is limited and how vending makes the school money.

Water: how pupils have access to free, fresh drinking water throughout the day and are encouraged to drink it frequently.

Food allergy: the procedures for meeting the needs of children with allergies, and how it is ensured that children do not come into contact with allergens unexpectedly in school (for example in lessons).

Curriculum: how nutrition education is included in the curriculum.

Encouraging healthier food choices

It's good practice to make children aware of healthy foods and how good they are for their bodies. This establishes the link between food and health. It's generally considered appropriate to make children aware that no foods are completely unacceptable, but that sugary foods (such as sweets and many drinks) and those which are high in saturated fats (such as cakes) should be regarded as occasional treats. Ways in which you can encourage children of various ages to eat healthily include:

Discussing healthy food and making a display or book about them as a reminder.

Introducing children to fruits and vegetables that may be new and interesting to them, for example star fruit.

Role modelling healthy choices, for example saying, 'I'm going to choose a lovely healthy apple for my snack today.'

Drawing older children's attention to the diets of role models such as athletes.

Involving children in shopping for and preparing healthy foods (see page 449).

Good practice

You must understand the food policy at your setting and work in line with it at all times.

- Letting children see practitioners frequently drinking water – ask whether children would like to do the same.

- Introducing children to multicultural healthy foods thay may be new and interesting.

Encouraging children to eat the food provided

In group settings, mealtimes can feel hectic unless practitioners plan well. It is good practice to present food attractively to children and this can be achieved by setting the table so that it looks pleasant, having all of the right utensils in place, and creating a calm atmosphere (quiet, gentle music playing in the background can help to settle children at lunchtime after a busy morning). Consider how much food you put on children's plates. You don't want children to go hungry, but too much food can be overwhelming and put a child off. Consider how the food looks.

Involving children in the planning and preparation of food

Involving children in the planning and preparation of food is a good way to ensure you are providing things they like and it's a good opportunity to discuss healthy foods. Children are often much keener to eat food they have helped to prepare. Children are even more eager

You can role model healthy choices

when they have grown vegetables themselves. Even settings without access to a garden can grow herbs and cress in pots. Children can help in many ways depending on their age by:

- washing fruit
- scrubbing vegetables
- cutting fruit (soft fruits such as bananas can be easily cut or mashed with children's knives)
- peeling fruit
- putting spread on bread or toast
- making sandwiches
- preparing salad
- growing vegetables
- harvesting vegetables
- mixing drinks
- pouring out drinks
- sharing out food
- setting the table
- washing the dishes.

Involve children in the preparation of food

FOCUS ON

... being able to support hygiene during mealtimes or snack times

In this section you'll learn about the importance of personal hygiene at mealtimes and snack times. You'll also learn about demonstrating good hygiene practice in relation to your own role in food handling and waste disposal. Lastly, you'll learn about ways of encouraging children and young people's hygiene at mealtimes and snack times. This links with **Assessment Criteria 4.1, 4.2, 4.3.**

Unit MU 2.4 Contribute to children and young people's health and safety.

Unit MU 2.8 Contribute to the support of positive environments for children and young people.

The importance of personal hygiene

The personal hygiene of practitioners and the children and young people themselves is extremely important at mealtimes and snack times. It protects everyone's health by preventing the spread of infection.

Encouraging children and young people's personal hygiene

The following guidelines and the reasons why they are important (to prevent the spread of infection) should be taught to children and young people:

■ Hands must be washed thoroughly with antibacterial soap before eating or drinking. In settings, they should be dried with paper towels or by an air hand dryer.

■ They should only touch the food they are going to eat (for example no picking up food and putting it back – if they don't want it after all they can leave it on their plate).

■ They should not eat food from other people's plates, or share cutlery or take bites from food that someone else has bitten.

- They should not drink from the same cup, bottle, glass or straw as someone else.

- They should not eat food that has been dropped on the floor or use cutlery that has fallen on the floor.

- Any open wounds to the hands should be covered with a plaster.

- They should avoid sneezing, coughing, yawning or blowing their nose near food.

Good practice

To ensure personal hygiene, strategies are built into the daily routines of most settings. For instance, everyone will be sent to wash their hands before mealtimes and snack times. But do you remember to tell children why they need to wash their hands? Making the most of these regular opportunities helps children to want to wash their hands before eating, even when an adult isn't there to tell them! Children will also need reminding about certain guidelines when they are about to breach them – you may have to stop a child from using a knife that has fallen on the floor for instance. Again, use this as an opportunity to explain the reason. Remember that children learn through repetition, and they may not drop their knife that often!

Food handling and waste disposal

For information about food handling, see the food safety section in Unit MU 2.8, Learning outcome 4. For information on waste disposal, see Unit MU 2.4, Learning outcome 6.

Link Up!

Unit MU 2.8 Contribute to the support of positive environments for children and young people.

Unit MU 2.4 Contribute to children and young people's health and safety.

LEARNING OUTCOME

... being able to support the code of conduct and policies for mealtimes or snack times

In this section you'll learn about codes of conduct and policies for mealtimes and snack times. You'll also learn about techniques for supporting and encouraging positive behaviour in dining areas, and skills and techniques for dealing with inappropriate behaviour in dining areas. This links with **Assessment Criteria 5.1, 5.2, 5.3.**

Codes of conduct and policies at mealtimes and snack times

Many settings have:

■ a policy that explains the setting's ethos on mealtimes and snack times. This is for the attention of practitioners, parents, carers and regulatory bodies such as Ofsted. This is separate to the food policy described in Learning outcome 3, which focuses on the food provided rather than on the activity of having a meal or snack

■ a code of conduct for older children and young people on how they should behave and what they should do at mealtimes and snack times. These are most common in schools.

Snack and mealtimes promote children's learning

A mealtime and snack-time policy

A policy is likely to cover the atmosphere that will be promoted at mealtimes and snack times as well as the learning and skills that will be promoted. There may also be a separate set of procedures for practitioners to follow.

Practical example

Fiona's policy

Fiona's pre-school is planning to introduce a mealtime and snack-time policy, so Fiona is thinking about the learning and skills that can be promoted at mealtimes and snack times. So far, she's made the following notes:

- Communication skills – chatting to others at the table.
- Social skills – table manners.
- Numeracy – counting out the cups and plates when laying the table.
- Physical development – using cutlery, pouring drinks.
- Personal development – independence in eating and drinking.

Question:
Can you suggest further notes for Fiona's list?

Codes of conduct

Codes of conduct are likely to tell children and young people:

- how they are expected to enter and exit from the dining area, for example they may have to queue up to get in and wait to be excused before they leave

- how they will get their food. They may have to collect it, or it may be served to them

- what level of noise is considered acceptable

- about conduct in the dining area, for example the positive behaviour expected

- about conduct at the table, for example the positive behaviour expected

- what to do when they finish eating, for example whether they should clear their trays, wipe their table, etc., and how this should be done.

Older children and young people may have a code of conduct to follow

Supporting and encouraging positive behaviour

As you saw in the Practical example on page 453, mealtimes and snack times are rich opportunities for early years children to learn and practise a number of skills. It's best for a practitioner to sit at the table with the children to promote a calm, pleasant atmosphere, and to support and encourage positive behaviour. If it's possible for a practitioner to eat with the children, then positive table behaviour can also be role modelled. Examples of positive behaviour that should be encouraged and supported are shown on the diagram on page 455.

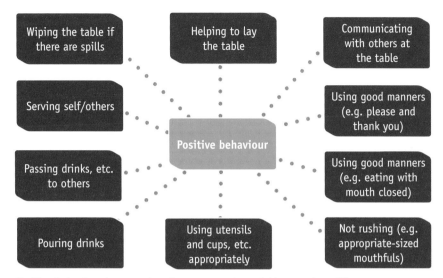

Positive behaviour to support and encourage at snack times and mealtimes

Dealing with inappropriate behaviour

When dealing with inappropriate behaviour in the dining area, the strategies and techniques you learnt in Unit MU 2.2, Learning outcome 3 can be applied as appropriate to the situation. It's particularly useful to try to find out the reason behind the behaviour. It could be that a child or young person is trying to avoid eating their meal or snack because they don't like it, or for some other reason.

In a school setting, older children and young people are not closely supervised in a large dining hall, so inappropriate behaviour can escalate quite quickly if an adult doesn't step in. This is particularly the case if several children sitting together are involved in inappropriate behaviour such as throwing food or flicking water.

How are things going?

▶ Progress Check

1. Describe six healthy snacks for children and young people. (1.2)

2. Give one example of how each of the following might impact on food choices:
   a Culture.
   b Religion.
   c Health conditions. (1.3)

3. What are the key benefits of healthy eating? (2.1)

4. What are the signs and symptoms of an allergic reaction to food? (2.3)

5. Name three key points likely to be covered in a food policy. (3.1)

6. Describe two ways to encourage children and young people to eat the food provided for them. (3.2)

7. What are the guidelines that children and young people should follow to ensure their personal hygiene at mealtimes and snack times? (4.3)

8. What is the purpose of a code of conduct for mealtimes and snack times? (5.1)

9. Describe two techniques that you might use to encourage positive behaviour in the dining area. (5.2)

10. Describe two techniques that you might use to deal with inappropriate behaviour in the dining area. (5.3)

Are you ready for assessment?

Learning Outcomes 4 and 5 must be assessed in a real work environment.

CACHE

Set tasks:

■ An in-depth task in which you produce an information pack for parents and carers. Covering three sections you should demonstrate that you understand the principles of healthy eating, the benefits of healthy eating, as well as how to encourage children and young people to make healthier food choices. You can prepare by reviewing the food policies and procedures of your workplace setting.

City & Guilds

You can prepare for assessment by reviewing the food policies and procedures of your workplace.

Edexcel

You can prepare for assessment by reviewing the food policies and procedures of your workplace.

UNIT 2.15

TDA

Support children and young people with disabilities and special educational needs

LEARNING OUTCOMES

The learning outcomes you will meet in this unit are:

1 Know the rights of disabled children and young people and those with special educational needs

2 Understand the disabilities and/or special educational needs of children and young people in own care

3 Be able to contribute to the inclusion of children and young people with disabilities and special educational needs

4 Be able to support disabled children and young people and those with special educational needs to participate in the full range of activities and experiences

INTRODUCTION

It's essential that all practitioners understand how to meet the individual needs of the children and young people who they work with. Often a basic adaptation to an activity is all that is needed to empower a disabled child or young person to participate fully during a play session.

... knowing the rights of disabled children and young people and those with special educational needs (SEN)

In this section you'll learn about the legal entitlements of disabled children and those with SEN. You'll also learn about the assessment and intervention frameworks, and about the benefits of early intervention. Lastly, you'll learn about individual plans and the principles of working with disabled children and those with SEN. This links with **Assessment Criteria 1.1, 1.2, 1.3, 1.4, 1.5.**

Legal entitlements

Thanks to legislation that has been gradually brought in over the years, disabled children and young people now have significant legal rights. Both settings and individual practitioners must be aware of these entitlements, and work in ways which ensure that disabled children and young people's rights are promoted at all times.

Key pieces of legislation/requirements include:

- UN Convention on the Rights of the Child.

- Every Child Matters.

- Disability Discrimination Act 1995 and 2005.

- Equality Act 2010.

Link Up!

Unit SCH 23 Introduction to equality and inclusion in children and young people's settings.

You can read about these in Unit SHC 23. Settings must also comply with the Special Educational Needs Code of Practice 2001 (see page 459), and the requirements of frameworks that apply in the home country. For example, in early years settings in England this is the Welfare Requirements.

Special Educational Needs Code of Practice 2001

The Special Educational Needs Code of Practice (SEN Code) was implemented in 1994 and revised in 2001. It applies to schools and early years settings. Children with **special educational needs** are identified as children who learn differently from most children of the same age. They may need extra or different help to learn. The SEN Code sets out procedures to be followed in order to meet the requirements of children with special educational needs.

Under the SEN Code, early years settings (even those in which there are currently no children with special educational needs) must:

■ adopt the recommendations of the SEN Code

■ train staff to identify and manage children with special educational needs

■ devise and implement a Special Educational Needs policy in line with the SEN Code. This must explain how the setting promotes **inclusion**, which means how it includes children with disabilities and/or special educational needs within the mainstream setting. (You should be familiar with how inclusion works within your setting and your local area, and the reasons for this)

■ appoint a Special Educational Needs Coordinator (SENCO), who will have particular responsibility for overseeing the setting's practice with regard to meeting the needs of children and adhering to the SEN Code.

Did you know?

In addition, settings will implement graduated action and intervention when working with children with special educational needs, known as Early Years Action and Early Years Action Plus. You'll learn about these on pages 460–2.

key terms

Special educational needs children with special educational needs learn differently from most children of the same age. These children may need extra or different help from that given to other children. (*National Occupational Standards.*)

Inclusion children with disabilities or special educational needs belonging to mainstream settings. (*National Occupational Standards.*)

Did you know?

At the time of writing, the Government is in the process of reforming the current approach to special educational needs and disability. You can view the Green Paper which sets out the new proposals at https://www.education.gov.uk/publications/eOrderingDownload/Green-Paper-SEN.pdf. This means that there will soon be changes in regard to what is currently required of settings under the SEN Code of Practice 2001. You can keep up to date by reading industry journals and visiting the Government's education website. Planned changes include a new single assessment process and 'Education, Health and Care Plan' by 2014. This will bring together the support on which children and their families rely across education, health and social care. Services will work together with the family to agree a straightforward plan that reflects the family's ambitions for their child from the early years to adulthood; this will be reviewed regularly.

Disabled children and young people now have significant legal rights

Assessment and intervention frameworks

Under the SEN Code, two models of graduated action and intervention are recommended to early years settings working with children with special educational needs:

- Early Years Action. This is the initial stage in which children's special educational needs are identified. The setting should then devise interventions (strategies) that are additional to or different from those provided under the setting's usual curriculum.

- Early Years Action Plus. This is the stage in which practitioners feel it's appropriate to involve external specialists/professionals. They can offer more specialist assessment of the child and advise the setting on strategies.

Early Years Action

Practitioners working in the early years settings are often the first to notice that a child may be experiencing difficulties with their learning and/or development, although sometimes it is a parent or carer who first expresses a concern about their child. When it is suspected that a child is having problems, practitioners need to make focused observations of the child to see if they can identify specific difficulties. These observations should be documented.

When there is cause for concern

The SEN Code explains that practitioners will have cause for concern when, despite receiving appropriate early education experiences, one or a combination of the following criteria applies to a child:

- They make little or no progress, even when practitioners have used approaches targeted to improve the child's identified area of weakness.

- They continue working at levels significantly below those expected for children of a similar age in certain areas.

- They present persistent emotional and/or behavioural difficulties that are not managed by the setting's general behaviour management strategies.

- They have sensory or physical problems and continue to make little or no progress despite the provision of personal aids and equipment.

- They have communication and/or interaction difficulties, and require specific individual interventions (one to one) in order to learn.

When concern has been established

Once it has been established that a child meets one or more of the above criteria, practitioners should:

- arrange a time to meet with parents or carers to discuss the concerns and to involve them as partners in supporting the child's learning. The practitioner should explain the role of the setting's SENCO, and discuss the involvement of the SENCO with the parents or carers. The practitioner should ask the parents and carers for their own observations of their child's learning and, if appropriate, for information about health or physical problems or the previous involvement of any external professionals such as speech therapists. Parents are the prime source of information in many cases

- meet with the SENCO. Practitioners should make available as much helpful information as possible, such as observations, assessments, health details, etc.

- work with the SENCO, liaising with the parents and carers to decide on the action needed to help the child progress in light of the observations made. The SEN Code states that action should 'enable the very young child with special educational needs to learn and progress to the maximum possible'.

Practitioners need to make focused observations of the child

- devise an Individual Education Plan (IEP) for the child. You'll learn about IEPs on page 464.

Early Years Action Plus

The decision to implement Early Years Action Plus (that is, to involve external support services and professionals) is generally taken in consultation with parents or carers at a meeting to review a child's IEP. At this stage, a CAF assessment will also be carried out (see Unit MU 2.9, Learning outcome 2). The SEN Code identifies that Early Years Action Plus is likely to be triggered when, despite receiving support tailored to their needs, a child:

- continues to make little or no progress in specific areas over a long period

- continues working at a level substantially below that expected of children of a similar age

- has emotional difficulties that substantially interfere with the child's own learning or that of the group, despite an individual behaviour management programme

- has sensory or physical needs and requires additional equipment or regular specialist support

- has ongoing communication or interaction difficulties that are a barrier to learning and social relationships.

Link Up!

Unit MU 2.9 Understand partnership working in services for children and young people.

Did you know?

The type of support services available to settings under Early Years Action Plus varies according to local policy.

Statutory assessment

In some cases, children do not make the expected progress despite the intervention of Early Years Action Plus. At this stage it is appropriate for the parents, carers, practitioner, SENCO and external professionals to meet to discuss if a referral should be made to the local authority (LA) requesting a statutory assessment of the child. If it is agreed, an application for assessment is made.

The LA will require all relevant documentation including observations, IEPs and assessments. These are considered and the LA decides (within 26 weeks) whether the child should be made the subject of a Statement of Special Educational Needs. The statement is legally binding. It sets out a child's needs and outlines what special educational provision must be made to meet them. The LA concerned is then legally obliged to provide this for the child. This applies to all LAs in England. The nature of the provision will depend on the child's need, but some examples of provision include:

- A transfer to a specialist setting.

- A place at a mainstream setting with additional one-to-one support.

- A place at a mainstream setting with additional resources and equipment.

- Support of an educational or clinical psychologist.

Did you know?

The same procedures will be followed in schools. The terms 'School Action' and 'School Action Plus' are then used.

A child may require additional equipment or aids

Did you know?

Statements for children under the age of five must be reviewed by the LA every six months. Because of the time it takes to go through the stages of intervention, most children are not referred for statutory assessment until they are over the age of five, by which time they will have started school.

The benefits of early recognition and intervention

These are explained in the section on concerns about development in Unit TDA 2.1, Learning outcome 2.

The purpose of individual plans

A disabled teenager may have a participation plan at their youth club

Plans to support learning, play or leisure needs can be devised for children and young people in many different ways. For instance, a Saturday morning sports club might draw up a 'play plan' to identify the goals that a disabled child has and how the staff will support the child in achieving them. Or a youth club may agree a 'participation plan' with a disabled teenager, which outlines what they want to achieve and the support they'll receive to enable equality of access to activities and outings. However, most early years settings use the IEP method of planning which is required if graduated action and intervention is in place under the SEN Code.

Individual education plans (IEPs)

An IEP should concisely record three or four short-term targets set for a child, and detail the strategies that will be put in place. The IEP should only record that which is additional to or different from the general curriculum plan of the setting. The IEP should be discussed with parents, carers and the child concerned.

Good practice

IEPs should be working documents, kept continually under review. They are primarily for checking the effectiveness of strategies implemented and the progress made towards targets.

Information recorded

The diagram on page 465 shows the information that will be recorded on the IEP:

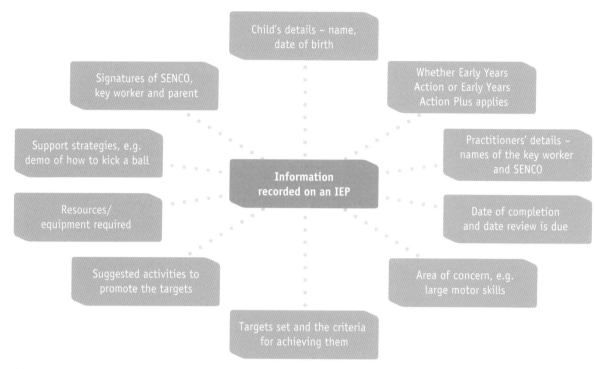

Information recorded on an IEP

Support strategies

Strategies to support children and young people in achieving targets may include:

- Extra adult support for some activities.

- Provision of special equipment.

- Provision of different materials.

- Staff training and development.

- Allowing extra staff time for planning interventions.

- Allowing extra staff time for monitoring progress.

Good practice

It's important that all practitioners working with a child or young person are aware of the strategies planned to support them. This enables a consistent approach to the implementation of plans.

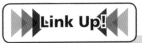

Unit SHC 23 Introduction to equality and inclusion in children and young people's settings.

The principles of working inclusively

You were introduced to inclusion and inclusive practice in Unit SHC 23, Learning outcomes 1 and 2. You are advised to reread the information now.

Medical model of disability

Disabled people have a right to be included in society and to participate within it. But things have not always been that way. Although disabled people have always been part of society, they have not always been treated equally.

Did you know?

There were times when disabled children spent their lives locked away in institutions. The way disabled people lived was dictated by non-disabled people and their attitudes towards disability.

Assumptions

In the more recent past there has been the assumption that disabled people (children and adults) have a problem. Their impairments have been regarded as personal tragedies. It has been seen as the responsibility of non-disabled people to either cure or care for the disabled person, taking steps to fit them into society. Treating disabled people as sick patients in this way is not empowering. This way of thinking is known as the '**medical model of disability**'.

key terms

Medical model of disability this reflects the traditional view that disability is something to be 'cured', treating the child as a sick patient.

The social model of disability

There is a worldwide organisation called the Disabled People's Movement. The British Council of Disabled People (BCODP) is a branch of this, formed in 1981. The BCODP believe that disability is not an inevitable consequence of a person's impairment, but that disability arises from the negative way in which disabled people are treated by society. They believe that disabled people are disabled by society's structure, its attitudes and its lack of access, which exclude disabled people from activities that non-disabled people take for granted. It is believed that society should change to meet the needs of disabled people. This gives disabled people rights and choices. This is known as the '**social model of disability**'.

Did you know?

The Disability Discrimination Act 1995 and 2005 supported the social model of disability by giving disabled people (children and adults) rights regarding the way they receive services, goods and facilities.

key terms

Social model of disability
this considers that it is society that needs to change and that disabled people have rights and choices. (*National Occupational Standards*.)

Principles central to inclusive working

The following principles are central to inclusive working:

■ **Respect**:
Disabled children and young people and their families should be shown respect at all times. They should never be patronised or spoken down to. Respect underpins all of the other principles. For example, there is no point consulting disabled children and young people if you don't respect and value what they say in response.

■ **Empowerment**:
Disabled children and young people may experience times in their lives when they are expected to be passive receivers of services, as you learnt in the section on the medical model of disability on page 466. So it is particularly important that practitioners empower disabled children and young people to express their views, make decisions and be in control of what they do and what happens in respect of meeting needs. This is part of a child/young person-centred approach (see page 469).

■ **Enablement**:
This is about the practical things that you do to enable empowerment, such as the ways you find to consult children and young people about the purchase of new equipment, or how you consult them about the effectiveness of the adaptations made to an activity.

Extra adult support may be provided for some activities

■ **Empathy:**

Being empathetic means understanding someone else's feelings and point of view. This informs the way in which you go about your practical work and your interactions with others. For instance, empathy helps practitioners to ensure that the dignity of disabled children and young people is maintained when their physical-care needs are met. Empathy is completely different to sympathy. It most certainly is not about feeling or acting on pity for disabled people. Empathy fits in with the social model of disability. Sympathy fits in with the undesirable medical model.

■ **Organisation culture and ethos:**

Organisations should have a culture and ethos that promotes inclusive working as a matter of course. This means that services will be child and young person led.

■ **Policies:**

The organisational culture and ethos should be underpinned by inclusive policies that promote the legislation and requirements that apply in the home country.

■ **Training:**

Practitioners should have access to high-quality training on inclusion and matters relating to disability.

Unit SHC 23 Introduction to equality and inclusion in children and young people's settings.

Dignity must be maintained when physical-care needs are met

Ask Miranda!

Q How can I take a child/young person-centred approach to inclusive working?

A **By encouraging the disabled children and young people who you work with to express their views and to make decisions about the way in which they experience the setting, and how their needs are met. Examples of how this may be achieved on a day-to-day basis include:**

- **Asking a child which member of staff they'd like to work with them as their PA (personal assistant) on a group outing.**

- **Asking a young person how they'd like to adapt a game so that they can participate fully.**

- **Consulting a child when evaluating activities to understand how effectively their needs were met and how this can be improved in the future.**

LEARNING OUTCOME 2

FOCUS ON

... understanding the disabilities and/or special educational needs of children and young people in own care

In this section you'll learn about the relationship between disability and SEN. You'll also learn about knowing the nature of the particular disabilities/SEN of children with whom you work, and the special provision that is required by them. This links with **Assessment Criteria 2.1, 2.2, 2.3**.

Disability and special educational needs

Impairments

Impairments are conditions within an individual that may affect the function of their body, their behaviour and/or the way their brain works. This means there are differences in terms of the usual expected patterns of development. The following impairments are common:

- Physical impairments.

- Visual impairments.

- Hearing impairments.

- Communication/speech difficulties.

- Emotional/behavioural difficulties.

- General learning difficulties or developmental delay (for which there is no specific name).

- Specific learning difficulties (such as dyslexia).

- Medical conditions.

Did you know?

Learning difficulties were once called 'mental impairments', but this language is no longer used.

Good practice

It's good practice to use the term 'usual' rather than 'normal' when comparing the patterns of development of a disabled child to the usual expected patterns of development. This avoids implying that a child who develops differently is 'abnormal' or has 'something wrong with them'.

Disability

As you learnt in Learning outcome 1, an impairment may give rise to disability due to society's attitudes and lack of access.

Special educational needs

Children and young people with special educational needs learn differently from most children of the same age. They need extra or different help compared to that given to other children. This special provision may be provided for them in a mainstream setting or in a special setting such as a special school. There's more about this on page 473. Special educational needs are commonly due to a learning difficulty, and this will be the first thing many adults think of when special educational needs are mentioned. But special educational needs can be due to any of the impairments listed in the bullet points on page 470.

Some children and young people attend special schools

The children and young people with whom you work

Practitioners should develop a good knowledge of particular disabilities and/or special educational needs as they affect the children in their care. It's important to acknowledge that the same impairment can be experienced by different individuals in very different ways. You need to understand how the children you are working with are affected so that you can meet their needs appropriately. You'll learn more about this in Learning outcome 3. Practitioners should also be aware of the expected pattern of development of the children they work with. Further information is provided in Unit TDA 2.1.

Link Up!

Unit TDA 2.1 Child and young person development

Down's syndrome is caused by chromosome differences

The nature of particular disabilities and special educational needs

Genetic make-up

Genetic make-up starts to influence a child's development at the moment of conception. All cells in our bodies contain 46 chromosomes, which are made up of 23 pairs. Each chromosome consists of long chemical threads, which we know as DNA. Each of the threads contain genes. The father's sperm and the mother's egg each carry their genetic information, and when the sperm and egg fuse, the chromosomes pair off, with the baby getting half of their chromosomes from the mother and half from the father. Some impairments (such as cerebral palsy and cystic fibrosis) are genetic.

Pregnancy and birth

Further factors can arise during the pregnancy and birth. If the mother picks up certain infections, they can affect the baby's development. Harm can also be caused by drinking alcohol or taking drugs during pregnancy. If a baby is born prematurely, the usual full-term development will not be complete, and this can also have long-term effects. There can also be difficulties at birth that can impact on development, including a lack of oxygen, which can cause learning difficulties. But it's important to stress that the majority of pregnancies and births are healthy.

Medical conditions

Some medical conditions that cause impairments, such as certain heart problems, are present at birth, and the child will be affected by them to some extent from the start of their lives. There can be a disposition for other conditions, but a child will only develop them if they are triggered by external factors. For example, asthma can be triggered by living in a damp house or in an area with high levels of traffic pollution. Medical conditions acquired in childhood can also lead to impairments. For instance, diabetes and meningitis can both lead to visual impairments.

Accidents and injury

Some children and young people have impairments as a result of an accident or injury. For example, a young person may become a wheelchair user as a result of a road traffic accident, or a child may acquire a brain injury falling from a tree they have climbed.

Good practice

You should understand the nature of the particular disabilities and special educational needs that are experienced by the children and young people who you work with. Your SENCO will be able to answer any questions you may have.

The special provision required

You should understand the special provision required by the children and young people who you work with. This enables you to support them effectively, and to contribute to the process of delivering any special interventions. Read Learning outcome 3 to learn how to obtain information about the special provision required by individual children and young people.

LEARNING OUTCOME 3

FOCUS ON

... being able to contribute to the inclusion of children and young people with disabilities and special educational needs

In this section you'll learn about ways of supporting participation and equality of access. You'll also learn about the use of specialist aids and equipment. Lastly, you'll learn about reviewing and improving the activities provided for disabled children and young people and those with special educational needs. This links with **Assessment Criteria 3.1, 3.2, 3.3, 3.4**.

Obtaining information

While it's helpful to have knowledge and understanding about impairments and medical conditions, this doesn't tell you anything about the way in which individual children or young people experience them. For example, knowing about Down's syndrome doesn't give you any information at all about the support that an individual child with Down's syndrome may need. It certainly won't tell you anything about the child's learning and development, their personality, their preferences, their interests and past experiences. But this information can be obtained from:

- children and young people themselves
- family members
- colleagues within the setting
- external professionals/support agencies working with the family (for example the speech and language therapist)
- individual plans made for the child or young person.

Did you know?

You are likely to offend a disabled person or their family if you assume that you know about them without getting the relevant information in the appropriate way, as outlined above. Assumptions fit the negative medical model of disability.

Barriers to participation

Barriers to participation are factors that can cause difficulties for families, children and young people, preventing them from accessing your setting's services or activities. Barriers fall into three categories:

- **Environmental:**
  These barriers are caused by features of the environment such as steps, poor lighting or lack of space.

■ **Attitudinal:**
These barriers are caused by the attitudes of practitioners.

■ **Institutional:**
These barriers are down to organisational policies or procedures
that do not promote inclusion, or the lack of policies and
procedures that do promote inclusion.

Working to remove barriers

In order to have an inclusive setting, practitioners must identify
barriers to inclusion and find effective ways to remove or overcome
them. Attitudinal and institutional barriers are often based on
practitioners' worries and anxiety. They may be concerned that they
will not be able to meet the needs of a disabled child adequately, or
that they will not understand how to give the right cultural respect
to a family. These things can be overcome with equality training
and support.

Environmental barriers can be identified and removed or overcome in a
number of ways. Examples include:

■ **Steps (for example, a parent who uses a wheelchair cannot get
into the setting):**
A ramp could be built from concrete, or a free-standing ramp could
be used.

■ **Poor lighting (for example, a child with a visual impairment is
experiencing more difficulty than usual due to inadequate light):**
In consultation with the family, practitioners can find out what
lighting works effectively for the child and introduce it.

■ **Lack of space (for example, a setting does not have enough
space for a child who uses crutches to manoeuvre between
activities):**
The furniture can be moved to a better position. It may be
necessary to put out fewer activities at one time, but change them
more frequently.

For information on overcoming/removing barriers to activities and
experiences, see Learning outcome 4.

Did you know?

Action taken to remove
or overcome barriers
should be monitored
and reviewed to ensure
that it is effective.

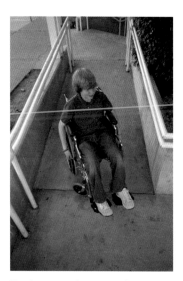

Barriers must be removed or
overcome

475

It's good practice for settings to work in partnership with children and young people when planning how to remove or overcome barriers. They should also consult them when monitoring and reviewing whether the action taken has been successful. This supports the social model of disability.

Supporting inclusion and inclusive practices

For this Learning outcome, you're required to demonstrate ways of supporting inclusion and inclusive practices in your own work. Examples are given in the section on principles central to inclusive working in Learning outcome 1. Also see all of the practical advice in Learning outcome 4.

LEARNING OUTCOME 4

FOCUS ON

... being able to support disabled children and young people and those with special educational needs to participate in the full range of activities and experiences

In this section you'll learn about making adaptations to activities and experiences, and supporting children to use specialist aids and equipment. You'll also learn about supporting participation, equality and access. Lastly, you'll learn about working in partnership to review and improve activities and experiences. This links with **Assessment Criteria 4.1, 4.2, 4.3, 4.4**.

Adapting the physical environment

It's likely that your setting will have already identified and overcome some of the barriers to participation that occur within your physical environment. However, it's still necessary for practitioners to consider and eliminate any potential barriers that may affect new disabled children or those barriers that become apparent as the needs of existing disabled children change over time. Some environmental barriers may only come to light when different activities or experiences are planned (see below). By considering the layout of a room carefully you can overcome barriers effectively. For instance:

- Furniture of different heights may be used to ensure that wheelchair users can participate in tabletop activities.

- Furniture may be positioned and activities set out to allow easy passage for children using wheelchairs, crutches or other aids.

- Furniture and equipment may be kept in the same position to assist children with visual impairments to locate and navigate.

- Equipment and resources may be stored at a height that makes them accessible to all.

- Scent clues or bright colours may be used to mark out certain areas (for example lavender in the book corner).

- Adequate task lighting may be employed in activity areas.

- Comfortable soft areas may be provided for children who need to rest during play sessions.

Furniture of different heights may be used

Adaptations to support participation in activities

It is part of the practitioner's role to consider the needs of children and young people in relation to every activity and experience that the setting offers. This can be done at the activity planning stage. Once barriers to participation have been identified, practitioners can consider ways of overcoming or removing them. Specialised aids or pieces of equipment may be available to assist children. However, simple strategies can often be used effectively to enable full participation. It may be appropriate to:

- devise your own adaptations

- implement adaptations that a child or young person suggests or has used successfully before

- change your working practice by altering the way an activity is organised (this may include changing the way adult support is given)

- swap the activity for an alternative activity or experience

- make changes to the environment.

Good practice

It's good practice to consult children and young people about the way in which barriers are tackled if this is appropriate to their age and ability. Remember to consider the grouping of children during activities and the support available from practitioners.

Table TDA2.15.1 below gives examples of simple strategies that could be implemented to overcome some barriers to participation in everyday activities.

Table TDA2.15.1: Adaptation

Activity	Barrier	Adaptation strategy
Painting with rollers	Child with a physical impairment cannot grip the roller effectively	Mould thick plasticine around the handle. The child grips it, altering the shape of plasticine to suit their grip. The roller has been easily adapted to suit the child's individual grasp
Game of catch to be played in pairs	Child with a visual impairment has difficulty seeing the ball approaching, and therefore difficulty preparing to catch it accurately	Practitioners attach a tail of bright ribbon to some of the balls, and tie bells (from a textile shop) securely to the ends. The balls are now more easily located, and they can also be caught by the tail
Game of musical bumps	One child with a hearing impairment cannot hear the music, and a wheelchair user cannot sit on the floor and get up again easily	Practitioners arrange to play musical statues instead, and devise two hand signals, one that is used to indicate when children should dance, and another for when they should freeze like statues
Singing songs	A child with communication difficulties has difficulty joining in	Practitioners encourage the group to come up with actions they can do as they sing. They also slow the pace of the singing. They allow time to play along with musical instruments too

Practical example

Will's adaptation

Playworker Will works at a holiday club. Ten-year-old Jade, a wheelchair user, has recently started attending the club. The staff have planned some parachute games and Will needs to ensure that Jade can participate. He thinks that she could join in effectively if the other children played kneeling down instead of standing up. He asks Jade what she thinks of this idea. Jade says her teacher plays parachute games in the same way at school, and that this adaptation works for her.

Supporting the use of specialist aids

Make sure that you are aware of the relevant specialist aids and pieces of equipment that are available for the children and young people who you work with. You must be confident that you know how to use these/how to support children to use these safely and, if appropriate how to keep them clean/sterile and functioning properly and safely. Your SENCO will be able to advise you. Some children and young people will already be using aids and equipment at home, in which case they and their families will be the main source of information.

Types of aids

There are many specialist aids and pieces of equipment available for children. What individuals use will of course depend on their needs, but you may come across:

- specially angled cutlery designed for children with physical impairments who experience difficulty feeding themselves

- non-slip matting that has flexible use – it can be placed under plates or bowls at mealtimes to stop them sliding away, or perhaps under pots of paint at the craft table

- light boxes that can be used to backlight objects so that they can be seen by children with visual impairments

- voice-activated computers

- hearing loops that can be installed for those with hearing impairments

- communication boards that can be used by those with communication difficulties

- prosthetic limbs

- mobility aids including wheelchairs, rollers, crutches, callipers (leg braces) and walking frames

- feeding tubes

- catheters.

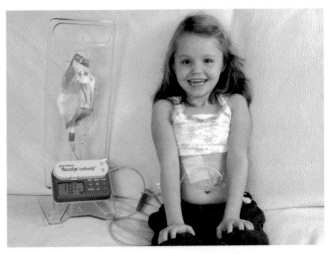

Some children and young people use a feeding tube

Working in partnership to monitor, review and improve

It's important for practitioners to monitor, review and improve the:

- activities and experiences offered to children and young people

- success of adaptations made to enable participation in activities and experiences

- effectiveness of their own practice in terms of supporting children and young people and promoting inclusion.

This should be done in partnership with:

- children and young people

- families

- colleagues

- external professionals/agencies that work with the family, if appropriate.

Good practice

Children and young people know best about how well their needs are being met in terms of the activities and experiences. Asking for and listening to their views is always of the utmost importance.

You should work in partnership with colleagues

Techniques for monitoring, reviewing and improving

You learnt about reflection techniques for monitoring, reviewing and improving in Unit SHC 22, Learning outcomes 2 and 4.

Supporting participation and equality of access

For this Learning outcome you're required to demonstrate ways of supporting participation and equality of access in your own work. You've learnt ways of doing this throughout the unit.

Link Up!

Unit SHC 22 Introduction to personal development in children and young people's settings.

How are things going?

▶ Progress Check

1. Describe the assessment and intervention frameworks. (1.2)

2. What are the benefits of early recognition and intervention? (1.3)

3. What is the purpose of individual plans for children and young people? (1.4)

4. What is the definition of 'special educational needs'? (2.1)

5. Give an example of how 'special provision' may be made for a child or young person. (2.3)

6. Describe the ways of obtaining information about an individual's needs, capabilities and interests. (3.1)

7. What must practitioners do if they identify a barrier to participation? (3.2, 3.3)

8. Give an example of an adaptation you may make in your setting to meet the needs of a wheelchair user. (4.1)

9. Give five examples of specialist aids and equipment that you may come across. (4.2)

10. Describe a technique you might use to review an activity provided for a disabled child. (4.4)

Are you ready for assessment?

Learning Outcomes 3 and 4 must be assessed in a real work environment.

CACHE

Set tasks:

■ You are asked to produce a resource folder demonstrating that you understand the legal rights, intervention frameworks, benefits of early intervention, purpose of individual plans, and can describe the principles of inclusive working with regards to children and young people with disabilities or special education needs. You should also describe the relationship between disability and special education needs, the nature of particular disabilities and/or special education needs of children and young people with whom you work, as well as any special provisions required. You can prepare by talking to your SENCO about the individual needs of the disabled children with whom you work, and how these needs are met.

City & Guilds and Edexcel

You can prepare for assessment by reviewing the policies at your workplace setting relating to equal opportunities, inclusion and special educational needs. You can also talk to your SENCO about ways of obtaining information about the individual needs, capabilities and interests of the disabled children you work with (including those with SEN).

UNIT 2.16

Support children and young people's play and leisure

LEARNING OUTCOMES

The learning outcomes you will meet in this unit are:

1 Understand the nature and importance of play and leisure

2 Be able to support children and young people's play and leisure

3 Be able to support children and young people in balancing risk and challenge

4 Be able to reflect on and improve own practice

INTRODUCTION

Play and leisure are so important to the well-being of children and young people that they have been given a legal right to it. Play is also the most effective vehicle for young children's learning and development. Children are driven to play.

You will have noticed children and young people in all sorts of situations finding a way to play without any help from adults and with no props or toys – skidding up and down on a nice shiny floor in the supermarket for example. So just imagine the rich world of play available when practitioners provide access to a range of exciting resources and high-quality play spaces, and let children choose how to play for themselves.

... understanding the nature and importance of play and leisure

In this section you'll learn about the importance of play and leisure, and how it contributes to children and young people's development. You'll also learn about children's rights for relaxation and play. Lastly, you'll learn about the characteristics of freely chosen, self-directed play. This links with **Assessment Criteria 1.1, 1.2, 1.3, 1.4.**

The importance of play and leisure

Play and leisure provide children and young people with the opportunity to interact with both adults and their peers, at whatever level is appropriate for them. This helps children to gain the social skills they need to get on with others and become part of a group. Children learn and practise a wide range of skills when they're playing, for example how to ride a tricycle. They also make discoveries and learn concepts. At the water tray they may learn that pebbles sink, for instance. The activity, game or experience will finish when children stop playing, but the learning will eventually be remembered. These are long-term benefits of play, which develop over time. Other long-term benefits gained through play include increasing:

- independence

- self-esteem

- knowledge and understanding

- well-being, health and development

- creativity

- capacity to learn.

Children make discoveries and learn through their play

Short-term benefits of play

The short-term benefits of play occur at the time a child is playing. They include the opportunity to:

- enjoy freedom

- have fun

- test boundaries

- explore risk

- exercise choice

- exercise control over their body

- exercise control over their actions and emotions.

Social skills and relationships

Play acts as a bridge to social skills and relationships. Young children need to gain skills such as:

- sharing

- taking turns

- cooperating

- making and maintaining friendships

- responding to people in an appropriate way.

The stages of child development influence children and young people's play needs and behaviours. Practitioners must remember that all children develop at different rates and so their play needs and behaviours will also vary. For example, children tend to have different interests and be drawn to different types of play as they grow up and develop, and the amount of independence that children are comfortable with increases over time. A good knowledge and understanding of children's development is essential to the provision of good, appropriate play opportunities.

Parten's five stages of play

In 1932 researcher Mildred Parten was studying the play of children aged between two and five. Despite her research being carried out so long ago, her findings are still valid today and are generally accepted. She focused on the children's social interactions during their play. She identified five stages of play that children pass through:

Solitary play

This occurs when a child plays alone, completely independent of others. Very young children only play alone.

Spectator play

The word 'spectator' means someone who is watching. Spectator play occurs when a child watches another child or children at play but does not join in. The spectator either will not be playing themselves, or will be doing a different activity to the one they are watching. This is sometimes called 'onlooker play'. Toddlers can often be observed watching others from a distance.

Parallel play

This stage occurs from around two years of age. The child plays alongside others and may share resources, but they remain engrossed in their own activity. The child has companionship, but even in the middle of a group, the child remains independent in their play. They do not look at other children when they are playing.

Felix wants to watch

Shobna is a new learner on placement. She's at the water tray with a group of children. She notices two-year-old Felix watching nearby. She invites Felix to come and play. He doesn't. Shobna doesn't want to just leave him there. She thinks he must want to join in but is too shy. She tries hard to persuade him again but he wanders off.

Question:
Shobna inviting Felix to play was fine. But what should she have done when he didn't want to join in? Give the reason for your answer.

Parallel play

Associative play

This occurs from between the ages of three and four years. Children share resources and talk to each other. But they each have their own **play agenda** (their own idea of what they want to do). The children don't coordinate their play objectives or interests. This means there will be trouble! Conflicts arise when children have ideas that others do not share. Children especially have trouble when trying to play imaginatively together.

key terms

Play agenda what a child wants to achieve in their play.

487

Cooperative play

This occurs when children fully interact, and can participate together in play with specific goals in mind. They can play their own imaginary games, organising themselves into roles, etc. for example: 'You be the doctor and I'll be the patient.' The older children in Parten's study were capable of cooperative play from the ages of four to five years.

Young people's leisure activities

As children mature into young people, their play usually evolves into leisure activities. They may:

- belong to formal, organised groups such as sports clubs, dance classes or youth theatre

- spend time relaxing with their friends, hanging out in public or at one another's houses.

You may not think of these leisure activities as 'play', but they fulfil many of the same purposes as play – socialising with peers for instance, developing skills and making discoveries. Almost all pursuits also have a playful element to them.

Have a go!

Bob Hughes is a leading modern theorist who studied older children and young people's play extensively and identified different types of play, known as the 'taxonomy of play types'. The taxonomy is widely used within playwork and youth work. You can find out more with a quick web search.

Children enjoy playing!

How play and leisure contribute to development

Children learn through play. Play is an effective vehicle for children's learning because:

- children enjoy playing, which means they will enjoy learning

- children are intrinsically motivated to play (they are internally driven), which means they are also driven to learn and develop

- children can make their own discoveries through play

- children can initiate their own activities and explore their own thoughts and ideas through play

- children can actively learn through play – the learning is a real, vivid experience

- play is necessary for children's well-being in a way that being 'taught' in other formal ways is not.

Did you know?

It's widely accepted that early years children should learn through a play-based curriculum. In settings, most practitioners no longer find it desirable for pre-school children to be given formal worksheets and the like.

Types of play

We can see how play is linked to development by considering how early years curriculum frameworks, which are designed to promote children's learning and development, are delivered through play activities. For our example, we'll use the EYFS that applies in England. We'll look at the types of play that contribute to children's learning and development in each of the six areas of learning. You'll see there is some overlap, which demonstrates how children's learning and development occurs holistically.

Personal, social and emotional development

Here are some examples of play that contribute to personal, social and emotional development:

- Playing board games (learning to take turns and to emotionally deal with winning and losing).

- Playing with others (learning social skills – sharing, communicating, getting along, understanding other people's feelings and needs, negotiating, resolving conflict).

- Imaginary play without props.

- Imaginary play with props such as puppets, dolls, home corner resources, dressing-up resources or items that 'become' something else, for example a box becomes a car or a desk (learning to cooperate and share an imaginary world with others, assigning roles and organising, acting out and developing ideas, feelings and recent learning).

Communication and language

Here are some examples of play that contribute to communication, language and literacy:

- Playing with others (developing language skills, increasing vocabulary, exploring meanings of words, learning to listen and respond appropriately to communications from others).

- Imaginary play (developing language linked with feelings and ideas and for expression).

- Making a den with sheets and tables (language for thinking and negotiating).

A box becomes a boat

Literacy

- Mark-making, for example with pencils, chalk, paint, fingers (learning to hold mark-making materials, learning the control needed for writing later, attempting writing).

- Enjoying books alone and with others (learning that print has meaning, how books and stories work, developing a love of books and stories, learning from story events, learning from non-fiction, learning to read).

Mathematics

Here are some examples of play that contribute to problem solving, reasoning and numeracy:

- Sharing out resources for play (learning skills for counting up, dividing, using vocabulary used for number operations).

- Printing with an ink pad and stampers, vegetable printing, making handprints (learning to recognise and create patterns and use associated language).

- Singing number songs and rhymes (learning to do number operations of adding and subtracting).

- Playing bingo (learning to recognise numbers).

> **Did you know?**
>
> Babies love to be read to. They enjoy the tone and pitch of your voice, even though they do not yet understand the words.

- Playing hide and seek (learning to count to higher numbers while players hide, learning to problem solve mathematically when considering what hiding places they and other players may fit into).

- Cooking, making play dough (learning to use numbers when weighing out ingredients).

Understanding of the world

Here are some examples of play that contribute to knowledge and understanding of the world:

- Exploring living things, for example picking daisies, having a look at a snail found in the garden, playing with a pet, digging in earth (developing awareness of the wider world, learning how to care for living things).

- Playing on computers, with programmable toys or using MP3/DVD players (developing knowledge, understanding and ability to use ICT (information and communication technology).

- Playing with magnifying glasses in the garden (learning from observing things closely).

- Playing in new places, for example trip to the park or beach, playing with a range of natural objects such as pebbles, logs and fir cones (finding out about features of the natural world they live in).

- Building with bricks, blocks and other materials and using tools (learning techniques to join, assemble and shape materials).

Physical development

Here are some examples of play that contribute to physical development:

- Playing on playground equipment – climbing, swinging, sliding, balancing, riding trikes, bikes and ride-on toys; pushing objects, for example a baby walker or trolley; pulling objects, for example wagons, toys on strings (developing large motor skills/locomotive skills, coordination and balance).

- Making things using tools, for example scissors, rolling pins, cutters; mark-making, for example with pencils, chalk, paint; playing with malleable materials, for example play dough, corn flour paste, plasticine (developing fine motor skills).

Did you know?

Children can learn about ICT when they're out and about by noticing traffic lights, pedestrian crossings, cameras, etc.

- Making collages with natural objects, for example seeds, pasta, or craft resources such a sequins, fabric scraps (developing fine motor skills and hand–eye coordination).

Expressive arts and design

Here are some examples of play that contribute to creative development:

- Playing with natural and man-made materials (learning to respond to what they see, touch, feel, hear, taste and smell, developing creativity, becoming inspired, playing or moving in new/ interesting ways).

- Mark-making, for example with pencils, chalk, paint, fingers (developing creativity, learning about colour and texture).

- Making recycled models (developing creative thinking and problem-solving skills, learning about shape and space in three dimensions).

- Singing, dancing, playing instruments (developing imagination, creative expression, learning to match movement to music, learning to recognise and repeating sound patterns).

- Imaginary play, small world play (developing imagination and ability to tell and interpret stories).

Link Up!

Unit OP 2.17 Contribute to the support of children's creative development.

Have a go!

Because there are so many wonderful opportunities for play, it's only possible to list a few types of play for each area of learning above. Can you think of at least three more play activities that promote each one?

Ask Miranda!

Q Can all of the learning and development listed above really happen just as a result of play?

A **Absolutely. But play is facilitated by practitioners who ensure that a range of opportunities and materials are available to support a range of play types, and through this they support diverse learning. Skilled practitioners will also enhance play by choosing the right moments to demonstrate a skill, offer a suggestion, provide encouragement or ask a question. But they will also recognise when children are deeply engrossed in their freely chosen, self-directed play and should not be needlessly interrupted. Judging this successfully comes with experience. You'll learn more about this as you work through this unit.**

Instruments promote creative expression

Leisure activities for older children and young people

Many popular leisure activities for older children and young people still fall into the traditional play types and promote learning and development in the same way as the examples we have looked at for younger children in the EYFS. Consider these examples:

- Drama is linked to imaginary play.

- Sport is linked to physical play.

- Playing an instrument is linked to creative play.

- Reading is linked to literacy, which also underpins learning in many other areas.

- Camping is linked to learning about the world (many older children go to Scouts/Guides and the like).

- Cooking is linked to science and maths.

- Hanging out with friends is linked to social development.

When you were an older child or young person, what leisure activities were you into? How did they promote your learning and development? Make some notes in your reflective diary.

Younger children

The Practical example below shows an effective way of promoting free play with interesting objects with younger children.

Practical example

Tansy's treasure basket

Tansy is a student on placement in a nursery toddler room. She has recently learnt about heuristic play – a term first used in the 1980s by child psychologist Elinor Goldschmeid to describe what happens when babies and children explore the properties of real objects (as opposed to toys). For babies and toddlers, this play centres on a 'treasure basket' filled with a diverse collection of objects, which babies can explore from the time they are able to sit up unaided. Tansy makes her own treasure basket. She gathers both natural and man-made objects from the real world, including a whisk, a large pebble, a sponge, a hairbrush, a wooden spoon, a metal sieve, a cardboard tube, a square of fun fur and a woollen glove. She ensures the items are clean. She leaves the basket on the playroom floor, then moves away. She watches from a distance as children discover the basket and explore the items.

Treasure baskets promote free play for younger children

UN Convention on the Rights of the Child

The UK government made this convention law in 1991. It contains Articles that refer to the rights and needs of children. Some of these are relevant to play and leisure:

■ **Children have the right to rest, play and leisure, and opportunities to join in with activities including those that are cultural and artistic:**
For many countries, this gave children a right to play and leisure for the first time. In our settings, we should value play and leisure as both a right and a need. We should offer a range of different cultural activities for all children, whatever their own culture. See Unit OP 2.17 for more information about creative, artistic activities.

■ **Disabled children have the right to live as independently as possible, and to take a full and active part in everyday life:**
We must make sure that disabled children and young people have full access to all play and leisure activities.

■ **Children have the right to have their views heard:**

Unit OP 2.17 Contribute to the support of children's creative development.

Practitioners should consult with children, particularly about decisions affecting them, and take notice of what they say. They should seek out and respect the views and preferences of children. You'll learn more about this in Learning outcome 2.

- ■ **Children need a strong self-image and self-esteem:**
  Children should feel valued and accepted for who they are within the setting. This is achieved in part through showing an interest in children, giving them respect and supporting them with praise and encouragement. You'll learn more about this in Learning outcome 2.

Freely chosen, self-directed play and leisure

Freely chosen, self-directed play is a natural and spontaneous activity. It's essential for children's growth and development – it is not just enjoyable but vital to children and young people's well-being. Good play opportunities and environments can make a real difference to a child's quality of life. That is why children have been given the legal right to play.

Did you know?

It is accepted that it would not be practical for some settings to offer a free choice of whether to play indoors or outdoors because of the physical restrictions of the premises or lack of access to an outdoor play space. In these settings, an 'everyone out or everyone in' approach may be necessary.

Common misunderstandings

There is sometimes confusion about free play. For example, some people think free play is occurring if they set up three or four activities and let children decide which to play – but this is a very limiting approach. Or, they may allow children to choose 'any board game' or 'any of the hoops, balls and bats', or 'any of the resources on the bottom shelf'. Again, this is limiting. Sometimes where children can play is restricted. For example, children may only be able to look at books in the book corner, or have the bricks out in the construction area, or wear the dressing-up clothes inside. All of these things are about the adult directing play rather than supporting it. This is not giving children access to freely chosen, self-directed play.

Good practice

Many settings start the day with a free-play session. This allows children to come in and settle down to the important business of play right away. It also means that children don't keep arriving part-way through an activity such as story time. Most of these settings will set up the room with a number of play areas and activities, as you've learnt in other units. This is absolutely fine, and children's free play need not be limited by this approach as long as they have access to any other resources they want and can move around the setting freely, playing as they choose (provided their behaviour remains safe and acceptable).

Twelve features of play

Tina Bruce (1996) identified the 12 features of play, stating that if more than half of them can be observed in action, then high-quality play is present.

1   In their play, children use first-hand experiences from their lives (for example experience of people, places events and objects).
2   Children make up their own rules as they play, and so keep control of their play.
3   Children make play props.
4   Children choose to play. They cannot be made to play.
5   Children rehearse the future in their role play (for example they pretend to be adults – cooking, driving, being a parent, etc.)
6   Children pretend when playing.
7   Children play alone sometimes.
8   Children and/or adults play together, in parallel, associatively, or cooperatively in pairs or groups.
9   Each player has a play agenda, although they may not be aware of this.

10 Children playing will be deeply involved, and difficult to distract from their deep learning. Children at play wallow in their learning, feelings and ideas.

11 Children try out their most recent learning, skills and competencies when they play.

12 Children at play coordinate their ideas and feelings and make sense of relationships.

Children playing will be deeply involved

LEARNING OUTCOME 2

ᶠᴼᶜᵁˢ ᴼᴺ

... being able to support children and young people's play and leisure

In this section you'll learn about your role in supporting play and leisure activities, and about giving attention sensitively to play and leisure activities. You'll also learn about undertaking routine safety checks and supervising play and leisure to ensure children and young people's safety. This links with **Assessment Criteria 2.1, 2.2, 2.3, 2.4, 2.5.**

Your role in supporting play and leisure activities

It's the role of the practitioner to:

■ support children and young people's play

■ enrich children and young people's play

■ effectively manage risk involved in play.

Supporting not directing

Because of the benefits of freely chosen, self-directed play, it's good practice for practitioners to intervene or interfere with children and young people's free play as little as possible, as long as they remain safe and engaged and their behaviour is acceptable. The emphasis is more on supporting children and less on directing them. But practitioners always remain on hand to join in with play and to interact with children if the children want them to.

Did you know?

This approach is sometimes called 'low intervention, high response'.

Enriching

It's up to practitioners to enrich play and leisure activities by providing children and young people with suitable, stimulating environments that give rich opportunities for play of different types (see Learning outcome 1). This means providing appropriate play spaces and a wide variety of resources.

Good practice

Practitioners must also foster positive attitudes to play and leisure within the setting. Attitudes are a key element of the environments that children experience, and they form the culture and atmosphere of a setting. Practitioners can also enrich play and activities by sensitively giving attention to them, as described on page 500.

Managing risk

Practitioners must manage risk by balancing the benefits of play and leisure activities with levels of risk during risk assessments. You'll learn about this in Learning outcome 3.

Sensitively giving attention to activities

You must balance the benefits of activities with levels of risk

Practitioners should of course be attentive to children and young people. An important part of this is giving attention to their play and leisure activities and often joining in. It may also be appropriate to make a suggestion, provide resources or offer support or encouragement – these are all ways in which we can enrich play.

But we need to be aware that when free play is interrupted, important benefits of play can be affected. Interruptions can disturb or destroy the play 'world' that children have created and are playing within. A child may not be able to recapture this. Also, ideas or trains of thought can be lost in an instant when interruptions occur. So before you intervene look for signs that a child does want you to join in with them. These may be communicated through eye contact, facial expressions and touch as well as language. Also see the play cues below.

Did you know?

Practitioners can be valuable role models who introduce children to new and different play and leisure activity ideas.

Good practice

Practitioners should not show children or young people what they perceive to be 'better' or 'proper' ways of doing things when they're playing unless they ask to be shown or behaviours are potentially dangerous (the dangerous misuse of a tool for instance). Play isn't about the right or wrong way of doing things. It's about exploration, discovery and individual creativity.

Have a go!

Think of a time when you've been interrupted and you've lost track of what you were doing or thinking about. How did you feel? Was it frustrating, or annoying perhaps?

Play cues

Play cues are wonderful signals that a child or young person gives to show that they want to play. They're hoping their cue will get a favourable response. For instance, if a child kicks a ball towards you they're indicating that they want to play – they're hoping you'll give them a 'play return'. This is a signal that you're willing to play. In our example, you would kick the ball back as a 'play return'. There may be a natural end to the play you engage in – perhaps a board game has finished or a model has been made. Whenever possible you should follow children's lead in terms of the end of play. This is demonstrated in the Practical example on page 501.

Amy's play cue

Seven-year-old Amy has been playing alone with a balloon. She has been hitting it around the room with her hand. As playworker Leanna passes by, Amy hits the balloon towards her. Leanna hits it back then stands still to see how Amy responds. Amy hits the balloon back to Leanna again. Leanna recognises the play cue and continues to play the game with Amy. After a few turns Amy begins to hit the balloon in the air. She claps her hands before she catches it. The play engagement is over, and Leanna moves away as Amy carries on alone with her new game.

Unit OP 2.17 Contribute to the support of children's creative development.

Routine safety checks

As you learnt in Unit MU 2.4, Learning outcome 2:

■ risk assessments will have been carried out on the premises of a setting

■ in addition, routine safety checks will be carried out on a daily basis.

You may like to reread the information now as part of your study of this section.

Unit MU 2.4 Contribute to children and young people's health and safety.

Supervising play and leisure

Practitioners must supervise children and young people safely at all times and maintain the minimum staff-to-child ratios, although many settings aim to exceed these ratios in the interests of quality. In day-care settings in England (without a qualified teacher) the minimum ratios are as follows:

■ Children under two years: one adult to three children (1 : 3).

■ Children aged two years: one adult to four children (1 : 4).

■ Children aged three to seven years: one adult to eight children (1 : 8).

For some activities, adults can keep a general eye on things

Levels of supervision

For safety, the deployment of staff (where and how staff work) should be carefully considered throughout the session. Generally, the younger the children or the more challenging an activity, the closer the supervision will need to be. For some activities, children and young people can safely play independently as long as there are adults in the room keeping a general eye on things. Children and young people can approach them if they need assistance. Other activities would be unsafe without one-to-one support from an adult – when a child is learning to use woodworking tools such as a hacksaw, for instance.

Changing levels of risk

Although risk assessments will be carried out prior to activities (see Unit MU 2.4, Learning outcome 2), the level of risk can change. This is due to the way children and young people choose to play and use the resources. Practitioners must continually monitor the changing levels of risk. There's no need to intervene in play unless the level of risk becomes unacceptable. But in this case it's the duty of practitioners to intervene and bring the level of risk back to an acceptable level.

Interacting with children and young people

It is important that you interact with children and young people in a way that shows:

- you're interested in what they say, experience and feel

- you have respect for their privacy and freedom to make choices for themselves

- encouragement and praise for play and leisure activities.

We'll look at these in turn.

Showing that you're interested

In other units you've learnt that whenever you interact with children and young people you should listen actively to what they say (see page 18). This shows that you are interested in what they say, experience and feel, and that you value their communications. This impacts on their self-esteem and self-confidence.

Unit MU 2.4 Contribute to children and young people's health and safety.

Did you know?

An effective technique to keep intervention to a minimum is to encourage children and young people to develop an awareness of hazards and how to manage risk themselves. This is also an important life skill. You'll learn more about this in Learning outcome 3.

When you interact during play, you also have opportunities to connect on a deeper level by sharing in what children are experiencing and feeling. For example, if a child is having fun, you can show that you're having fun alongside them – you can smile back at them, or join in with the laughter. Or, for example, you may share an 'Oh no!' moment with a young person when the tent you've been trying to pitch falls down, followed by a 'Eureka!' moment when someone has a brilliant idea to fix it.

Show that you're having fun with children

Showing that you have respect

■ As we've discussed, you shouldn't interfere with free play or interrupt needlessly. This is one of the best ways to actively demonstrate that you have respect for children and young people's privacy. All types of play can be very personal and meaningful to children, and they may not wish to share that with you.
This is entirely their right. It's perhaps most common to come across this when children are playing imaginatively in a world they have created for themselves.

Did you know?

You can also show that you respect children and young people's freedom to make choices for themselves through consultation. (You were introduced to consultation in Unit TDA 2.7).

Link Up!

Unit TDA 2.7 Maintain and support relationships with children and young people.

Why not try one of the following evaluation techniques with a group of older children or young people:

- Draw out a large bullseye target and ask each person to place a cross on it to indicate how they felt about a particular experience. The nearer to the bullseye the cross is, the better they enjoyed the experience. See the diagram below.

- Draw up a list of play experiences. Children are given a gold, silver and bronze sticker. They place the stickers next to the experiences on the list, awarding them first, second or third in terms of their favourites.

- Draw a list of numbers, perhaps one to five. Next to the relevant numbers the children write or draw on their top five play experiences of the session.

- Four corners of the play space are identified as 'really liked it', 'liked it', 'didn't like it' and 'really didn't like it'. Practitioners call out play experiences and children run to the relevant corner depending on how they felt about the experience.

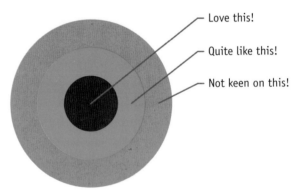

Love this!

Quite like this!

Not keen on this!

Evaluation target

Encouragement and praise

In Unit TDA 2.9, Learning outcome 2, you learnt about the value of encouragement and praise and how you can give them to children and young people. You may like to reread this as part of your study of this section.

Link Up!

Unit TDA 2.9 Support children and young people's positive behaviour.

You can make good use of praise and encouragement to motivate children and young people to persevere with tasks that they find challenging during play and leisure activities. It's also important to show that you value having a try by praising effort as well as achievement.

Mikey offers encouragement

Mikey works at a holiday club for teenagers. As part of a funded music scheme, the setting has been given some instruments to borrow over the summer holidays. Three times a week, some volunteer music tutors drop in to give on-the-spot music lessons to anyone who's interested. Thirteen-year-old Kaz had never picked up a guitar before, but now she loves it!

In-between the music lessons Kaz has been practising hard. But she's struggling to get a chord right, and she's obviously frustrated. As Mikey approaches she says, 'Why can't I do it? I just can't get it! I'll never learn to play at this rate!' Mikey praises Kaz for persevering. He reminds her that she'll need a lot of practice over a period of time, but that it will be worth it in the end. Kaz smiles but looks downhearted. He suggests she takes a break and comes back to it later. He adds that she can always ask a tutor to help her with the chord next time.

Encouragement is often needed when a task is challenging

LEARNING OUTCOME 3

FOCUS ON

... being able to support children and young people in balancing risk and challenge

In this section you'll learn about the value of risk and challenge in play and leisure activities, and what is meant by unacceptable risk. You'll also learn about why it's important for children and young people to manage risk, and the ways they can be encouraged to do so. This links with **Assessment Criteria 3.1, 3.2, 3.3, 3.4**.

Unit MU 2.4 Contribute to children and young people's health and safety.

The value of risk and challenge

You learnt about the risk and challenge in children's play and activities in Unit MU 2.4, Learning outcome 2. You are advised to reread this now as part of your study of this section.

Unacceptable risk and challenge

In Unit MU 2.4, Learning outcome 2, you were also introduced to the process of conducting risks assessments to decide whether risks and challenges are acceptable or unacceptable. We'll look at this in more detail here.

Rights and choices versus health and safety

There's a tricky dilemma to balance the rights and choices that belong to children and young people in terms of the freedom to play, and the health and safety requirements of settings and services. However, children and young people should be allowed to experience and explore *appropriate* risk during their play. There are four types of hazard/risk that should be considered in terms of play. These are:

- physical
- environmental
- emotional
- behavioural.

You learnt about physical hazards (tangible items, such as a stack of chairs) and environmental hazards/risks (such as water or stairs) in Unit MU 2.4.

Emotional risk

Emotional risk-taking is a life skill. Children and young people (and adults) take emotional risks whenever they pluck up the courage to do something that stretches them emotionally or that risks personal failure or rejection. Examples of emotional risk-taking include:

- Speaking in front of a group of peers or adults.
- Auditioning/performing in public (singing, acting, dancing, playing musical instruments).
- Trying to make a new friend.

Emotional risk-taking is a life skill

Saying no to friends or refusing to give in to peer pressure.

Showing others your own creative work (art or creative writing for instance).

Entering a competition.

Suggesting your own ideas to peers/adults.

Telling a joke.

Applying for a college course or a job.

Doing something independently for the first time (for example using public transport, living alone).

Taking a physical risk in front of others (for example going on a skateboard ramp for the first time).

Comfort zones

The things that children are comfortable with are sometimes referred to as being within their 'comfort zone'. But if children and young people are to continually move on and progress in their development, they need to step out of their comfort zone every so often, and take an emotional risk. Those with good levels of self-esteem and confidence are generally more willing to take emotional risks. You can support this by providing activities that foster confidence and self-esteem, such as:

- team activities
- trust games
- games that give everyone the opportunity to be the 'leader'
- activities that involve a physical challenge
- consultation (see the ideas and suggestions section on pages 426–7)
- displays of art/craft work.

Behavioural hazards

Behavioural hazards occur when children and young people behave in a way that could cause harm to themselves or others. For example, practitioners may provide clay and tools for modelling. Although the tools may be pointed, this would generally be considered a relatively low-risk activity. However, if a young person began throwing these tools at 'targets' in play, or even deliberately using them as weapons during a disagreement, the risk would be raised significantly to an

Did you know?

Activities that feel like a risk to one person may come easily to another because children and young people are individuals who are comfortable doing different things.

Good practice

Ensure you offer children plenty of praise in general terms, and specifically for 'having a go' or 'trying hard'. This helps to communicate that stepping out of your comfort zone is worthwhile, whatever the result of taking the risk. You'll learn more about this in Learning outcome 4.

Always judge if and when to intervene

unacceptable level. Practitioners would need to intervene quickly (that is, step in and take action) to curb the behaviour and therefore the risk. A child or young person's behaviour during play or leisure activities can also harm others emotionally.

Examples of unacceptable challenge and risk

Examples of unacceptable challenge and risk in children and young people's play and leisure activities include:

- A young person who wants to do 'free-running' around the premises of a group setting (in free-running street stunts are used to navigate obstacles and move from place to place at speed).

- A group of children want to swim in the sea on their holiday club's daytrip to the beach.

- An older child who is enjoying raising money for her school wants to sell raffle tickets door to door to people she doesn't know.

- A six-year-old wants to play in his 12-year-old brother's football league team.

The importance of children and young people managing risk for themselves

Children and young people will not always be under the close supervision of adults, and as they grow older they will become entirely independent. So it's essential that they learn to recognise and manage risk for themselves. This enables them to make good decisions and keep themselves safe, without being overly cautious or worried.

Encouraging the management of risk

It is good practice to involve children and young people in thinking about safety, and encourage them to tell an adult if they see something unsafe. One of the most effective and simple ways to teach children about safety is to explain to them why you feel that an activity, a situation or someone's behaviour is potentially dangerous. (See the Practical example on page 509.)

Did you know?

Experience of recognising and managing risks for themselves should increase as children and young people mature.

Try designing your own moral dilemma game to help young people to consider how to handle potentially dangerous situations. You'll need to:

■ compile a list of appropriate dilemmas. For example, what should a young person do if their lift home from a disco or club doesn't turn up? Or if someone offers them alcohol or drugs? If you're currently working with young people, why not consult them and include their dilemma ideas too

■ write or print the dilemmas on to individual pieces of card

■ try the game out with a small group of young people. (Players will take it in turn to choose a card at random. They must then read it out and tell the group what they would do in the situation they have selected.)

Young people can also help adults to check appropriate areas of the premises for safety and assist in carrying out risk assessment informally. Moral dilemma games and role plays can also be an effective way to encourage young people to think about how they should handle potentially dangerous situations. These are best done in small groups of three or four.

Practical example

Harry's warning

Stuart and his colleague Karin have taken a group of children out to play ball games on the local playing field. This is something they do quite often as the field has a basketball hoop mounted on a freestanding pole. Seven-year-old Harry is attempting to jump up and swing from the hoop. The whole pole is leaning and could easily tip over. Karin has told Harry not to do this before. She's about to remind him again, but Stuart gets in first.

Stuart says, 'Please don't do that, Harry. It's dangerous. Do you know why?' Karin is surprised to learn that Harry has no idea that he's in danger of knocking the heavy pole over and it could land on him or someone else. With hindsight, Karin realises that in the past she has not explained the reason why Harry must not try to swing from the basketball hoop. So Harry has not learnt to keep himself safe in this type of situation.

... being able to reflect on and improve own practice

In this section you'll learn about reflecting on your own practice in supporting play and leisure. You'll also learn about identifying your own strengths and where practice could be improved, and about describing how reflection has improved your practice.
This links with **Assessment Criteria 4.1, 4.2, 4.3.**

Reflecting on all aspects of your practice

Link Up!

Unit SHC 22 Introduction to personal development in children and young people's settings.

You learnt about reflection techniques in Unit SHC 22, Learning outcomes 2 and 4. You can choose a range of techniques to reflect on all aspects of your role in supporting play and leisure activities.

Key aspects to cover when reflecting include evaluating:

- how effectively you support play/leisure activities with children and young people of different ages
- how well you support play of different types
- how well you support play in various locations (for example indoors/outdoors or in different types of setting)
- how effective the play setting is
- how well you judge when to intervene in play.

Identifying strengths and areas for improvement

Once you have reviewed all of your information, it's time to draw some conclusions about your strengths and areas for improvement.
You learnt how to act on these to improve your practice in Unit SHC 22. It will help to ask yourself the following questions:

You can consult with colleagues

- Did children/young people enjoy the instances of play or the activity?

- Were they engaged and interested?

- Could everyone participate equally in activities?

- Did I give individual support effectively when it was needed?

- Did I interrupt play needlessly?

- Did I enrich play *when appropriate* by offering suggestions and encouragement or by demonstrating skills?

- Did I notice and respond to play cues?

- Was the play child/young person led, or did I direct it?

- Would I do the activity again?

- What would I do differently next time?

How your practice has been improved following reflection

For this assessment criteria, you're required to demonstrate that your practice has been improved following reflection. So it's a good idea to get into the habit of tracking your progress in your reflective diary. This will also inform your future personal development.

How are things going?

▶ Progress Check

1. Why is play and leisure important for children and young people? (1.1)

2. What rights does the UN Convention on the Rights of the Child give children in regard to play and leisure? (1.3)

3. Describe what is meant by 'freely chosen, self-directed play'. (1.4)

4. Describe the key aspects of your role in supporting play and leisure activities. (2.1)

5. Give an example of how you may impact negatively on free play if you do not intervene sensitively. (2.2)

6. Explain why you may need to alter your level of supervision during a play activity. (2.4)

7. Explain a way in which you can demonstrate respect for children's:

   a privacy in play

   b freedom to make choices for themselves. (2.5)

8. What is the value of risk and challenge in children and young people's play and leisure? (3.1)

9. Give an example of how you can encourage children to manage risk for themselves. (3.4)

10. Describe a technique that you might use to reflect on how you support play and leisure activities. (4.1)

Are you ready for assessment?

Learning Outcomes 2, 3 and 4 must be assessed in a real work environment.

CACHE

Set tasks:

■ You are asked to produce a resource file of evidence to show that you can describe the characteristics of different types of play and leisure, the importance of play and leisure, and how they contribute to children and young people's development. You should also outline the requirements of the UN Convention on the rights of the Child in relation to relaxation and play. You can prepare by rereading pages 484–498 and making relevant notes.

City & Guilds and Edexcel

You can prepare for assessment by reflectng on your own role in supporting children and young people's play and leisure activities and making notes in your reflective diary.

UNIT 2.15
Contribute to the support of children's communication, language and literacy

The learning outcomes you will meet in this unit are:

1 Understand the importance of communication, language and literacy

2 Be able to contribute to children's learning in communication, language and literacy

3 Be able to evaluate own contribution to children's learning in communication, language and literacy

INTRODUCTION

Children's communication, language and literacy is a large area of development that encompasses learning to interact with others and to talk, read and write. These are skills that underpin much of children's learning in other areas as you'll learn throughout the unit.

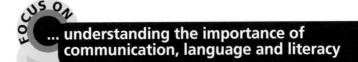

FOCUS ON

... understanding the importance of communication, language and literacy

In this section you'll learn why communication, language and literacy are important to children's learning. You'll also learn how communication, language and literacy links to other areas of learning and development within the framework related to your own work setting. This links with **Assessment Criteria 1.1, 1.2**.

Why communication, language and literacy are important to learning

Communication, language and literacy is a huge area of development. Let's look at each component in turn.

Communication

This is an umbrella term that covers all forms of communication, including:

■ Speech.

■ Listening.

■ Gesture.

■ Sign language.

■ Facial expression.

■ Reading.

■ Writing.

Children's skills in these areas will be constantly developing in many different ways in response to the ongoing communication experiences that they have every day.

Why communication is important to learning and development

Communication is vital to learning and development because it's at the heart of all children's interactions with others. It underpins the relationships that they make and how well these work. This impacts on children's social and emotional development. Young children are learning the communication skills that they will depend on throughout their lives to connect with others and to understand the feelings and thoughts of those around them. Communication skills enable children to be social beings rather than isolated individuals. Even the simple acts of making eye contact, smiling or saying hello make a huge a difference in terms of children's experience of the world. Communication is also central to children's learning across all areas of development because we build on children's ability to relate to us in order to teach and guide them and to support their learning. For instance, a simple facial expression can tell children so much about the way adults feel about their current behaviour.

Eye contact, smiling or saying hello makes a huge difference to children's experience of the world

Language

Language is essentially the things that children say and how they say them. This covers everything from the gurgles and babbles that babies make as they are learning to speak, to the language that children use to describe their feelings, thoughts and ideas. Listening is an important part of language development because children learn to understand and use language by listening to those around them using language.

Why language is important to learning and development

Acquiring language is hugely important in terms of learning and development. It enables children to understand what others mean. Just think how much children learn from what we say to them. The amount of information we give to children verbally is vast. We also use language to support learning in many other ways – to ask questions that encourage children to think for instance. Language also enables children to make themselves understood. This fulfils many needs for children. A good example of this is the fact that before they are able to express themselves in language, toddlers can be expected to display behaviour linked to frustration. This includes tantrums

> **Did you know?**
>
> It's important to remember that some children will learn sign language instead of or alongside speech.

Before they can express themselves in language, toddlers often display frustration

and behaviour such as biting. But once they are able to talk and use language to express what they want, feel and need, these behaviours generally begin to fade away.

Did you know?

Children learn a lot of language in a short space of time. They generally say their first word at around 12 months of age. By the age of two to three years, children are speaking in simple sentences and using language to find out things. Who, what and why questions are asked frequently. By the age of four most children are speaking well, and by five, most children are speaking fluently.

Other important factors

Language is also important for:

- playing

- thinking

- socialising.

Playing

Children use language to communicate with others in their play. Imaginary play is a wonderful example of this because children use language to:

Did you know?

Language enables children to say these very important words to adults and another child: 'Do you want to play with me?'

- assign roles (for example, 'You be the baby and I'll be the mummy.')

- communicate their thoughts and ideas ('The mummy's going to work; she has to take the baby to nursery.')

- make their games work ('Come on baby, time to have your dinner! Sit down here with me.')

Language opens up a world of play opportunities.

Thinking

We use language to think, both out loud and in our heads. For example, imagine you see a letter on the table at home and it occurs to you that you need to remember to post it tomorrow. How does that thought actually occur? It would be unusual if you were to look at the letter and then visualise yourself walking to the postbox and posting it. Normally, someone would think to themselves – in words, inside their head – something along the lines of, 'I must post that tomorrow.' This is language for thinking in action. Because of the way our brains do this, we can use language to prompt children to think and therefore learn. For instance, we may say to a child, 'I wonder what will happen if ...' See Unit OP 2.17, Learning outcome 2 to learn more.

Unit OP 2.17 Contribute to the support of children's creative development.

You be the child and I'll be the mummy

Socialising

Language is linked to social skills. Language is important to socialising because it enables children to express themselves and to understand what other people say. Communicating through language also supports children to display more cooperative behaviours and less frustrated behaviours, as we've discussed.

Literacy

Literacy is being able to read and write. It takes children several years to be able to read and write, and in the early years children practise and use the skills that will eventually enable them to master reading and writing fluently. For example, children learn to recognise the sounds that letters make, and they learn how to hold and control mark-marking materials such as crayons.

Reading and writing

Many children will have mastered the basics of reading and writing by age seven, and they will be fluent by 11. But there are wide variations. Some children experience difficulty learning to read and write and may struggle in this area throughout their education and beyond. Children with strong language skills tend to be the most confident readers and writers, and tend to show the most motivation to begin writing and reading.

Good practice

In the early years, practitioners can support children's future literacy by providing many varied language opportunities, fostering a love of books and stories (which motivates reading) and ensuring there's access to a range of mark-making activities and resources (which supports the skills needed for writing). You'll learn how to do this through the provision of equipment and activities in Learning outcome 2.

Why literacy is important to learning and development

Literacy is one of the cornerstones of education. Whatever the subject, older children and young people will be required to read and write. Those who do that well are likely to do better not only in English, but whenever they're required to express their learning in assignments, essays, reports and exams. Because reading and writing is something that most adults do naturally throughout their everyday lives, it's easy to take for granted just how important it is. But without literacy skills, we wouldn't be able to email or text, get information online or from books, read a timetable, write a message, read our post, follow an instruction manual or even understand what items are on sale when we go to the supermarket.

Did you know?

Children who grow up without good literacy skills are at a big disadvantage in the modern world.

Ask Miranda!

Q I understand why communication and language skills go together, but why are they linked to literacy in one area of development?

A Because they are inseparably linked. Communication and language are linked to literacy because children cannot progress with reading and writing unless they are progressing in terms of their understanding and use of communication and language. Children won't make sense of what they read unless the words have meaning for them. For example, learning to read the words 'shouted angrily' in a story is of little use unless a child understands what the word 'anger' means, and knows what it's like to communicate anger to another person.

When communicating verbally, children are limited by the amount of language they have acquired to express themselves. Writing is another form of communication. Children will only be able to write down the language they have acquired.

How communication, language and literacy links with other areas of learning and development

You learnt about the learning frameworks that apply to your home country in Unit MU 2.8. Each framework has its own way of covering the learning that children should do in the area of communication, language and literacy:

▪ In England, there are two relevant areas of learning within the Early Years Foundation Stage. These are called Communication and language and Literacy.

▪ In Wales, this is the area of the Foundation Phase called Language, literacy and communication skills.

▪ In Scotland, the practitioners will promote Languages throughout the Curriculum for Excellence.

▪ In Northern Ireland (where there's no formal early education framework) children will undertake Language and literacy when they begin following a framework at school.

For our example of how communication, language and literacy links with other areas of learning and development, we'll take a closer look at the Early Years Foundation Stage (EYFS).

Early learning goals for Communication and language

By the end of the EYFS (the end of the reception year), most children are expected to have reached the following early learning goals:

- Listening and attention: Children Listen attentively in a range of situations. They listen to stories, accurately anticipating key events and responding to what they hear with relevant comments, questions or actions. They give their attention to what others say and respond appropriately, while engaged in another activity.

- Understanding: Children follow instructions involving several ideas or actions. They answer "how" and "why" questions about their experiences and in response to stories or events.

- Speaking: Children express themselves effectively, showing awareness to listeners' needs. They use past, present and future forms accurately when talking about events that have happened or about to happen in the future They develop their own narratives and explanations by connecting ideas and events.

The Early Years Foundation Stage goes on to tell us that Communication and language development involves giving children opportunities to:

- Experience a rich language environment

- Develop their confidence and skills in expressing themselves

- Speak and listen in a range of situations

Early learning goals for Literacy

By the end of the EYFS (the end of the reception year), most children are expected to have reached the following early learning goals:

■ Reading: Children read and understand simple sentences. They use phonic knowledge to decode regular words and read them aloud accurately. They also read some common irregular words. They demonstrate understanding when talking with others about what they have read.

■ Writing: Children use their phonic knowledge to write words in ways which match their spoken sounds. They also write some irregular common words. They write simple sentences which can be read by themselves and others. Some words are spelled correctly and others are phonetically plausible.

By the end of the EYFS, most children will write simple regular words

The other areas of learning

Now you're aware of the content of Communication and language and Literacy as EYFS areas, we'll look at how they link to the remaining five EYFS areas. Examples are given in Table OP2.15.1 below and on page 522. There are some overlaps as, in practice, children's learning is holistic rather than compartmentalised, as you've learnt in other units.

Table OP2.15.1: How communication, language and literacy links with other areas of learning

EXAMPLES HOW COMMUNICATION, LANGUAGE AND LITERACY LINKS WITH:
Personal, social and emotional development
Using communication and language skills to form and maintain relationships with other children and with adults. Expressing own ideas, feelings and thoughts, and learning to listen to and understand the ideas, feelings and thoughts of others. Learning to behave in more socially acceptable ways as language is acquired, for example getting less frustrated, using manners, etc. Gaining confidence and self-esteem through positive relationships with others.
Mathematics
Learning, understanding and using the language for numbers and number operations, for example how many, take one away, add two more. Learning, understanding and using the skills and language for mathematical thinking and problem solving. This includes the language to question and make choices, identify problems, generate a number of imaginative solutions, try out and apply ideas, for example how can we measure, how can we weigh, shortest, shorter, heaviest, heavier, etc.

Understanding of the world

Learning, understanding and using the skills and language for thinking and problem solving. This includes the language to question and make choices, identify problems, generate a number of imaginative solutions, try out and apply ideas, for example why do things happen and how do they work? Learning the skills and language connected with IT, and learning to follow the verbal instructions and symbols necessary to use computers and other IT equipment.

Physical development

The development of fine motor skills aid the control needed later for writing. Children learn and use the rich language associated with movement, for example slithering, hopping, rolling, skipping, trotting, etc., and the language associated with dance. Children communicate with language to discuss being healthy and the way their body feels – tired, hungry, etc.

Expressive arts and design

Children use language to express themselves during imaginary play, and they will communicate and express their thoughts, ideas and feelings in a number of creative ways. This includes art, crafts, dance and music. Mark-making activities give children opportunities to control implements such as paintbrushes, crayons and pencils. This control is needed for writing later on. Mark-making enables children to understand that marks carry meaning, and children will begin 'emergent writing' (see Learning outcome 2). Singing and rhyming encourages language and communication skills.

Have a go!

If your home country is Wales, Scotland or Ireland, have a go at producing a table similar to the one on page 521 and above which shows how children's learning and development in communication, language and literacy links to other areas of the framework. If your home country is England, add to the table by suggesting two more links to Communication, language and literacy for each of the other five areas of learning shown.

LEARNING OUTCOME 2

FOCUS ON

... being able to contribute to children's learning in communication, language and literacy

In this section you'll learn about the equipment and activities used to support communication, language and literacy, and about engaging attention and interest through a variety of methods. You'll also learn about using clear language, encouragement and praise to support communication, language and literacy. This links with **Assessment Criteria 2.1, 2.2, 2.3, 2.4**.

Equipment and activities that support communication, language and literacy

Communication, language and literacy is a big area of learning and there are many exciting, new and well-loved ways to promote it through the equipment and activities you provide. We'll continue to use the EYFS area of Communication, language and literacy as an example of how these can be used as part of a learning framework. In the EYFS, Communication, language and literacy is made up of six aspects. These are:

- language for communication
- language for thinking
- linking sounds with letters
- reading
- writing
- handwriting.

We'll look at some equipment and activities for supporting these aspects. Writing and handwriting are very closely linked, so we'll look at those together.

Unit OP 2.17 Contribute to the support of children's creative development.

Language for communication

Babies and young children learn to communicate by being communicated with. The most important thing by far in this aspect is the quality of your communications with children and the frequency of them. Using a 'commentary' approach works very well – you simply give a running commentary on whatever you're doing, and involve a child in it. See page 551 for an example. Activities and equipment that promote communication include role-play resources, puppets, imaginary areas, telephones, tabletop games (for encouraging playing together), circle time, songs and rhymes, sharing picture books and shared mealtimes.

Using puppets at story time

Language for thinking

Again, the way in which practitioners interact with children is more important than the resources provided. The commentary approach works well to introduce language for thinking, for example you may say, 'I'm just wondering if I can think of a way to stick this lolly stick to my paper'. Good use of questioning is important to encourage children to use language for thinking both aloud and to themselves (inside their heads). To read a Practical example, see Unit OP 2.17, Learning outcome 2, page 552. A good all-round range of free-play and adult-led activities across all areas of learning will promote this aspect.

Linking sounds with letters

Children usually recognise their own name first. You can help by providing children with plenty of opportunities to see and look for their name. For instance, you may have names displayed above the coat pegs or have names written on pieces of paper for the children to find at craft time. You can also provide labels on familiar objects (on your boxes of resources for instance) or in familiar places (such as the book corner). Songs and rhymes support learning in this area, and musical activities will help children to spot the rhythms and patterns in word and letter sounds.

Reading

Sharing stories and books and giving children plenty of opportunities to see adults writing for real purposes helps children to understand that print carries meaning. For instance, this can be demonstrated by making a list of the drinks that children would like at snack time and giving it to the practitioner who will fetch the drinks. When sharing books on a one-to-one basis with children, practitioners can run their finger along the sentences as they read, demonstrating that they are following text. In settings that do this, children may be observed 'playing reading', copying the technique when 'reading' to a doll or

> ### Did you know?
>
> You should aim to introduce new vocabulary as children's language develops.

> ### Good practice
>
> Help children to learn both the names of letters and the sound that they make. This aids learning to read phonetically. Magnetic letters are popular in settings, and letter posters and friezes are also used frequently.

Every child should have the opportunity to share books every day

Emergent writing

Unit OP 2.17 Contribute to the support of children's creative development.

teddy. Every child (whatever age) should have the opportunity to share books on a one-to-one basis every day. Time should be taken to look at the pictures and absorb the vocabulary. Matching games are very useful for developing recognition skills which are key to reading – snap and picture lotto are examples.

Writing and handwriting

Plenty of early opportunities to make marks in a range of ways are needed, for example with pencils, pens, felt-tips, paint and brushes, and by printing, finger painting, chalking, tracing marks in the sand, etc. These help children to learn how to make and control the arm and hand movements necessary for writing. It also helps them to learn how to hold mark-making implements. It's useful to encourage children to make patterns, perhaps by sitting at the painting table and making some yourself. This also helps children to understand that marks can be used to communicate with other people. Practitioners can comment on children's pictures and patterns to demonstrate this. Children can make marks from the time they are babies.

Emergent writing

When children first attempt to write, they tend to draw rows of patterns and shapes that look similar to letters. They will eventually include some letters amongst the patterns and shapes, although they may be muddled – perhaps back to front. This is known as 'emergent' writing. Children benefit from lots of practise at emergent writing, and this can be provided effectively as children play. You can supply envelopes and paper (a good use for junk mail) and encourage children to write 'letters' and post them in an imaginary post office area for instance. You can provide a notepad when the imaginary area is turned into a restaurant, and encourage children to take orders. Give children opportunities to see words and letters in the areas in which they mark-make so that they can try to copy them. For instance, you may place children's name cards on the drawing table and invite children to find their seat. They may then attempt to copy their name since all the materials will be at hand. For examples of how to introduce mark-making opportunities into role play, see page 546.

Engaging children's interest and attention

The activities and opportunities you provide should engage children's interest and attention. Here's some guidance on achieving this when using a variety of methods to promote communication, language and literacy.

Reading

Firstly, choose books that are suitable for the children you are working with. Think about their ages and stages of development, and their interests and preferences. If the whole group is focusing on a theme for instance, you may like to choose a book that's connected to it in some way. However, it's absolutely great to also make choices based on fantastic illustrations, characters that children will fall in love with or fun use of language. In fact, over time, you should aim to introduce children to as many different types of books as possible.

Listen to the way skilled practitioners read stories to children. Their voice will rise and fall in a lively, engaging way, and they will vary their pitch, tone and level. There is energy in their voice. They may whisper sometimes to create effect, or talk more loudly in some parts. They'll pause to let children see the pictures, they'll slow down when there are a lot of words to take in, and they'll speed up for excitement when the story warrants it – if they are reading about a character running in a race for example.

Early years workers read with books facing outwards towards the group

Ask a colleague if you can carry out an observation of them reading a story. Take note of all they do. Then reflect on your own reading aloud. What improvements can you make? Make notes and then monitor how well you put your new learning into practice after your next story-telling session.

Good practice

When reading to groups, you should always allow time for everyone to sit comfortably before you begin, otherwise there will be some distracting fidgeting. Also, ensure that everyone can see the pictures. Early years workers soon learn to read with books facing outwards towards the group. Try to choose the right time for stories – children should be ready to settle down. Many settings plan story time to follow a period of physical play.

Puppets and other visual aids can be wonderful for engaging children during a story. When you're happy that you're reading stories well, why not try introducing them? You can always carry out another observation on a colleague doing so first to learn the technique.

One to one

When looking at books with children on a one-to-one basis, let the child set the pace. Use the time well to give the child a chance to linger over each picture for as long as they like. Talk about the pictures too. You can also ask them questions such as, 'What do you think happens, next?' or, 'Do you think the rabbit in the story is happy today? Why is that?' Also, encourage parents and carers to read to their children every day if they can. Bedtime is a lovely time to settle down together with a book.

Telling stories

Storytelling is telling a story without a book. The art of storytelling is ancient and still very valuable. Storytelling can take a number of forms, for instance:

■ You may tell a well-known tale from memory – Goldilocks and the three bears perhaps. This could be informal and spontaneous, as shown in the Practical example on page 529.

- You may tell stories about things that have happened, for example: 'When I went to the zoo, guess what I saw the monkeys doing? They were swinging from trees and they were ...'

- Running commentary is a way of telling the story of an unfolding event. For example, 'Look at Morgan. She's going behind the counter in our shop. Do you think she's going to serve the customers? Oh yes, she's taking Laurel's basket from her.'

Practical example

Goldilocks and the three bears

Practitioner Ben is playing in the home corner with some children. He notices that there are three bowls of different sizes on the table. He says to the children, 'Look at this. There's a small bowl, a medium-sized bowl and a large bowl. Can anyone guess what story that reminds me of?' Kieran answers, 'Goldilocks!' Ben says, 'That's right. In the story, Goldilocks goes into the three bears' cottage doesn't she? And on the table she sees three bowls of porridge.'

Songs and musical activities

To do a good job and to engage and interest children in singing and musical activities, you need to understand – to really believe – one important thing. *It is not about you!* No one is interested in whether or not you can carry a tune. What they do care about is the energy and enthusiasm you put into joining in and leading these types of activities. Singing and music should be fun, joyful and infectious in the early years. Nothing spoils a song like an adult who is reluctant to join in. If you are self-conscious about it, try to focus on the children's experience instead of your own feelings. After the first few singing sessions, most new practitioners completely overcome any initial reservations.

Good practice

Try to introduce children to a range of songs, music and musical instruments to keep the experience fresh. You can sing in various situations. How about singing hello to everyone at circle time, or singing and playing musical instruments outside like a marching band? The possibilities are endless!

Singing and music should be fun, joyful and infectious in the early years

Rhymes, poems and finger play

The advice given for songs and musical activities also applies here. Poems and rhymes are great for introducing children to new vocabulary and for having fun playing with words. You'll find many children's books of poetry in the library. Why not see if the group can extend the ones that you introduce by coming up with extra words that rhyme? This is an effective way to extend the activity for those who are ready for it.

What are finger plays?

Finger plays are rhymes with actions, and they are loved by babies and toddlers. Examples include:

- This little piggy went to market.

- Round and round the garden.

- Two little dicky birds.

A lot of the pleasure is the close one-to-one interaction and waiting for the fun bit at the end – for the tickle in Round and round the garden, or for the birds to come back in Two little dicky birds. For this to be appreciated by younger children, finger plays need to be repeated often. There should also be a sense of excitement and delight in the delivery of the adult.

Have a go!

Why not try reading a poem to a small group of children aged 3–5 years. Humorous poems go down especially well with this age group, and you will probably enjoy them too!

Finger plays are loved by babies and toddlers

A creative approach

For further information on supporting many activities and experiences linked to communication, language and literacy, see Unit OP 2.17, pages 538–46. You'll learn how engaging and exciting a creative approach can be for children *and* practitioners.

Using clear language to support learning

You need to use clear language that children understand in order to support learning effectively. Also, children learn communication and language from those around them, so you are an important language role model. You need to ensure that you:

- **Use an appropriate level of language:**
  Pitch your language to suit the child or group, as you learnt in the vocabulary section on page 16.

- **Use language that is grammatically correct:**
  This is important as children will copy you. Avoid phrases such as, 'When I went up the shop'. It should be 'When I went to the shop'.

- **Make good use of facial expression and gestures:**
  Make sure that your facial expressions and gestures match your language. For instance, if you're saying that you're pleased about something a child has done or that you like something they have made, look happy! There's more about facial expressions and gestures in Unit SHC 21, on pages 21–2.

- **Check children's understanding:**
  This ensures messages are understood and checks a child's level of understanding. You may find that you need to alter your level of communication. You learnt how to do this on pages 415–16.

Using encouragement and praise to support learning

You learnt about this in Unit TDA 2.9, Learning outcome 2. You're advised to reread this as part of your study of this unit.

Link Up!

Unit OP 2.17 Contribute to the support of children's creative development.

Link Up!

Unit SHC 21 Introduction to communication in children and young people's settings.

Unit TDA 2.9 Support children and young people's positive behaviour.

LEARNING OUTCOME 3

FOCUS ON

... being able to evaluate own contribution to children's learning in communication, language and literacy

In this section you'll learn about reviewing how your own working practice has contributed to children's learning in communication, language and literacy. You'll also learn about adapting your practice to meet individual children's needs. This links with **Assessment Criteria 3.1, 3.2.**

How own working practice contributes to children's learning

You learnt about the benefit of reflection in Unit SHC 22. It is hard to be objective about your own practice in supporting communication, language and literacy, so observation can be a valuable tool. It's helpful for someone to record you or to record yourself as you work with children, either using a video camera or an audio recorder. (Make sure you have written permission from your supervisor and the children's parents or carers first.) Alternatively, you can ask a colleague to make a written observation of you for a period of time. You can then analyse the recordings or observation notes.

To do this, you can reflect on how well you engage children's interest and attention when carrying out the following:

■ Reading to children in groups.

■ Reading to children on a one-to-one basis.

■ Telling stories.

■ Singing songs.

■ Sharing poems.

■ Sharing finger plays.

Did you know?

It can also be helpful to ask colleagues to give you feedback on how they feel you do in terms of supporting children's communication, language and literacy. If you do this, ask for both strengths and weaknesses to be shared.

Unit SHC 22 Introduction to personal development in children and young people's settings.

You can improve your own practice by learning more about communication, language and literacy. There are plenty of books dedicated to the subject. There are also short courses and seminars, so why not find out what is available locally. You can also learn from skilled colleagues, and visits to other settings are a wonderful way to become inspired and pick up tips.

Meeting individual children's needs

When promoting communication, language and literacy, it's good practice to give all children the opportunity to participate fully and to be effectively supported. To do this effectively, you need to consider children's individual needs.

Think carefully about:

■ **the resources you offer:**
For example, you may need to adapt mark-making implements such as paint brushes or crayons. Or you may work with a child who has a hearing impairment and will benefit from learning some songs and rhymes in sign language. Or perhaps you may work with a child who has a learning difficulty who may learn to sing using Makaton signs.

■ **access to activities:**
You may need to adapt the way you make activities available. For instance, by lowering the table height to meet the needs of a wheelchair user, or providing plenty of room for manoeuvring in imaginary areas.

■ **the adult support available:**
Children will need differing levels of adult support according to their needs, and they may also need extra time. This will be the case with some children who have learning difficulties and/or communication difficulties for instance. You may communicate with children via sign language, or use of a communication board or deck of cards. Also see page 28 for more information about meeting children's language and communication needs.

How are things going?

▶ Progress Check

1. Why is communication, language and literacy important to children's learning? (1.1)

2. Describe how communication, language and literacy development links to other areas of children's learning. (1.2)

3. Why is it important to use clear language to support communication, language and literacy? (2.3)

4. What are the benefits of using encouragement and praise to support children's communication, language and literacy? (2.4)

5. How can observations help you to review how your working practice has contributed to children's communication, language and literacy development? (3.1) (2.3)

6. Give three examples of ways in which you might make adaptations to the way you provide communication, language and literacy activities/experiences to meet children's individual needs. (3.2)

Are you ready for assessment?

Learning Outcomes 2 and 3 must be assessed in a real work environment.

CACHE

Set tasks:

■ You are asked to produce a leaflet to describe why communication, language and literacy are important to children's learning, and how they link with other areas of learning and development within the framework of your own work setting. You can prepare by rereading pages 514–522 and making relevant notes.

City & Guilds

You can prepare for assessment by gatherng evidence of times when you have engaged children's interest and attention in communication, language and literacy activities through a variety of method (e.g. plans, evaluations or reflective accounts of activities such as storytelling or using puppets).

Edexcel

You can prepare for assessment by gatherng evidence of times when you have engaged children's interest and attention in communication, language and literacy activities through a variety of method (e.g. plans, evaluations or reflective accounts of activities such as storytelling or using puppets).

UNIT 2.17
Contribute to the support of children's creative development

LEARNING OUTCOMES

The learning outcomes you will meet in this unit are:

1 Understand the importance of creative development

2 Be able to contribute to children's creative development

3 Be able to evaluate own contribution to children's creative development

INTRODUCTION

Creativity and creative development are extremely important because they can positively influence all aspects of children's learning and development. Practitioners can use some interesting techniques to support children's creative development. It can be very rewarding for practitioners to provide and work in a stimulating, vibrant, creative environment that offers plenty of varied creative opportunities.

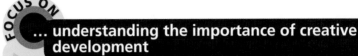

FOCUS ON ... understanding the importance of creative development

In this section you'll learn why creative development is important to children's learning. You'll also learn how creative development links to other areas of learning and development within the framework related to your own work setting. This links with **Assessment Criteria 1.1, 1.2.**

The importance of creative development

Creative development has two aspects. These are concerned with:

■ how children engage in creative activities

■ children's **creative learning**.

We'll look at each of these aspects in turn and explore the benefits to children.

How children engage in creative activities

We can define 'creative activities' as activities that:

■ allow children to express themselves creatively *and*

■ are linked to the traditional creative arts.

key terms

Creative learning the development of imaginative thinking skills and problem-solving skills.

Creativity play and exploration related to the traditional creative arts.

Good practice

The main focus of **creativity** for young children should always be the *process* of making or doing things, rather than the *product* or end result (for example a painting).

The traditional creative arts are shown in the diagram below.

```
                    ┌──────────────┐
                    │  Visual arts │
                    └──────────────┘

┌──────────┐      ┌──────────────┐      ┌──────────┐
│ Theatre  │      │ Traditional  │      │  Music   │
│          │      │ creative arts│      │          │
└──────────┘      └──────────────┘      └──────────┘

        ┌──────────────┐   ┌──────────────┐
        │  Literature  │   │    Dance     │
        └──────────────┘   └──────────────┘
```

The traditional creative arts

Play, exploration and discovery are key to creativity. Since children are naturally motivated to play and explore, we can give them rich opportunities to be creative by providing the right activities. Examples of children's activities linked to the traditional arts are shown in Table OP2.17.1 below.

Banging on pots and pans is a musical activity

Table OP2.17.1: Examples of children's activities linked to the traditional arts

Area of the traditional arts	Examples of children's activities
Visual arts This area of the traditional arts includes painting, drawing, etc. as well as three-dimensional work, such as sculpture and design.	■ Mark-making in any way, for example with a paintbrush or making finger trails in a tray of sand. ■ Messy play and exploring a range of media (materials), including malleable materials such as play dough, plasticine or cornflour paste.
Music This area of the traditional arts includes playing instruments and singing.	■ Banging on some pots and pans with a wooden spoon. ■ Singing songs or rhymes, or humming their own made-up tunes.
Dance	■ A toddler swaying instinctively when music is played. ■ Any creative physical movement, for example pretending to be a lion and crawling along on all fours with a swagger.

Area of the traditional arts	Examples of children's activities
Literature/theatre The area of the literature is about the writing of fiction. It's linked closely to theatre, which is about acting out the written word as well as improvisation.	<ul><li>Imagining what might happen next when a storybook is read to them.</li><li>Retelling a story they know or making up their own – this could involve role play, puppets, etc. This includes assigning character traits to dolls and figures, and giving them something to do. For example, the little girl figure is unwell so she's going to the doctor.</li><li>Imaginary play/role play and dressing up, particularly when items such as long pieces of fabric are used creatively to make a sari or a cape or a skirt, as opposed to 'off-the-peg' dressing-up costumes such as a nurse's uniform.</li><li>Representation of objects in play. For example, a piece of string becomes a snake or a wedding ring, a cardboard box becomes a car or a house.</li></ul>

Have a go!

As you've worked through the other units you have learnt how important it is for children to express themselves. Why not see if you can explain this to someone else.

Children's creative learning

'Creative learning' refers to the process of developing:

■ **thinking skills:**

These include the skills we use to remember, to develop ideas and to understand new things.

■ **problem-solving skills:**

These include the skills we use to work out what we should do, how we should do things and how we can make things work. It also includes divergent thinking (see page 539).

These key skills are used throughout our lives and across all of the curriculum areas, so they are extremely important in terms of children's overall development. In recent years, these skills have been increasingly valued in:

- mathematics

- science

- design.

Divergent thinking

'**Divergent thinking**' is a term you will hear in connection with children's creative learning. It's the name given to the thought processes we use to generate creative ideas by exploring many possible solutions. You may often use this sort of thinking yourself. For instance, when planning a theme for children, you may start by thought storming related ideas. This is great example of divergent thinking in action.

Creative activities promoting creative learning

Although creative activities and creative learning are quite different, *many creative activities will promote creative learning*. For instance, you learnt on page 538 that dressing up is a creative activity. Yet a child making a skirt from a piece of fabric will need a way to keep the skirt on. They may try tying the fabric in a knot or using sticky tape, before successfully using a clothes peg from the home corner. This means they've used both imaginative thinking skills and divergent thinking skills within the creative activity.

> **key terms**
>
> **Divergent thinking** the thought processes used to generate creative ideas by exploring many possible solutions.

Dressing up is a creative activity

How creative development links to other areas of development

As well as promoting children's creative development, creative learning and engaging in creative activities can also support children's:

■ emotional development

■ social development

■ intellectual development

■ communication development

■ physical development.

Examples of this are shown in Table OP2.17.2 below.

Table OP2.17.2: How creative learning and creative activities support areas of development

Creative learning and engaging in creative activities supports:
Emotional development Responding to experiences and self-expression through creative activities relating to visual arts, music, dance, literature/theatre and design. Gaining confidence through the development of thinking and problem-solving skills. Experiencing both success and failure when trying out own ideas and through this developing perseverance, which leads to increased self-reliance.
Social development Learning and using skills to contribute their own imaginative ideas to a group (for example during role play or shared artwork) and to listen to, understand and respond to the imaginative ideas given by others. Developing the ability to be creative and to engage in creative learning within social boundaries and environmental limitations. For example, it is fine to draw on the ground outside with chalk, but it is unacceptable to paint on the carpet inside.
Intellectual development Learning and using the skills of imaginative play, thinking and problem solving. This includes the skills to question and make choices, identify problems, generate a number of imaginative solutions, try out and apply ideas.
Communication development Learning and using the language associated with thinking and problem solving. Responding to creative questions and asking creative questions (see Learning outcome 2). Singing and rhyming. Using language for expression in role play. Learning and using the language associated with storytelling. Learning and using the language associated with behaviour and emotions.
Physical development Large motor skills – moving imaginatively and in new ways when role playing (for example slithering along the floor like a snake) and when dancing, etc. Using fine motor skills – controlling mark-making implements such as paintbrushes and pencils, handling small objects such as sequins and beads when creating artwork, fastening zips, buttons, etc. when dressing up.

Early years frameworks

Creative learning and engaging in creative activities will also promote creative aspects of the early years framework that applies in your home country. In England, this is the Early Years Foundation Stage (EYFS), and the area of learning most closely linked is Expressive arts and design. The EYFS tells us that Expressive arts and design involves enabling children to explore and play with a wide range of materials, as well as providing opportunities and encouragement for sharing their thoughts, ideas, and feelings through a variety of activities in art, music, movement, dance, role play, and design and technology.

The early learning goals for Expressive arts and design

By the end of their reception year most children following the EYFS are expected to be able to fulfil the following Creative Development early learning goals:

- Exploring and using media and materials: Children sing songs, make music and dance and experiment with ways of changing them. They safely use and explore a variety of materials, tools and techniques, experimenting with colour, design, texture, form and function.

- Being imaginative: Children use what they have learned about media and materials in original ways, thinking about uses and purposes. They represent their own ideas, thoughts and feelings through design and technology, art, music, dance, role play and stories.

Links to other EYFS areas of learning

As you've learnt in other units, children's learning is holistic, not compartmentalised. This means that Expressive arts and design is linked to the other areas of learning included in the EYFS framework.

Think of one more creative activity and one more creative learning opportunity to promote each of the areas of learning included in the curriculum framework that is followed in your home country.

Table OP2.17.3 below lists all seven areas of learning. There's an example of how each one can be promoted through a creative activity and a creative learning opportunity.

Table OP2.17.3: Links between creative activities, creative learning and the EYFS areas of learning

Area of learning and development	Creative activity	Creative learning opportunity
Personal, social and emotional development	Sharing a story about an impatient gardener who can't wait for his plants to grow.	Pausing part-way through a story to discuss how the character is feeling and what they might be thinking in light of events, their expressions in the pictures and their behaviour.
Communication and language	A visit from a dancer who will be leading a dance session with the children.	Coming together at circle time and thinking up questions to ask the dancer.
Literacy	Group discussion following a visit from a dancer.	Writing down dance words the children have learnt (e.g. leap, step) and displaying them on the wall to create a dance word bank.
Understanding of the world	Planting flowering bedding plants in the nursery garden.	What will happen if we water one plant and not the other? Let's try it and see.
Mathematics	Sharing out our sunflower plants so that everyone has their fair share to plant in the garden.	We've built a tower next to our sunflower with the Mega Blocks – it's 10 blocks high. What else can we use to measure it?
Physical development	Making play dough and developing fine motor skills to shape the malleable material.	What will happen if we put food colouring in the water before adding it to the dough? What will happen if we add two colours? What will happen if we add peppermint essence?
Expressive arts and design	Making our own robots from found items.	What will happen if we plot a course for a programmable robot, then place it in a shallow tray of sand? Will it leave footprints? Let's try it and see.

Link Up!

Unit MU 2.8 Contribute to the support of positive environments for children and young people.

Did you know?

Adult-led opportunities such as those shown in the table above should be offered within a programme that also promotes child-led activities and experiences.

LEARNING OUTCOME 2

... being able to contribute to children's creative development

In this section you'll learn about the equipment and activities used to support creative development, and about setting out and implementing activities with children. You'll also learn about using clear language, encouragement and praise to support creative development. This links with **Assessment Criteria 2.1, 2.2, 2.3, 2.4.**

Equipment and activities that support creative development

In environments that successfully support creative development, children will be given access to a wide range of materials and resources. They will have many varied opportunities to be creative and to think creatively during:

- child-initiated activities
- adult-initiated activities.

Building on your learning

You were introduced to the basic activities and equipment for supporting children's creative development in Unit MU 2.8, Learning outcome 1. You may like to recap on this as part of your learning towards this unit. So to build on this learning, what equipment and activities might you expect to find in an environment that really supports young children's creativity and creative learning well? Let's look at different areas of the setting in turn.

Link Up!

Unit MU 2.8 Contribute to the support of positive environments for children and young people.

Displays

You would find plenty of visual and sensory inspiration in a display. This might include interest tables as well as displays of the children's own individual work. There may also be a large piece of artwork that children have collaborated on. Interesting and inspirational visual

Did you know?

If potentially inspirational items such as paintings are not rotated regularly, children and adults alike will tend to stop noticing them.

artwork from a variety of artists may also be displayed as inspiration – there could be paintings, prints, photographs, posters, postcards, wall hangings, stained glass, sculptures, ornaments, etc.

Visual and sensory inspiration should be on display

Role play

Role-play areas are likely to feature real objects and artefacts to enrich imaginary play. There may be real pasta 'cooking' in the saucepans of a home corner for instance, and a real telephone to play with (disconnected!) The focus of imaginary areas will be changed regularly, providing many opportunities to bring the real world in. For instance, if the area is a corner shop, real cans and packets of food can be sold, along with real fruit and vegetables. If the area is a post office, real junk mail can be made available.

Music

Musical instruments will be made available during free play, not just at music time. This is likely to inspire children to move and think imaginatively. They might dance along while they play, or imagine they are part of a marching band, or that they are a musician performing on stage or on the television. Children might make their own simple instruments. For example, plastic bottles filled with pasta can become shakers, and pots and pans can become a drum kit with the addition of a wooden spoon. There will also be opportunities to hear recorded music from around the world, and live music played by musicians (perhaps a staff member or parent plays the guitar).

Good practice

In Learning outcome 1 you learnt how off-the-peg dressing-up outfits can inhibit creativity in imaginary play, so creative environments are likely to provide lengths of fabric, etc., which encourage creative use. Real items such hats, handbags, bangles, etc. will also be provided.

Children may be inspired to dance along as they play

Small world

Small world will be presented in exciting ways to maximise potential creativity. For instance, the train set may be set out with construction materials such as corrugated card and tape. If an adult models making their own tunnel for a train to pass through, children are likely to follow suit. A farmyard may be set up in a tray of real soil and turf, and sand, water and shells may recreate a seabed in which to play with small world marine life creatures.

Stories

A well-stocked, inviting book corner will be ready and waiting to whisk children off on an imaginary journey into another world, to meet characters and situations both familiar and new. Meanwhile, non-fiction books will stimulate creative learning. Children will explore and handle books freely outside of the set story time, and books will be rotated regularly. **Story bags** will add interest and extend learning, as will a range of sensory books. Practitioners will be skilled at reading aloud to children, making story time a rich and engaging experience. There will be opportunities to visit the local library.

Physical movement

A wide range of sounds – from music to animal noises – will inspire creative movement. Props such as ribbon and floaty scarves will be available, alongside role-play resources such as masks (children may make these themselves), fringed waistcoats and skirts that twirl when children spin. There may be exposure to a range of dance genres accessed via video clips, the internet, pictures and stories. There will also be opportunities to see live dance, for example a visit to the local school to see older children perform.

Mark-making

Mark-making will often be purely creative, and materials to support it will be varied and plentiful. This will include pencils, crayons, felt-tips, charcoal, chalk and paint, and there will also be opportunities to make marks in sand, foam, cornflour paste, etc. At the same time, creative opportunities will be provided for children to develop emergent writing skills by mark-making for real purposes. For instance, in the home corner children may use notebooks and pencils to create their own shopping lists. Outside they may chalk all over the playground, and 'paint' the walls with water (not paint!), paintbrushes and rollers.

Creative opportunities to mark-make for real purposes will be provided

Art, craft and design

Art, craft and design resources will be interesting, varied and plentiful. There will be opportunities to use natural and recycled objects as well as manufactured supplies. Many opportunities will be child led and purely inspired by the materials – collages for instance, or models made from clay.

Good practice

The practices and attitudes held by staff set the all-important tone and atmosphere of the environment. Environments that support young children's creativity and creative learning promote exploration and play without undue limitations. Boundaries are of course necessary, but in a creative environment the atmosphere supports acceptable risk-taking, doing things in unconventional ways, making mistakes, and a certain level of untidiness and noise during sessions. Flexibility and a willingness to go with the flow of children's ideas is also necessary.

Free space

There will also be some free space in creative environments. Children can use this as they wish. They can get out new resources, or use the space to bring together items from around the setting that they'd like to explore together in one place. This supports joined-up thinking and discovery. However, it's important to understand that children's freedom to choose and mix up resources won't be limited to this one dedicated free space – it just helps to ensure that there is room within the overall layout for extra, spontaneous things to happen in the environment.

Children may sometimes collaborate during creative activities

Setting out and implementing activities with children

Whatever creative activity you are planning to provide, it's important to consider the following factors.

Flexibility and spontaneity

To support children in being creative and using creative thinking skills, you must have a flexible approach to activities and play, and accommodate the spontaneous ways that children play and explore.

Did you know?

Children often take imaginary activities in directions practitioners had not planned. For instance, you may set up an imaginary area as a hospital because it fits with the setting's current theme. But if children bring over soft toys and this captures their imagination, it could spontaneously be turned into a vet's surgery. It's important to value this sort of free-flowing imaginative play when it occurs.

Link Up!

Unit MU 2.8 Contribute to the support of positive environments for children and young people.

Providing options and allowing choice

You need to provide a wide range of resources and materials for children to explore and use in their creative pursuits, for example a varied collection of natural materials such as fir cones, shells and pebbles, and a wide range of art/craft resources such as tissue paper, cellophane and corrugated card. Further resources to support creativity and creative learning are given in Unit MU 2.8, in the resources table on pages 302–3.

Providing inspiration

Everyone needs inspiration in order to be creative, and the more children are exposed to a wide range of experiences, the more inspiration they will have to draw on. Visits and visitors are valuable. It's inspiring for children to hear a brass band in the park for example. Trips unconnected to the traditional arts can be just as inspiring – handling animals at a city farm or visiting the coast for instance.

Experiences such as a trip to the theatre are valuable

Good practice

Children should also be exposed to a diversity of cultures and ways of thinking. It's good for them to see the different approaches that people take to specific problems and to everyday life. Inspiration can also be provided through visual stimulus in the setting – via pictures on the wall for instance.

Encouraging collaboration

Collaboration can drive creativity and creative learning to a new level. You will have experienced this yourself, perhaps in a meeting when the ideas are flowing and one person's suggestion triggers you to have a related idea. You can encourage young children to develop these skills by giving them opportunities to collaborate with one another, perhaps to build a den or to make a giant collage for the wall.

Encouraging idea generation

You can promote imaginative, divergent thinking and problem-solving skills by encouraging children to come up with lots of ideas. When working with young children, these will often be connected with what the group might do, or how to do something. For instance, if a child floats a large piece of corrugated card in the water tray, you could encourage the children at the water tray to suggest as many ways as possible to sink it.

Wonder and excitement are signs of creativity in action

Finding wonder and excitement

When children respond with wonder and excitement to the activities and experiences that you provide, this often indicates that creativity and/or creative learning is taking place. Different children will be drawn to different aspects of creativity, and it is part of a practitioner's role to help children experience a full range of opportunities, and also to help them find out what excites them and gives them that creative spark.

Extended and unhurried periods of time

Creativity and creative learning cannot be rushed. When children first participate in an activity or experience, they are likely to do something familiar, something they have done before. They need extended, unhurried periods to really get into activities and experiences, and to engage at a deeper level. This is when new connections and new explorations and discoveries tend to be made.

Ask Miranda!

Q Won't children become bored if activities aren't changing frequently?

A Young children will be accessing creative activities and experiences as part of their free play, so opportunities to engage for extended periods will be offered within an environment that also facilitates moving on to the next thing when children are ready. In fact, an important part of making creative connections for young children is joining and mixing up what is on offer to them – taking some water to the sand tray for instance, or taking a toy car to the drawing table and subsequently drawing a road.

Good practice

A key difference between bought toys and gathered items is that the gathered items do not come with safety marks or age guidelines. So it's up to practitioners to make sensible, safe judgements about what materials are suitable for children in light of their age and stage of development.

Age appropriateness

As you've learnt, environments that support creativity and creative learning provide access to a range of resources, materials, and real objects and artefacts.

Using language to support creative development

We need to help children to develop the vocabulary to express themselves in conversation and in role play by promoting language relating to:

- feelings

- behaviour

- action.

You can expose children to this language by modelling it yourself. An effective method is to provide a running commentary on events in real life, in storybooks or even on television. Within this running commentary, you can:

- give information to extend children's learning

- ask open-ended questions that require a response and make children think

- introduce new vocabulary.

Here's an example of a running commentary shared with a three-year-old. It promotes language related to feelings, behaviour and action. 'Look, Jacob's rubbing his eyes and yawning, I think he must be tired. Yes, he's snuggling up with his teddy and having a cuddle with his mum. What do you think?'

Children also need support to develop the language of:

- thinking

- problem solving.

Using thinking and problem-solving questions

Asking children questions that encourage them to think creatively is perhaps one of the most effective ways of all for practitioners to promote creative learning, and it can be applied to any activity or experience right across the curriculum, whatever age range you are working with. You should use the following types of questions:

Have a go!

The table on page 542 includes several examples that promote language connected to feelings, behaviour and action. Turn back to the table now, and see if you can identify them.

Have a go!

Pay attention to the way in which skilled colleagues ask questions and learn from the reaction that they get from children.

- What if?

- What will happen next?

- How can we change?

- Why?

- Why not?

Practical example

Lucien's questions

Lucien works in a pre-school. He's making play dough for the group with four-year-old Ruby. Lucien says, 'This dough is a bit too dry to knead. What can we add to the mixture to solve the problem?' Ruby says, 'A little bit more water.' Lucien replies, 'Good idea, let's try it.' It works. Lucien asks, 'What do you think would have happened if we added a lot of water?' Ruby doesn't know. Lucien realises that she's picked up from making dough before that water should be added in small quantities, but that she doesn't know the reason for this. Lucien breaks off a section of the dough for Ruby and says, 'How can we find out using this piece of dough?'

Encouragement and praise

As you learnt in Learning outcome 1, it's important that children develop:

- the confidence to express themselves

- the self-reliance and self-esteem that comes from believing that they can think and learn effectively and solve problems for themselves.

These attributes will nurture children throughout their lives. So it's important for you to notice and praise children's creativity and creative learning. Let them know that you value their expression, ideas and thoughts, and that you believe they are good at conveying them (putting them across). A key part of this is valuing *process* over *product*, as mentioned in Learning outcome 1.

Notice and praise children's creativity and creative learning

Displaying work

When you display children's creative work, you are demonstrating that you value it. So make sure that:

- **everyone has opportunities to have their work displayed:**
  Don't just pick the 'neatest' or 'brightest' or most 'eye-catching' work. (These things are subjective in any case.) Value everyone's process and expression rather than the end product.

- **work is treated with respect:**
  Mount work carefully and remove any displays that become tatty. Let children take home their work – don't throw it in the bin! Involve children in the display of their work where possible. That way you can be sure that you aren't making an error such as displaying an abstract painting the wrong way up. Also, never be tempted to cut a picture so it 'fits' a display, or worst of all, to 'tidy it up' by changing things, for example moving the eyes on a face made from collage materials so that they are straight.

- **attention is drawn to children's work:**
  Spend time looking at displays with children, and point them out to children's parents, carers and other visitors to the room. This will increase the amount of praise and attention that children receive for being creative.

Have a go!

When you visit other rooms within your setting, take the time to pay attention to children's creative work that you come across. Ask your colleagues to do the same when they visit your room.

When you display children's creative work, you are demonstrating that you value it

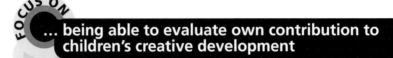

LEARNING OUTCOME 3

FOCUS ON

... being able to evaluate own contribution to children's creative development

In this section you'll learn about reviewing how your own working practice has contributed to children's creative development. You'll also learn about adapting your practice to meet individual children's needs. This links with **Assessment Criteria 3.1, 3.2**.

Reviewing your practice

As you know from Unit SHC 22, reflection brings many benefits. It is hard to be objective about your own practice in supporting creativity and creative learning, so observation can be a valuable tool. It's helpful for someone to record you or to record yourself as you work with children, either using a video camera or an audio recorder. (Make sure you have written permission from your supervisor and the children's parents or carers first.) Alternatively, you can ask a colleague to make a written observation of you for a period of time. You can then analyse the recordings or observation notes.

To do this, you can refer to the practical techniques that promote creativity and creative learning, which you've learnt about in this unit. Reflect on how well you:

■ provide children with options and allow choice

■ model creativity and creative thinking

■ emphasise process over product

■ provide inspiration

■ support language development

■ make use of creative thinking questions

■ build children's self-confidence and self-reliance

■ provide opportunities that result in wonder and excitement.

Link Up!

Unit SHC 22 Introduction to personal development in children and young people's settings.

Did you know?

It can also be helpful to ask colleagues to give you feedback on how they feel you do in terms of supporting children's creativity and creative learning. If you do this, ask for both strengths and weaknesses to be shared.

Good practice

You can improve your own practice by learning more about creativity. There are plenty of books dedicated to the subject of promoting children's creativity, and even more on how to promote your own creativity and creative thinking skills. The most effective practitioners develop their own creativity as well that of children. There is an increasing number of short courses and seminars on promoting creativity. Some focus solely on theory, while others introduce activity ideas and practical techniques. You can also learn from skilled colleagues, and visits to other settings are a wonderful way to become inspired and pick up tips.

Did you know?

Creativity thrives on trial and error. Regularly experiment with new ways of working by introducing new activities or resources, or make alterations to your old ones. Monitor children's responses. Repeat things that go well. If something doesn't work, simply try something else next time.

Meeting individual children's needs

When promoting creative development, it's good practice to give all children the opportunity to participate fully and to choose and make decisions for themselves. To do this effectively, you need to consider children's individual needs.

Think carefully about:

■ **the resources you offer:**
For example, you may need to adapt tools such as paintbrushes or use specialist versions of items such as scissors to enable a child with a physical impairment to use them. Or you may work with a child who has a visual impairment and will benefit from experiencing materials with different textures, sounds and smells.

■ **access to activities:**
You may need to adapt the way you make creative activities available. For instance, by leaving plenty of space for a child who uses crutches to manoeuvre around floor activities. Or you may need to lower the table height to meet the needs of a wheelchair user, or provide good task lighting for a child with a visual impairment. You may also need to tailor the opportunities for creative expression to suit individual needs. For example, a child may make paint prints with their elbow rather than their hand, or hold a crayon between their toes.

Link Up!

Unit TDA 2.15 Support children and young people with disabilities and special educational needs.

■ **the adult support available:**

Children will need differing levels of adult support according to their needs, and they may also need extra time. This will be the case with some children who have learning difficulties for instance. Adults can also carry out tasks under the instruction of children to test out children's ideas. For instance, a child who has limited use of their arms may instruct an adult to pour sand on a boat in the water tray for them, to see if it sinks.

■ **how you ensure real choice and that children's voices are heard:**

Be careful to ensure that children with communication difficulties have equal opportunities to share and express their ideas, preferences and opinions. Also ensure that you find an appropriate way to communicate to them the language used for creative expression, creative thinking and to praise creative efforts. This links with your learning in Unit SHC 21.

Link Up!

Unit SHC 21 Introduction to personal development in children and young people's settings.

How are things going?

▶ Progress Check

1. What is meant by the following terms?
   a Creative activities.
   b Creative learning. (1.1)
2. Describe how creative development links to other areas of children's learning. (1.2)
3. Identify five creative activities that promote children's creative development. (2.1)
4. Explain three important factors to consider when setting out and implementing creative activities with children. (2.2)
5. Explain how you can use language to promote children's thinking and problem-solving skills. (2.3)
6. Why is praise important when supporting children's creative development? (2.4)
7. How can observations help you to review how your working practice has contributed to children's creative development? (3.1)
8. Give three examples of ways in which you might make adaptations to the way you provide creative activities to meet children's individual needs. (3.2)

Are you ready for assessment?

Learning Outcomes 2 and 3 must be assessed in a real work environment.

CACHE

Set tasks:

■ You are expected to create notes for parents and carers detailing why creative development is important to children's learning and how it links to other areas of learning and development within the framework of your own work setting. You can prepare by rereading pages 536–542 and making relevant notes.

City & Guilds

You can prepare for assessment by gathering evidence of times when you have set out and implemented creative activities with children (e.g. plans, evaluatons or reflective accounts of activities such as imaginative play).

Edexcel

You can prepare for assessment by gathering evidence of times when you have set out and implemented creative activities with children (e.g. plans, evaluatons or reflective accounts of activities such as imaginative play).

REFLECTIVE PRACTICE

SHC 21

Spend some time thinking about how well you listen and how you show you are listening when:

1. children or young people are communicating with you
2. adults are communicating with you.

Now return to the list of active listening strategies on pages 18–19. Think about how you could incorporate them into your current practice.

Next, consider the bullet points that list behaviour that could indicate you do not value children's ideas and feelings. Are there any behaviours that you need to eliminate from your current practice?

SHC 22

Turn to pages 63–4 and recap on the reflection techniques. Now think about your own reflective practice. Are you using a range of techniques effectively? If not, what will you do to change this?

SHC 23

Spend some time thinking about your own prejudices and the stereotypical beliefs that you may hold, and write them down in a list in your reflective journal. You may find it useful to reflect on the list of common reasons for discrimination on page 85 as part of the process. Now, focusing on each item, consider the following:

1. Where the view came from and what it is based upon.
2. How you feel about the view now you have learnt about equality and inclusion.
3. The ways in which someone holding the same views may inadvertently discriminate within a setting.
4. The ways in which someone holding the same views may intentionally discriminate within a setting.
5. What you will do in practice to ensure that you promote equality and inclusion and do not discriminate.

TDA 2.1

Spend some time thinking about the last time you provided a play activity for children. This may have been a planned activity, or you may have set out toys or resources informally. Did you successfully consider the age and stage of development of the children beforehand to ensure the activity was appropriate? If not, what will you do differently next time? (You may want to refer to the development tables on pages 113–131.)

MU 2.2

You've learnt that in your role as a practitioner you support children and young people's development in many ways. Referring to the bullet points on page 189, spend a few minutes thinking about how well you currently support development. Where could you improve, and how?

TDA 2.2

As you've learnt, some children and young people disclose abuse to practitioners. To handle this situation effectively, what skills and attributes do you think a practitioner needs to have? Make notes in your reflective diary.

MU 2.4

Spend some time thinking carefully about the health and safety policies and procedures at your setting. Do you fully understand them all, and do you work in line with them at all times? Are you clear about your own roles and responsibilities? If not, make a list of queries and arrange a time to talk with your workplace supervisor.

TDA 2.9

Reread the Practical examples on pages 270 and 275. In both cases, the adults do not initially respond well to the children's inappropriate behaviour. In fact, they unintentionally make it worse. But the adults do learn from their mistakes.

Now think about your own experience of dealing with inappropriate behaviour. Are there mistakes that you can learn from? (It would be very unusual if there were none at all.) Consider how you can respond differently in the future and make notes in your reflective diary.

MU 2.8

Spend some time thinking carefully about how you praise children and young people for individual achievements. Do you praise them for trying as well as succeeding? Are there any ways in which you could improve your practice? Make notes in your reflective diary.

MU 2.9

Many new practitioners say they feel a little nervous when they interact with parents and carers. But it's important to keep up the interaction, as this will build your relationships and also your confidence. Spend some time thinking about the way you currently interact with parents and carers. Is there anything you can do to improve? For example, would it help you to spend a few moments thinking through what you want to say before you approach parents? (You could even make a note of the key points you want to discuss.) Make notes in your reflective diary.

PEFAP 001

It's important for a first-aider to keep calm under pressure. Can you remember a time when you've been under pressure at the setting? How did you respond? Is there anything you can learn from the situation? Make notes in your reflective diary.

MPII 002

Spend some time thinking about how well you ensure children cannot access poisonous substances and plants. Do you consider the full range? Are you careful about the access that children have to bags belonging to adults? Is there anything you can do to improve your current practice? Make notes in your reflective diary.

TDA 2.7

Spend some time thinking carefully about how effectively you respond to a child or young person's questions, concerns or ideas. Are there any ways in which you could improve your practice? Make notes in your reflective diary.

TDA 2.14

Does your setting have a food policy or a policy for mealtimes and snack times? If so, ask your supervisor if you can read a copy. Go through it carefully and consider how well you meet the policy in practice.

TDA 2.15

Using reflective practice techniques, review an activity or experience you have provided for a disabled child. Work in partnership by consulting with the child and your colleagues if possible. (You will need permission from your setting to do this.) Make notes in your reflective diary.

TDA 2.16

Turn to the 12 features of play on pages 497–8. Think about each one in turn. How many of them do you see occurring frequently at your setting? What does this tell you about the quality of play?

OP 2.15

Spend some time thinking about how well you use clear language, praise and encouragement to support children's learning in communication, language and literacy. Where do your strengths lie? Where could you make improvements? Make notes in your reflective diary.

OP 2.17

Spend some time thinking about how well you use the practical techniques that promote creativity and creative learning. You can do this by considering each of the 'Reviewing your practice' bullet points on page 554, and making notes in your reflective diary.

GLOSSARY

Barriers to effective communication factors that prevent effective communication.

Bilingual able to speak two languages.

Cascading the passing on of new information or learning from one colleague to another.

Child protection the measures taken to keep children and young people safe from abuse and harm from others.

Compliance children co-operating with requests. (National Occupational Standards).

Confidentiality this refers to the rights of people to have information that is held or known about them kept privately and safely.

Creative learning the development of imaginative thinking skills and problem-solving skills.

Creativity play and exploration related to the traditional creative arts.

Disclose pass on confidential information in certain circumstances, in line with confidentiality procedures.

Disclosure when a child reveals to an adult that they have been abused.

Divergent thinking the thought processes used to generate creative ideas by exploring many possible solutions.

Excessive risk taking taking inappropriate risks.

Excessively risk adverse prone to avoiding risk altogether.

Expected development rates the approximate ages at which most children will achieve key developmental milestones.

Fine motor skills these are sometimes called 'small motor skills'. They are the delicate, manipulative movements that are made with the fingers.

Free play a period of time in which children freely choose what resources to play with and how to play with them. Practitioners usually set the room up with a range of resources to choose from. Children will also be able to select additional resources if they prefer.

Full disclosure when a child says who abused them and goes into the history and nature of the abuse.

Gross motor skills sometimes these are called 'large motor skills'. They are whole-body movements, such as walking.

Hazard an item or situation that may cause harm.

Inappropriate behaviour actions that conflict with the accepted values and beliefs of the setting and society. Inappropriate behaviour may be demonstrated through speech, writing, non-verbal behaviour or physical abuse.

Inclusion children with disabilities or special educational needs belonging to mainstream settings. (National Occupational Standards.)

Incubation periods the amount of time between an infection and the onset of signs and symptoms.

Indirect disclosure when a child discloses indirectly, for example through their play or in a letter. This may be intentional or unintentional.

Induction programme the system by which an employer or placement supervisor introduces a new staff member or student to the setting.

Key person a person appointed to take a special interest in the welfare of a particular child.

Medical model of disability this reflects the traditional view that disability is something to be 'cured', treating the child as a sick patient.

Multidisciplinary working when professionals with different job roles work together, in this case for the benefit of children and young people.

Multilingual able to speak three or more languages.

Neonate newly born baby.

Non-participant observer someone who observes unobtrusively, without interacting with children.

Partial disclosure when a child begins to tell of abuse but does not continue, or when they do not give full details, such as the name of the abuser or the nature of the abuse.

Participant observer an observer who interacts with a child during the observation. They may ask or encourage a child to do things.

Person specification part of a job description which lists the knowledge, experience and attributes a practitioner will need to fulfil a job role.

Personal assistant workers who support disabled children, young people or adults in an enabling, empowering role. They provide practical support to enable them to achieve the things they want to do but with which they need help.

Personal development plan a plan that details how a practitioner will gain new knowledge and skills.

Play agenda what a child wants to achieve in their play.

Prone the position a baby is in when lying on their front.

Reflective practice the process of thinking about and analysing your work to improve your practice.

Reflective practitioners workers who use reflective practice regularly.

Reflexes physical movements or reactions that neonates make without consciously intending to do so.

Risk the likelihood of a hazard actually causing harm.

Safe working practices the ways in which practitioners work to protect children and to protect themselves from allegations of abuse.

Safeguarding an umbrella term used here to describe measures taken to keep children and young people safe from a wide range of dangers.

SENCO Special Educational Needs Coordinator. An appointed practitioner within a setting who is responsible for ensuring that the individual needs of children and young people are met.

Sequence of development the expected order in which most children will achieve key developmental milestones.

Small world small world play resources represent the real world in miniature, for example a farmyard with animals or a doll's house with figures.

Social model of disability this considers that it is society that needs to change and that disabled people have rights and choices. (National Occupational Standards.)

Special educational needs children with special educational needs learn differently from most children of the same age. These children may need extra or different help from that given to other children. (National Occupational Standards.)

Story bags also called 'story sacks', these are a collection of items relating to a particular story, which are used to enhance storytelling and/or to extend learning. For example, a Goldilocks story bag may contain three different-sized teddies, three different-sized bowls and spoons, etc.

Supine the position a baby is in when lying on their back.

Index

ABC (airway, breathing, circulation)
check 360–1
abuse 208
responding to evidence of 214–17
types of 208–14
accidents
recording 254
reporting 251–2
see also first aid
acknowledgement, giving 7
active listening 18–19
activities and experiences
of choice 300–1
communication, language and
literacy 302, 523–7
creative 536–7
creative development support 303,
543–50
evaluation of 167–8
observation of 165–6
planning 161–3, 178–9
sensory 303–4
space for 291–5
support participation in 477–9
to meet individual needs 164, 301
to support learning and development
132, 165, 301–3
adults
communicating with 17
as role models 180, 276
see also parents and carers;
practitioners
advocacy services 37
after-school clubs 244
aggression 282, 285
airways
checking casualty's 360, 362–3
obstructions 368–70
allergies
food 320, 443–4
severe reactions 375–6, 408, 444
anaphylactic shock 375–6, 444
anecdotal records observation method
157
animal bites 408, 410–11
animals, handling and keeping 259
appraisals 66, 70
arguments, between children 283
art, craft and design 294, 546
assessment
of activities 167–8

of children's development needs
158–61
observation methods 150–8
and personal development 64–7
reviewing own contribution to
187–8
special educational needs 460–3
assessors 70–1
associative play 487
asthma 392–4
attendance, and behaviour policies
268
attention
engaging children's 527–31
giving fairly 423–5
to play activities 500
attention seeking behaviour 282, 286
attitudes, personal 58–60

babies
bathing and washing 306
building relationships with 420–1
development 108, 112–18
first aid 357
barriers
to effective communication 31–4
to participation 474–5
BCODP (British Council of Disabled
People) 466–7
behaviour
at mealtimes 454–5
changed as sign of abuse 210, 211,
212, 213
consistency and fairness dealing
with 269–70, 274–6
group agreements on 432–3
inappropriate 265, 268, 277–83
individual plans 186, 269
policies and procedures 185, 264–9
positive 175–82, 271–3
realistic expectations 274
reasons for behaviour problems
183–5, 287
referrals 284–7
reflecting on own role in promoting
positive 187
role models 180, 276
to avoid when communicating 19–
20
transitions and 145–6
behavioural development 111–12

development tables 113–31
behavioural hazards 507–8
beliefs
personal 58–60
respecting others' 97–8
bias, and assessments 160
bilingual children 31, 41–2
bites and stings 408–11
biting 285
bleeding 372–3
blue spots 209
body language 22, 39
body maps 209
bones, broken 379, 380–1
book corners 294, 545
books 525–6, 527–8
boredom and behaviour 178
boundaries 180–1, 266–7, 432–3
brain injuries 385
breathing, checking casualty's 361,
363
British Council of Disabled People
(BCODP) 466–7
bruises 209
bullying 217
behaviour referral 285
effects of 219
policies and procedures 219–20,
268
reasons for 219
supporting children and young
people 220–1
types of 197, 199, 218
burns and scalds 403–4
Byron Review 2007 197

CAF (common assessment framework)
337–40
calcium 318
carbohydrates 315, 316
carers see parents and carers
cascading of information/learning 70
cerebral compression 382, 383
challenges
balancing with risk 234–5, 506–9
providing 162, 178
checklist observation method 155
chickenpox 203
child development
activities to support 165, 301–3
age-appropriate approach to
relationships 422–3

age-related boundaries 266–7
aspects of 107–12, 132
communication, language and
    literacy 514–33
concerns about 141–2
creative development 536–55
development tables 112–31
environments supporting 296–7
and health and safety 238–40,
    501–2
influences on 134–41
nature and nurture 133–4
needs 158–64
observing 150–8
patterns of 106–7
play and leisure and 489–94
practitioners supporting 189–90
transitions and 146–7
child protection 193
abuse 208–17
agencies involved in 200–1
bullying 217–22
concerns about a colleague 222–3
e-safety 196–9
legislation 193–4
policies and procedures 195–6
reporting accidents or injuries 252
Children Act 1989 94, 193, 229
Children Act 2004 94, 194, 229
children and young people
challenging their discrimination
    98–9
and choices 140, 179, 279, 428
codes of conduct 265, 432–3, 452,
    453–4
communicating with 16–17, 18–20,
    414–16, 502–5
information from 102
managing risk 508–9
and observation and assessment
    159
preparing for transitions 170–5
relationships with 417–28
safeguarding 193–223
their relationships with others
    429–33
choices
and development 140
giving children 179, 428
limiting children's 279
choking, first aid for 369–70
chromosomes 135, 472
chronic medical conditions
asthma 392–4
diabetes 390–2

sickle sell anaemia 394–5
circulation, checking casualty's 361
cleaning routines 255–6
clothing
children's 308
personal protective 257, 355
codes of conduct
child/young person 265, 432–3,
    452, 453–4
staff 265
cognitive development 110–11
development tables 113–30
cold, extreme 398–9
collaboration, and creativity 549
colleagues
challenging their discrimination 99
reporting concerns about 222–3
source of information, advice and
    support 70, 102
comfort zones 507
common assessment framework (CAF)
    337–40
common cold 203
communication 28
with adults 17
with babies, children and young
    people 18–20, 414–16, 502–5
barriers to effective 31–4
children and young people with
    others 429–30
confidentiality 44–51
diversity and equality and 38–43
and emotional well-being 7–8
ensuring understanding 35, 416
everyday 10
good manners and 26–7
of ideas, thoughts, opinions and
    concerns 8–9
importance to learning and
    development 515
of information and instructions
    5–6, 278
information and support services
    36–7
language for 524
methods and styles 2, 10–17, 514
needs 27–30
own reaction to others when
    communicating 24
and partnership working 329,
    330–1
reactions to 21–4
reasons for 3
and relationships 3–4, 25–6
communication development 110

creative learning and 540
development tables 113–30
communication, language and literacy
    297
activities resources 302, 523–7
clear language to support learning
    531
encouragement and praise to
    support 271–3
engaging children's interest and
    attention 527–31
importance to learning 514–18
meeting individual needs 533
observation of own practice 532
and other areas of learning and
    development 519–22, 542
play and 490–1
compliance, rewarding 280
concussion 382
confidence, and communication 40
confidentiality 44
confidential records 47
data protection 47, 336
in day-to-day communication 12,
    48–50
'need-to-know' basis 45–6
observation and 159
passing on/sharing confidential
    information 48, 51, 215, 334
seeking advice about 51
types of confidential information 45
conflict
children resolving 182–3
practitioners responding to 268
consistency, importance of 181,
    269–70, 274–6
construction areas 294
Control of Substances Hazardous
    to Health Regulations 1994
    (COSHH) 227
convulsions 367–8
cooperative play 488
CPR (cardiopulmonary resuscitation)
    366–7
creative development
activities and resources for 303,
    543–7
activity setting out and
    implementation 548–50
encouragement and praise 552–3
importance of 536–9
language to support 551–2
meeting individual needs 555–6
and other areas of development and
    learning 522, 540–2

play and 493–4
reflection on practice 554
creative learning 536, 538–9
creativity 536
Criminal Record Bureau (CRB) 194
cultures, different
  and communication 32, 33, 39
  and food 319
  and personal care 306–7
  respecting 97–8
curriculum frameworks 160, 296–7,
    301–3
cyber bullying 197, 199, 218

Data Protection Act 1984/1998 47,
    336
de-escalation of situations 280
deliberate discrimination 85
destructive behaviour 282
development see child development
diabetes 390–2
diary observation method 151
diet
  advice on dietary concerns 444–5
  benefits of a healthy 442
  consequences of unhealthy 442
  encouraging eating of food provided
    448–9
  encouraging healthier food choices
    447–8
  food allergies and intolerances 320,
    443–4
  food policies 445–7
  a healthy 315–18, 436–8
  healthy meals and snacks 438–41
  specific dietary requirements
    319–20
differences see diversity
direct discrimination 86
disability 93
  adaptations and aids to support
    inclusion 477–80
  assessment and intervention
    frameworks 460–3
  barriers to participation 475–6
  early recognition and intervention
    141–2
  impairments and 470
  inclusive working 88–9, 91–7,
    467–9
  individual information 474
  individual plans 464–5
  legal entitlements 458–9
  models of 466–7
  partnership working 481

reasons for 137, 472
special educational needs 470, 473
Disability Discrimination Act (DDA)
    1995 & 2005 93
disclosure 51, 215–17
discrimination 82
  challenging 98–100
  effects of 87
  occurrences of 85
  types of 86–7
dislocations 379–81
displays 294, 543–4, 553
divergent thinking 539
diversion tactics 280
diversity
  challenging discrimination 98–100
  discrimination and 82, 85–7
  discussing 96
  information, advice and support
    100–3
  respecting 84
  support children and young people
    to understand 430–1
  see also inclusion
DNA 135
dressing and undressing 308
dysentery 203

e-safety 196–9
Early Years Action 460–2
Early Years Action Plus 462
Early Years Foundation Stage (EYFS)
  communication, language and
    literacy 520–2
  creative development 541–2
  curriculum frameworks 160, 296–7,
    519
  play 490–3
  welfare requirements 229–30
Early Years Workforce Qualifications
    Audit Tool 78
ears, foreign bodies in 386–7
education
  and child development 140
  see also learning
electricity, incidents involving 401–2
email 14
emergencies
  coping with 246, 361
  medical 207, 247–9
  non-medical 241–2
  recording 254
  reporting 251–2
  see also first aid
emergent writing 526

emotional abuse 210–11
emotional development 111–12
  activities and resources 302
  communication, language and
    literacy and 521
  creative learning and 540
  development tables 113–31
  play and 490
emotional risk 506–7
empathy 468
empowerment of disabled children and
    young people 467
encouragement, importance of 7, 304,
    504–5, 552–3
environments, positive 290
  activities 300–4
  adapting for disabled children 477
  and curriculum frameworks 296–7,
    301–2
  different kinds of 290
  food safety 321
  integrated 325–6, 327
  meeting and greeting 299–300
  nutritional requirements 315–20
  personal-care needs 305–14
  practitioners and 298
  praise and encouragement 304
  regulatory requirements 298
  stimulating and challenging 178
  use of space 291–6
equality 82–3
  challenging discrimination 98–100
  discrimination 82, 85–7
  information, advice and support
    100–3
  interacting with respect 95–8
  legislation 91–5
  promoting 88–90
  see also inclusion
Equality Act 2006 94
Equality Act 2010 95
equipment and materials
  safety and hygiene 256
  specialist for disabled children
    479–80
  to support communication, language
    and literacy 523–6
ethnicity
  and food 319
  and personal care 307
event recording observation method
    154–5
Every Child Matters: Change for
    Children 93, 229, 325
exercise 312

expected development rates 106
experiences *see* activities and
    experiences
eye injuries 387–9

face-to-face conversation 13
facial expressions 21, 278, 531
fairness, importance 269–70, 423–4
family backgrounds
    and child development 138–9
    and communication 39–40
    valuing diverse 343–4
fats 315, 316
febrile convulsions 367–8, 400
feedback and personal development
    65–7, 75–6
feelings
    expressing 7–8, 171–2
    talking about 177–8
feely bags 303
fever 367
fibre 315, 317
fine motor skills 109–10
finger plays 530
Fire Precautions (Workplace)
    Regulations 1997 227–8
first aid
    asthma attacks 393–4
    bites and stings 408–11
    burns and scalds 403–4
    calling for help 249, 361
    choking 368–70
    CPR 366–7
    diabetic hypos or hypers 391–2
    ears, nose and eyes 386–9
    electric shocks 401–2
    first-aid kits 356–7
    fractures and dislocations 379–81
    head and spinal injuries 382–5
    hypothermia 398–9
    infant and child definitions 357
    infection control 255–7, 258–9,
        355
    medical attention needed 247–9
    meningitis 396–7
    overheating 399–400
    paediatric first-aiders 354–5, 376
    poisoning 406–7
    primary survey on infant/child
        360–1
    priorities 362–5
    reports and records 251–2, 254
    rescue breaths 365–6
    scene surveys 358–9
    seizures 367–8

shock 374–6, 444
sickle cell crisis 394–5
wounds and bleeding 371–3
fits (seizures) 367–8
fluoride 318
food
    advice on dietary concerns 444–5
    allergies and intolerances 320,
        443–4
    benefits of healthy eating 442
    consequences of an unhealthy diet
        442
    encouraging eating of food provided
        438, 448–9
    encouraging healthier choices
        447–8
    meal and snack times 438–41,
        452–5
    nutritional requirements 315–18,
        436–8
    policies 445–7
    safety and hygiene 257, 321
    specific dietary requirements 319–
        20
Food Handling Regulations 1995 227
food poisoning 203
Food Safety Act 1990 227
foreign bodies (in ears, nose or eyes)
    386–7, 388–9
fractures 379, 380–1
free play 291, 292, 296, 496–8, 499,
    500
free space 547
frozen watchfulness 210
full disclosure 215

gastro-enteritis 203
genetics 135, 472
German measles 204
gestures 22, 39, 531
good manners 26–7
GPs, safeguarding children 200
grasp reflex 108
gross motor skills 109
group agreements 432–3

hair care 305
hand-eye coordination 109–10
hands, washing and drying 258–9
handwriting 526
hazards 236–7, 237, 507–8
head injuries 382–5
head lag 114, 115
health
    and child development 136–7

    see also illness
health and safety
    and development stages 238–40
    documentation 254, 261
    food safety 257, 321
    infection control 255–7, 258–9
    legislation 226–30
    medical attention needed 247–9
    medicines 260–1
    non-medical incidents and
        emergencies 241–2
    personal protective clothing 257,
        355
    policies and procedures 231–2
    reporting procedures 251–3
    risk assessment 236–8, 502
    risk/challenge balance 234–5,
        506–9
    roles and responsibilities 233, 250
    security 244–6
    supervision levels 501–2
    waste disposal 259–60
Health and Safety at Work Act 1974 &
    1992 226–7
Health and Safety Executive (HSE)
    251
Health and Safety (First Aid)
    Regulations 1981 227
Health and Safety (Young Persons)
    Regulations 1977 229
health visitors 200
heat, extreme 399–400
high temperatures 206–7
hospitals, safeguarding children 200
Human Rights Act 1998 94
hygiene
    food 257, 321, 450–1
    infection control 255–6, 258–9,
        355
    personal 259
hyperglycaemia ('hyper') 390, 392
hypoglycaemia ('hypo') 390, 391–2
hypothermia 398–9

ideas
    children's 426–7, 549
    expressing 8–9
IEPs (individual education plans)
    464–5
illness
    and child development 136–7
    chronic conditions 390–5
    common illnesses 203–4
    meningitis 395–7
    needing medical attention 207,
        247–9, 351

practitioner's role and
responsibilities 205–7, 250
recording 254
reporting 251
signs and symptoms 202–3
see also first aid
imaginary areas 294
impairments 29–30, 470, 472
inadvertent discrimination 85
inappropriate behaviour 265, 277
behaviour referrals 284–7
common 282–3
dealing with 265, 268, 269–70,
277–81
in the dining area 455
reasons for 183–5, 287
incidents and emergencies
coping with 246, 361
medical 207, 247–9
non-medical 241–2
recording 254
reporting 251–2
see also first aid
inclusion 84
challenging discrimination 98–100
and child behaviour 181
and disability and SEN 459, 466–9,
474–6, 477–81
discrimination 32, 85–7
encouraging family participation
346–7, 348–9
information, advice and support
100–3
interacting with respect 95–8
legislation 91–5
promoting 88–90
incubation periods 203
independence, promoting 172, 311–12
Independent Safeguarding Authority
(ISA) 194
indirect disclosure 216
indirect discrimination 86
individual plans 464–5
individuality, support 430–1
induction programmes 57
infection control 255–6, 258–89, 355
information
about individuals with disabilities
and SEN 474
confidentiality 44–51, 334, 336
gathering for assessment 161
recording 334–6
sharing 5–6, 332–3, 344–6
inhalers 393
injuries

bites and stings 408–11
burns and scalds 403–4
electric shock 402
eyes and ears 387–9
fractures and dislocations 379–81
head and spinal injuries 382–5
needing medical attention 247–9,
361
poisoning 405–7
reporting 251–2
insect bites and stings 408, 409–10
inspections 67
inspiration, providing 548–9
institutional discrimination 86
instructions, giving and receiving 5–6
insulin 390
intangible rewards 272
integrated working 325–6, 328–9
intellectual development 110–11
creative learning and 540
development tables 113–30
interaction
and child development 141
respect during 26–7, 95–8, 277,
418
see also communication;
relationships
interest, engaging children's 527–31
internet
for communication 14
e-safety 196–9
for information 103
interpretation services 36
intervention
physical 281
and SEN 460–3
to support child development
141–2
intolerances, food 320
iodine 318
iron 318
ISA (Independent Safeguarding
Authority) 194

jargon 31
job descriptions 54–6
job roles *see* work roles

key persons 342, 344, 420
knowledge and understanding of the
world 297, 302, 492, 522, 542

language 28
barriers 31, 33, 39
clear to support learning 531

for communication 524
impairments 29–30
importance to learning and
development 515–17
and nature and nurture 133
needs 27–9
play and 490–1, 516
for thinking 524
to support creative development
551–2
using appropriate 16–17, 96
languages, learning two or more 41–2
learning
and child development 141
communication, language and
literacy 514–33
creative 536, 538–9
play and 162, 489–94
space for 291–5
supporting 296–7, 301–3
see also child development
legislation
disabled children entitlements
458–9
environments 298
health and safety 226–30
inclusion and equality 91–5
play and leisure rights 495–6
safeguarding children 193–5
leisure
importance of 484, 488
and learning and development 494
legal rights 495–6
supporting 499–501
letters (documents) 13
listening, active 18–20
listening, to children 177–8
literacy 40, 490–1, 517–19
locomotive movements 109

Makaton 13
manners, good 26–7
mark-making 490, 526, 546
mealtimes
behaviour at 452–5
encouraging children to eat food
provided 448–9
healthy meals and snacks 438–41
hygiene at 450–1
measles 204
medical model of disability 466
medicines 260–1
meeting and greeting 299–300
meningitis 395–7

mentors 70–1
messy play areas 294
milk teeth 309
minerals 315, 317, 318
mirroring 24
missing child procedures 246
mongolian spots 209
moral development 112
  development tables 123–31
motor skills 109–10
movement, creative 545–6
multi-agency working 325, 328–9,
    337–40
multidisciplinary working 94, 325–6,
    328–9
multilingual children 31, 41–2
mumps 204
music 529, 544

names
  children recognising 525
  using correctly 27
nappies 306
narrative observation method 151–2
National Occupational Standards (NOP)
    57
nature and nurture 133–4
needs
  and behaviour 179–80
  care 306–7
  development 158–64
  expressing 7–8
  see also special educational needs
neglect 212–14
neonates 108, 113
'no', saying 279
non-participant observers 155, 157
non-verbal communication 10–11,
    21–2
NSPCC 201
numeracy see problem solving,
    reasoning and numeracy
nutrition
  advice on dietary concerns 444–5
  basic requirements 315–18
  benefits of healthy eating 442
  consequences of an unhealthy diet
    442
  encouraging eating of food provided
    448–9
  encouraging healthier food choices
    447–8
  food policies 445–7
  a healthy diet 436–8

healthy meals and snacks 438–41
  specific dietary requirements
    319–20

object permanence 117
observation 150
  of activities 165–6, 167–8
  children and 159
  confidentiality and 159
  methods of 150–8
  obtaining permission for 159
  of your own practice 532
off-site visits 245–6
offensive language 283
online safety 196–9
opinions
  expressing 8–9
  valuing children's 177–8, 426–7
outings 245–6
over-sexualised behaviour 212
overheating 399–400

paedophiles 196
palmar grasp 110, 116
parallel play 486
parents and carers
  challenging their discrimination 99
  and child development 138–9
  permission for observation and
    assessment 159
  working in partnership with 341–51
Parten's five stages of play 486–8
partial disclosure 215
participant observers 155, 158
partnership working
  communication and 330–1
  and disability 481
  effective 328
  information sharing 332–6
  multi-agency and integrating
    working 324–7, 328–9
  in own work setting 327
  with parents and carers 341–51
  referrals between agencies 338–40
  see also communication
person specifications 55–6
personal assistant workers 469
personal care
  balancing physical activity and rest
    312–13
  bathing and washing babies 306
  dressing and undressing 308
  independence and self care 311–12
  individual needs 306–7
  nutrition 315–20

routines 314
  showing respect in 310
  skin and hair care 305–6
  sun protection 307–8
  teeth 309–10
  toileting 308
personal development plans 61
  agreeing 72–3
  assessment/feedback and 64–7,
    75–6
  drawing up 68–9
  methods of learning and
    development 71–2
  personal attitudes and beliefs 58–9
  personal development cycle 74–5
  recording progress 76–8
  reflection and 61–4
  sources of support 69–71
personal hygiene 259, 450–1
personal protective clothing 257, 355
Personal Protective Equipment at Work
    Regulations 1992 228
personal, social and emotional
    development 297
  activities and resources for 302
  communication, language and
    literacy and 521
  creative learning and 542
  play and 490
personality, and communication 40
pertussis 204
phosphorus 318
physical abuse 208–10
physical development 108–10
  activities and resources for 302
  communication, language and
    literacy and 522
  creative learning and 540, 542
  development tables 113–30
  play and 492–3
pincer grasp 110, 117, 118, 120
pitch of voice 16, 23
play
  and creativity 537–8
  five stages of 486–8
  free play 496–7
  high-quality 497–8
  importance of 484–5
  interacting during 502–5
  language and 516
  and learning and development 141,
    162, 489–94
  legal rights 495–6
  safety and risk 234–40, 501, 506–9
  space for 291–6

supervising 501–2
supporting 499–501
play agendas 487
play cues 500–1
poems 530
poisons and poisoning 405–7
police, safeguarding children 200
policies and procedures
  behaviour 185, 264–9
  environments 58
  food 445–6
  health and safety 231–2
  information sharing 5–6, 332–3
  mealtimes 452–3
  safeguarding children 195–6
positive behaviour 175–6
  at meal and snack-times 454–5
  encouraging 176–86, 271–3
  reflecting on own role in promoting
    187
positive images, promoting 88–9
positive relationships
  with children and young people
    176–7, 417–20
  and transitions 169–70
potassium 318
poverty and deprivation, and child
    development 137–8
practitioners
  assessment of meeting standards
    64–7
  behaviour codes of conduct 265
  duties and responsibilities 54–7
  giving individual attention 424–5
  having concerns of abuse 214–17
  and health and safety 233, 250
  observation of 532, 554
  personal attitudes and beliefs
    58–60
  personal development plan 68–78
  and a positive environment 298
  reflective practice 60, 61–4
  standards influencing job role 57–8
  support SEN 471, 473, 475–6
  supporting development 189
  supporting play 499–505, 510–11
praise, value of 304, 504–5, 552
pregnancy and birth, and child
    development 135–6, 472
prejudice 81
primary survey, first-aid 360–1
probation services, safeguarding
    children 201
problem solving, reasoning and
    numeracy 297

activities and resources 302
communication, language and
    literacy and 521
creative learning and 538–9, 542,
    551–2
play and 491–2
prone position 112, 113, 115, 116
Protection of Children Act 1999 193
proteins 315
pseudo-sexual behaviour 212
psychology services 201
puberty 128, 130

questions 425–6

Race Relations Act 1976 94
Racial and Religious Hatred Act 2006
    94
rapport 4, 419–20
reading 518–19, 525–6, 527–8
reassurance, giving 7
recovery position 363–4
referrals 337–40
reflective practice 61
  areas for reflection 62–3
  assessing how well standards are
    met 64–7
  assumptions and discrimination 85
  on contribution to assessment
    187–8
  on promoting positive behaviour
    187
  reflecting on new learning 74–5
  reflection methods 63–4
  suggestions for 558–62
  on supporting creativity 554–5
  on supporting play 510–11
  what practitioners do 61–2
  when to reflect 67
reflexes 108
registers 243
reinforcement, of positive behaviour
    182
relationships
  with children and young people
    176–7, 417–28
  children and young people with
    others 429–33
  communication and 3–4, 25–6
  during periods of transition 169–70
  see also partnership working
religion
  and food 319
  and personal care 306–7

Reporting of Injuries, Diseases
    and Dangerous Occurrences
    Regulations 1995 (RIDDOR)
    228
rescue breaths 365–6
respect
  during personal care 310
  and inclusion 467
  interacting with 26–7, 95–8, 277,
    418
  and play 503
  teaching children and young people
    431–2
responses, supportive 425–7
rest 312–13
rewards 182, 272–3, 280
rhymes 530
risk 237
  assessment 236–8
  balancing with challenge 234–5,
    506–9
role models 180, 276
role play 544
rooting reflex 108
routines 314
rubella 204
running records observation method
    152–3

safeguarding children and young
    people 193
  abuse 208–17
  agencies involved in 200–1
  bullying 217–21
  concerns about a colleague 222–3
  confidentiality 44–51
  e-safety 196–9
  illness 202–7
  legislation 193–5
  policies and procedures 195–6
  see also health and safety
salt 318, 319
sanctions, use of 279
scalds and burns 403–4
scarlet fever 204
scene surveys, first-aid 358–9
School Food Trust 436
security 243
  arrivals and departures 243–5
  during sessions 245
  missing child procedures 246
  off-site visits 245–6
segregation 86
seizures 367–8
selective ignoring 280

self-esteem 40, 496
SEN *see* special educational needs
SENCO *see* Special Educational Needs
    Coordinator
separation anxiety 172
sequences of development 106–7
sexual abuse 211–12
shock 374–6
shock, electric 401–2
sickle cell anaemia 394–5
sign language 13, 36
skin care 305–6, 307–8
skull fracture 382
sleep 312–13
slings 381
small motor skills 109–10
small talk 4, 5
small world 545
SMART objectives 68–9
snack times
    behaviour at 452–5
    healthy snacks 438–9, 440
snake bites 408, 411
social, emotional and behavioural
        development 111–12
    activities and resources 302
    communication, language and
        literacy and 521
    creative learning and 540
    development tables 113–31
    play and 490
social model of disability 466–7
social services 200
social skills 485, 517
sodium chloride 318
solitary play 486
songs 529
sound lotto 303
space, use of 291
    balanced approach to 292–3
    common dedicated areas 294
    factors affected by layout 295
    free space 547
    location of areas 294–5
    playing and learning 291
Special Educational Needs Code of
        Practice 2001 459
Special Educational Needs Coordinator
        (SENCO) 29–30, 102, 459, 461
special educational needs (SEN) 471
    adaptations and aids to support
        participation 477–80

assessment and intervention
        frameworks 460–3
    barriers to participation 474–5
    communication, language and
        literacy 533
    creative development 555–6
    inclusive working and 88–9, 91–7,
        467–9
    individual information 474
    individual plans 464–5
    legal entitlements 458–9
    partnership working 481
spectator play 486
speech 28
speech and language services 37
spinal injuries 364, 384–5, 385
staff-to-child ratios 501
standards
    external and internal 57–8
    meeting 64–7
    personal 58–60
standing reflex 108
startle reflex 108, 114
Statement of Special Educational
        Needs 463
stereotypes 81
stimulation 141, 178, 312
stings and bites 408–11
stories 525, 545
    reading aloud 527, 528
    telling 528–9
story bags 545
sun protection 307–8
supervision levels 501–2
supine position 112, 113, 115, 116
swearing 283

tangible rewards 272–3
target child observation method 156
teamwork 60
    see also partnership working
teeth 309–10
telephone calls 13
temperatures, high 206–7
text messages 13
thinking 538
    divergent 539
    language for 516–17, 524, 551–2
time out 280, 281
time sampling observation method
        153–4
toileting 308–9

tone of voice 15–16, 23
tonsillitis 204
touch 24, 421
traffic lights food labelling system
        441
transitions
    effects of 145–7
    losing familiar people 147
    support strategies 169–75
    type of 141–3
    who experiences? 144
translation services 36
trips 245–6
truancy 269
trust 417, 419
tutors 70–1

UN Convention on the Rights of the
        Child 92–3, 495–6

values
    personal 58–60
    respecting others' 97–8
vegan diets 320
vegetarian diets 319
verbal communication 10–11, 15–16
Vetting and Barring Scheme 194–5
victimisation 86–7
vitamins 315, 317
vocabulary, using appropriate 16–17
voice, tone and pitch of 15–16, 23

walking reflex 108
waste disposal 259–60
water, drinking 437–8
'whistle-blowing' 222–3
whooping cough 204
work placement guidelines 55
work roles
    duties and responsibilities 54–7
    and personal attitudes and beliefs
        58–61
    standards that influence 57–8
    see also practitioners
Working Together to Safeguard Children
        2006 194
wounds and bleeding 371–3
writing 518–19, 526

young people *see* children and young
        people

Acknowledgements

The author and publisher would like to thank the following for permission to use or adapt copyright material:

p221 © Kidscape, www.kidscape.org.uk; p258 © Crown copyright 2007 283373 1p 1k Sep07 reproduced under PSI licence no. C2009002012; p338 © This publication is the copyright of the Children's Workforce Development Council 2009; p340 Department for Children, Schools and Families © Crown Copyright 2009 reproduced under PSI licence no. C2009002012; p395 © Meningitis Trust 2011. If you would like further information regarding this organisation please visit www.meningitis-trust.org; pp437, 441 Food Standards Agency © Crown Copyright reproduced under PSI licence no. C2009002012; p439 © School Food Trust 2011; pp439-440 Reproduced by kind permission of the Department of Health, © 2011; pp446-447 'Food Policies in Schools' © 2007 National Governors' Association. Produced in association with Foods Standards Agency © Crown copyright 2007 reproduced under PSI licence no. C2009002012; pp495-496 from UN Convention on the Rights of the Child © UNICEF 2011.

Many thanks to the parents, children and staff at Churchdown Day Nursery, Churchdown and Little Hoots Preschool, Bishops Cleeve.

Photo Acknowledgements

Alamy: © Rob/Alamy p36; © Picture Partners p42; © Image Source / Alamy pp62, 75; © Jeff Gilbert / Alamy p138 (top); © mediablitzimages (uk) Limited / Alamy p172; © Sally and Richard Greenhill / Alamy p181; © Bubbles Photolibrary / Alamy p206; © Medical-on-Line / Alamy p209; © Leila Cutler / Alamy p210 (top); © Tony Watson / Alamy p214; © Angela Hampton Picture Library / Alamy p218; © David J. Green / Alamy; © Image Source / Alamy p249; © Science Photo Library / Alamy p260; © Anne-Marie Palmer / Alamy p266; © Ian Canham / Alamy p347; © Author's Image Ltd / Alamy p383; © SHOUT / Alamy p386; © Graham Ella / Alamy p393; © Bubbles Photolibrary / Alamy p432; © Malcolm Case-Green / Alamy p438; © Indigo Images / Alamy p444; © Robert Johns / Alamy p446; © MBI / Alamy p454; © Paul Doyle / Photolibrary pp464, 468; © Janine Wiedel Photolibrary / Alamy p471; © Siegfried Kuttig - RF -2 / Alamy p500; © Darrin Jenkins / Alamy p506; **fotolia:** © Vladimir Mucibabic - Fotolia.com p28; © rnl - Fotolia.com p120 (top); © pressmaster - Fotolia.com p127; © Michael Ireland - Fotolia.com p193; © matka_Wariatka – Fotolia.com p295; © Sergey Galushko - Fotolia.com p430; **Getty:** © Lihee Avidan p39; © Echo p143; Fuse p268; **:** ©Vanessa Davies / Getty Images p303; © Stockbyte p366; © Gary Ombler p397; © Echo p415; © Realistic Reflections p460; © Trish Gant p537; © Ableimages pp550, 552; **www.heathergunnphotography. co.uk:** pp1, 7, 17, 24, 60, 66, 93, 101, 105, 116 (bottom), 117 (bottom), 123 (bottom), 124, 125, 126, 129 (top), 134, 155, 168, 169, 179, 221, 225, 238, 245, 253, 271, 291, 292, 293, 294, 297, 300 (bottom), 308 (bottom), 321 (bottom), 325, 328, 331, 333, 335, 418, 421, 424, 427, 449, 452, 481, 485, 502, 503, 511, 515, 544, 545, 546, 547; **Connie Handscombe:** p114 (top); **iStockphoto:** © Rouzes p8; © Valua Vitaly p15; © Lise Gagne p18; © imagebroker/Alamy p19; © drbimages p22; © malerapaso p32;